Visions of Sound
Musical Instruments of First Nations Communities in Northeastern America

Visions of Sound
Musical Instruments of First Nations Communities in Northeastern America

Beverley Diamond,
M. Sam Cronk, and Franziska von Rosen

The University of Chicago Press
Chicago and London

Beverley Diamond is Associate Professor of Music at York
University. She is the co-editor of *Canadian Music: Issues of
Hegemony and Identity* (1994). M. Sam Cronk and Franziska von Rosen
are currently graduate students in music at
the University of Michigan at Ann Arbor and Brown University respectively.

The University of Chicago Press, Chicago 60637
Wilfrid Laurier University Press, Waterloo, Ontario, Canada N2L 3C5
Copyright © 1994 Wilfrid Laurier University Press
All rights reserved. Published 1994
Printed in the U.S.A.

Cover and interior design by Jose Martucci, Design Communications

Front cover photograph: Naskapi caribou shoulder blade rattle with star
design (HEY 23/6638). Photo by Franziska von Rosen.
Back cover photograph: The purple flower next to the yellow flower.
Photo by Sandra Woolfrey.

03 02 01 00 99 98 97 96 95 94   1 2 3 4 5

ISBN: 0-226-14475-5 (cloth); 0-226-14476-3 (paper)

Library of Congress Cataloging-in-Publication Data

Diamond, Beverley.
    Visions of sound : musical instruments of First Nations
communities in Northeastern America / Beverley Diamond, M. Sam Cronk,
and Franziska von Rosen.
      p.   cm. – (Chicago studies in ethnomusicology)
    Includes bibliographical references (p. 197) and index.
    1. Iroquoian Indians – Music – History and criticism. 2. Algonquian
Indians – Music – History and criticism. 3. Musical instruments,
Primitive. I. Series.
ML3557.D5 1994
784.1974'08997—dc20

                                                                94-10337
                                                                CIP
                                                                MN

This book is printed on acid-free paper

The consultants and musicians from the First Nations communities
were our primary teachers. They entrusted us with stories and teachings,
with aspects of their history and their science. We hope that we have met their trust
with respect. Several elders who became our mentors will not see
the completion of this project, but their spirits live on.
We dedicate this book to their memory.

Royalties from the sale of this book will go to support
scholarships for research or study proposed by First Nations
musicians, filmmakers, or artists. The scholarships will be
administered by Native organizations in the regions in which the
authors worked. For further information, please contact either
the publisher or one of the authors.

SGENO.
GANO:NYONK ENDWASHNYE:TAK DEYONWEDA:GE
NIDZO:SA DAENYADANO:NYO.

Greetings.

Thanks we are going

to talk about;

two persons,

where it starts,

greet each other.

Contents

List of Figures

Acknowledgements

This project extended over nine years, fifteen Native communities, twenty-four museums and archives, three computer systems, four universities (two of which served as host institutions), and four cities of residence. We were helped by so many generous individuals that the task of bringing them all together into this section is extremely humbling.

The project would never have taken place except for the generous financial support of the Social Sciences and Humanities Research Council of Canada, who supported us through the Research Grants programme and later the Major Research Grants programme. We were especially grateful that they were willing to take some risks in funding the style of collaborative research which we were increasingly interested in moving toward. In particular, they agreed to sponsor a series of visits by Native scholars, elders, and cultural spokespersons to the Queen's University campus. This enabled us not only to have several days of fairly intensive discussion (including work with photos, language materials, etc.) with knowledgeable consultants, but also to introduce our students and colleagues to our distinguished guests who spoke in classes, attended faculty lunches, and helped present, on one occasion, a social which brought university and community together in a very good feeling social space. Thanks to Bernie Francis (University College of Cape Breton), Peter Christmas (Director, Micmac Association for Cultural Studies), Jim Dumont (Native Studies, University of Sudbury), Art Solomon, Tom Paul, as well as Amos Key (Woodland Cultural Centre) and his colleagues from Six Nations—Hubert Buck, Sr., Hubert Buck, Jr., Sadie Buck, Sue Jacobs, Tom Hill—who participated in this programme, and to Mary Lou Fox (Ojibwe Cultural Foundation, West Bay) and Nicole Obomsawin (Musée Abenaki) who worked with us to try to arrange other events which, eventually, did not take place. Thanks also to Queen's University for supplementing resources and providing space for events that were spinoffs from the research visits. York University provided additional funding through the Minor Research Grants programme of the Faculty of Fine Arts for the preparation of illustrations for the book, and the Association of Canadian Studies supported the manuscript preparation with a Writing Award for which we were extremely grateful.

Sam is deeply grateful to his many teachers and colleagues and their families, and would like particularly to thank the families of the late Hubert Buck, Sr., Elijah Harris, Reg Henry, and Richard JohnnyJohn for their kindness, encouragement, and unfailing humour. Sam offers thanks to Kevin and Letha JohnnyJohn and family, Lyford JohnnyJohn, Dr. Hazel Dean, Amos Key and family, Dar Dowdy and family, Beatrice Thomas, William Crouse, Sr. and family, Shirley Williams, Gesso Thomas, Evelyn Bomberry and the Grand River Champion of Champions Powwow Committee, Old Mush Gang, the Allegany Men's Singing Society, the Six Nations "Old Timers," Huron Miller, Gordy Buck, Mike Doxtator, Anne Jock and family, Louise Dallaire,

Dr. Michael K. Foster, Dr. Trudy Nicks, David Maracle, Sheila Staats, Harriet Boots, Teresa Doxdtator David and Leroy David, Anne General, Mark Phillips, Dr. Mary Black, Marilyn Spruce, Amelia Boots Watt, George and Martha Abrams, and James Skye, always Ogwali. For sharing their knowledge and for access to archival materials, thanks to James Corsaro (New York State Library), Ray Gonyea (New York State Museum), the late Dr. Ed Rogers (Royal Ontario Museum), Rayna Green (National Museum of American History, Smithsonian Institution), Judith Gray (Federal Cylinder Project, Library of Congress). Particular thanks also for Sally Kope, her compassion and teaching.

Although Bev visited the Abenaki community of Odanak only a few times, the gracious assistance of museum curator and dance instructor Nicole Obomsawin and, on one occasion, an important conversation about musical instruments with Thérèse Obomsawin were key to understanding the cultural challenges faced by members of this community, which has been buffeted by so many external forces. We are grateful to the Innu consultants who tolerated Bev's mediocre French and agreed to respond to her strangely formulated requests: especially to Annette Vollant and her family, whose friendship is really valued, Jean-Baptiste and Alice Jean-Pierre, Daniel Vachon and family, Alexandre and Alice Michel, and various personnel associated with the Innu Nikamu festival, including Florent Vollant and Cyrille Fontaine. Conversations with many others, including Philippe Pietashu, Helen Mollen, and Zacharie Mollen at Mingan were valued experiences. Bev benefited enormously from discussions with knowledgeable teachers and museum curators in both Innu and Abenaki com-

munities and for their help in accessing materials in local archives: Céline Bellefleur in Sept-Îles/Maliotenam, Marcelline Canape in Betsiamites, Madame Carmen Gill Casavant (and family) in Pointe-Bleue, André Michel in Sept-Îles, Ann Casavant at I.E.C.A.M. in Village Huron, Quebec, Monsieur Picard and Mario Gros-Louis at Village Huron, and Bertha Tenasco in Maniwaki (who helped both Bev and Sam). In the early stages of the project we benefited from Esther Wesley's help at the Ojibwe-Cree Cultural Centre in Timmins. Later, during a week-long tour of northern Ontario Cree communities, the patience and efficiency of Esther Wesley, Bertha Mathat, and Dennis Austin, and other members of their staff, as well as elder James Carpenter, were valuable informative experiences.

Before the official beginning of the SPINC project, Bev's sabbatical in Davis Inlet, Labrador, was formative in developing her understanding of some issues relating to the Innu struggle for cultural survival. For a fondly remembered introduction to Labrador, thanks to Doris Saunders (Goose Bay/Happy Valley) whose extraordinary creation of *Them Days* is an inspiration. In Davis Inlet, the friendship and interpretive skills of Emma Piwas as well as her mother Agathe and aunts Mani Shan Nui and Charlotte Gregoire made her feel welcome in their homes and at the Craft house where they often talked together. To Thomas Noah—that experienced teacher of academics and other "outsiders"—Philip Rich and family, Gilbert Rich, Marianne Noah, John Poker, Sam and Elizabeth Napeo, Simon Noah, Charles James (Tshenish) Pasteen and his wife Thérèse, Pien and Mary Charlotte Katchinak, Mary Josette Mistanapeo, Joachim and Edith Jacobesh, as well as David Nui and Jacqueline Rich who assisted with interpreting on several occasions—Bev says thank you. For their gracious hospitality and extensive knowledge, special thanks to Sisters Martha Groffen, Lieve Bosmans, and Evelyn Kane, as well as Bridget Murphy and Pitt Catrie, who put up with an unexpected room-mate.

Franziska is especially grateful to a number of special consultants and assistants, including Michael W. Francis who, among other things, collaborated with her on the production of the video *River of Fire*, and his wife Ada Francis for her hospitality; the late Tom Paul of Eskasoni, Nova Scotia, whose role in bringing the big drum tradition to the Maritimes was of great importance and who helped the SPINC project in many capacities; Alma Brooks and Margaret Paul who generously shared their knowledge, music, and hospitality; Sarah Denny and her wonderful daughters whose work in revitalizing Micmac music and dance in Eskasoni and elsewhere has served her people; and Dr. Marie Battiste who articulates issues of language and culture so eloquently. Our thanks also go to all members of the Birch Creek Singers from Big Cove.

Among other academic colleagues, we are very grateful to Dr. Robert Leavitt who read parts of our manuscript, and gave access to materials at the Micmac-Maliseet Institute, University of New Brunswick. Thanks to Dr. Mildred Milliea (Big Cove) and Bernie Francis (Sydney) who also helped Franziska extensively with language issues. Franziska also thanks Dr. Harold McGee, who was generous in sharing information and personal photographs with us, and Dr. Ruth Holmes Whitehead, who gave access to important archival materials at the Nova Scotia Museum, Halifax, and shared her own vast knowledge of Micmac culture. Thanks to Dr. Robert Morgan

who enabled Franziska to carry out her work at the Beaton Institute, University College of Cape Breton, Sydney, Nova Scotia. We are grateful to other members of the Micmac-Maliseet and Passamaquoddy communities for meetings or interviews: thanks to William Nevin, Donna Nevin (Augustine), Rebecca Simon, Pat and Joey Joseph, Henry Augustine, the late Edward Kabatay, the late Emmerson Sock and family, the late Simon Marshall, Dr. Peter Christmas and his staff at the Micmac Association of Cultural Studies, Anthony Francis, Eva and Jane Milliea, Joseph Nicolas, the late Dr. Peter Paul, Romi LaBillois, René Martin, Nicholas Smith, and the late Dr. Helen Creighton.

We want to give special recognition to two individuals who were exceptional friends of this project, guiding us all at numerous stages and sharing their knowledge generously. To Amos Key and Jim Dumont, both of whom have so many responsibilities within their communities and many professional circles, we thank you for many hours together during which we learned so much.

Within our own communities, a number of Aboriginal organizations and individuals encouraged and assisted us. We thank Patricia Monture, members of the Medicine Hoop Drum, the Native Sisterhood, and the Native Canadian Centre in Toronto.

Two undergraduate (at the time of their participation) student projects were associated with SPINC. It felt good to see Kevin Hamlin's enthusiastic work during two summers in Moose Factory and Connie Heimbecker's initial residence at Lobstick Lake turn into experiences that really changed their lives. Both became educators with a much-needed awareness of Aboriginal issues. Connie's subsequent work in curriculum development with the Innu Nation has been an inspiring example of collaboration. Thanks to both Kevin and Connie for their important contributions to the project and to Connie for her hospitality and introductions to many of her friends in Sheshashit and for her continuing friendship. We are especially grateful to members of the Otterhead and Young Eagle Drums and to those who agreed to participate in interviews with Kevin or Connie, especially Geraldine Nadgewan, whose words we have used in this book. In addition, our thanks go to a number of students at Queen's University who worked for short periods of time in the SPINC office, hopefully learning a bit about data bases in the process. We especially acknowledge Al Price, Maureen Bracewell, and Marie von Rosen.

When SPINC worked as a group in museums and archives, in particular, our demands often occupied considerable staff time and energy. Nevertheless, we were given gracious assistance. We are grateful to both the Canadian Museum of Civilization, especially Judy Thompson, Judy Hall, and their staff, and the McCord Museum (especially Conrad Graham) who gave us access to materials at awkward moments in their institutional history, when they were in the process of being moved or transferring to new computer cataloguing systems. Special thanks go to Dennis Slater, Beth Carter, and staff (Glenbow Museum in Calgary, Alberta) whose sensitivity to the concerns of Native researchers and elders greatly impressed us. More recently, at the Glenbow, Clifford Crane Bear's assistance to Bev was much appreciated. We were especially grateful for the patience and helpful assistance of Marie-Paule Robitaille at Quebec's Musée de la Civilization

and Kathryn Skelley at the Peabody Museum, Harvard. We were treated graciously by Martha Kriepe and Nancy Rosoff at the Heye Foundation, and we thank James Smith for access to the artifact collection of that institution. For information from the Metropolitan Museum in New York, we are grateful to Kenneth Moore.

Several York University graduate students assisted with later stages of the project. Thanks to Charles Fairchild for bibliographic checking, to Claude Gallant for French interview transcriptions, to Karen Pegley for a summer of highly creative work on computer drawings, and Bish Sharma for assistance with copyright permissions.

The essential, behind-the-scenes support of office staff was, in the case of this project, truly extraordinary. We have had the good fortune to have the assistance of several skilled individuals in secretarial positions. Particular thanks to Kathryn Brownsey for keeping the project finances straight and helping with a myriad of other tasks, all the while being capable of discussing Foucault or Barthe, in preparation for her own scholarly career. Thanks also to Nan Sawyer; her involvement was less direct but her support in recent years has helped to complete the project and her knowledge of the challenge of respecting ethnocultural difference has been immensely important for the research programmes at York University, of which this project was one.

It is difficult to single out the personal and professional contacts who may have influenced the development of our thinking. But we certainly wish to acknowledge Bruno Nettl and Charlotte Frisbie who gave us valuable comments on a draft of the manuscript. Bev is grateful to her colleagues at York for providing such a stimulating intellectual environment in which to work, and Sam and Franziska have, as the writing of the project proceeded, benefited from the mentoring of their supervisors, Judith Becker and Jeff Titon, respectively.

Special thanks to the staff of Wilfrid Laurier University Press, especially Sandra Woolfrey whose friendship and personal involvement with this project have made the complex production a great pleasure. For their patience and professionalism special thanks also to Maura Brown and Doreen Armbruster. We are also grateful to Martin Dowding for his work as indexer.

Finally to the families and friends who sustained us through this huge undertaking, we offer gratitude and affection.

We are, of course, responsible for any errors, omissions, or misrepresentations which remain in the text.

Megwetch

Tshi naskumitin

Nya:weh agwe:g¿

Thank you

Permissions

We are grateful to the following museums and archives for permission to publish our photographs of artifacts from their collections:

Agnes Etherington Art Gallery, Kingston, ON (Photo 144).

Canadian Museum of Civilization, Ottawa/Hull, Canada (Photos 8, 9, 10, 13, 26, 40, 41, 42, 44, 52, 59, 60, 75, 84, 88, 89, 92, 94, 97, 101, 102, 111, 115, 116, 118, 127, 146, 156, 157, 158, 159, and Colour Plates 3, 4, 12, 22).

Glenbow Museum, Calgary, AB (Photos 6, 11, 50, 53, 58, 62, 63, 65, 85, 117, 128, 135, 136, 161, and Colour Plate 2).

Heye Foundation, Museum of the American Indian, NY—now the National Museum of the American Indian, Smithsonian Institution, Washington, DC (Photos 3, 15, 31, 34, 46, 48, 49, 54, 64, 68, 69, 70, 83, 103, 110, 113, 114, 120, 125, 126, 134, 137, 138, 140, 141, 147, 150, and Colour Plates 5, 6, 10, 17, 20, 21, 26).

Isaacs/Innuit Gallery, Toronto, ON (Photos 107, 108, and Colour Plate 9).

McCord Museum of Canadian History, Montreal, PQ (Photo 43, 71, and Colour Plate 11).

Musée amérindien de Mashteuiatsh, PQ (Photos 29, 66, and Colour Plate 25).

Musée Arouane, Village Huron, Wendake, part of the collection of the Conseil de la Nation huronne-wendat (Photo 2).

Musée de la Civilization, Quebec, PQ (Photos 5, 23, 47, 67, 93, 98, 104, 123, 143, and Colour Plates 18, 19).

Musée des Abénakis, Odanak, PQ (Photos 33 and 155).

Peabody Museum at Harvard, Boston, MA (Photo 87 and Colour Plates 7, 15, 16).

Peabody Museum at Salem, MA (Photos 45, 56, 73, 78, 99, 100, 106, 131, 145).

Royal Ontario Museum, Toronto, ON (Photos 57, 72, 74, 76, 139, and Colour Plate 8).

Rochester Museum and Science Center, Rochester, NY (Photo 95).

Smithsonian Institution, Washington, DC (Photo 86 and Colour Plate 23).

Seneca Iroquois National Museum, Salamanca, NY (Photo 105).

We are also grateful to the following individuals for permission to publish our photographs of privately owned instruments: Alma Brooks, Eddie Kabatay, Alexander Michel, and Donna Newell .

We are grateful to the following institutions for permission to publish their photographs or illustrations:

American Museum of Natural History for their photo 178379 (our Photo 61).

Archives Obedjiwan for Photo 151.

Canadian Museum of Civilization, Hull, PQ, for their photo 48803 (Photo 14) and negative 24972 (Photo 156).

Chicago Field Museum (Photo 36).

L'êquipe d'Amérindianisation des Services êducatifs, Betsiamites, PQ (Figure 9).

Heye Foundation, Museum of the American Indian, NY—now the National Museum of the American Indian, Smithsonian Institution, Washington, DC, for their photos 11760 (Photo 12), and 12063 (Photo 150).

Kitigan Zibi Anishnabeg Cultural Education Centre, Maniwaki, PQ (Photo 122).

Musée des Abénakis, Odanak, for their photos 3583 (Photo 160) and 3560 (Photo 162).

Notman Photographic Archives of the McCord Museum for their photo MP2030 (Photo 153).

Promotions Innu Nikamu for the reproduction of their festival logo (Figure 18).

Public Archives of Canada for their C60659 (Photo 7), PA 74611 (Photo 18), PA 120191 (Photo 25), PA 181704 (Photo 28), PA131709 (Photo 109).

Smithsonian Institution for Figure 15, a drawing made from the birch-bark scroll, catalogue number 153136, from the *Handbook of the North American Indians*, vol. 15 (Trigger 1978: 755).

Thanks to the following individuals who permitted us to use their artistic work:

Dr. Hazel Dean for images in Chapter Two.

Jim Dumont for lecture segment in Chapter One and images in Chapter Two.

Michael W. Francis for the drawings and narration of the Mi'kmwesu legend (Figure 12) and for the drawings of how to make a hemispheric drum (Figure 16).

Rita Joe for the poem that opens Chapter One.

Ken Syrette for the cartoon in Chapter Two.

Connie Heimbecker (Photo 35).

This book has been published with the help of a grant from the Social Science Federation of Canada, using funds provided by the Social Sciences and Humanities Research Council of Canada, as well as funding received from Multiculturalism and Citizenship Canada and the Canada Council.

All possible care has been taken to trace the ownership of all works in copyright reprinted in this book and to make acknowledgement for their use. The authors and publisher will welcome information that would enable them to rectify any errors or omissions.

Abbreviations of Archival Collections

AGE	Agnes Etherington Gallery, Kingston, ON
AMNH	American Museum of Natural History, NY
BM	British Museum
BRA	Brant County Museum, ON
CFM	Chicago Field Museum, Chicago, IL
CMC	Canadian Museum of Civilization, Hull, PQ
GLE	Glenbow Museum, Calgary, AB
HEY	Heye Foundation, Museum of the American Indian, NY (now the National Museum of the American Indian, Washington,DC)
HUR	Le Huron, Village Huron, PQ
MAB	Musée des Abénakis, Odanak, PQ
MAPB	Musée amérindien de Mashteuiatsh, PQ
MAR	Musée Arouane, Village Huron, PQ
MCC	McCord Museum of Canadian History, Montreal, PQ
MCQ	Musée de la Civilization, Quebec, PQ
MIN	Musée Mingan, Mingan, PQ
MSI	Musée Vieux Poste, Uashat (Sept-Îles), PQ
NYSM	New York State Museum, Albany, NY
PAS	Passamaquoddy Museum, MA
PEAH	Peabody Museum at Harvard, Boston, MA
PEAS	Peabody Museum at Salem, Salem, MA
RDCEC	Kitigan Zibi Anishnabeg Cultural Education Centre, Maniwaki, PQ
RMSC	Rochester Museum and Science Center, Rochester, NY
ROM	Royal Ontario Museum, Toronto, ON
SI	Smithsonian Institution, Washington, DC
SINM	Seneca Iroquois National Museum, Salamanca, NY
WICEC	Woodland Cultural Centre, Brantford, ON

My words fall,
Arousing inquisitiveness,
Hoping to stir
Different opinions.

If Indians today
Are not fictitious,
Then know them.

I am not
What they portray me.
I am civilized.
I am trying
To fit in this century.

Pray,
Meet me halfway—
I am today's Indian.

—*Poems of Rita Joe* (Halifax: Abenaki Press, 1978)

Chapter One

Cultural Knowledge: Searching at the Boundaries

I If we can only begin in the way we're supposed to begin, then it changes whatever we're talking about. That meaning, that understanding, and the truth of it somehow, it gets beyond just the words, and our hearing and our seeing.

—Jim Dumont, Birch Island, August 1986

The Boundaries of Beginning

A beginning is a boundary, but beginning in the right way often seems to involve a search beyond that boundary. A search for motives or reasons, for the roots of one's thinking/feeling, or for the sources from which one learned. A search for the right moment, the best place or truest emotion. Such searches take different forms, of course, in different contexts.

An academic book concerning sound-producing instruments in First Nations communities in Northeastern America might indeed be expected to begin with "motives or reasons," probably labelled "objectives" and frequently outlined in general, sometimes abstract terms. In academic discourse, we might say that this book aims

(a) to explore the symbolism of sound and image as expressed in the musical instruments of Aboriginal communities in this broad geographic area by reflecting on the processes of interpretation used by Native consultants;

(b) to examine how such instruments facilitate interaction and relationship among all parts of the living world;

(c) to represent information in a multivocal manner and to engage in a reflexive examination of the dialogic relationship of different voices, both to avoid the homogenization of Native perspectives and to uncover some of the bases and biases of our own interpretive tools.

In the context of Native communities, on the other hand, we are often challenged to search for motives and reasons not as "objectives" but "subjectives"—to look within. Why did we *need* to do this research? Or as we were so often asked by Native acquaintances in the course of the project, "Why are *you* so interested in Native culture?" Trying not to sound self-righteous, we sometimes responded: "Cross-cultural understanding is surely a good and necessary thing. Respect for the dignity of another way of being is the objective." But then we were sometimes asked, "Why do you think you should *write* about a culture other than your own? Is it not better to offer respect by continuing to listen to what others say?"

All of us in this dialogue are aware of the Euro-American heritage which attempted to legitimize the presumed cultural supremacy of the European in part by drawing a stereotypic picture of a simultaneously savage and naïvely noble North American Indian. That awareness has been articulated by many writers, including the poet Rita Joe, whose challenge is printed opposite this text. While perhaps our fascination with Native culture is, in part, a continuation of the Euro-American search for self in the mirror of another way, it is also an attempt to listen accurately and respond in a manner which will, in turn, arouse inquisitiveness and stir different opinions. For us, this book is part of a pathway which continues.

On a personal level, it is difficult to define—simply and relevantly—the position *from* which we speak or write. Even a small "we" such as the SPINC Research Group[1] involves three individuals with different backgrounds, interests, and personalities. To what extent do our Irish, Scottish, and German ancestors shape our thinking? In what ways were "we" formed by the Ontario farms and towns where we grew up? How does the fact that one of us was born in Europe, the other two in Canada, contribute to the identity of SPINC? What are the structures of class, age, or gender which support or constrain us, making us who we are? Who are our most influential teachers and friends? What music do we listen to? What do we read, eat, dream, wear? While we won't bore our readers with answers to these and other questions, neither will we discount such factors. Individual styles and ideas emerge in our words, and we hope, by recognizing this, that we also offer respect for the individuality of the consultants and musicians with whom we worked.

On the other hand, the position *in* which we research and write, our position as social actors in the often uneasy relationship between museums and archives, on one hand, and First Nations consultants on the other, can and must be addressed. Various Aboriginal curators and writers have explicitly voiced critiques of museums. George Horse Capture, former curator of the Plains Indian Museum of the Buffalo Bill Historical Center, Cody, Wyoming, describes the "strange and special link" between First Nations and museums "as a love/hate relationship. . . . The hate aspect comes from the fact that the museums and materials often are inaccessible" (1991: 50). Gloria Cranmer Webster, Director of U'Mista Cultural Centre, Alert Bay, Vancouver Island, is equally direct about the return of cultural materials:[2]

My question to museums out there is, "Why would you want to keep objects that you know, or even suspect, may have been stolen or otherwise illegally acquired." If you can't answer that honestly, don't talk to me about your ethics. (1988: 44)

Of course, many museum personnel have a strong commitment to support the interests of Native communities.[3]

Nevertheless, it is uncomfortable to work among certain "privileged" institutions knowing that Native colleagues might be far less welcome, to study instruments so restricted that they cannot be discussed in the homes from which they were obtained, to encounter drums taken from unprotected grave sites. It is unlikely we would analyze, photograph, poke and prod (however respectfully) instruments in a friend's home as we did those in museum collections, and we simply would not have access to many restricted materials outside these institutions. Native colleagues did not instruct us *not* to study certain collections; they may have felt

that would be culturally inappropriate. Some strongly encouraged us to continue; at the very least, we could help locate significant material resources of value to their communities. But discrepancies between that which is culturally appropriate and that which is institutionally accessible have left us uneasy.

While we are deeply grateful to museum staff at each institution for the opportunity to research, we have struggled to achieve a text which recognizes the integrity and priority of Native concerns. What we present reflects the perspectives of Native colleagues, elders, teachers, and friends to the best of our understanding. As such, photographs of certain instruments are not included, certain private information is not transcribed and several instruments are omitted altogether. We do not seek to justify our work but to respond in a way which recognizes that the discovery of hard truths is part of the learning process.

Beginning with Boundaries

Within the academic context of ethnomusicology, a book about sound-producing instruments in the context of Native communities might present sources of our thinking/feeling by referring to the history of organology—the English term used to describe the study of musical instruments—or by acknowledging important publications in ethnography, Native studies, or social scientific theory. Within academic work we often discuss music as if it were separable from the events and experiences of our daily lives. In the teachings of Native consultants, on the other hand, music is integrated with dance, spirituality, and life; the discourse about all these things often focuses on personal experience; and the right way to begin more often involves celebration and thanks than rigorous explanation or analysis.

These differences are, of course, not just distinctions between Native and non-Native approaches but also between cultural outsiders and insiders or theorists and practitioners. As Pierre Bourdieu said, "in taking up a point of view on the action, withdrawing from it in order to observe it from above and from a distance, he [the scholar] constitutes practical activity as an *object of observation and analysis, a representation*" (1977: 2). He likens the scholarly enterprise to the creation of a repertoire of rules and observes that:

It is significant that "culture" is sometimes described as a *map*; it is the analogy which occurs to an outsider who has to find his way around in a foreign landscape and who compensates for his lack of practical mastery, the prerogative of the native, by the use of a model of all possible routes. The gulf between this potential, abstract space, devoid of landmarks or any privileged centre—like genealogies, in which the ego is as unreal as the starting-point in a Cartesian space—and the practical space of journeys actually made, or rather of journeys actually being made, can be seen from the difficulty we have in recognizing familiar routes on a map or town-plan until we are able to bring together the axes of the field of potentialities and the "system of axes linked unalterably to our bodies, and carried about with us wherever we go," as Poincaré puts it, which structures practical space into right and left, up and down, in front and behind. (Ibid.)

Native consultants who challenged us to identify why we needed to study their culture as well as critical theorists such as Bourdieu suggest, as we read their meaning, that the right place to begin is with an awareness of reasons for which boundaries (such as Native/non-Native, outsider/insider, or theoretician/practitioner) were created and of ways in which they have been defined. To understand the theory of our own academic practices and the conditions which make our project possible is, in our view, a necessary part of this study.

The problematizing of boundaries is pervasive in both the content and organization of this book. The scope of the study and of subjects within it are

not easily delimited, for one thing. We undertook archival research in two dozen museums in Canada and the United States, research encompassing a larger range of artifacts than in any previous study of this kind; as well as community research with elders, musicians and other consultants in fifteen Iroquoian and Algonquian communities in Ontario, the Maritimes, and the Northeastern United States. The anthropological label, the (North)Eastern Woodlands, which denotes both a huge geographic area and several dozen First Nations, facilitates a comparative perspective. But the boundary is arbitrary and imposed. The Cree and Ojibwe Nations, in particular, span areas called Eastern Woodlands and Plains; Western Native teachings are shared in Eastern Canada. While the instruments we documented were, primarily, in the "Eastern Woodlands" collections of most institutions, we examined one Plains collection (the Glenbow), which was of particular relevance to Eastern communities because of its Midewiwin collection.

People move! Area boundaries are also crosscut by socio-political and linguistic ones; intertribal gatherings have often taken different forms in Quebec, for example, from those in provinces on either side, or in Iroquoian as compared with Algonquian communities. As the short historical accounts in Appendix A indicate, the building of confederacies, the interrelationship of people

Nations and Communities
The following map series shows the approximate location of Nations and communities referenced in this book. More extensive maps may be found in the *Historical Atlas of Canada* (Toronto, 1993), vols. 1 and 2; see especially vol. 2, Plates 31-33. For complete listings of communities in Canada, see Indian and Northern Affairs Canada, *Schedule of Indian Bands, Reserves and Settlements Including—Membership and Population, Location, and Area in Hectares* (Ottawa, 1987).

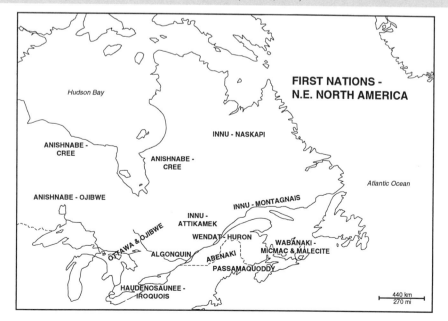

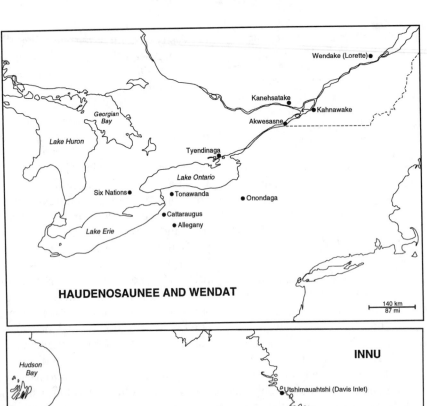

Wendake (Lorette)

Kanehsatake

Kahnawake

Akwesasne

Georgian
Bay

Lake Huron

Tyendinaga

Lake Ontario

Six Nations

Tonawanda

Onondaga

Cattaraugus

Allegany

Lake Erie

HAUDENOSAUNEE AND WENDAT

140 km
87 mi

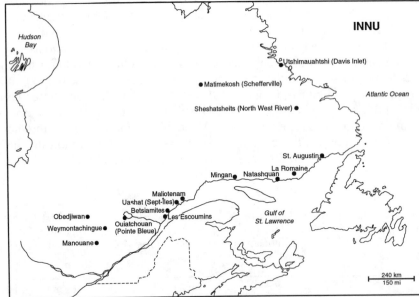

INNU

Hudson
Bay

Utshimauahtshi (Davis Inlet)

Matimekosh (Schefferville)

Atlantic Ocean

Sheshatsheits (North West River)

St. Augustin

La Romaine

Mingan   Natashquan

Maliotenam

Uashat (Sept-Îles)

Betsiamites

Obedjiwan

Les Escoumins

Weymontachingue

Ouiatchouan
(Pointe Bleue)

Gulf of
St. Lawrence

Manouane

240 km
150 mi

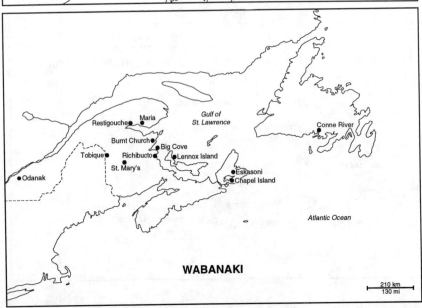

Gulf of
St. Lawrence

Maria

Conne River

Restigouche

Burnt Church

Big Cove

Tobique   Richibucto

Lennox Island

St. Mary's

Eskasoni

Odanak

Chapel Island

Atlantic Ocean

WABANAKI

210 km
130 mi

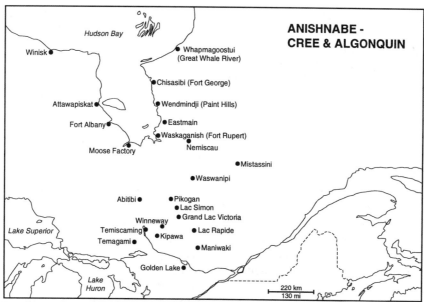

through alliance and cultural exchange, is exceedingly complex. The residence of the Delaware, Tutelo, or Mississauga among the Iroquois, the continuing co-residence of Odawa with Ojibwe or Eastern Cree with Naskapi are examples of international and cross-cultural interaction within communities and households.[4] At the present time, the recognition of "mixed" languages such as Oji-Cree, the sharing of traditions at intertribal gatherings such as powwows, festivals, or summer games, the building of institutional structures which span Nation to Nation facilitate continuing interaction.[5]

The space between Native and non-Native identities is of a different order again. The imaging of this boundary reflects several different political positions. For some, the area between Native and non-Native cultures is a "fertile, liminal ground where new meanings germinate and where common experiences in different contexts can provoke new bonds" (Lippard 1990: 9). For others, the image of the double-row wampum belt depicting parallel histories which maintain their own course, never overlapping, is fundamental.

In order to juxtapose ideas which contribute symbolically to either boundary-making or boundary-crossing, each chapter of this book is organized around an abstraction. While these metaphors are the authors' creation, they were selected because they seemed to facilitate a dialogue across boundaries, encounters between concepts which were our consultants' and our own, or between issues among consultants. In this way, "theory" (ours/theirs, yours/mine, Iroquois/Algonquian, etc.) and "practice" are placed in dialogue, thereby problematizing the processes of representation in which we engage. The abstractions are expressed as follows: "relationship, complementarity, and twinness," "real," "languages of sound," "languages of image, design, and structure," and "motion, cycles, and renewal."

In the second chapter, we consider instruments as reflections of different concepts of "relationship," particularly concepts of family, clan, and cosmos articulated within individual First Nations, and beliefs about the complementarity of difference (the "twinness of all things" as described in many Anishnabe contexts). Wherever appropriate, musical instruments are presented as "beings," alive and sentient; we explore processes of working with natural materials as ways of relating to the environment in a manner consistent with traditional teachings.

Chapter Three explores a wide and disparate array of meanings which we came to associate with the concept of "realness." These include issues of "authenticity," shaped historically by non-Natives writing about Native culture. But we also consider very different emphases voiced by Native consultants who described the "real" as things "given by the Creator." And we explore the constraints and contingencies of using "real" to distinguish between conscious and unconscious (or dream) realms, as well as between human and spirit beings.

Chapter Four looks at verbal discourse—in languages of both the Iroquoian and Algonquian families—relating to musical instruments. Naming practices, ways of verbalizing use and function, and both morphemically and lexically based connections between sound and other domains such as "motion" and "dressing" are discussed. Verbal and non-verbal language are juxtaposed. That is, the sonic vocabulary of instruments is explored in relation to metaphors for sound and sound-production.

Chapter Five shifts the emphasis to elements of visual design and physical structure. A structuralist presentation is framed by discussions of larger theoretical issues such as "what draws attention" and "percept ambiguity." Consultants' interpretations are discussed as a system in which meaning is emergent.

Chapter Six looks at the abstraction of "motion" in its three English-language senses: motion in time, in space, and in thought/feeling. Fundamental images and topics from earlier chapters return here; in

particular, the basic connection between sound and motion is examined in both its physical and philosophical senses. Again, the multifaceted nature of the abstraction takes us to rarely connected subjects: the integral unity of music and dance, the life cycles of individual musical instruments, contrasting paradigms for exploring the history of both artifacts and processes of interaction among First Nations and between Aboriginal and Euro-American communities.

In Appendix A, a summary account of the historical contexts and development of musical traditions within each of the Nations concerned in the study is presented.

A Catalogue of Musical Instruments of First Nations Communities in Northeastern America is forthcoming on disk from Wilfrid Laurier University Press. It contains short physical descriptions, provenance and other museum documentation, and consultants' comments where available. The catalogue is prefaced with information regarding database design, institutions, and an index of instrument makers.

Sources of "Knowing": Elders

First Nations Elders

To acknowledge the intellectual traditions which form the underpinnings of any study is an awesome task. There are so many!

Within the context of university study, Native intellectual traditions are just beginning to make a significant impact. The work of writers and cultural theorists Rayna Green and Paula Gunn Allen as well as historian Deborah Doxtator were particularly influential at various stages of the project. Autobiographers (Ron Geyshick, Dominique Michel, An Antane Kapesh, Daniel Vachon, Mistanapeo),[6] as well as numerous playwrights, novelists, and poets[7] who are finally achieving the recognition they have been denied for so long helped us see the place we were speaking from with more clarity because they wrote of themselves with such honesty and power. At later stages the publication of histories from First Nations' perspectives produced a long-overdue revision: Métis historian Olive Dickason's *Canada's First Nations* (1992) is a landmark example.

But it was most certainly the elders[8] and consultants who worked with us on the project who were the major theorists, the philosophers who challenged the straitjackets of our minds, who encouraged us to respond with heart and mind together. In the oral tradition, we are indebted to many speakers at Elders Conferences and gatherings, but especially to a number of people who worked individually with us. Anishnabe Jim Dumont, Art Solomon, and Gladys Kidd and Cree elder James Carpenter together with Esther Wesley and Bertha Mathat at the Ojibwe Cree Cultural Centre worked with us on the definition of the project and on specific problems of instrument interpretation. Within the Iroquois communities, many respected singers and speakers are our teachers, working closely with Sam Cronk: they include Seneca singers Elijah Harris, Fidelia Jimerson, Richard JohnnyJohn and family, Chief Hubert Buck, Sr., Sadie Buck, Dennis Lay, and linguist Dr. Hazel Dean, Cayuga linguist Reg Henry as well as Mohawk linguist David Maracle and linguist/musician Amos Key and family. Museum curator and art historian Tom Hill, also Seneca, advised us on numerous matters. Wabanaki from both the East—Micmac storyteller and musician Michael W. Francis, singer Tom Paul, linguists Bernie Francis and Mildred Milliea, educator Marie Battiste, elders Sarah Denny and Peter Christmas, as well as Maliseet advocate Alma Brooks, and Passamaquoddy singer Margaret Paul—and the West—Abenaki curator and musician Nicole Obomsawin similarly assisted us. Innu singers, instrument-makers or dancers from Sept-Îles—Jean-Baptiste Jean-Pierre, Alexandre Michel, Annette Vollant and family, contemporary singer/songwriter Cyrille Fontaine, educator Céline Bellefleur—and Labrador singers—Agathe Piwas, Mani Shan Nui, and Thomas Noah—were patient consultants. Museum curator Carmen Gill Casavant gave us valuable assistance and information about the collection at Pointe Bleue; Marcelline Canape introduced us to the work of the Comité Educatif at Betsiamites; Emma Piwas assisted as an interpreter in Davis Inlet, Labrador.

To search for a uniform "Native perspective" is ludicrous, of course. Nevertheless, certain shared values and ideas emerge in the diversity. One of these was a challenge to embed our study within broader philosophic questions: not just what it means to know about musical instruments but what it means to know. In our experience, only trained philosophers could approach such huge and significant questions without risk of utter naïveté and extreme arrogance. We met such philosophers, trained within their own First Nations cultures, and they convinced us to be perhaps a little less afraid of the questions or perhaps a little more convinced that we could not relegate responsibility for the answers to the elites of a single academic discipline.

For Anishnabek, a perspective on "knowledge" is often integrally related to a four-part circular design which is sometimes called the Medicine Wheel. Its cardinal points are multiple symbols: among other things, for the races of humanity, for the four directions, for colours, for physical elements and for various qualities associated with each of these. While the teachings of the Medicine Wheel are often associated with Plains culture and many people read aspects of these teachings in the words of Black Elk (an Oglala Sioux whose "vision" has been published in several editions), the life "in the four directions" is widely prevalent in Ojibwe and Cree communities and has a following in Micmac and Maliseet communities.

In a course on Culture, Identity and Behaviour of the Native Person, Ojibwe elder and Laurentian University professor Jim Dumont explains the place of knowledge within this circle as follows:

"First of all, we begin with 'seeing.' Everything begins here. Simply understood, it refers to the day: VISION applies to the sunrise. At this beginning place we can *see* the whole day—the whole picture. We can see what is ahead of us and have a view of what it is that we are to do and the direction we have to go. From this stance, how we *see* the day and the picture of life will determine everything else that unfolds and how we will come to understand it.

"TIME refers to the length of 'day' itself—from the time the sun begins to move following the 'moment' of sunrise to the point of sunset. During this *time* we experience the whole length of the day and *relate* to the world around us. First we 'see' life ahead of us and then we 'relate' to what we see, in terms of the reality around us as we respond to and experience it.

"At the end of the day we look back on our day and consider our experiences and remember our first thoughts at its beginning. When we do this, we can understand our response by relating our 'vision' to the actual experience of everyday life. The 'vision' gives meaning to our experience in 'time' and when we apply reason and feeling to this we have KNOWLEDGE. We understand.

"Now, in 'knowing' what it means, we can *act on it*. We can behave in such a way that is appropriate to the intention of life itself. DOING follows understanding. Understanding depends upon our experience in 'time.' Experience is of quality when it emerges from out of the right 'vision' in the beginning.

"DOING, then, is acting on the original VISION with the KNOWING and the understanding that

comes from the everyday experience of life in TIME.

"This way of understanding the progress of the day applies to everything in life: from the process of the four stages of life to the way in which an idea or flash of insight is tested by reality, is rationalized by the meaning it gives to everyday experience, and is finally realized in concrete actuality."

Some Algonquian Nations do not regard the Medicine Wheel or the teachings of the four directions to be part of their heritage. And yet, certain ideas have a similar resonance. There are different Montagnais words for "knowledge" said Céline Bellefleur, education consultant for IECAM. One— *n'tsessinan*—means that you hear about and understand the words about something. On the other hand, you can "know" because you experience. Knowledge for the Montagnais people, she continued, is a place. That place is *nutshimits*. Usually translated as "the country," it refers to the heavily forested, rugged interior of Labrador and Northern Quebec. The metaphor of reading is not so foreign to the knowledge of place. You learn to "read" the natural phenomena there; each plant or animal is like a book. Indeed, some elders know the "languages" of animals and can replicate them.

Hubert Buck, Sr., an Iroquois singer and Confederacy Chief from Six Nations reserve also spoke of learning to "read" the world around him. There are also many ways to express "knowing" and "understanding" in Iroquoian languages. In Mohawk, for example, *kahronkha'* translates "I know (and thus use) a language"; *keweien:te*, "I know how to do something." The root of *wake'nikonhraien:ta's*, "I understand something," is *o'nikon:ra'*, which implies spirit, character, thought, belief, and consciousness, depending on the context (Maracle 1985: 227). Mohawk linguist David Maracle stated that all these terms imply direct experience or first-hand knowledge. To know means, then, that you use or have personally experienced something.

Closely related to these ideas are others from different First Nations which stressed similar kinds of response to one's environment. Manitoban Native educators Margot Flanagan and Ellie Iverson write:

Native philosophy and religion, language, historical perspectives and contemporary approaches to life are wholistic in nature. That is, Native thinking sees the world and its elements in a certain totality, with a whole-to-part mode of consciousness. This high-level mode focuses on the whole pattern, the whole concept, the overall picture, of the perception of stimuli. Rela-

tionships among the parts making up the whole pattern are intuitively felt, but are not specifically obvious nor important. Logical, temporal, factually detailed components of the overall perception do not command attention in themselves, but are derived as divergent conclusions from the whole picture. As Momaday has observed, the Native person sees . . . with both his physical eye and the eye of his mind; he sees what is really there to be seen, including the effect of his own observation of the scene. . . . There at the centre, he stands in good relation to all points in the wide circle of the world." ("Integrated Approach to Native Education," in Mokakit Indian Education Research Association 1988)

In other instances, we were reminded of the double nature of knowledge. Jim Dumont advises that knowledge has two sides: "It can be best *for* you or get the best *of* you." In other instances, when asked why we "needed" to know something, we came to realize that knowledge has responsibilities.

The tools of learning in different institutional contexts were sometimes compared. Micmac educator Marie Battiste, for example, has explored the ideological framework of a writing-based education system:

When Mi'kmaqs' curiosity and ingenuity prevailed over missionary restrictions and they learned how to use the new phonemic scripts for their own purposes, they were presented not only with another writing form but also with access to another paradigm of knowledge not based on information acquired through ritual and ceremony. The objective world of tribal knowledge was challenged by writing specialists or ruling elites. Western knowledge posited a new paradigm; it was man-made, incremental and segmented, hierarchically divided, and ever-changing. Authority for Western knowledge was not of the spirit world but was acquired by specialists and elites who formed socially and politically acceptable paradigms which changed with society through time. Preserved in books, knowledge was accessible to only a small group of literate elites. Societal and political structures further determined who learned to read and who had access to knowledge, as well as who was to contribute to the knowledge. (1982: 110-11)

All of these authors emphasize that interactive personal experiences and reciprocal living constitute the knowledge of a group.

In parts of North America remote from the Northeastern Woodlands Nations and communities, complementary stories have been published. Like the statements cited above, these reiterate the need to respond personally and individually to the world around us. Soge Track, a young woman from Taos Pueblo, is quoted in P.V. Beck and A.L. Walters, *The Sacred: Ways of Knowledge, Sources of Life*, as follows:

All through this time I never asked of them (grandmother and grandfather) or anyone, "why?" It would have meant that I was learning nothing—that I was stupid. And in Western Society if you don't ask why they think you are stupid. So having been raised to not ask why but to listen, become aware, I take for granted that people have some knowledge of themselves and myself—that is religion. Then when we know ourselves, we can put our feelings together and share this knowledge. (1977: 51)

A very similar point of view has been published in a curriculum statement from the "Sacred Circle Project" in Edmonton:

Elders emphasized listening and not asking WHY. There isn't any word in the Cree language for "why." A learner must sit quietly and patiently while the elder passed on his wisdom. Listening is considered to be very important. Questions were not encouraged. Asking questions was considered rude. Clarification of a certain point or comment was considered okay.

Learners were also encouraged to watch and listen to what was happening around them. Eventually with enough patience and enough time the answer would come to the learner. When this happened, the learning was truly his own. (Quoted in Medicine 1982: 148)

A number of ethnomusicologists have reported similar perspectives in explorations of the processes of learning/acquiring Native ceremonial knowledge, including song. In Charlotte Frisbie's study of Navajo medicine bundles or "jish," for example, she reports on Navajo styles of learning. The process can be a very long one—four or five years usually but perhaps as many as twelve. Her Native collaborators emphasize the importance of choosing a good teacher, of getting the proper instruction rather than picking up or stealing songs. One must wait to acquire the appropriate songs at the time when one is ready.

Once you learn Blessingway, you have to perform it in the presence of your teacher. After it's decided that you really are sincere and are going to perform the ceremony correctly, then you have the privilege of asking your teacher for those especially sacred songs. You do not learn those right at the start. . . . When you are learning . . . and you suddenly begin asking questions about the secret songs, they always put you aside and say, "No, I can't tell you that. You're not ready for it. You are not prepared for it. I haven't seen how you conduct your ceremonies. " (Quoted from Frank Mitchell, Frisbie 1987: 89)

These statements, emanating from different regions, demonstrate that Native processes of acquiring knowledge differ quite radically from many aspects of education acknowledged in institutions of the dominant society, institutions of which we are a part. Recently, however, an increasing number of individuals in mainstream universities have also turned to engage in styles of teaching and learning which seek to integrate experiential and hence individualized learning with received tradition.

Non-Native, Academic Elders

Logically, all studies are necessarily products of coincidence, although scholars may rarely think of them as such. In the case of the SPINC project, however, coincidence was a subject we frequently discussed. The issues raised by the elders we have just cited intersect, perhaps coincidentally, with many ideas current in social scientific and humanistic "theory" in the last decades of the twentieth century: the emphasis on meaning as a dialogic construction (exemplified in the passage quoted earlier from Bourdieu but indebted to Russian literary critic Mikhail Bakhtin 1934); attention to the specific historical moment and geo-cultural milieu which nurtured specific academic questions (see, e.g., the argument for late twentieth-century ethnography as an "experimental moment" in relation to intercultural relationships in a post-colonial world in Marcus and Fischer 1986 or Appadurai 1988); reflexive critiques of ethnographies (see Clifford 1986, Said 1977, or Marcus and Fisher 1986) and art or literary forms (see Clifford 1988, Lippard 1990, hooks 1990, Spivak 1988; for music, see Said 1991, McClary 1991, Solie 1993); multivocal representations (Lippard 1992, Tedlock 1992, Seeger 1987); and more richly textured studies of "identity" as fluid and relational (Kondo 1990, Clifford 1992), as well as many other issues in "cultural studies" (as exemplified in Grossberg et al. 1992). All these interrelated themes enable us to see the social groundedness of our thought, knowledge, and expression.

Within both North and South American Native studies, these themes resonate in a number of recent works which influenced or paralleled aspects of our own. As a study of artifacts as symbolic universes and as sites of political and intercultural negotiation, ethnomusicologist Charlotte Frisbie's *Navajo Medicine Bundles or Jish: Acquisition, Transmission, and Disposition in the Past and Present* (1987) served as a model of interdisciplinary range and synthesis as well as social responsiveness. The need to work interdisciplinarily, indeed the impossibility of isolating one domain—such as music—from other expressive forms or experiences, is widely acknowledged by many other contemporary ethnomusicologists working in First Nations contexts. Barbara Tedlock's work on intertextual aesthetics (1985), her insistence on the association between "the arts that stem from the voice" and those that "stem from the hand," each an "intertext," a gloss on other texts which speak within it, is, in our view, a profoundly important concept for organology. Her recent ethnography, *The Beautiful and the Dangerous* (1992), challenges the genres of writing which ethnography normally draws upon and sets challenging standards in its rich detail and evocative writing. Interdisciplinary approaches (indeed the recognition that music, dance, ceremony and worldview are inseparable) as well as evocative presentation are equally hallmarks of *Native American Dance: Ceremonies and Social Traditions* (Charlotte Heth, ed., 1992) the first publication of the Smithsonian Institution's National Museum of the American Indian.

Studies of metaphor and language-based worldview influenced our work on verbal concepts and discourse styles. These include classics such as Witherspoon's *Language and Art in the Navajo Universe* (1977), Dennis Tedlock's exploration of myth performance in *The Spoken Word and the Work of Interpretation* (1982) as well as Regina Harrison's *Signs, Songs, and Memory in the Andes: Translating Quechua Language and Culture* (1989). Near the end of our study, the publication of Robin Ridington's *Trail to Heaven: Knowledge and Narrative in a Northern Native Community* (1988) presented another non-Native's pathway from academic study to a knowledge which did not divorce either experience or artistic expression from "social science."[9]

As an exploration of multivocality, Judith Vander's presentation of five Shoshone women's perspectives on their musical repertoires in *Songprints* (1988) demonstrates one means of respecting the individuality of consultants, while Tony Seeger's *Why Suya Sing* (1987) enables us to see how several different styles of research writing could be synergistically juxtaposed. Lucy Lippard's *Partial Vision* (1992) presents a varied array of elders' and consultants' commentaries on their favourite photographs of First Nations people and places. All these authors offer alternatives to monolithic or univocal pictures of cultural expression and experience.

Within the narrower field of organology, a number of recent studies, some focusing on North and South American Native contexts, seem coincidentally to have moved in parallel directions to ours. First, they regard musical instruments interdisciplinarily, not isolating the art historical from the technical or interpretive. Second, they reflect recent emphases on the interpretation of metaphoric and symbolic codes, particularly anthropomorphic and zoomorphic codes. Third, several studies have used unusually broad ranges of data (historically, geographically, and morphologically—i.e., museum and contemporary instruments, ceremonial and commercial instruments) in order comparatively to explore processes and systems of thinking, classifying, and evaluating images and sound.

Margaret Kartomi's *On Concepts and Classifications of Musical Instruments* (1991), for example, looks at types of classificatory systems—particularly "culture-emerging" systems—of categorizing musical instruments, ways which are rooted in different linguistic and conceptual worlds,[10] thereby seeking to debunk the "assumption that it was correct to use Western categories for the study of a non-Western instrumentarium" (1991: 9).

Both Kartomi and Sue Carole DeVale (in *Issues in Organology*, 1990) are concerned with the wide range of culturally defined phenomena which the study of musical instruments can access. DeVale acknowledges her debt to her teacher Klaus Wachsmann whose organological model placed the instrument at the centre of a converging stream of musical and contextual elements, as in the diagram below:[11]

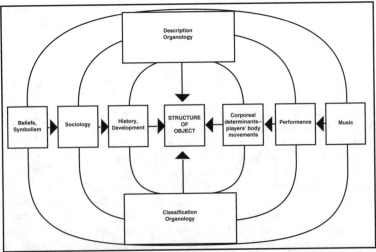

Fig. 1. A model for the study of musical instruments. After K. Wachsmann, "Classification," in S. Sadie, ed., *The New Grove Dictionary of Musical Instruments* (London: Macmillan, 1984), vol. 1, p. 407.

Among recent explorations of instrument form, particularly as a reflection of the human body and of various species of beings in the cosmology, are studies in *Sounding Forms: African Musical Instruments* (1989), which, like the aformentioned *Native American Dance*, draws together scholars and practitioners, contemporary interpreters and museum collections. Ethnomusicologists have also addressed the link between cosmological explanation and musical instruments. Judith Becker's exploration of the relationship between "Earth, Fire, Sakti and the Javanese Gamelan" (1988) emphasizes the breadth and depth of metaphoric references which musical instruments embody:

Musical instruments, throughout the world, come to have meanings associated with them that far surpass their pure physicality as sound producing objects made of wood, metal, or clay. Their use in ritual brings them into association with whatever ideas concerning man and the sacred are suggested by the ritual. As sound producers, as instruments which are capable of the miracle of producing form without substance, they can powerfully suggest and support ideas of the sacred. (1988: 385)

She examines Indonesian belief in a sacred earth, an earth which is transformed by fire (literally by volcanic eruption). She then looks at the process of mining and forging the bronze used for instruments, a process which both mirrors and creates the transformation of earth through fire; hence, mining is "spiritual" in that miners or blacksmiths must communicate and placate the forces with which they are tampering. The third metaphor in her title, *sakti*, or the combination of male and female elements, also reflects in the structures and sounds of instruments, reinforcing the link between cosmic and social energies and the value placed on the inherent balance among them. We were drawn to Becker's exploration of intertextual metaphors, to her discussion of the spirituality of process, and her emphasis on the coincidence of iconic systems as powerful creators of meaning.

In other geographic areas, instruments both represent and elicit different metaphors. Kartomi's discussions of Mandailing discourse relating potency and completeness (ideas which also govern musical performance where types of ensembles have more or less completeness) or her representation of Mora's work on the T'boli metaphors of strong and gentle in relation to musical instruments are cases in point. Also relevant to our work are studies which explore the legend-based origins of music or other relationships between instruments and myth (see, e.g., Hugo Zemp's *Musique Dan*, 1971 or Feld's *Sound and Sentiment*, 1982).[12]

Within the Americas, organological studies focusing on "culture-emerging" symbolic interpretation have been more prevalent in the South than in the North American context. Izikowitz's *Musical and other Sound Instruments of the South American Indians* (1970 [1935]) emphasizes interpretation and symbolism at an early point in the history of organological study. More recently, the metaphoric extensions of musical instruments have been a central theme in several studies: the relation of Kamayura flutes to gender structures and to the human body (Hill 1979) or zoomorphic and anthropomorphic iconization by the Waiapi of Brazil (Fuks 1990). An aspect of Fuks' research procedure which resonates with ours is his examination of symbolic concepts of place. In his conclusion, he summarizes the implications of Waiapi beliefs about musical instruments:

Musical instruments imitating animal sounds and behaviours stand in a shifting relationship to both the realm of human society (where their use in ritual helps assure the constant flow of necessary resources and social relations) and the realm of nature (of which they are considered to be a metaphoric representation). (1990: 168)

On the other hand, North American research focusing on the symbolism and interpretation of musical instruments is scant, although early twentieth-century anthropologists including Hallowell, Speck, Skinner, Harrington, Parker, Goldenweiser and others recorded many fragmentary accounts. A rare study which does focus on musical instruments is Voegelin's description of Shawnee musical instruments (1943). These works often omit precise contexts and sources of information, unfortunately, creating an impression of a rigidly defined symbology rather than demonstrating individuality operating in relation to a field of shared values and practices. The richness of symbolic information from these sources, however decontextualized, has been represented and extended in later ethnographies and ethnomusicological studies (e.g., Merriam 1967). To date, the most extensive exploration of a North American Aboriginal instrument is Thomas Vennum's *The Ojibwe Dance Drum: Its History and Construction* (1982). Working both in archives and with drum-maker William Bineshi Baker, Sr. (with whom Vennum also produced a film to accompany the book), he explores a single instrument type, the dance drum, from its late nineteenth-century origins through the twentieth century.[13]

Most other research on North American Native musical instruments has not emphasized culture-emerging classifications or interpretations. Distributional studies (e.g., Haefer 1976, Brown 1967) have sought to map instrument types in order to determine historical interaction or to define regional differences.[14] Performance practice explorations have enabled us to contextualize instruments, or to trace their uses and functions (see, e.g., Speck 1935, Gessain and Victor 1973, Conklin and Sturtevant 1953). Processes of instrument construction have been the focus of other studies (Conklin and Sturtevant 1953) while still others have examined the means by which instruments may be acquired (Merriam 1967).

In sum, however, our academic approach to Native musical instruments was indebted to early North American Native studies more for the comparative data they document than for their methodological premises. Recent organology, however, as well as "post-modern" theory and multivocal representations in ethnomusicology and other domains have been highly influential. The most fundamental developments of our thinking have ultimately taken shape within the confluence of ideas developed by critical theorists of the past decade and those of the elders and consultants with whom we worked in the course of the project.

The Moment and the Research Process

We began[15] this project at a significant moment in our collective histories. The critical need for a new relationship between the First Nations and Canadian governments, both federal and provincial, was evident. Preoccupying our emotions and our thoughts as we worked on this book were conflicts over injustices in the legal system, over the continuation of third-world poverty levels within this affluent country, over Constitution and land claims—at Kanehsatake and Kahnawake, Temagami, Goose Bay, Old Man River, and Meech Lake. "Symbolic" studies may enable a better understanding of a cultural worldview, yet not only differences of outlook and concept, but real differences of power and access, real problems of justice and human dignity, are at issue.

In the same historical "moment," an amazing process of healing and renewal had begun within Native communities. A new generation had turned to their elders, turned to their original teachings and in many areas now lead a cultural renewal that is possibly unprecedented in post-colonial Canada. In some areas, the Maritimes and Ontario for example, events such as Elders Conferences, or traditional Gatherings, provide opportunities to hear these spiritual leaders. We have been privileged to attend many such events and subsequently to work with several of the elders. In the province of Quebec, a somewhat different direction has been taken; particularly among the Montagnais, where the Innu lan-

guage remains strong, programmes designed to teach cultural traditions have been established in Friendship Centres and on University campuses but also in forest camps—the places of traditional knowledge. Simultaneously, a popular song movement is giving voice to First Nations concerns.[16]

Both for practical purposes and because of our previous association with specific Nations, each member of our group attempted to keep contact with a different range of communities. Franziska spent part of each year in the Maritimes, in Micmac communities or travelling with a drum group. When back in Ontario, she was active in the intertribal events scheduled there and in the work of the Native Sisterhood. Usually several days a week, Sam continued his long-time friendships and professional association with people at the Six Nations reserve in Brantford, Ontario, as well as Allegany and Cattaraugus reservations in New York State and with the Native Canadian Centre in Toronto. Like Franziska, he participated in a wide range of Ontario activities, studying Ojibwe as well as several Iroquoian languages. Bev spent part of an early 1980s sabbatical in the Innu community of Davis Inlet and travelled several times a year in the late 1980s primarily to the Montagnais communities of Maliotenam and Uashat, and occasionally to Betsiamites and Pointe Bleue as well as to the Western Abenaki community of Odanak; she also participated in Ontario events including the Native Sisterhood.

The differences among us created healthy intellectual tensions within the group. While Bev was aware, on a daily basis, of her need as a university teacher to communicate with students and colleagues who generally privileged Mozart or Boulez above non-European music and printed sources above oral transmission, Sam and Franziska were more deeply involved on a regular basis with finding ways to communicate effectively with Native friends and associates. We saw all "needs" as legitimate and important but we were constantly aware of forces which pulled us simultaneously in different directions.

We had opportunities to hear a considerable range of music-making, from powwows and socials, gatherings, and private visits to special recording sessions. The contexts of our community work were quite varied. When it was appropriate we were sometimes participants in ceremonies whose repertoires were somewhat restricted. More frequently, we heard social dance songs, certain drum repertoires as well as fiddle and contemporary music performed at public festivals or recorded privately.

In many communities, hymn-singing was a particularly important type of music, both in and outside of the context of Christian church services.

We all had opportunities to hear speech events in which some of the Nations' culturally important texts were performed. We were also each privileged to have an opportunity to work with Native speakers on some of these texts. In the Iroquois context, Native linguists at the Woodland Cultural Centre initiated, in 1988, a project to record the interpretations of such texts as the Handsome Lake Code or Great Law by respected elders. Sam was invited to assist at these sessions. He also worked with individual linguists and elders and, at the same time, produced an "edukit" on music for the Woodland Centre, a joint exhibit (" The Sound of the Drum") as well as two powwow videos. Both Franziska and Bev had opportunities to hear performances of a wide variety of myths and stories. Franziska worked extensively with one storyteller, Michael William Francis, over several years making a full-length video as well as discussing the nuances of his stories and storytelling skill. Bev recorded a collection of myths, traditional songs, and hymns in Davis Inlet, Labrador,[17] from some of the most respected narrators in the community. She subsequently worked with elders on translations and explanations of several of these.

The archival phases of our work were sometimes joint and sometimes individual ventures. Where possible we liked to work together, using Franziska's photographic skill while Sam and Bev prepared notes and drawings of musical instruments. Because we soon found that the profiles of various collections were radically different (see the *Catalogue*, forthcoming on disk) we elected to extend our archival documentation to a large number of collections. Time, funding, and institutional constraints, however, militated against the "complete" documentation of everything in the large collections. In most cases, however, we saw the majority of artifacts (all that could be located for us within the time available) and checked catalogue information for the remainder; we also searched out manuscript and photographic materials. In a few cases (e.g., the Smithsonian Institution where other ethnomusicologists have made or are making comprehensive studies), we documented selected instruments.[18] In retrospect, we feel that our criteria for selection, in these cases, were biased slightly toward objects which were "old," "unusual," or "individualized" with regard to structure, sound, or image. While we realize the problems inherent in these biases, we think that the size of our sample makes our documentation representative of a wide range of musical experience.

We then attempted to share photographs of archival instruments with elders and consultants. They generously offered interpretations and additions/corrections to documentation. We asked few specific questions, preferring instead to listen carefully to whatever our guests wished to share with us about the images they saw. There was not a single group of "selected" photos shown in this manner. Some people saw several of the major collections and spent considerable time looking at them with us. Others saw only a few or commented on local instruments about which they knew something. We arranged for a number of consultants to visit our university campus where they spoke in classes and public lectures, participated in a community social, and worked with us in the SPINC offices. We were honoured to have with us Micmac linguist Bernie Francis, Micmac singer/drummer Tom Paul, as well as Maliseet elder Alma Brooks and drum keeper Margaret Paul, Ojibwe elders Jim Dumont and Art Solomon, and from Six Nations, Iroquoian linguist Amos Key, curator and art historian Tom Hill, singer Sue Jacob, singer and Confederacy chief Hubert Buck, Sr. together with his son and daughter Hubert Buck, Jr. and Sadie Buck. Their comments often suggested new lines of research about instrument types, terminology or discourse, and historical development.

Just as every boundary is both fictitious and real, every boundary both facilitates and constrains. In our case, the broad boundaries of our archival work did, indeed, allow us to see relationships and "developments," but the managing of such a large body of documentation prevented us from following up on a myriad of smaller research problems which predictably arose in the process of our work. Many of these remain for the future.

The final phase, of course, was the writing of the book itself.[19] Fundamental was our belief that we should try to keep individual voices—ours and others—intact. Among the reasons for this was our view that complicated abstract issues are best presented from multiple perspectives. Furthermore, our own emotional and intellectual responses to some of these matters differed and we did not want to homogenize these differences. In addition, we wanted this book to represent a kind of "authoring" which invited continuation.

One strategy for achieving this multivocality was the creation of a series of dialogues intended to serve as a stimulus for further "dialogue." Just how they came about was a second matter. We tried tape-recording actual dialogues and working from the transcripts—rewriting the ideas which were not clear and editing/rearranging sections to improve comprehensibility. In other cases, we made notes during an actual meeting which were later transformed into a written "dialogue." We then rewrote parts and extended the discussion via computers and FAX. While they initially preceded the writing of the chapters, they were subsequently re-edited.

In the pre-publication stages of this project, the dialogues received the most varied reception. While one Native consultant thought they were a strong and important part of the book, as well as the most fun, an academic colleague found them diffuse and self-indulgent. These responses reflect, we think, the fact that monologic authority is itself so contested at present and that individual authority is still ambiguous within the context of academic writing. We hope that the contentious readings of the dialogues may stimulate further "negotiation" of some of the issues they raise.

A more important concern about multivocality was our wish to respect the individuality of the musicians and consultants with whom we worked. Quotations from consultants are minimally edited and separated typographically in boldface print; different kinds of texts are placed side by side, shifting styles from colloquial and subjective to mythic to more academic and distanced, or changing modes from verbal to imagal (through the use of extensive drawings and photos).

In sum, we have often been reminded of the words of the Cochiti potter, Helen Codero, as reported by Barbara Babcock (1987: 392). Babcock was impressed by "her repeated denial of anything resembling singular artistic authorship and control":

"I don't just get up in the morning and start making potteries. First I talk with Grandma Clay and she tells me what to do." "It's not me, it's the fire, he decides how they'll come out." "It's my grandfather, he's giving me these. He was a wise man with lots of stories and lots of grandchildrens and we're all in there, in the clay."

Our collaboration relied on many grandfathers and grandmothers, some of them very young. It relied also on one another, the process of bouncing ideas around the group or even reacting with discomfort to the hard lessons we learned in the course of the work. Together, the "authors" of this book gave voice to the larger body of "Authors" who contributed to its creation. Clearly, we must follow our own pathway across many boundaries from the familiar to the unfamiliar. In each chapter, for each

of five abstract metaphors—relationship, realness, languages of sound, languages of image, and motion—we first examine concepts which emanate from our experiences in Euro-American society, especially the "societies" defined by academic disciplines. We then present a range of ideas and concepts which were shared with us by consultants and musicians who participated in the project, and finally, we comment on differences and relationships among the multiple perspectives as we see them.

To Whom We Speak

As we have stated, the boundaries of groups, communities, nations, and regions are not fixed and definable. Neither are the boundaries of the sources of our knowledge. But the most mutable and unpredictable of all are surely the boundaries of our readership.

We, the writers, are rather like shells on the seashore: the "waves" break on us in a certain manner, we return their energy and send it out, yet we each have a distinctive voice. The book is, in effect, a series of gifts (stories, teachings, drawings, access to artifacts) made from members of the Native community to us, reflected on by us, and passed on with their permission to you, the reader.

The wave goes out . . .

Notes

1 The anagram SPINC stands for Sound-Producing Instruments in Native Communities. The research group, formed by Beverley Diamond, operated out of Queen's University from 1985 to 1988 with the financial support of the Social Sciences and Humanities Research Council of Canada. We are grateful for their generous sponsorship of our work. Sam Cronk and Franziska von Rosen were full-time research associates in the group for four years. The archival materials collected and generated in the course of our research are now housed in the Ethnomusicology Archive at York University, Toronto, Ontario.

2 In this case, she speaks of materials removed during the Potlatch seizures, but her comments are more broadly applicable.

3 As of 1991, American federal legislation is in place to effect the repatriation of Native American sacred materials, and a Royal Commission is currently exploring government policy for museums in Canada. During the past decade, numerous museums, including the Royal Ontario Museum in Toronto, Ontario, have collaborated positively through co-operative exhibits, research, and repatriation.

4 Furthermore, attention to the contrasts between Nations is in itself politicized. Lippard has observed the irony of the fact that "just when new nationalisms

are emerging the dominant society is decentering subjectivities" (1990: 12).

5   What came to interest us were the different contexts and emphases by which we construct differences. Within Euro-American society, for example, a preoccupation with difference can, at times, resist the strength of the political solidarity of Aboriginal people. (We encountered one grant programme, for instance, which would not fund a performance using the big powwow drum—associated with intertribal gatherings—although it offered support for performance specific to individual Nations.) An emphasis on sameness, on the other hand, might result in reductionism and stereotyping.

6   Ron Geyshick's stories are compiled in *Tebwewin: Truth*, compiled by Judith Doyle (1989). Several Montagnais autobiographies have been published in bilingual (Montagnais/French) editions: An Antane Kapesh/Anne André, *Eukuan Nin Matshimanitu Innu-Iskueu/Je Suis une Maudite Sauvagesse* (1976); Daniel Vachon/Tamien Pashau,*Umue Tipatshimun Innut Ute Uashat/L'Histoire Montagnaise De Sept-Îles* (1985); Mathieu André,*Moi Mestanapeu* (1984). Note also a French translation of Michel Gregoire's autobiography with commentary by Richard Dominique: *La Langage de la Chasse* (1989). Excerpted stories of a Micmac elder are published in Ruth Whitehead's *The Old Man Told Us: Excerpts from Micmac History, 1500-1950* (1991).

7   While we cannot, of course, present a complete list of the fictional writings of recent years we might suggest, for readers who seek a starting point, several anthologies of short stories and poetry: Rayna Green, ed., *That's What She Said: Contemporary Poetry and Fiction by Native American Women* (1984); Beth Brant, ed., *A Gathering of Spirit* (1984); Thomas King, ed.,*All My Relations: An Anthology of Contemporary Canadian Native Fiction* (1990); Jeanne Perreault and Sylvia Vance, eds.,*Writing the Circle: Native Women of Western Canada* (1990).

8   The boundaries implied by this subtitle and the next one, "Academic Elders," do not imply exclusive categories. A number of Native scholars who are colleagues in the professoriate are quoted or referred to in both sections. Furthermore, other personal "elders" are not given credit for shaping our perspectives here. The division indicates, however, that our major sources and ways of knowing during the course of this project were, on one hand, individuals whom we met within Native communities and at gatherings who helped us understand Native perspectives and, on the other hand, the traditions of academic study in which we are working.

9   Of his thirty-year association with the Dunne-Za (commonly called the Beaver Indians) of northern British Columbia, Ridington has written as follows: "I had been socialized to think about people, particularly Indian people, as the proper and inevitable subjects of an objective and imperial [*sic*, 'empirical'?] social science. More significantly, I did not question the style of that science. I assumed that the people I

had come to study were, if not my personal subjects, surely subjects of the kingdom of science whose unquestioned objectivity ruled both their experience and mine. Objectivity required that what I did as a person and what I reported as a social scientist were related only in that one was instrumental to the other. I expected the experience of fieldwork to be entirely different and separate from the results.

"Gradually, sometimes painfully, often comically, it dawned on me that this instrumental separation of experience from accomplishment made no sense at all to the people with whom I was living. Knowledge, for them, was something a person integrated immediately into a shared thoughtworld through the authority of his or her own experience. Knowledge, I came to learn, was a primary form of individual empowerment" (1988: ix-x).

10   She creates several dichotomies, taking care not to align them with the culture-emerging/observer-imposed pair. One of these is an attempt to establish a continuum between societies oriented toward oral and literate transmission. Although she is careful to stress the overlap among systems and the "shading" between oral and literate, she believes that systems rooted in oral transmission tend to have a plurality of schemes, to exhibit parallels between the main classification scheme and other spheres of thought such as cosmology, social organization, or historical discourse, to classify prestigious instruments more closely than lesser ones and to use both paradigmatic and single-character logic (p. 12). Another is a distinction between "downward" classifications (those which assume a hierarchical framework which will have sub-divisions as needed) and "upward" typologies (those which examine a wide range of detail and then create a system on the basis of the information). She suggests that downward systems have been used within both culture-emerging and observer-imposed schemata, while upward schemes are always observer-imposed. In this regard, she offers clear definitions for "taxonomies and keys" (a downward system which groups entities logically by applying one criterion at each level), "paradigms" (a multidimensional classification system which derives from the simultaneous intersection of several facets or dimensions), and "typologies" (a multidimensional, "upward" system, always observer-imposed, created by scanning all the variants and grouping them).

11   DeVale applies and extends this system in an analysis of the gamelan at the Field Museum of Natural History in Chicago. She researched the physical and acoustic structure of the instruments, as well as five contextual elements (i.e., the manufacture of the bronze and wood parts in relation to other gamelans, the cosmological significance of the design, the historical and commercial process by which the gamelan came to the World's Columbian Exposition at Chicago in 1893, the documented responses to performances in 1893, the restoration of the instruments in the 1970s). Her reconstruction of these aspects of the "meaning" of this one ensemble demonstrates

that attention to the unique rather than the norm can be an illuminating approach.

12 Ethnomusicologists have also studied instruments as manifestations of social ideology (see, e.g., Hassan's *Les Instruments de Musique en Iraq,* 1981), and, of course, as products of historical processes (see, e.g., L. Picken's *Folk Musical Instruments in Turkey,* 1975).

13 Vennum accepts Wissler's attribution of Pawnee origins (in the "Iruska") for the drum dance and Plains grass dance. Tara Browner has recently done further study of the Grass Dance complex and has corrected some earlier errors in confusing the two ceremonial events (paper presented to the Society for Ethnomusicology, 1990). Her work indicates the need for more intensive historical research.

Nevertheless, historical studies (as opposed to acculturation studies) of delimited aspects of specific Native music cultures have become increasingly numerous in recent years. Some are reconstructions using archeological evidence: e.g., see Donald Brown "Ethnomusicology and the Prehistoric Southwest" (1971); or Beverley Cavanagh, "Problems in Investigating the History of an Oral Tradition: Reconciling Different Types of Data about Inuit Drum Dance Traditions" (1987). Others are largely dependent on archival materials (e.g., Bruno Nettl, *Blackfoot Musical Thought: Comparative Perspectives* [1989], especially chap. 3; or Robert Witmer, "Stability in Blackfoot Songs, 1909-1968," in Blum *et al.,* eds., *Ethnomusicology and Modern Music History,* 1990). Still others are based on oral history: e.g., Victoria Lindsay Levine, "Arzelie Langtry and a Lost Pan-tribal Tradition" (in ibid.).

14 The emphasis in ethnomusicology on distributional studies seems to vary both historically and geographically. Such approaches seem to have remained important in studies of indigenous cultures in the Americas, possibly as extensions of the culture area concept. As applied to "music," for example, Bruno Nettl's delineation of music culture areas (1954) retains a prominent place as a framework for study in several standard music reference works. (See, for example, Randel 1986). Distributional studies continue to hold a prominent place with regard to European folk music instruments, styles, and genres and have received new emphasis in conjunction with Hypercard applications.

On the other hand, the purposes of distributional studies have varied considerably. The SPINC research group also engaged in distributional mapping, as a result, not of the early diffusionist studies, but of suggestions by two Algonquian consultants that the mapping of instruments would be a useful research strategy. At the root of their suggestions was, we came to realize, a completely different concept of mapping, one which did not divide the "map" of North America or Turtle Island from the symbolic "teachings" of the turtle's back, one which saw historical process and human experience as a reflection of mythical teaching at some level.

15 Throughout this book the past tense is used whenever we speak about specific work conducted during the late 1980s. We are uneasy that the use of the past tense is often read, in relation to First Nations cultures, as if the cultures were frozen in the past. We caution readers that our use of the past tense is intended rather to attend to the specific historical moment of the work with some care. As we have already stated, however, our association with many communities and individuals involved as consultants in this project continues. Hence, the present tense is used for more general issues which are ongoing.

16 In 1994, the vitality of Native music will be recognized with the establishment of a special award category within the competition for Junos; it recognizes the best recording by Aboriginal musician(s) at each annual awards ceremony.

17 Copies of the collection were given to the local school and subsequently to the Curriculum Development Centre in Sheshashit, Labrador.

18 Some institutions place a three-day limit on access to their collections, obviously restricting comprehensive documentation.

19 At this point, the problems of working together were complicated by the fact that Bev had now moved to Toronto, Franziska to Providence, Rhode Island, and Sam to Ann Arbor, Michigan. Further coincidences facilitated the completion of the project. Here we refer to the advantages of computer technologies and communications systems which enable university electronic mail links throughout North America.

Chapter Two

Relationship, Complementarity, and "Twinness"

Dialogue

FvR:

I think it was one of the last days we were together this summer that Michael Francis[1] was talking about "clan" and he got really emotional about it. First he talked about clan as a choice: "Well, you get together and you choose something that's important to you, you know, bear, otter or whatever." Then it came out more and more that it's as family that clan is so meaningful. Mike's clan is the raven. Through the raven he connects to his father and his grandfather and great-grandfather. The clan is always ongoing. He also related this to patriotism, saying that clan is "something like your flag to us."

MSC:

A major point here, I think, is that without family you will be physically and emotionally bereft and you will die. Have you ever read the many Iroquoian stories about lost or abandoned children who were adopted by bears or birds, turtles or spirit beings? If you are alone, you will not thrive. There have to be reciprocal relationships, obligations, and connections. In Iroquoian diplomacy newcomers were formally adopted and thus connected to the Confederacy so that they would, in effect, be related.

BD:

What has often surprised me is that there seems to be no dichotomy between this strong sense of connectedness and one's individuality. In fact, as I understand it, individuality is defined through complementary relationships.

FvR:

Do you mean duality when you say "complementary"? I've been wondering whether "duality" implies things in opposition, things in conflict, or mirror images—different perspectives on the same thing? I am thinking of the double curve motif, a frequently used Wabanaki design. That is sometimes interpreted as symbolizing the blurred boundary between reality and illusion.

BD:

I prefer "complementarity" or "twinness" to "duality." I don't hear opposition implied when individuals speak of families or clans or other relationships.

MSC:

I sometimes use "duality" intentionally.

BD:

It depends what you're talking about, doesn't it? When duality is used for, let's say, the double-row wampum belt or when elders talk about the "white" road and the "red" road, that's perhaps duality. That's talking about parallel paths, I think. Each of us has a path, and we try to follow it or we try to go off on the other path.

MSC:

With one foot in both boats, on both roads? We can't do that—not comfortably at least. They're separate paths.

FvR:

Are they really regarded as separate or—I'm just wondering—is it the same road only seen from different perspectives?

Zen Buddhism, for example, sees apparently different concepts as one. You can turn an idea, like a crystal, and you can look at different sides—but it's basically all one. Our world has really stressed division: of the mind and spirit, the real and the illusory, the object and the subject. I'm wondering if I'm still often hearing these polarities when I hear duality; what am I bringing to what I hear?

MSC:

You're question is a good one but, as I understand it, Haudenosaunee do see our Native and non-Native roads as separate. They do not share a Buddhist belief in oneness.

FvR:

But within Iroquoian tradition you read myths of the twins, one being good and the one bad.

MSC:

Who can't exist without each other. Both are children of Sky Woman—I see what you mean. But both are related more to *Ongwehonwe* rather than white culture. That's what I meant about separate paths.

FvR:

But are they actually different or are they one with different sides?

BD:

Saying they're one is too simple. Elders emphasize that some things which are good in one situation can become bad in another.

FvR:

Poison can be medicine or medicine can be poison depending on how you use it.

MSC:

I know, at least in my understanding of Iroquoian thought, that there are examples of duality and twinness. Remember those bone combs with mirrored clan animals, or the silver brooches with mirrored patterns? That may be duality if not "twinness" engaging you in design. But the most important thing that I take from this is the sense of essential relationship between the two parts. For example, each Longhouse has a moiety system, dividing the clans into animal (earth) side and bird (sky) side. They're *not* the same, they're not mirrors of each other. They say slightly different speeches and they have slightly different responsibilities during ceremonies. But it is the sense of responsibility to each other that binds the Longhouse together. "Complementarity"—that's a little bit different from "duality" and twinness, I think.

Returning to cosmological stories about the Elder and Younger brothers—certainly it depends on the interpretation—again it's up to the individual to define good and evil. There are gradations of things related to what we consider negative. But whether death and destruction or decay are pejorative . . . ? These words aren't defined in any dictionary or any discussion I've shared; they're part of a natural cycle. (Violence or witchcraft, on the other hand, *are* considered evil.)

Younger brother is linked with death, but he's not completely evil. Is the Elder brother completely good, or are these terms relevant? I repeat: they simply couldn't exist without each other, and being twins, they are connected to each other in a very obvious way.

FvR:

They are the mirror image of each other as twins. Are they not?

MSC:

They were born differently, the Younger brother emerging from underneath his mother's arm, which killed her. They chose different paths at the very first point in life.

FvR:

The same person with different sides going in different directions, like the Anishnabe lodge of life where women's paths face west and they see life moving away from them while men see life coming toward them.

MSC:

But there is a necessity and obviousness in this. When I talk with Iroquoian people about our interest in complementarity and duality, they look at me, well, not exactly in a bored fashion but as if to say, "Of course this exists. This is reality; this is related to the natural world." There is always interaction; it's just that we don't always recognize or acknowledge it.

I usually hear about concepts of twinness in terms of the story of Sky Woman. Otherwise, I don't hear "twinness" raised in conversation unless people are referring to living twins—one's children, for example. But I certainly don't know every speech or song and there may well be references I don't recognize.

BD:

I've heard discussions of complementarity as a broader concept, one which celebrates "diversity." When an Anishnabe elder speaks of the yellow flower standing beside the purple flower, the birch beside the cedar—all in perfect harmony, part of the message is surely that the diverse elements of the environment, including the human environment, are "needed" for all to survive.

FvR:

That's something like a story that Mike tells about Creation—about the beginning when everything was green; there was no diversity, no red, yellow, and purple flowers until the Creator made it rain and the water droplets absorbed the colours of the rainbow and fell to the earth. Then the earth sprouted flowers in all the colours of the rainbow.

MSC:

Talking about flowers and trees: the experience of where people are situated geographically—the expression of that *physical* experience of the landscape is so central to philosophy, music, culture. I keep thinking about the many Iroquoian metaphors related to trees, the bush, the forest's edge, to kinds and uses of wood—at Stirring Ashes, for example (a renewal ceremony at Midwinter), at Condolence ceremonies, or annual ceremonies acknowledging *wahda*, maple trees; or the use of wood for masks, lacrosse sticks, baskets and of course the Longhouse itself. The abundance of this substance shapes their culture.

FvR:

In a similar way, I think, Maritimers use the sand and the beach as a constant theme. *Wta'nuk* ("out to sea") is the summer camp on the sand dunes, a place, I was told, which is important for story-telling. It seems to me that the the "ashes stirring" of Iroquoian culture is analogous to the "sand stirring" which is the action of the ocean.

BD:

The bush, *nutshimits*, which is usually translated as "the country" is, I think, the same kind of cultural heart for the Montagnais.

Recently, however, another sort of complementarity was mentioned to me by a Montagnais friend. For her, the Ojibwe are responsible for maintaining Native spiritual values, the Montagnais, for maintaining their language through the medium of popular song and so on. History, socio-political context, all these things also seem to shape the complementarity of the Nations.

Her words reminded me of a comment made by Montagnais elder Alexandre Michel that "instru-ments are like flags." He was, I think, expressing a deep sense that every group of people has a responsibility. That seems to be getting clearer and clearer for me. As I understand it, the close association with a particular geographic location means that certain people know about certain physical aspects of the environment and have a responsibility for them. It might be related to the clan responsibilities—we have heard Anishnabe elders speak about the clans being jointly responsible for different parts of the earth's surfaces—or it may be more specifically related to region. On a visit to Pointe Bleue, I was told that the neighbouring Attikamek were really skilled in the treatment of skins; they were the ones who really knew those materials. I didn't visit any of the Attikamek communities, but it is apparent from the museum artifacts we documented that they also have developed a technology and aesthetic for birch bark. Together the knowledge of materials, the knowledge of environment, enables the physical and spiritual survival of the nations.

MSC:

For me, it's the relationship between communities that gives these different areas of knowledge meaning. The emphasis must be on the connections; it's my responsibility to you, our responsibilities to each other.

Note

1   Michael W. Francis is a Micmac storyteller, artist, and musician with whom Franziska has worked extensively. Their video co-production, *Micmac Story-teller: River of Fire* (1991), is one product of their collaboration.

Now another thing, in the air and wind,
He created in the air the fluttering of the birds
And the different sounds of the birds.
This is for them to hear.
This is for when they are lonely.
This is for them to enjoy, the ones I have created.
Now this time of the day,
Now we give thanks for the birds that are fluttering in the air.
This is the way it should be in our mind.

—From the "Ganohonyonk"—Thanksgiving Address —as spoken
by Richard JohnnyJohn and translated with Jerome
Rothenberg, 1968, and M. Sam Cronk, 1989

Relationship, Complementarity, and "Twinness"

A nd it is here in the Western Hemisphere that
the knowledge
Still remains intact
Of how we are to walk in peace and harmony
With the Creation,
That knowledge was here
Before the strangers came and it is here still.

—Art Solomon, "What We Say We Are," in *Songs for the People:
Teachings on the Natural Way* (1990)

S omebody asked me once where they could go and photograph
Indian churches. I said, "Go and take a picture of the sky. Go and
walk out and thank the Maker of breath that you are in a church.
An Indian church is all around us. There are special places of course. . . .

—Rayna Green, radio broadcast in conjunction with the Smithsonian Institution's
programme honouring the Seneca Nation, April 1987

All My Relations

Within a Native American ceremonial or social context, within a speech-event or written document, as a salutation or cadence point, when the phrase "all my relations"[1] is uttered or written, a notion of relationship that is broader and deeper than any we have learned within Anglo-American society is invoked. This struck us forcibly when we first spoke about writing a chapter on "connections and relationships" among the musical instruments we had studied. We first thought in human-centred terms. What could artifacts tell us about the relationships of people, their regional differences, the cross-influences and interactions among them? But Native consultants immediately conceived of our title in terms of all living entities in the universe. We began to see that in relation to their interpretation, our human-centredness was a narrower vision, a Euro-Canadian-centric vision. Though voiced and lived in diverse ways, "all my relations" is a vision

shared by Aboriginal North Americans. Some speak about symbolic representations of "relationship"; others emphasize the practical or experiential. We continue to struggle to understand this Native concept of relatedness, an ideal which generates co-existence and mutual respect among all living things. Without knowing this, little can be understood about Native song, music, instruments, or worldview.

In this chapter, we begin by presenting Innu, Anishnabe and Iroquoian perspectives of relationship to one's community and environment. Phrases which serve as subheadings—"The One and the All," and "The Twinness of all Things"—are heard most often in Anishnabe contexts, but similar concepts seem to underlie many Iroquois and Innu worldviews.

"The One and the All": Identity, Family, and Relatedness

Identity and its host of attributes—gender, age, ethnocultural background, economic class, religious affiliation, and many others—have been extensively discussed by social scientists from many disciplines.[2] Recent academic explorations have rejected the notion that identity is "coherent, seamless, bounded and whole" (Kondo 1990: 14), relating the "Eye" and the "I," and demonstrating the partialness of individual perspectives (see Kondo 1990, chap. 1). Scholars have suggested that experience fragments or subverts notions of identity as often as it confirms them (e.g., Butler 1990). The elusiveness of the boundaries of identity reminds us of one of the metalogues written by Gregory Bateson as if in conversation with his young daughter, Mary Catherine. She queries why things have outlines. Bateson (1972: 2) responds with a theoretical problem: how one can draw the boundaries of a flock of sheep or a conversation. "Things," like discourse or experience are often in motion and their qualities are of course different from one moment to another.

Like these academic explorations, the words of First Nations consultants recognize and express the complex, fluid play of relationships. They frame concepts of individuality somewhat differently, however—not as separate from and contrasted with the world around, but surrounded and supported by and connected with that world.

At traditional gatherings and conferences, Aboriginal speakers usually choose to begin with a statement about who they are. They often indicate their Nation and clan affiliation or, less frequently, their Native name. Such statements, however, have less to do with defining identity boundaries than with establishing their relatedness to the world around.

Sometimes an image is used to represent this relatedness, but just as discourse is fluid and in motion, design and design interpretations vary among individuals and contexts, as well as over time. Some years ago at a conference on Iroquoian culture in Rensselaerville, New York, Allegany Seneca Wolf clan mother, Longhouse faithkeeper and linguist Dr. Hazel Dean emphasized that, first of all, she was alive, then she acknowledged her

clan and her role as clan mother, that she was Seneca, then Iroquois, and then Indian. These seemed to be the circles of importance for her.

This image of concentric circles reflects a distinctive way of situating individuality, not in contradistinction to (or in confrontation with) other individuals but encircled by rings of relations. The concept it represents is widely shared among First Nations.

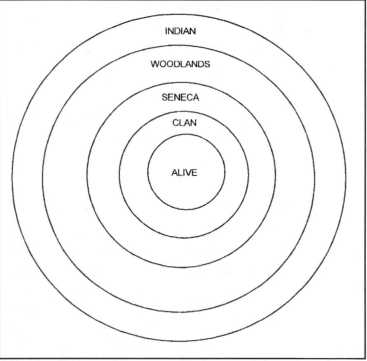

Fig. 2. Circles of relationship.
Drawing based on presentation by Dr. Hazel Dean at a conference on Iroquoian culture, 1989.

An Iroquoian illustrator drew Fig. 3 to interpret her words, depicting a non-hierarchical array of elements in a network of relationships.

More recently, during a private conversation with Sam Cronk, Hazel described an alternative design, one similar to that drawn by William Fenton (see Foster 1974: 107) who worked with many members of her family. Framed within the skydome and supported by the earth, she exists as part of a world shaped by reciprocal relationships—with the natural environment: water, plants, four-legged beings, trees, birds, winds, the sun, the cosmos—and with spiritual forces. Similar drawings have been used by Iroquoian speakers throughout this century as mnemonic devices for remembering the *Ganohonyonk* ("Thanksgiving Address"), a traditional opening and closing speech which acknowledges all these elements. At a conference, Hazel must

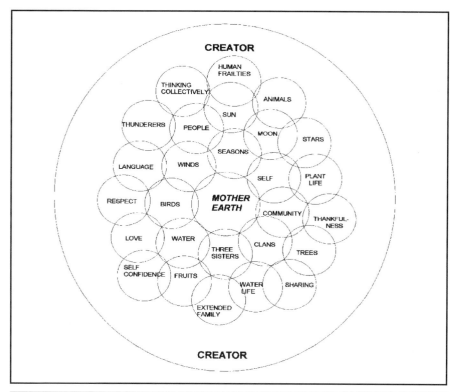

Fig. 3. Ögwehöwe:ka:? Wholistic way of life.
After *Ögwehöwe:ka:—Native Languages for Communication*, New York State Syllabus (Albany: University of New York, State Education Department, 1987).

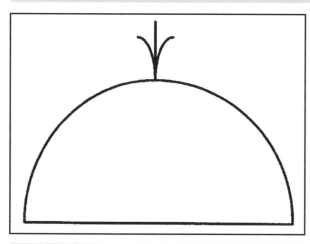

Fig. 4. Skydome: Enclosing "All my relations."
Draw *your* world.

Photo 1. Rattle with sky-dome (MSC 87/10).

acknowledge her many roles to those who do not know her. But at home at Allegany, she is immediately recognized by and recognizes all those physical and spiritual forces which make up an Iroquoian worldview and she is an integral part of her environment.[3]

Ojibwe elder, Keeper of the Eastern Door of the Three Fires Midewiwin lodge, Laurentian Univer-

sity professor Jim Dumont used a comparable image to explain each human's relationship to other beings in a presentation about the Ojibwe clan system at the Third Annual Traditional Awareness Gathering, at the Native Canadian Centre, Toronto, March 1989.

Some of Jim's explanatory comments are paraphrased below:

You have to know your whole family to know who you are.

You should actually start from the outer circle and move in, but from where we are on this Earth, it is easier to start from ourselves and move out.

In a family, a mother's love is unconditional because her child moves away from her from the moment he is born. A father sees the child coming toward him. He can see when the child goes off the path and must correct him.

You have to know your clan because you are related to all of creation which belongs to this clan. They are your family.

The earth family includes rocks and trees and animals; the cosmic family, stars and the spirit world.

In Jim's image, the first circle surrounding the self is the family, a word indicating blood relatives[4] on the chart but extending, as his comments make clear, to indicate the relationship of all living things. There are many contexts in which kinship terms and concepts of family are used by Aboriginal speakers to describe broad socio-political concepts which are not separable from "spiritual" belief. A nation may refer to another by a kin-

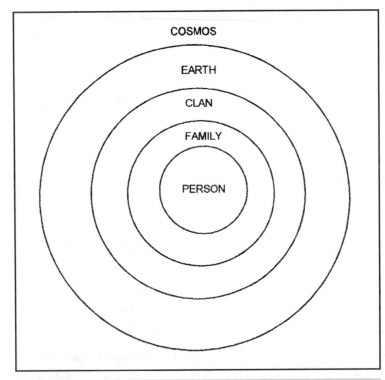

Fig. 5. Relationship.
Drawing and comments after presentation by Jim Dumont on the "Ojibwe Clan System" at the Third Annual Traditional Awareness Gathering, Native Canadian Centre, Toronto, March 1989.

ship term. Ruth Whitehead provides an etymology for the name "Micmac," explaining that it was actually "nikmaq," meaning "my kin-friends" and was the greeting with which Europeans were welcomed to North America in the sixteenth century (1989: 1).

Within the Iroquois Confederacy, the smaller nations, the Oneida and Cayuga (and later the Tuscarora) are the "younger brothers." In treaty alliances, British and American governments have similarly been addressed as "younger brothers,"not with reference to the size of their populace but rather to the status of their relationship with the Confederacy and indeed with this continent:

Onondaga	
Elder Brothers	Younger Brothers
Seneca and Mohawk	Cayuga and Oneida (Tuscarora have no voice)

Perhaps more familiar references to this extended family are phrases such as "Mother Earth," "Grandmother Moon," and "Grandfather" (spoken in reference to a drum, an animal, or other natural phenomena—a river, the sun, or the thunderers). In

print, words such as "Mother Earth" seem to have little emotional quality. As a literary conceit, the phrase has been reduced to describing analogous qualities between two components—the creation and sustenance of life, of nurturing and dependability. However, "Mother Earth" is not just an abstract concept for many Native people, but a deeply *experienced* relationship.

The affirmation of this relationship may take place in special circumstances. In some Anishnabe families, young boys begin at about the age of eight to go on a series of solitary fasts in a designated spot away from other human beings. At a certain point, they may receive a special dream, a visit from an animal or spirit, or an experience which becomes a "vision," a lesson or power or simply a knowledge of self which will serve them well throughout their lives. For girls, the traditional Anishnabe preparation for adult life takes different forms: during an entire year they abstain from certain social relationships or foods such as berries; they conduct themselves and dress in a certain manner as they learn to know themselves and their responsibilities to those around them; to mark the end of their fast they are first given a strawberry—the "heart" berry—in which a small piece of charcoal has been placed. Adults are encouraged to go out and "spend time alone with Mother Earth" whenever they feel that their lives are out of balance.

To return to Jim's imagery, relationships to non-human beings are recognized within the "clan" circle. Although clan systems differ among Nations, virtually throughout North America, Native people are affiliated with other species. Early ethnographies described these connections as "totemism," cast as a "pagan" religious system which pre-dated Christianity. Contemporary Native elders describe this as a system of governing and organizing the responsibilities of all creatures in the world. Jim Dumont's representation of the Ojibwe clan system in words and images is represented in Figure 6.

Jim Dumont stresses the importance of complementary responsibilities. There are also practical care-giving functions within a clan. If, for example, one travels to other communities, people are expected to treat a fellow clan member as family. Clan,

Each group has a role to play. Together they look after Creation.

When the Crane and Loon people can't agree, they come to the Fish clan for help. The Turtle is at the head. They are the mediators and philosophers.

The Crane and the Loon are at the head because together they have the responsibility of leadership. Their distinctive voices can be heard over both land and water. Their roles are complementary, with one responsible for "internal affairs" and one for "external affairs."

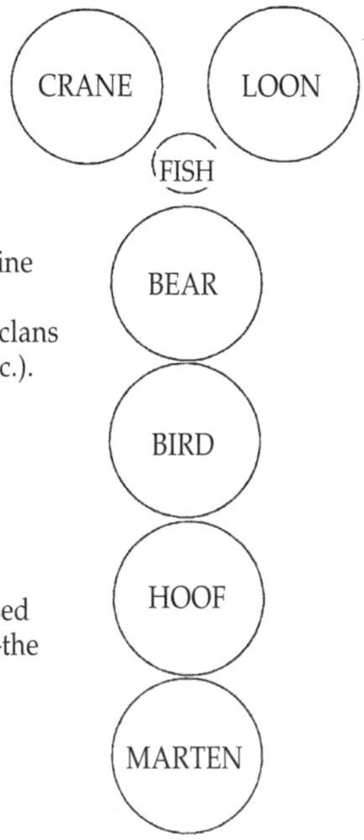

The Bear people are the guardians and the Medicine people. Unlike the Fish clans, which are named for different species (eel, sturgeon, etc.), the Bear clans have names of different parts of the Bear (paw, etc.). There is also a Grizzly Bear clan.

The Bird clans are the educators.

The Hoof clans are good dancers and singers. Caribou skin has a good voice; that is why it is used for the drum. They are the poets and musicians—the "arts" people. Their leader is the moose clan.

The Marten clans know the lay of the land. They are often silent and unobtrusive; they can slip away like the otter. They are the planners. If a child didn't have a clan because his father was a non-Native, the Marten people took him in.

CRANE — LOON — FISH — BEAR — BIRD — HOOF — MARTEN

Fig. 6. The Ojibwe clan system: A system of government.
Diagram and paraphrased comments after presentation by Jim Dumont at the Traditional Awareness Gathering, Toronto, March 1989.

in turn, is associated with place in that certain clans in Anishnabe thought have responsibility for certain parts of the earth. The Anishnabe "fish" clans (led by the turtle clan) are responsible for the waters of the earth. So, too, is the bear clan associated with the earth and regions under the earth; the earth is regarded as the source of many medicines and, hence, bear clan members may be regarded as healers.[5]

Photo 2. A moose hoof rattle identified as a clan rattle (compare catalogue entry for SPINC ID:F.3006.r). Musée Arouane, Village Huron, Quebec (MAR. BD 87/5/2).

Photo 3. Menominee water drum with green and red painted rings possibly indicating clan. Collected by A.B. Skinner in Wisconsin, ca. 1918 (HEY 8/2999. FvR 88/43/5).

Clans are structured differently within Iroquoian Nations. Names for the Cayuga clan animals are as follows:

hnyagwai:	bear
ganyade:	snapping turtle
odre i:ga:	painted turtle
dewahohde:s	deer
dewenhega:	ball deer
deyojia:ne do:t	large deer
otahyo:ni	wolf
go:deh	eel
onehsi:yo	sandpiper
duwisduwi:	killdeer
ohswegai:yo	hawk
naganyayo	beaver
sganyadi:ga:	heron

Special characteristics are also associated with matrilineal Iroquoian clans, though these connections seem less generalized. People joke affectionately about a Heron's love of fishing, the deliberateness of Turtles, or the bearlike walk and growling mannerisms of some Bear clan members. They may also comment on the role of Bear people as healers or on the leadership acumen of the Turtle clan, but to our knowledge these roles are not formally stated in traditional speech or song. Iroquoian Nations have different numbers of clans (the Mohawk have three, Wolf, Bear, and Turtle, for example). Within the political structure of the Haudenosaunee (or Longhouse) Confederacy, each clan of each Nation has both a Clan Mother and hereditary Chief (chosen by the Clan Mother). Within the traditional religious structures of Iroquois communities, clans are divided into two moieties or "sides" of the Longhouse (usually the "birds" side and "animals" side). Members of your own clan are sisters or brothers; members of other clans are your cousins. The moieties have clearly prescribed reciprocal obligations to assist their cousins during Longhouse ceremonies, weddings, funerals, and condolences for Chiefs.

Haudenosaunee people almost invariably own some symbol or image of their clan family—pictures of wolves on the living room wall, for example, or turtle potholders in the kitchen, bears carved in silver and bone, or beaded images of clan animals on baseball caps and key rings. Clan symbols are also prominently featured in traditional bone combs, in beadwork on traditional outfits and *gustoweh* (men's headdresses) and other ceremonial objects such as wooden stirring paddles. Although the turtle is indeed a clan "animal," the turtle rattle is not, per se, a clan object; its role is for the benefit of the entire community. Neither this nor any other Iroquois musical instrument is restricted in terms of clan use or ownership.

The Haudenosaunee system of reciprocity and relationship is clearly expressed by Cayuga Headfaithkeeper (Bear Clan) and linguist Reginald Henry from Six Nations.[6] His acknowledgement makes reference to living things on the earth, in the sky, and beyond, a sequence which is more elaborately unfolded in each varied recitation of the *Ganohonyonk*, the Thanksgiving Address which begins and ends every Longhouse event. He speaks of the significance of the Ashes Stirring which similarly "performs" this deeply felt concept of relationship at major Longhouse ceremonies.

"For us Natives, most anything that lives and grows has a purpose and a spirit, for the purpose of communication in times of need and in appreciation in meeting these needs. The needs are many; it could be for food or it could be for medicine. Weeds, bushes, trees, animals and running waters are only a small part of what mother earth provides for us. The medium we have been given for communicating with any spirit is Indian Tobacco.

"The world could not function without the sun, the moon, the stars, the winds and the thunder Gods and so we give thanks to their spirits also.

"In the beginning the Creator gave us Clans, divided into moieties, to form two main groups, to organize, to function as a people in times of rejoicing and in times of sorrows and in times of misunderstanding. Then, the Creator gave us women and men of wisdom to form a Chieftainship to carry out the peoples' wishes (for) a religious ceremony.

"This one religious ceremony that the Chiefs [did] was for the people; they represented the people in this ceremony. The stirring of tree ashes [was shared] between the two clan groups of people. The people of that time revolved around the forests, the animals, the firewood, the numerous game, the sugar in their homes, their means of transportation on lakes and rivers. Their entire livelihood was dependent upon the forests. So the tree ashes became a symbol of life."

Not all Aboriginal people know their clan, though many are actively searching for that knowledge. Contemporary Innu who are linguistically related to the Anishnabek, for example, do not speak about clan structures, although there is some evidence that one may have existed at an earlier period; for Innu consultants an intensive relationship with the environment is enacted differently. Men do not undertake a "vision quest" but, like the Anishnabek, they pay close attention to dreams, which serve as sources of practical information and spiritual direction. Dreams are the source of traditional hunting songs or *nikumana*. In many instances an intensive knowledge of and relationship with the natural world is maintained for pragmatic reasons. In northern Labrador, for example, a story about a dramatic incident which occurred in the early 1980s affirms this: a local Innu hunter was thought to be lost in a winter white-out, but he knew the locations of the species of each tree in the area so well, it was said, that he managed to find his way home by feeling the bark on one tree after another. The incident demonstrates how an intense connectedness to the world around is expressed and lived on a personal basis.

Vastly wider on Jim's relationship circles are all physical and spiritual beings in the universe.[7] Here another frequently misinterpreted word surfaces: "spirit." Are we speaking of "ghost," of "energy and vitality" or perhaps other things to which the English word is applied? We invariably hear the word "spirit" in Native discourse through a veil of romanticism created by our cultural backgrounds. In contrast, Native teachers are often pragmatic. For them, the practical and spiritual are inextricably linked. A spirit enters each new human life, is born as a human baby, and departs at death. Some spirit forces are familiar; the wind, thunder, and lightning are unseen but felt sources of energy. Native elders resist describing any spirit force (such as *Hadui*, the Wooden Face being, or *Mistanapeo*, the Innu hunter's spiritual aid) as myth since they are considered to be as tangible and conscious as any other living force. In practical gestures of common sense and goodwill, friends provided us with protection, with tobacco ties or sweetgrass as we worked among museum collections where they felt unknown spirit forces were certain to exist. Yet we were shocked and left disoriented when occasionally we encountered the rationally unexplainable. Our experiences made us aware that certain individuals could call upon realms of mind and body, could connect with spirit forces whose existence we had been socialized to dismiss.

Outside Native communities, English speakers rarely use the word "beings" without the adjective "human" before it. Even where we are in awe of or reject potential life-forms, as in the case of UFOs, we refer to "Unidentified Flying *Objects*," not "Unidentified Flying Beings." Objects are defined by their inanimateness. Of course, we recognize "life" in plants and animals but we have been encouraged to regard human life as "higher," more important, and uniquely sensate. There have been many ways of creating a rationale for that value system. Berger and Luckmann (1966: 4), for example, differentiate between the human and non-human worlds using the terms "world-openness" and "closed world." "In this sense [biologically fixed character of the animals' relationship to the environment], all non-human animals, as species and as individuals live in closed worlds. . . . By contrast, man's relationship to his environment is characterized by world-openness."

Unlike Berger and Luckmann (whose book title affirms that they believe in the "social construction of reality"), First Nations consultants with whom we worked saw the relationships among all beings as reciprocal. All life might be described as world open. Struggling between the Euro-Canadian concepts we were taught and the perspectives we were learning, the SPINC group preferred to speak not about the social construction of reality, but about socially constructed attention to reality.

Place

The final circle on Jim's relationship drawing, "cosmos," indicates a sort of relationship which we have arbitrarily separated from the category of "beings" and relabelled "place." "Arbitrarily," because where the environment is regarded as alive and active in the establishment of a "relationship," the concept is, on one level, indistinguishable from that of "beings." We make the separation, however, to highlight the importance of this sort of relationship for the subject that we write about as well as for current discussions in the social sciences about the significance of place.

The attachment to place has, no doubt, been felt by every human being of every culture. The places one finds beautiful, frightening, or com-

Photo 4. Dreamer's Rock on Manitoulin Island in Georgian Bay, Ontario (FvR 86/4/1).

forting are each of those things because of the "relationship" we feel to them. In Native cultures, certain physical formations are important sites because they may show a certain kind of "power"—a strong wind, the sound of an underground stream, a clear vision of the morning sun.[8]

That certain physical spaces have special characteristics is obvious to any individual regardless of cultural background. No doubt, for example, both Innu and Jesuits were drawn to Tadoussac, not only because of the practical value of establishing a mission and a trading centre at the confluence of the St. Lawrence and Saguenay Rivers, but because the drama of the shadow-shrouded rocks at sunset, the marbling of the sheer vertical surfaces that fall to the sea, the winding shoreline that presents a new, strikingly beautiful view over each hill crest, the abundance of sea mammals—probably all of these things compelled the hearts and souls of sixteenth-century people from such vastly different socio-cultural backgrounds as they continue to awe contemporary travellers. Similarly, it is no surprise that Dreamer's Rock on Manitoulin Island is regarded as a place which may inspire a personal vision. Or that the Moisie River, called "Mistashipu" by nearby Innu residents is also called "grandfather" and regarded with respect and love. For both visitors and residents, this countryside is a place of beauty, a home for some, and a source of strength and enjoyment for all. For Native consultants, it is their flesh and blood, their mother. They understand the less dramatic qualities which might imbue a place with spiritual significance, and the ways not just of recognizing, but of honouring, such places.

In the Midewiwin migration myths of the Anishnabek, the "seven fires" (although their exact geographic referents are interpreted differently)[9] help us understand the relationship between place, thought, and life. Each "fire" represents, simultaneously, a stopping point, a teaching or prophecy, and a period within the life of the Anishnabe people.

Recent scholarship has explored this sort of relationship with regard to Native art and religion. The importance of place is overt and dramatic with regard to Anishnabe rock art, for instance, where the sun's rays, the natural markings, or the environmental sounds may be powerful images in themselves, images which may inspire enhancement. In Ontario, for example, the slab of white rock facing east at the petroglyph site near Peterborough may have been selected for decoration because it faces the sun, because its whiteness has a special colour energy, or because the sound of water flowing beneath it makes it seem "alive"; a fissure along which many petroglyphs range may represent the earth's vagina (see Vastokas and Vastokas, 1973; also see Paper, 1988: 8). Design may have been added after the fact to point up the mythic importance of a place or to call beings to a specific site (e.g., Young 1985: 29).

The relationship to place, the feeling that place is "alive' or "sacred" can be easily oversimplified, however. Joan Vastokas warns us of the double-edged reductionism of Eliade's categorization of Native cultures as "cosmic," where an "eternal present" or "cyclical return" governs perception of the phenomenal world—in contradistinction to Euro-American, linear concepts of time and space. She correctly observes that such reductionism can make us insensitive to "experiential phenomena" and "individual response," and she urges us to recognize "that it is experience of the physical environment itself which gives rise to Native cosmology and its symbolism. Archetypal meaning, in short, is generated in experience" (1990: 56-57).

This fundamental affirmation of the "individual" is implied in the image of concentric circles in the diagrams by Hazel Dean and Jim Dumont. This image suggests that the one *is* the all. The whole—the circle—is embodied in the single ring in the middle, the single life cycle, just as it is repeated in each outer ring. Just as the rings have the same form, physical places, beings, and mythic space (or everyday objects) may "map" unto one another.[10] A well-known case in point is the Iroquoian-based identification of North America as Turtle Island, an identification

Fig. 7.

SOUPBONE and SKAWNDAWG   by Ken Syrette

From *Native Canadian* 4/3 (June/July 1991).

which emanates from a version of the Iroquois Creation story.[11] This same story, which tells of the creative/destructive gifts of Elder and Younger brother, introduces the concept of complementarity.

Complementarity and Twinness

This cursory exploration of concepts of relationship has already raised problems of definition and differences in application and emotional response to specific words or ideas. If the bases of "relationship" are construed variably in different cultures, then one must look carefully at how criteria for describing relationship may also diverge.

Our Euro-Canadian backgrounds conditioned us to expect that, regardless of linguistic or cultural background, individuals would use "sameness" and "difference" in a similar manner, as criteria for defining the boundaries of related things or beings. Even this assumption proved fragile, however. We tended to see these criteria as opposites while understanding that this is a deceptively simple opposition. If, for example, we introduce the concept of "identity" in relation to sameness and difference, we begin to see an integral tension. Does "identity" relate to features which are "identical" or "the same," or is it more dependent on features which are "individual" or "different"? At each moment of our lives, we try to balance these two poles with delicacy and appropriateness. At times, we stress individuality, at times solidarity with others with whom we share something (whether that be age, gender, ethnic background, place of residence, occupation, preference for certain movies/songs/books, and/or a huge number of other factors). The emphasis shifts with changes in context.[12]

Some Algonquian languages, on the other hand, don't dichotomize sameness and difference as English does. Innu translators sometimes used the same word *tapiskut* to replace either sameness or difference in an English sentence. The word suggests a comparison, an observation of two things "in a similar way"[13] but the speaker does not impose a specific interpretation. The fact that the balance shifts with changes in context is embedded in language. (See Colour Plate 1.)

Shifts which Native consultants made helped us understand the delicate balance as they saw it. A Micmac drummer and lead singer, for example, stressed the musical traditions of his own Nation when he spoke to Micmac school children in Conne River, Newfoundland, saying that the intertribal

Plains traditions were "not theirs." However, in private conversations he expressed a preference for Plains-style musics, finding a satisfaction here in the shared experience that was important to his "Native" identity. An Iroquois friend who is widely sought as a lead dancer at powwows told us that he felt some tension at such events because they are sometimes competitive, unlike Iroquoian traditions, and because in relation to Iroquoian tradition, the dancers move in the wrong direction (clockwise rather than counter-clockwise). The joy of participating in powwows, however, outweighs his concerns. A Montagnais drum-maker used a newly designed flag for his Nation to distinguish, during an interview, symbols such as the pipe which belonged to other Nations. He did not seem concerned by the borrowing provided it was understood that some symbols were not specifically those of his Nation.

Rather than "sameness and difference," a phrase which we frequently heard in Algonquian gatherings as a means of describing contextually dependent relationships was "the twinness of all things." In one conversation the phrase emerged in relation to gender. Excited by a number of recent feminist publications, we were considering a chapter in this book about gender and sound-producing instruments. Perhaps it would be better, suggested the Anishnabe elder with whom we were discussing the idea, to enlarge the concept to "the twinness of all things": left/right, male/female, sky/earth, day/night . . .

On other occasions, "twinness" was implied by an emphasis on mid-points rather than boundaries. The day, for example, divides into before noon and afternoon or into light and dark. Anishnabe stories often make reference to dividing or turning points with different "directions" on either side. In the migration story, it is said that Anishnabe went out but after four "fires" he turned back toward the Creator. Similar turns may be observed in nature. We were taught that the bear turns in its den halfway through the winter; he turns and faces the door when his fast is half over. Young thunderbirds turn at a certain time of year.[14] The concept of turning is fundamental to the notion of relationships, emphasizing their dynamic and non-static qualities as integral.

Related to the emphasis on middles rather than boundaries is the notion that the parts on either side are fundamentally complements of one another. In some cases, the complementary parts complete a circle or cycle, as in the case of the bear or thunderbirds. In other cases they are reflections. The Anishnabe religious institution known as the Midewiwin is regarded as a reflection of the fourth universe of the spirit world.[15]

Similar though distinct concepts are evident in Iroquoian belief and lifeways. The twins of the Creation story, the Elder and Younger brother, are related to Night and Day, although summer and winter are not so twinned. The centre of space in the Longhouse is marked by the singers' bench, demarcating, in turn, the dividing line between clans and moieties and between men and women. A Seneca perception of time with an emphasis on midpoints has been explained by McElwain as follows:

The Seneca day is not perceived in terms of sunset and sunrise as might be expected, but rather in terms of the meridian noon. The beginning and ending of the day (defined here as one complete rotation of the earth) is midway between two noons, but this is not an important point of time in Seneca perception and is not sharply defined. The important point of time is noon which is called *ha'tewe:nishe:h*, "the middle of the day." Noon divides the day into two parts. In theory these two parts are very different in quality and this quality has an effect on everything that happens. Ritually it can be noted that certain ceremonies must be performed before noon and others after noon. The forenoon ceremonies include most of the public rituals or thanksgiving rituals and the recitation of the Good News of Handsome Lake at Midwinter. The afternoon (in practice we would say evening) ceremonies include most of the medicine society rituals, whether at Midwinter or otherwise. Certain kinds of stories belong traditionally to winter and to afternoon rather than forenoon. The colour of a falseface mask is determined as red or black depending on whether it was made in the forenoon or afternoon. (1989: 22)

All My Relations and Musical Instruments

Thus far, readers may wonder whether we have lost our subject—sound-producing instruments—in the broad discussion of relationship. Concepts of "family," of "the one and the all" as well as "the twinness of all things" underpin the design, use and interpretation of musical instruments since, regarded in some instances as sensate, they are part of "all my relations." Metaphors of relationship are reflected in instrument design and enacted in performance.

Instruments, "Family," and "The One and the All"

Images of circle upon circle are evident in the design of many instruments. They may take the form of painted rings on a membrane, wooden disc, or vessel; or we may see circles of dots, each a multiplication of the last. The layers may be the multiple rims of a frame drum or carefully layered cloth wrapping a water drum rim or dressing a rattle handle or drum frame. Such images can be explained and interpreted in many ways, as we discuss in more detail in Chapter Five. In some instances (see, e.g., HEY 2/9537), Anishnabe interpreters describe this image as "the one and the all."

Photo 5. Montagnais disc rattle (drumstick) and frame drum with double rims, top and bottom. The membrane has four concentric circles of red dots (MCQ 87-3654-1 and 2. BD 88/8/7).

Photo 6. An Ojibwe frame drum with yellow and blue circumference rings and a central blue circle. The drum was collected by Fred Blessing in the 1950s in Mille Lacs, Minnesota (GLE AP3220. FvR 88/21/16).

Such images are also realized in performances of course. In some locations (at Chapel Island, Cape Breton, or Indian Island, New Brunswick, for example), the earth itself bears the imprint of a ring of dancers, moving year after year, generation after generation, over the same circle which is in turn a small dot on the sphere of the earth itself. At a powwow, a drum is surrounded by a circle of drummers, perhaps surrounded by a circle of women who are said to "hold the circle together"; the drum arbour is surrounded by a circle of dancers inside a circle of onlookers, who are probably ringed by food concessions and craft booths. What do these images mean? How does it feel to be part of the image?

Photo 7. Ojibwe powwow held during the Algoma Legislature Tour at Barwick on the Rainy River, Ontario, June 23, 1899. Public Archives of Canada (C60659).

The feeling of dancing in such a circle conveys one sort of answer to these questions as was eloquently described, in relation to Iroquoian social dancing, by Cherokee scholar, author, and poet Rayna Green:

For most people who participate, something happens when you're dancing together with your own community. Something happens to bring you together. And it is the coming together that is part of the beauty. Seeing other people, out of the corner of your eye or in front of you, moving in the way they move, the "in" way of moving. And we like to see that; it pleases us.

We dance to please the Creator. We dance to express joy in the Creation. That's what dancing's about. Prayer if you will. It's an act of prayer.

So when you see people moving with you, your whole community with you, joining in the same beat over and over again—it's like for a Buddhist chanting a mantra, the repetition and the beauty.

That dancing in a circle is important, to bring the circle back in. That's an expression of togetherness, of community, of on-goingness. When outsiders see that, they think "oh how dull. They just go round and round the circle, the same old thing all the time."

For us something else is happening. (Rayna Green, radio broadcast in conjunction with the Smithsonian Institution's honouring of the Seneca Nation in April 1987)

The structure of a powwow song has been described using similar imagery:

"So the first part is the one where the leader sings. He comes on really high and he's alone and he starts off the song. That's the part where he calls on the Creator. That's what that part represents. He calls the Creator and says come and listen; we're gathered here the way you intended us.

"Then there's a second part when all the singers come in. And that one calls all the spirits of the animals and plants to come and listen—asks them to join in.

"And the third part calls on the men, people to come.

"Then the last part—the last part always goes. . . . It sort of goes down like that. That's the part they say that blesses all of nature like—asks all of nature and gives thanks.

"I've just been told that by an elder." (Interview conducted by Kevin Hamlin with Geraldine Nadgewan, Moose Factory, May 1986)

In these images, each "one" is both part of the whole and, in some senses, replicates the "all." Similar ideas are conveyed by the stories of the origins of certain types of sound-producing instruments, such as the "grandfather" water drum of the Anishnabek. Such teachings or stories can be heard at Elders Conferences and traditional gatherings in many regions of Eastern Canada (and elsewhere) where they are told by respected elders as part of the process of healing within Native communities and in response to worldwide environmental problems. Each element of this Anishnabe drum represents a part of the living universe and together, the parts are "all you need" (Colour Plates 2 and 3).

There may be other senses in which the one is the all, that is, in which one living entity "maps" unto another. A woman's body is often described by members of Algonquian Nations as a drum, the heartbeat of the baby she carries, the drum-beat. Conversely, some drums are living entities which may be compared to the human body. Garland Augustine, Micmac drum keeper of the Birch Creek drum of Big Cove, New Brunswick, explained this relationship as follows:

"The drum is the heart. It's a heart. And the stand is like the legs. You know you got legs. And the rope, it's your veins. That's why [the drum] is not on the ground. The heart's not on the ground. And it's not in a dirty or dusty place. It has to be always up from the ground." (Workshop presentation to young Micmac students at Conne River, Newfoundland, 1987)

Fig. 8. "Grandfather" water drum of the Anishnabe Nation.

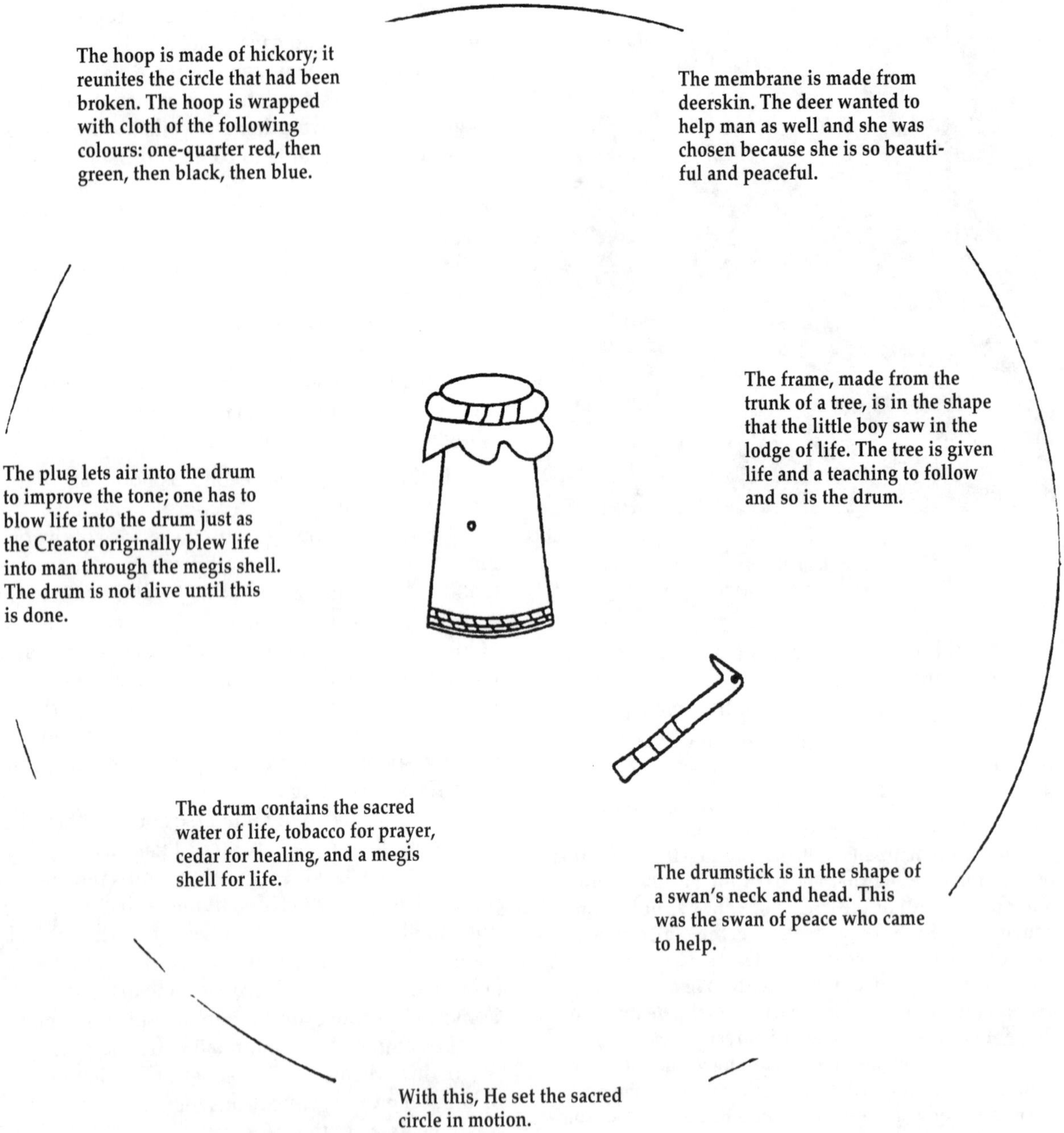

The hoop is made of hickory; it reunites the circle that had been broken. The hoop is wrapped with cloth of the following colours: one-quarter red, then green, then black, then blue.

The membrane is made from deerskin. The deer wanted to help man as well and she was chosen because she is so beautiful and peaceful.

The frame, made from the trunk of a tree, is in the shape that the little boy saw in the lodge of life. The tree is given life and a teaching to follow and so is the drum.

The plug lets air into the drum to improve the tone; one has to blow life into the drum just as the Creator originally blew life into man through the megis shell. The drum is not alive until this is done.

The drum contains the sacred water of life, tobacco for prayer, cedar for healing, and a megis shell for life.

The drumstick is in the shape of a swan's neck and head. This was the swan of peace who came to help.

With this, He set the sacred circle in motion.

After presentations at several Elders Conferences and gatherings.

Photo 8. Ojibwe water drum from Parry Island, Ontario. Collected by Diamond Jenness in 1929. The inset bottom is painted white and pink. Distinctive are the six round wooden plugs wrapped with black thread and coloured cloth and tied to the rim.Multicoloured, ropelike strips of cloth are attached to these plugs (CMC III-G-404. FvR 88/2/6).

Photo 9. Ojibwe water drum from Wisconsin (CMC III-G-843. FvR 88/6/22).

"The rings of colour on water drums may indicate clan or may come from a personal dream or the order of the colours may indicate a male or female drum. Both men and women have red but only men have blue or black. If the order is reversed, the drum may be for the opposite sex." (Jim Dumont)

Photo 10. Ojibwe water drum from Mole Lake, Wisconsin. Collected from John Pete by John Shalloch in the 1940s. Wooden rims are wrapped with navy, printed, and white cotton cloth and burlap, each tied with a layer of string. The inset bottom has a swimming turtle figure which is outlined and partially filled with black paint with a red head/heart line. Black and faded gold rings encircle the lower edge. Black, red, green, and gold rings encircle the vessel half way up (CMC III-G-743. FvR 88/2/23).

In the 1920s, Frank Speck was offered a similar explanation by a Mistassini Cree teacher.

That the drum is more than a mere object, that it has the form of a living entity, is shown by the statement of a Mistassini informant who spoke of it as having a head and a tail; one side being the head, the hoop being the body, the other side, the tail. In this case the Mistassini drum has two heads. Life symbolism in form may be of common distribution throughout the peninsula, but it has not been mentioned to me elsewhere. The informant, in the instance noted, compared the drum to the pack string or *ni.ma'ban* in having its parts correspond to head, body and tail. In speaking further of the drum and its spirit personification I shall use the expressions as they were given to me. "It can speak to him who understands its language when it is beaten. It talks, but all do not understand. When it is beaten by one whose soul is strong, it reveals what is going to happen. Sometimes during sleep the drum will address itself to the soul of a man and urge him to rouse himself and consult its meaning by attacking it with his drumstick. Whereupon it utters forth its message, to be grasped, if possible, by the imagination of the spectator." (1935: 176-77)

The head, body, and tail analogy continues to be used by Innu hunters. See, for example, William-Mathieu Mark's description of the *teueikan* in Serge Jauvin's *Aitranu* (1993: 106).

At powwows, similarly, the sound of the powwow drum is described frequently as "the heartbeat of the Indian Nation."

Rattles may also be compared to the body. One drawing in our collection shows a disc rattle as a human head (where a frame drum is the body). In other instances, a rattle or a drum might be given a "mouth" so it could breathe; we have heard this terminology applied to the wide end of an Algonquian horn rattle, to Wabanaki, Innu, and Anishnabe drums or to small holes made in an Iroquoian bark rattle. Iroquois bark and turtle rattles used in *Hadui* (Wooden Face) curing doings are sometimes described as the hands of the Hadui spirit beings.[16]

The concept of family is also reflected in the naming of musical instruments, at least in Anishnabe practice. As we have seen, Midewiwin water drums are referred to as "grandfather" and "little boy." Analogies may be drawn between the "little boy" and the Younger brother of Nanabus (a legend paralleled in Iroquoian mythology by the story of Sky Woman's two sons). A lesser known family label within the Midewiwin tradition is a name for the gourd rattle—*ogwissimanishigwan* or *ogwissima* ("I have him for a son")—recorded by R.R. Bishop Baraga from Minnesota Ojibwe in the 1870s (see Baraga 1973).

Instruments: Complementarity and Twinness

We have most often heard the metaphor of "twinness" applied to Anishnabe musical instruments. In other contexts, similar ideas may be practised if not languaged, performed but not named. The pairing of complementarities may be reflected in names, in aspects of instrument-making, in visual design (both apparent and hidden patterns), in performance practice, and even in the processes of historical change.

We have already seen instances in which naming reflects a deep respect for "twinness." The complementarity of the generations, of past and future, is reflected in the Anishnabe terms for grandfather and little boy water drums. In both Anishnabe and Haudenosaunee contexts, drums may be described as "wet" (water drums, usually with tanned membranes) and "dry" (rawhide drums in a variety of forms: e.g., frame, barrel-shaped). See also Colour Plate 4.

Complementarities exist in instrument structure and design, as well as in the symbolic interpretations of structural or design elements. An instrument may have interdependent parts—drum and stick, for example—or two sounds—drum-beat and snare, or rattle and handle bells or jingles. A drum and rattle may be paired (see, e.g., GLE AP412 and 413 or MCQ 87-3654); the rattle may serve as the drum-beater, or they may be used together or even buried together. In some cases, their relationship is marked by similarities of design. Elders told us, on

Photo 11. A Plains Saulteaux water drum and tin can rattle, collected by D.W. Light and V. Dusenberry from Pete George of Sakemay River, Saskatchewan. Elders recently gave the following information to the Glenbow Museum: **Peter George received the drum from his father "Old Blind George," whose Saulteaux name meant "Ten Wing Feathers on each Wing" and was sometimes translated to "Two Wings," about 55-60 years ago. Ownership before that is unknown.** Used in the Midewiwin, the water drum is a hollowed log vessel 29 cm high, with dark red dye on the top half and dark blue on the bottom half of the exterior. There is black paint on the inside bottom except for an unpainted central circle. The top rim (not shown) has a red and blue cloth wrap. The tin can rattle is a companion to the drum. Bark is left on the handle at the distal end. The handle has green, blue, and beige twisted yarn ties near the insertion point (GLE AP412 and 413. FvR 88/23/19).

several occasions, of other things a specific instrument needed—attachments, kinds of cloth, images. The museum documentation in our catalogue sometimes indicates things that go together with a specific instrument. The Ojibwe Peace (Dance) drum, for example, is usually associated with the pipe. Some Peace drums have specific songs which must be sung when they are used before anything else can occur. Certain drumsticks, medicine bags, stands, or blankets may be the property of the drum. The sweetgrass used to smudge the drum, to purify it before it is used, or tobacco offerings may also accompany this drum. Small bundles may be tied unto the lacing as gifts to the drum. These are things that are said to "belong" to the drum.

In performance, several aspects of complementarity may be represented. At the intertribal pow-wow, women encircle the men, forming an outer circle around their inner one. While the men are the singers, for the most part, women may join an octave above them to finish the song which the men start. Early twentieth-century photographs of Woodlands and Plains Cree or Ojibwe show similar performance arrangements.

Photo 12. Women encircling the drummers, a tradition shared by Plains and Woodlands Cree and Ojibwe. Photo by D.A. Cadzow at File Hills Reserve, Saskatchewan, in 1926. Heye Foundation (neg. 11760).

Dance directions are sometimes complements. Iroquois social dances are always performed in a counter-clockwise direction but at the *oghiwe*, or ceremony for the dead, the direction is reversed, since it is explained that the living and dead dance in opposite circles. A relationship is also sometimes expressed about Algonquian dance directions relative to the pathway of the sun; both Innu and Anishnabek dance in a clockwise direction, sunwise.

Another aspect of relationship which has recently attracted ethnomusicologists' attention is gender complementarity.[17] Earlier, we mentioned that the woman's body is sometimes referred to as the first drum, her baby's heartbeat as the first drum-beat. Some Anishnabek say that, for this reason, women do not have to drum. With regard to the powwow drum, a Cree consultant from Moose Factory, explained this as follows:

"Women are already considered sacred. She already has the power. The men they have to seek power. And the reason that she has it is the power to give life. She's the one to give birth. She's the life-giver. She's the one to suffer; she carries the pain. And she looks after the children as well. That was the gift that was given to her by the Creator. . . . They already have it, and so they don't touch that drum." (Interview by Kevin Hamlin, May 1986)

In other cases, the complementarity of male and female is reflected in the fact that they may use distinct instruments or share in the construction of instruments by taking responsibility for specific materials. Western Abenaki consultants, for example, associated drums with women and horn rattles with men (see SPINC ID:III.J.3006.d from MAB). Innu families collaborated to make drum or disc rattles in that the skins were usually prepared by women while the men worked with the wooden components.

Thus far, we have shared a number of examples from different Nations and communities which seem connected with the widely shared concept of reciprocal relationship (and the less widely shared metaphor of twinness) in First Nations communities. In the chapters to follow, some of these ideas will return in discussions of specific artifacts, sounds, or visual design aspects. It is important to recognize, however, that our perspective is necessarily shaped by the way in which we designed our research, a way which in itself reflects our own cultural backgrounds. By examining a wide range of instruments, by speaking with many elders and consultants, by participating in a limited number of circumstances, we learned by searching for relationships among the parts. The way we speak about our subject reflects this.

In contrast, we have asked permission to present to you a different vision of a musical instrument and the concept of "relationship," one which, in itself, embodies the "one and the all" and the complementarity of individuals.

An Anishnabe Perspective on the Peace Drum

"The Creation story, it is that very briefly, the Creator, he had put all of his powers in that place. He had already put in motion the sacred circle. We use that word 'the circle' a lot of times, in many ways. The drum is a circle. It's not only because it's round. There's more to it than that. The circle, it's not only because of its shape; there's more to it than that. The English word 'circle' can only define its shape. English terms and English words are limited to that. But the Anishanabe description of that is much more than that, much more beautiful, much more meaningful, and much more spiritual. But we use this language because it is the language of the day.

Photo 13. An Ojibwe dance drum with light blue and dark red sectors, separated by a black band. Collected in Bois Forts, Minnesota, by A.B. Reagan, in 1913 (CMC III-G-167. FvR 88/10/4-14).

"The Creation story which I'm going to hopefully give you to understand is that at a certain time after the Creator had finished the Earth and the Earth was teeming with our relatives, the ones that run about on the Earth, the ones that swim in the water, the ones that fly in the air, this Earth—is a womb. Therein lies the teaching that woman was here first, then man. The Earth she is the Mother of all living things. And water is her lifeblood. If there was not water there would be no life. It courses through her veins in the rivers that run over the surface. The Earth was given instructions by the Creator. And the Earth Mother she has been following those instructions without fail ever since the beginning. We do not know the spans of time—maybe it was ten million years—that this Earth Mother existed in peace and harmony and beauty before man started. . . .

"She was beautiful, the greatest beauty that you can imagine. But at a certain time the Creator said, I should like to send my children to the Earth and where did he turn, where did he look? (When I use the term 'he,' I do not know if that's correct because the Creator is neither man nor woman. He is both.) At that time, when the creation begins, he reached out to this beautiful Earth and he took four handfuls, four handfuls of the earth. What was in that. Those ingredients—what were they? Well science can tell us what our body is made of. He missed nothing. In his total creation, he forgot nothing. Nothing is forgotten. In those four hand-fuls, he took that, and he moulded it. When I say that he forgot nothing, he knew that [in] what he was creating, what was going to be set on Earth, what was going to have tracks on the Earth, there would be physical sickness. And so all of the things, of those things he held in his hand, that fell back down through his fingers, are all the medicines you will ever need.

"When he had finished moulding that figure he took the sacred megis shell, the megis shell that is still in the centre of the Midewiwin lodge, and through that shell he blew his breath upon it, he blew the breath of life. And he gave him, that fig-ure, that spirit/man, that figure that was part spirit and part physical of the Mother Earth, he gave it instructions. I'm going to lower you to the Earth. He was told his instructions. All of that is right here in this world. And it is said that when that took place—we do not know when that took place—I've asked a lot of anthropologists, they're supposed to know everything but they don't know. I've even asked a computer. I looked for that in the bible too. That's a different way there. Creation taught a different way there—It is said that as that being was coming down to the Earth from the reaches of the Creator, he looked down and he saw this most beautiful, beautiful Earth. Today when you look at true traditional dancers— and I'm talking about true traditional dancers— you see them, if you go to a big drum ceremony some day, if you go to sun dance, you will see them—the traditional dancers when they lift their feet and when they set their feet down ever so gently on the earth, that was the act of that man who was lowered to the Earth. He didn't want to land like this. It was so beautiful that he didn't want to disturb one blade of grass. Because it was

so beautiful. And so he touched the Earth lightly like a feather, and settled to the Earth like a feath-er. That's what some of those traditional dances— it has something to do with the grass dance. That's what took place. . . .

"After the world was populated, there came time among the Anishanabe people when anger came among us. Anger appeared among us; it's not part of our original make-up. The Creator did not give us anger; he gave us love, kindness, sharing, faith. That's what he gave us. He did not give us anger. He didn't give us conflict. He didn't give us the mentality of war. It's something else he gave us. And what this original man saw when he was coming to make his tracks upon the Earth, he saw this whole creation living in harmony. He saw the yellow flowers existing by the purple flowers in peace. He saw the birch and the maple existing side by side, each taking of the abundance of the sun as it was needed. He saw the rivers flowing where they needed to flow. He didn't see conflict. He didn't see the pine trees trying to take over the little trees. He didn't see the birds of one feather chasing off the birds of another feather. God's plan is not for conflict, war, destruction. That's man's. These are the things upon which our phi-losophy builds. From that, what this being saw as he was lowered to the Earth he was filled with that harmony, and as he walked off with his relatives, as he came upon the deer, he greeted them. As he came upon the different species he greeted them. He called them by their names.

"That's what he saw. That's harmony. That's peace. And that's how we were to live here on this Earth. We were not to take all, only that which we were to use. We were not to wholesale slaughter all of the moose, only that which would help us. But a time came when anger came, manifested itself. And conflict. And war. And this war among the Anishnabe people themselves, we don't know how long it lasted but it lasted a long time—cre-ated divisions among people. But at the same time, the maple still stood side by side with the birch. The yellow flower still existed with the red flower, each taking of the sun and the earth. The rest of creation did not war. Man did. Man made war. It wasn't God who made war. Man. He wasn't given that instruction: 'bring war and conflict to the earth, that's what I want.' It was the exact opposite of that. And this conflict that I talk about, when I heard that these conflicts were so terrible that it would make the largest rivers run red, whole fami-lies were decimated; whole clans were wiped out; that's how terrible it was. Then at a certain point in time, God the Creator looked down and he saw one Anishnabekwe sitting alone at the top of a hill. And she sat there for many many days without food, without water. She had tobacco in her hand, cedar in her hand. She had sage and sweetgrass. And it is said he looked down and he bent down close to her because she was very weak. He bent down close to her so he could hear her and she was praying. She was praying for the end of the bloodshed, the end of what was taking place among her people. She prayed for Anishnabe man to come to his senses, for Anishnabe man to get back to what he was supposed to be—a man of peace, a man of honour. That's what she was praying for. And it is said that he took pity on her and he gave her—and he said to her I will give you something that will bring peace. If you will take what I am going to give you and in turn give it in the way that I instruct you, what I shall give you will bring peace and the end of bloodshed. And it will always be a symbol of peace. That's the drum.

"Anishnabekwe in turn gave it to us with those instructions. And one of those commandments was that we, as Anishnabe men, was that we should sit around that circle, that we should circle that circle, and that it should be a circle of peace. No conflict. That we are to guard that circle. That certain way that we are to prepare for that drum, a certain manner that we are to gather ourselves around that drum. And from that grew many other kinds of society. But that first one [was] that Peace drum. And there are [as many] stories about other drums as there are other drums. And that [Peace] drum as we know—true ceremonial drums that we don't see at Indian Days, powwow, or at the grand opening of Canadian Tire, or on TV—they have certain markings on them. Those markings have great meaning. Because I can't draw all of it I'm going to share with you at least some of it.

"Across the middle you will see, on some of the drums, a series of stripes like that. It has a lot

Photo 14. Ojibwe drummers with peace drum. Canadian Museum of Civilization (no. 48803).

"And there's a whole beautiful story about how that drum was given. And he manifested it for her so that she could see it and it hung above the Earth—suspended above the Earth. And one of the instructions to her was that it should be suspended always. And when you see these traditional drums, those ceremonial drums, you see those four stakes upon which that drum hangs, that's what that symbolizes. That it should hang suspended above the earth. That's what that drum symbolizes. And from that grew other drums. But that drum that was given to that woman, she brought that. And we must remember that Indian myth. We must remember that. We must remember that the drum came to us through woman. It didn't come to us through a music store. It wasn't brought over here by pilgrims.

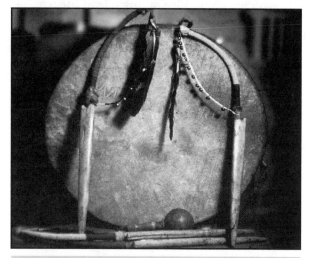

Photo 15. Ojibwe drum, late nineteenth century, "used in the Mide ceremony" according to the catalogue information of the Heye Foundation. Four curved supports, a solid wooden rattle and four rawhide rattles belong to the drum. On one membrane the following words are written in two different hands: "Chief-2/Moon-Drum/June 18.76" and "Mae/Da-I Guss/18.78." Collected by W. Wildschut on the Belknap Reservation in Montana (HEY 11/5864. FvR 88/40/15). See also Colour Plates 5-7.

"It might be a woman's drum because the moon is associated with woman. The red and blue exterior sometimes separates the male and female halves. This is usually also marked by a line on the skin but not here. While women don't drum, they are recognized as the keepers of the drum. If a woman who had dreamed the colours for a drum when she was a girl had not honoured the dream, as an adult, she might have problems until she had a drum made. Older stands (such as this) have the top part inserted into the bottom part." (Jim Dumont) of meaning. It says when you put this drum in place to begin your ceremony, that this road must always be east to west, because that's what it means, the road of life. And that there are two halves to this circle. That's why I was saying earlier today, 'Anishnabekwe'—that she's a part of it. This drum also by its colours and shape has other meanings. Some drums will be blue on one side and red on the other. Those two colours also represent something. They represent some part of that teaching. But this half is dependent on this half; otherwise you only have half a drum. This colour stripe depends on that colour stripe because it has something to do with something we hear so often—walking in balance. Another way that the teaching goes is that this represents the night side of life, the dark side of life, and this represents the good side of life. But in order to walk in balance, you must know of this side as well as this side. Because if you walk only on one side—only on the dark side—you're out of balance. That if you walk only with the knowledge of this side of life, you're out of balance, we are told. That's what those symbols, those colours they represent.

"They also have stakes on which the drum is suspended. Each one is a different colour. Each one of those represents one of the sacred directions. At the top of that pole, at the top of that stake, which is generally shaped like that, there's a little hook here where this loop will go on this stake. And thereby the drum is suspended just as it was in the beginning. Each one of those poles, it will be coloured in different colours, nowadays wrapped in coloured yarn—long ago they simply dyed the wood. That wood is a certain kind of wood for a certain purpose. I'm giving you a general description. I can't give you—you have to come to ceremonies, but I can tell you about it; I can describe it to you. Each one of those poles sits in one of the four sacred directions. And there's a spirit in each of those directions that is represented by this feather on each stake. This stake which is the west is a certain colour. This stake which is the east which is the source of light and knowledge is a certain colour. That's a general description of a drum. And in the beginning, the drum was made a certain way. I don't know how closely people carry that anymore. But one head had to be male, and the other side had to be female. And so generally, the one side was the female of the animal you were using. If it's moose hide, one side had to be from the female of the animal and the other side male, for a very specific reason. It was tied in a certain way. Nowadays, you

see drums being constructed here. There were a certain number of these [lacing points] that were cut into that hide so that they formed a pattern. There was also a certain way in which it was laced so that it formed a pattern and in that pattern you could see the four directions in-between. See these diamonds. That represents the four directions again. So everything about the drum symbolizes [something]. But it is the meaning of that drum that is the most important. Nowadays we have drums of every description. The drum society to which I belong, that drum will never leave that reserve because that's where it's given, that's where it will stay. Only woman could say it could be moved. And the drum represents one drum. There's only one drum, even though there are many."(Eddie Benton-Benai, drum workshop on Birch Island, 1986)

To Conclude

We have used an English-language abstraction, "relationship" to describe a concept which we believe is fundamental to understanding many of the explanations we have gathered in the course of our research. In some cases, instruments are described as symbolic representations of the natural world to which every living creature is related. It is important to emphasize again that not all Nations describe all instruments as symbolic representations of beings, cosmic spheres, bodies, or lodges. Most of these interpretations emanate from Anishnabe perspectives; a few from Innu, Micmac, or Maliseet. Iroquoian perspectives share an emphasis on relationship and on the use of musical instruments in the establishing of relationship but use other metaphors to express these connections. For all Nations, an intimate and detailed knowledge of natural materials and processes—knowledge which most urban dwellers lack—may point to or embody a deeply felt sense of relationship.

The concept of relationship cannot be discretely categorized as part of a religion or a belief system, as Eurocentric ethnography has tended to do, but rather as an ability to recognize spirit in all life. This calls into question distinctions between phenomena which are "natural" or, on the other hand, "supernatural." These English words are problematic. Spirit worlds are entirely "natural" from many Native perspectives. Many social scientists would say that different belief systems constitute different cultural *creations* overlaying the "natural." However, we think that a formulation which recognizes culturally constructed differences in the way we *attend* to the "natural" may be more compatible with the perspective of First Nations elders and consultants.

As we worked at documenting these richly varied and powerfully constructed instruments, we sensed their animation, and occasionally their power. We came to regard them as living players in this project. Perhaps, in saying this, we seem to claim nothing more than any researcher would probably claim about his/her research materials. To a medievalist, a fourteenth-century manuscript collecting dust in a European library might seem to have a similar "life" and vitality. What we experienced (for the most part) may be seen by some as the same active response of anyone who attends to their subject with intensity, intellectual care, empathy, and passion. What we learned is that life respectful of "all my relations" involves this same intensity, intellectual care, and passion on an ongoing, daily basis. But further, that actions and words have consequences throughout Creation, that "subjects" speak back.

Notes

1   The phrase "all my relations" is familiar to many readers since it occurs frequently in other publications. To cite two examples, it is the title of a recent anthology of Native literature, edited by Thomas King (1990) and a chapter heading in Jordan Paper's book about the sacred pipe (*Offering Smoke*, 1988). The non-Native representation of "all my relations" which most resonates with our own is that of Robin Ridington in *Trail to Heaven* (1988), a book which relates his experience in relation to Beaver Indian or Dunne-za people. As well as the substance of his words, the form of his writing, which circles back on the words of elders and on his own experiences, each circle offering a deeper understanding, embodies the concept. "The Trail to Heaven begins at the place where you meet your relatives. It begins when the people you knew from long ago come down to meet you. It begins when they give you a song. It begins when your own voice and their voices become as one" (p. 185). "The Dreamers speak of the Trail to Heaven as a song. They say a good person can grab hold of its tune with his or her mind. The good person is light and sensitive to messages coming from distant places. The animals recognize such a person and come to him in dreams. They give themselves to the person who gives to others. The Dreamers say if people are always together with one another, if they sing and dance together often, they will remain in perfect communication with the animals. The Dunne-za of old recognized Makenunatane as a Dreamer because he told them how to create a perfect surround. When each person knew his or her

place in relation to every other, they were able to walk up to a moose and kill it with an axe" (p. 29).

2   Recent landmark studies which recognize the fluidity of identity boundaries and the complex intersections of group affiliations include Dorinne Kondo, *Crafting Selves: Power Gender, and Discourses of Identity in a Japanese Workplace* (1990); Benjamin Lee, ed., *Psychosocial Theories of the Self* (1982); Edward Bruner, ed., *Text, Play and Story: The Construction and Reconstruction of Self and Society* (1988); and Judith Butler, *Gender Trouble: Feminism and the Subversion of Identity* (1990).

3   This is not to say Iroquoian people are disconnected from spirituality in urban settings. The earth, wind, water, trees, sky continue to exist despite the trappings of concrete and skyscrapers.

4   Native concepts of family and kinship may differ, even in their narrower sense, from those in Indo-European language contexts. Algonquian languages, for example, distinguish older and younger siblings of whichever sex, unlike the English labels, "sister" and "brother," which specify sex but not age.

5   Complementary relationships among other Nations are, in some respects, spoken about in similar terms. We were told, for example, that certain Nations have the teachings of one ceremony. The Menominee have the original teachings of the big dance drum. The Shawnee have the songs and rituals of the buffalo dance, but the Delaware have the dance itself (hence, together their knowledge can facilitate the use of this ceremony). The Buffalo dance is linked to the Corn dance, but also to one of the Midewewin ceremonies. This is interesting in light of Delaware borrowings and influences on Onondaga and Cayuga ceremonies and on all Longhouse social music. The Delaware, then, seem to be a bridge between Longhouse and Mide traditions. The dearth of careful historical research about the interaction among different Nations makes the task of sorting out such complementary relationships very difficult.

6   The statement is excerpted from his undated manuscript "Spiritual Evolution of the Iroquois," a document to which we will turn again in Chapter Six.

7   For the SPINC Research Group, our concept of family was stretched further with the realization that non-human, non-animal beings were also organized into families. An Anishnabe categorization of thunderbirds, for example, includes the "first one that comes in the spring," the "one that shakes the earth," the "one that lights up the sky," the "one that comes on a cloudless day," and the "one that makes a jingling sound way up high." The "little ones which precede the storm are testing their powers" and are the ones to create havoc. They are said to be followed by "the thunderbird mother" and then by a distant rumbling: "that's the old man—he sounds distant but you think if he was ever close, it would be the end of the world" (Jim Dumont, in conversation, May 1988).

8   See also James W. Mavor and Byron E. Dix, *Manitou: The Sacred Landscape of New England's Native Civili-*

zation (1989), which focuses on the "sacred land-scape" of New England drawing on cross-cultural data for comparative purposes.

9   Hickerson (1970) places the seven fires in a relatively close circuit around Lake Superior, while Anishnabe elders locate the starting point of the migration on the East coast of North America.

10   Other examples of relationships which are expressed by mapping the features of one thing unto another with which they may share a similar shape or character are discussed in Chapter Five. Naming practices which reflect such visual relationships are described in Chapter Four.

11   This story recognizes the physical layering of sky and earth worlds. Extending between the worlds is the Iroquoian tree of life. Anishnabe teachings similarly recognize a multilayered cosmos, with four universes above the surface of the earth, and four below. The burning of tobacco or sweetgrass may also serve to travel or communicate between worlds. In South American Native cultures, there are many parallels to North American Native cosmologies. In a detailed study of South American religions entitled *Icanchu's Drum* (1988), Lawrence E. Sullivan describes numerous instances. "The universe may consist of a differing number of significant levels: for example, the Pémon conceive of the universe as having three different levels. Good and evil may exist on any of these strata. The Tapirapé, according to Herbert Baldus, acknowledge the existence of four levels in the cosmos: a highest level, 'near the wild banana plants,' is known only to shamans; below that lies the level called the 'sieve' (Urupema); still lower is the earth, where the Tapirapé live; and finally, there is an underworld. The Waiwai cosmos exists in five different planes. Each level has a terra firma and forests as well as an opening that provides access to the other tiers. Each layer contains a different mode of being" (1988: 113). Sullivan's description of Chiripá cosmological structures has several points in common with one version of the Iroquoian creation story. "For the Chiripá, for example, earth is now separated from the level of heaven. The two realms are connected by an eternal palm tree, which sprang up when the universal flood destroyed the earth. This *axis mundi*, a symbolic feature connecting (and, at the same time, separating) heaven and earth, is a widely recognized feature of the religious landscape. The fragility of communication between cosmic realms is often symbolized by the difficulty of maintaining the *axis mundi* intact" (ibid.: 113-14).

12   As we write this, we are aware of the pitfalls of dichotomizing sameness and difference while realizing how often in this book we attempt to "compare and contrast" Native/non-Native, or Algonquian/Iroquoian, or perhaps MSC/FvR/BD in our efforts to understand the parallel and separate pathways which we follow.

13   José Mailhot glosses the word "également, de façon sembable" in her manuscript "Lexique Montagnais-Français" (n.d.).

14   Similarly, from a different culture area, the Beaver Indian legend of the culture hero, Saya, also called Swan, tells us that Swan's mother instructed his father before her death as follows: "You should look for a woman from where the sun is when it is highest in the sky. Sunup women are no good. Where the sun goes down is no good, You should just find a woman from where the sun is at dinnertime" (Ridington 1988: 12).

Ridington points out that "her country is forever balanced between the inclinations of rising and setting" (ibid.).

15   Again we note similarities with Dunne-Za concepts described by Ridington. The gathering place, called "Where Happiness Dwells" is a reflection of Heaven (ibid.: 24); the Muskrat who descended to the bottom of the waters to grasp a handful of earth which became the land is a reflection of the Swans who fly straight through the hole in the sky without dying (ibid.); our shadows are the other side of ourselves (ibid.: 8); the sound of underwater frogs are a reflection of drumming on the earth (ibid.: 181); one walks back along the Trail to Heaven to meet one's relatives (ibid.: 285). A song can be used for both good and evil (ibid.: 58); one learns that, although one has the power to kill one also has the power to refrain (ibid.: 26).

16   In Chapter Five, we explore other examples of musical instruments which serve as maps for other living entities: the duration of a human life, the lodge, the continent, the earth, the cosmos. We will also examine other ways in which instruments may serve as references for identity: as clan symbols, for example.

17   See articles in R. Keeling, ed., *Women in North American Indian Music: Six Essays* (1989).

Chapter Three

"Real"

Dialogue

BD:

The word "real" surfaces frequently in our conversations and it's rarely spoken without emotional intensity. Are issues of authenticity at stake here? If so, we might ask for whom, other than the self, is something authentic, or genuine.

MSC:

One thing that strikes me is our academic fear of data that can be interpreted by other academics as "not authentic," not right, not real. Iroquoian colleagues rarely place such importance in our detailed measurements for cowhorn rattles, or the precise location of a design on a water drum, or even the use of plastic materials in the construction of an instrument. There are norms, certainly, but they might regard a different way of doing something, not necessarily as right or wrong, but often as "individual" or perhaps as "amusing." Hurrah for laughter!

BD:

Maybe the humour escapes us academics quite often because the English language ties concepts of "authenticity" and "authority" so closely to "legitimacy." "Legitimate" implies social or moral rules which define the criteria of authenticity hierarchically. It is often not a matter of judging something right or wrong as much as distinguishing between that which is acknowledged to exist and that which is ignored or not noticed.

FvR:

In Micmac, according to Silas Rand, the word for "reality," *ketla'wa'uokn*, is closely associated with truth, belief, security, faithfulness, and power. The emphasis is not on the legitimacy of authority or law. Reality is rooted in personal stories and dreams that people share with one another. They are "real" because they come from the undisputed origin of personal experience. Surely, it is the way people themselves define the "real" that we want to focus on here.

BD:

Innu friends also stress personal experience as fundamental and they heed their dreams as vital sources of guidance. But in addition to personal stories, it is the classic myths, the *atnuhana*, which provide "authentic" bases for Innu reality. It is important to recognize that these legends are regarded as "true." They have extraordinary creatures—the giant who challenged Tshakapesh—and incomprehensible events—the transformation of Aiasheu into a bird—but such worlds are not discounted as unreal or surreal. Perhaps even more important is the emphasis people place on the contemporary relevance of the teachings of the myth—underlying lessons, values, encounters which may be played out in different ways in people's lives.

Rand's gloss for reality as "truth," however, raises another issue for me. I remember a conversation with two Maliseet guests with whom I was discussing a political issue. I commented that it was hard to sort out the different perceptions of the case and that the "truth" was a complex matter, depending on the point of view of the individual. "Oh, no" they said in unison, "the truth is simple." In effect, they were telling me, "Don't stumble over the surface details of different perspectives, while ignoring the fundamental 'truth' of our collective oppression." Here, it seems to me, they were suggesting that *my* focus on the authority of personal perspectives was actually derailing the "legitimacy" of their collective experience.

FvR:

But different perspectives are accommodated extremely well in some of the First Nations teachings we were told. One interesting aspect of this is the concept of order reversal and turning things. In comments about our photos we were told at one point that if, for example, you reverse the colours on something, that can mean that it belongs to the opposite sex. And sky and earth, if you reverse the colours, the sky view can become the earth view.

MSC:

I wonder if that has something to do with the different directions. The sky and earth face each other, touch each other. The earth is the skyworld from the perspective of the sky. The bear under the ground, holding up the Midewiwin lodge, may be reflected in the stars.

Sometimes, it is not clear which world we are in. There are, for example, two stories of Iroquoian creation. The better known story tells of Sky Woman coming down and the muskrat bringing earth up to the turtle's back, the birth of the twins, Elder and Younger brother.

But some very conservative Longhouse people at Six Nations don't speak this story at all. They believe the Creator made all people out of the earth, and that the image of Sky Woman falling to the earth is not correct—or at least, not their understanding. There is

Photo 16. Iroquois comb. Woodland Cultural Centre collection. Photo by MSC.

also some discussion suggesting that the former is the original story, while the narrative of Sky Woman is a story of "re-creation," of flood waters formed by the melting ice—the turtle's back existed for her to land on. Is that the Creation story doubling back on itself?

BD:

Like the "original sound" in the Anishnabe migration story and the sound before that. . . .

MSC:

Exactly! Which reverberation is that?

BD:

Reflection is not just a mirror but an echo.

MSC:

An echo before the sound?

BD:

Which is the sound and which the echo?

FvR:

I think we've been here before.

"Real"

"Get real or get lost!"

—Art Solomon, Traditional Gathering, Native
Canadian Centre, Toronto, 1990

"Only the dominant self can be problematic; the self of the Other is authentic without a problem, naturally available to all kinds of complications. This is very frightening."

—Gayatri Chakravorty Spivak,
The Post-Colonial Critic: Interviews, Strategies, Dialogues

In the context of our work, the word "real" surfaced in many contexts. It was often used in conjunction with a highly charged emotional issue and it was usually politically nuanced.

That dance troupe over there—are they REAL Indians? Can I touch one?
That's not REAL, that's acculturated.
Ongwehonwe—that translates as "REAL people." Everybody knows that, don't they?
That seed pod is a REAL instrument.
Did s/he dream that or did it REALLy happen?

This wave of comments— some spoken by Native participants in the project, some by ourselves, still others overheard among Native or non-Native observers—suggests (though by no means exhausts) a range of phenomena to which the label *real* could be applied. Native and non-Native people are deeply concerned about issues of "realness," although these issues are not always the same ones, nor the concern motivated by the same forces. Our dialogue hinted at some of these differences. We commented on a Western academic preoccupation with concepts of "authenticity," implying that this discourse was quite different from the Iroquoian and Algonquian stories which relate mythological origins and create a distinctive image of "reality." Do we still need to query, as Spivak implies in one of the epigrams which preface this chapter, why a discourse of colonialism and oppression lingers on? What can be learned by listening to the different and distinctive image of reality related in the cosmologies of First Nations people?

One issue voiced by all of us was the concept of "realness" in contrast to stereotypes and the racism which often accompanies them. As a context for examining musical instruments, we approach this issue by reviewing aspects of Eurocentred images of "Indianness." While non-Native researchers have contributed to the critique of these images, the heart of the matter has been most clearly identified by Native researchers, spiritual and political leaders, and creative writers. They challenge us, not just to identify problems accurately, but to commit to real social change. Within the context of this book, their statements help assess how "Western" constructions of "authentic" Indianness have affected evaluations and interpretations of musical instruments. But we move, in this chapter, to several other issues implicit in the wave of statements about the real. From issues of authenticity to contrasts between real-ness and manufacture and finally to considerations of the boundaries between real/ordinary/tangible and real/visionary/intangible, the shifts from one subject to another may initially seem arbitrary or disjointed. But these same disparate shifts hopefully enable a critical exploration of Eurocentred assumptions and a renewed hearing of the teachings of Aboriginal elders and consultants.

Real-ness and Authenticity

In recent decades, "post-modern" scholars (e.g., anthropologists Clifford 1986 and 1988, Marcus and Fischer 1986, Said 1978; literary theorists and feminists Spivak 1987 and 1990, hooks 1990, among others) have begun to untangle different perspectives on "realness," especially concepts of "authenticity," by critiquing the Eurocentric concern with the

Other. Many problems of the Us/Them dichotomy have been clearly articulated in virtually every academic discipline.[1]

Gayatri Spivak articulated a fundamental danger in the definition of a cultural Other: the very act of individuals from one group describing anOther has tended to homogenize their wide-ranging human experiences. This falsely implies that richness, diversity, and individuality are realized (or more fully realized) only in the society of the "describers." We are well aware that the "describers" were, in centuries past, the European colonizers and that the most privileged mode of their discourse—print—acquired a legitimacy which disempowered not just other modes of discourse (storytelling, for example) but other styles as well. Hence, the homogenized versions of non-European cultures became the ones labelled "true" or authentic. We also acknowledge the many ways in which this colonial legacy continues to be perpetuated.

Writing of her African-American heritage, literary critic bell hooks has extended our understanding of this fundamental problem.

Contemporary critiques of essentialism (the assumption that there is a black essence shaping all African-American experience, expressed traditionally by the concept of "soul") challenge the idea that there is only "one" legitimate black experience. Facing the reality of multiple black experiences enables us to develop diverse agendas for unification, taking into account the specificity and diversity of who we are. (1990: 37)

But she demonstrates, further, that recognition of multiple experiences must not be a dismissal of the shared history of a group:

Often folks evoke the experience of Southern rural black folks and make it synonymous with "authentic" blackness, or we take particular lifestyle traits of poor blacks and see them as the "real thing." Even though most black folks in the United States have Southern roots (let's not forget that for a long time ninety per cent of all black people lived in the agrarian South), today many know only an urban city experience. A very distinctive black culture was created in the agrarian South, by the experience of rural living, poverty, racial segregation, and resistance struggle, a culture we can cherish and learn from. It offers ways of knowing, habits of being, that can help sustain us as a people. We can value and cherish the "meaning" of this experience without essentializing it. (1990: 38)

First Nations writers[2] also address these issues articulately and poignantly. In the introduction to *All My Relations: An Anthology of Contemporary Canadian Fiction*, editor Thomas King writes:

"Authenticity" can be a slippery and limiting term when applied to native literature for it suggests cultural and political boundaries past which we should not let our writing wander. (1990: xv)

Historian Deborah Doxtator, whose book *Fluffs and Feathers* addresses Indian stereotyping in a wide range of media, including exhibitions, non-Native expressive culture, advertising, and historical writing, reminds us that

Every society creates its own images about itself and about other people that are connected to that society. Symbols of "Indianness" as used by both Indian and non-Indians are not universally "bad" or always destructive. Seeing how others see you, if done in the proper spirit, can be enlightening, once you stop laughing. The non-Indian use of Indian symbols operates within a hierarchichal society that is based on the principle of economic and social inequality. From the day children start school, they are ranked and judged according to their academic performance, their athletic abilities, their creative talents. It is not surprising, then, that non-Indian images of Indians are either at one extreme of the "ranking" spectrum or the other—either Indians are depicted as "savages" below Euro-Canadian "civilization" or as "noble savages" who are more moral, faster, stronger, kinder than any Euro-Canadian. Rarely have Indians been treated by Canadian society as equals.

This one fact alone is probably the key factor in understanding the destructive effects of the images created by non-Indians. It is not right that anyone should define someone else, tell them who they are and where they "fit in." You cannot do this to someone if you think of them as your equal. (1988: 67-78)

There are, however, other aspects specific to the Eurocentric stereotyping of Indianness. Referring to the North American habits of "playing Indian" when children act out Wild West fantasies, when tourists don Indian headdresses, or when Archie Belaney assumed the identity of culture hero Grey Owl, Doxtator observes that

[Other] Minority groups often endure discrimination but they never experience situations in which the discriminating group usurps their identity. (1988: 14)

Doxtator and Rayna Green, among others, have written about the appropriation of Indian symbols in the creation of an "American primal myth" (Green, 1988: 77).

The heritage of 19th- and 20th-century American romanticism, to some extent defined by its distinctly Indian "flavour," draws deeply on European and native born traditions refined by historical events. European immigrants brought with them folk traditions of belief in the wild man of the forest and the dark "bogeyman" and the intellectual traditions of "l'enfant sauvage" and the "natural man." The misnamed "Indian" seemed to fit neatly into these traditions, and thus became part of the

"New World." The Americas had an Indian identity from the outset. The earliest iconography representing the Americas was the late 15th- and 16th-century symbol of the Indian Queen. Later the symbol of America becomes the Indian Princess who eventually loses her Indianness as she is transformed into the Anglo-European and neoclassic Miss Liberty of the 19th century. The process of altering a cultural icon so that it conforms to the majority population's notions of itself was co-existent with nationalism and the development of a national culture. (Ibid.: 78)

A particularly severe homogenization still perpetuated is the denial of historical specificity to Native culture. Eleanor Leacock has described our propensity to "freeze Native culture in the past"

Photo 17. A Passamaquoddy Indian Band going to Boston in the 1930s. Passamaquoddy Museum collection (re-photographed FvR 87/14/20).

rather than to recognize growth and development (Leacock and Lee 1982: 167). Bruce Trigger has observed that the very disciplinary boundaries established by the Eurocentric academy accentuate (or reflect) this problem. Canadian "history," the discipline which traces development and interaction over time, has centred on the English and the French or regarded the First Nations as "prehistory," while "anthropology," concerned often with marginalized groups, has often cast them as "peoples who lacked their own history" (Trigger 1985: 4-5). (See the quotation which prefaces Chapter Six where historical issues are discussed more extensively.)

The problem of ahistorical representations is, not surprisingly, common in music publications as well. There are few dates in the chapters on Native music in American and Canadian music textbooks[3] although they abound in other chapters of the same books. Related to this problem, in our view, is the resilient perception that the Native response to Euro-American musics was "compartmentalization" in which no blending of styles occurred.[4] Styles such as hymns or band music which were introduced by Euro-Americans were, for a long time, dismissed as examples of acculturation, deculturation, or cultural impoverishment rather than examples of borrowing and creative adaptation.[5]

It is important to note that distortions may be unintentional results of the mismatch of concepts and values. Ethnomusicologists are keenly aware of the ways in which this has happened with regard to

Native music, for example. Because polyphony attained such a high value within the European composed tradition, many classically trained musicians who studied Native (or other primarily monophonic) musics were predisposed to regard them as simple. Furthermore, even the term "monophonic" (one part) reflects a cultural bias in that only pitched parts were considered relevant. Although many genres of Native music have accompanying rhythmic "parts" (either vocal or instrumental), these were not counted in a system which privileges pitch. Similarly, a culture which used predominantly drums and rattles was falsely viewed as musically and culturally simpler than one which had many types of string, keyboard, or wind instruments.[6]

These instances demonstrate what James Clifford has theorized, that notions of "authenticity" are often constructed by a colonially dominant culture in order to legitimate its own illogical notions of supremacy. He charts the very division of knowledge about expressive culture between ethnology (if the culture is non-European) and art (if the culture is European or Euro-American) in a system labelled "A Machine for Making Authenticity" (Clifford 1988: 224).

It is clear that such processes of categorization are different only in degree, but not in kind, from the stereotyping of a group through the use of a limited range of symbols. Where symbols have served as a means of dismissal rather than a means of recognition, they have little to do with "ways of knowing" and "habits of being," as hooks calls them.

How can we recognize and respect those "ways of knowing" and "habits of being" without homogenizing or "totalizing" Native experience, without using the machine for making authenticity? It seemed to us that several positive steps are possible:

(1) to pay attention to those contexts where public, even "stereotypic" symbols are used by Native musicians as positive empowering strategies or devices;

(2) to analyze the ways in which Natives and non-Natives have defined the acceptability of public symbols in specific contexts; and

(3) to explore the commodification of aspects of Native culture.

Clearly, symbols function in different ways and contexts. The image of a full feather headdress may embody "Indianness" to those insensitive to the rich variety of traditional dress in Native communities or it could represent a statement of First Nations political solidarity. A commercial bass drum could be an element of popular culture among rock groups; or turned on its side, it could become central to powwow culture, representing the political unity of First Nations who have transformed the power of a European military instrument to benefit Aboriginal people. The same drum embodies complex beliefs and ways of living. See "Different Perspectives on the Powwow" below.

Within Native events, boundaries defining the appropriateness of musical instruments may sometimes relate to the symbolism of sound or to process (also see "Real-ness and Manufacture" below). Practitioners frequently relate the "realness" of a musical instrument to the experience of making or using it. Special processes of construction or usage, rather than visual distinctiveness, may make an instrument "ceremonial" or "alive." At an Anishnabe drum workshop, for example, a man making a ceremonial drum worked alone; we were told that he used specially selected wood, and prepared the hide and vessel with hand tools. Such instruments may be blessed in a special ceremony and it is not appropriate to make them for sale.[7]

On the other hand, where a specific sound is essential or where proper conduct is important, the use of an "authentic" instrument may not be paramount. In one instance, at a Maritime Wabanaki gathering, when a dance troupe had forgotten to bring its drum, they found an old kettle, turned it upside down and used it instead. Here neither the sound nor object, but the fact that the event should go on was paramount.

The success or effectiveness—indeed, the "real-ness"—of events is evaluated on similarly diverse bases. In an Iroquoian context, for example, for a show to be "real" you need an audience but for a curing doing, there are a different set of requirements. The contemporary powwow exemplifies how a wide range of interpretive responses can coexist and intersect in a complex process within Native communities in relation to a single type of event. Responses to these intertribal and intercultural events indicate different kinds of attention to social or spiritual interaction, appropriate sound, movement, and visual symbolism.

Different Perspectives on the Powwow

The label "powwow," which some consultants trace etymologically to an Algonquian word indicating a person of power (cf. the Algonquin *pawaw* or medicine person), has been applied to different kinds of events historically as well as at the present time. Some regard the events as "shows," perhaps remembering occasions where they were part of local fairs or non-Indian celebrations. Some described occasions run by the Roman Catholic Church with bake sales and wheels of fortune.

Especially in Quebec, the label "powwow" was still sometimes used in the 1980s for a concert performance. Elsewhere contemporary powwows are most often events featuring intertribal dance and music; many, though not all, organize competitive dancing in specific categories: men's traditional, men's fancy, men's grass, women's traditional, women's fancy, women's jingle dress, and group dancing. Perspectives on the powwow vary.

Photo 18. The above photograph described in the catalogue of the Public Archives of Canada as an "Indian powwow and procession" may depict participants in such an event at Wikwemikong in 1885.

Photo 19. Powwow dancers. Photo by MSC.

For some, a powwow is analogous to popular culture. They love meeting friends at these weekend events and celebrating their pride as Indian people:

"There's a sense of community at a powwow—they all share the same values, it's like a big family. They enjoy being Indians so much that they come together every weekend to do this. We love being Indians, and they feel exactly the way we do. Everybody's telling jokes and laughing—you really want to be Indian, and that's where it all happens."
(Karen Deleary, *Sound of the Drum*, 1990: 21)

The most obvious aspects of a powwow may be deceptive, however. Some of the "spiritual" aspects may be less overt. An Anishnabe powwow, for example, may begin with a sunrise ceremony. The drums may be smudged with tobacco before public proceedings begin. For others, participation is part of a way of life which rejects drugs and alcohol and embraces traditional teachings.

Even the "commercial" aspects of a powwow may have other layers of meaning, meaning which derives from the manner in which an exchange takes place, for example. At powwows, people who "sell" items are often called "traders." A participant might trade an eagle feather for another piece of regalia, for Native jewelry, or medicine such as sweetgrass or sage. The question of value is negotiated at a personal level. Some powwows may distinguish or discourage traders who sell commercially manufactured objects, but the practice varies.

Photo 20. Drummer. Photo by FvR.

Photo 21. Powwow dancers. Photo by MSC.

Photo 22. Sour Springs booth. Photo by MSC.

Tourists and Shows

"Tourist" instruments may differ completely from those in community use. Such is the case with the small cylindrical birch-bark drum which continues to be the most widely sold tourist type. Similar to Algonquin-style drums, tourist drums were smaller, differently proportioned, and made without rims. An even smaller version of the same "drum" is now made as the vessel for a rattle. This rattle type is proportioned similarly to horn or can rattles, but the vessel is rotated 90° from the horn or can types, a process of turning which, by analogy with the aforementioned powwow drum (to cite one other example) changes the nature of the instrument. Some Iroquoian craftspeople make a claw rattle, another distinct type apparently constructed for the tourist market.[8]

In other cases, however, traditional instruments might be adapted to new purposes. Iroquoian turtle rattles made for sale are generally quite large;[9] most have leather strips wrapped somewhat loosely around the neck/handle. By contrast, smaller turtle rattles are more often used by Longhouse singers because of their good sound and light weight, a significant factor during a lengthy ceremony. For example, *Ostowagowah*, the Great Feather Dance enjoyed at major ceremonies, can last for more than

an hour—a strenuous event for singers who pound these rattles against a wooden bench. Smaller rattles may be wrapped with leather or splint (particularly pre-1960 instruments) or with electrical and hockey tape; the latter is efficient but evidently less appealing to tourists.

Another instrument type sometimes adapted in response to market forces is the birchbark moose call, made for sale by many Algonquin and Attikamek artisans. Catalogue information at the Musée de la Civilization (Quebec) indicates an increase in craft shop orders for moose calls during the 1970s; changes in construction and design seem to relate to the expanded "market." Craftsmen and women began using a staple-type construction and plastic lacing was substituted for root lacing as observed by collector Alika Webber for MCQ 74-127 and 74-129. During this decade the use of all-over floral or bird patterns on sale items contrasts with designs which show layers often by means of alternating negative and positive techniques. Compare, for example, the aforementioned MCQ 74-127 and 74-129 with MCQ (80)24-.5.73, HUR SPINC ID:III.?.1001.o, or MCQ 69-71. Finally, the addition of handles seems more prevalent from the 1970s on.

Instrument making for a craft-shop market may influence changes in construction techniques (Photo 23) or stimulate the development of new instrument types (Photo 24).

Photo 23. "Staple" technique used by moosecall-maker George Niqui from Sanmaur, Quebec, when he has a large order to fill. He told collector Alika Webber that his wife always sews rather than staples moose calls (MCQ 74-127. BD 88/8/32).

Photo 24. Iroquois turtle foot rattles are made in some areas for the craft market; this one is privately owned by a Maliseet consultant (FvR 85/4/13).

"Children start learning with 'used to be' shakers. There's Indian corn inside but sand, corn, and pebbles were all used depending on what sound you want. The turtle rattle was important." (Alma Brooks)

In still other cases, tourist instruments resemble those used within a community. At the Six Nations reserve, William Spittal's company, Iroqrafts, has become an important promoter in this regard. Spittal sells cowhorn rattles and water drums (used at social and ceremonial events) as well as bark and turtle rattles (used in ceremonial events) to the tourist market. These compare visually with traditional instruments, although many rattles feel cumbersome and less well balanced. Cowhorn rattles are generally thicker than those used by *hadreno:ta*; their sound is loud but not as clear. Tourist water drums are almost invariably made of wood and brightly painted; the plastic drain pipe or pvc kegs occasionally used by traditional singers are not in evidence. Ironically, these drums (like turtle rattle handles wrapped with hockey tape) are valued for their beautiful sound by an Iroquoian purchaser, but appeal less to the authenticity-seeking, non-Native tourist.

Another aspect of commodification related to the issue of authenticity concerns the marketing of dance shows or concert-style events. Once again, the boundaries of such events are not definable by a simple Native/non-Native dichotomy. These performances may take place in or outside a community and audiences can be remarkably diverse. Common to all shows and concerts, however, is a formal division of participants into "performers" and "audience," distinguishing these events from gatherings which take place for the benefit of a Native community.

For shows, repertoire and instrumentation varies, sometimes corresponding more or less to those used at community events. The Jim Sky Dancers from Six Nations, Ontario, and the Allegany River Dancers from New York perform brief excerpts of traditional Iroquoian social dances, music considered essential at Longhouse celebrations. On the other hand, dance groups may also include the "Ferry Dance" created especially for shows, or feature the boisterous "Alligator Dance" (which they state is borrowed from the Seminole), a song cycle currently heard less frequently at Longhouse socials. Although more common prior to 1985, some performers wear fringed leather clothing or parts of a powwow outfit rather than traditional Iroquoian dress, respecting opinions expressed by some Longhouse speakers that traditional "Indian clothes" should only be worn in the Longhouse, rather than for show or personal profit.

Similarly, in the Abenaki community of Odanak, the same social dances may be performed in a show context at the "Festival mondial de folklore" at nearby Drummondville, at the annual Fête des abénakis, where visitors are welcomed to the festival site on the Odanak Museum grounds, and at community-oriented spring and fall ("Indian corn") festivals. Individuals also choose to express different levels of Native identity through their outfits. Some dancers prefer fringed buckskin, but many women dancers wear black skirts encircled with coloured ribbons and beaded or embroidered collars and aprons characteristic of Abenaki clothing design. There are, of course, shifts in the "preferred" styles of outfits. Photographs from the 1940s and 1950s depict full feather headdresses while contemporary dancers prefer the Iroquoian *gus-toweh*. The fashion for powwow outfits similarly shifts rather quickly.

Like commercially marketed instruments, "show" instruments may differ from or be adaptations of traditional instruments used in community socials and ceremonies. A single-membrane frame drum with rawhide "spokes" on the underside stretching the membrane, a structural type more commonly used in Western (Plains) communities, was used as a show instrument by 1980s dance troupes from Huron, Abenaki, Maliseet, Micmac, Passamaquoddy, as well as Mohawk, and other Iroquoian Nations.[10] Coloured fluff feathers, or painted Indian heads in full feather headdress were common "decorations."

The choice of instrument type may be pragmatic. A large frame drum (equal in size to a powwow drum but played vertically like a military bass drum) was constructed a few years ago to accompany the Abenaki troupe *Mikwobait* (a name which means "Those who remember") because its loud sound carried better in open-air performances. Similarly, Seneca Confederacy Chief and singer Hubert Buck, Sr. used a large double-membrane drum for shows because the sound carried better and it was more visible for the audience than a water drum. Montagnais troupes, on the other hand, take pride in using the same instrument which serves hunters as a private tool, the traditional *teueikan*, for public, cross-cultural performances. One Montagnais drum-maker, however, uses two thicknesses of membrane for touring instruments so

Photo 25. Six Nations Dancers performing at Oswegen, Ontario, in the 1950s.
Public Archives of Canada (PA 120191).

Photo 26. The Iroquois "show" drum of Harold Thomas (CMC III-I-1260. FvR 88/1/25).

that, should the drum skin become damaged, it would be reparable.

Responses to the choice of instruments, repertoire, and costume selected for use in public cross-cultural performance contexts are governed by a complex array of factors. Indian "shows" can be uncomfortable events for non-Natives who are self-conscious about the colonial history of voyeurism in relation to Native culture and who perhaps view some symbols as "inauthentic." These reactions surfaced at the "Fluffs and Feathers" conference on stereotyping sponsored by the Woodland Cultural Centre in Brantford, Ontario, in 1988. At this event, academic disapproval of "inaccurate" stereotypic symbols (such as full feather headdresses in association with Eastern Woodlands culture) collided with Native participants sporting T-shirts with "headdresses all over the place." That many of these symbols are not essentially negative in themselves was not easily accepted by non-Indians; even less was the concept that an Indian's relationship to these images and ideas could be so different from a non-Indian's.

Obviously the symbols used as a kind of short form to represent "Indianness"—headdresses, tipis, canoes—are not "bad"; it is the context in which we place them, who manipulates them, the ways in which they are manipulated, the kind of Other ideas and relationships that non-Native people often associate with these images that creates havoc. The enjoyment of being part of a Wild West show or being crowned as "Indian princess" cannot be shared or understood if one's notions of "Indianness" are confined to such images, if we see Indians as defined by and limited to the frozen images of movies, romance novels, media, or advertising.

Anglophones often use the word "tradition" within a parallel "frozen" paradigm, connoting something from the past, something which is frequently no longer practised. Significantly, there is no exact equivalent for "tradition" in most Native languages—at least until quite recently. *Ongweowe:ka'*—which translates as the Indian way of being, of life, of living—is the closest Iroquoian concept. In recent curriculum materials, Montagnais educators use *innu aitun*, a word which translates approximately as "our ways," "things Innu do," "Innu matters." They speak of tradition, not as something which is fixed in the past, but as something which is ongoing and renewable through creative adaptation and response. With regard to dance, Huron dancer and cultural historian Marguerite Vincent has explained a similar distinction as follows:

Il y a les danses dites de cérémonies ou rituelles, celles dans lesquelles le danseur peut danser de la manière qu'il choisit, sans être réglé par un code spécifique. Par contre, les danses traditionnelles indiennes exécutées à l'occasion de festivités dites "pow-wow," exigent un mode d'exécution bien rigoureux. (1984: 275)[11]

Museum curator and director of the Abenaki dance troupe, *Mikwobait*, from Odanak, Quebec, Nicole Obomsawin offered an explanation consistent with Vincent's when she described a newly choreographed dance, the "Danse de la naissance," as "traditional." She explained that label was appropriate because the dance affirmed values which continue to underpin Native life: the importance of the family and the establishing of strong relationships with the newborn.

The following more extended comment from Nicole illustrates more fully how a show-style ensemble created for pragmatic reasons and without apparent "opposition" to stereotypes can be a force for renewing and strengthening a community's knowledge and pride in their history and identity:

"I was in a family of dancers and singers, and so I always loved to dance. I was part of a troupe myself—a non-Indian troupe off the reserve for four years. We performed in Quebec; it was before I had a family when I was a student. We did Spanish dances, Polish, Russian, Israeli. It is for that reason that the festival—my heart is really there—is not just for the troupe but also for the outside, because I love folklore; I began to do international folklore when I was twelve years old until I was twenty. The troupe demanded a lot of me; I had my "chum" in the troupe. When I came back here, they were doing "spectacles" for ourselves, "shows" for ourselves, but there were demands from outside for performances and we were not prepared. In any case, as I had seen, it is necessary for a troupe to practise; it is necessary that they are disciplined. I said to myself, it is necessary, perhaps, to do things which are more structured, more organized, in order to respond to these demands. The occasion that I chose for that was the 325th anniversary—the first time was to do promotion for the 325th anniversary of the reserve. With a troupe, one could be a good ambassador; by doing performances outside, one could say to people "Come to the reserve; visit the Abenakis" and then we could distribute brochures about the museum. That's how I did promotion; it was the first objective. Me, I loved dance and so I said to myself, I would have a good time. I loved it and decided to do something with that. I asked people "Do you want to dance?" Those who came wanted to and those who didn't come didn't want to. It began like that, but when the year was over and we had done seven or eight performances, we were very happy ourselves. The next year I said "If you're interested, I am ready to continue." That year we had more performances, more requests; we began to practise more and to go to other performances and the young people were hooked. Then I saw that this was a means of transmitting the culture to the young people. So that became my second objective; the first was the promotion of the village for the 325th anniversary but after that I said that it is the youth of fourteen or fifteen years who know nothing. They don't know their history; they don't know the culture that they are familiar with. They don't learn in their families; they don't learn at school. These are the people who know they are Indian because they live on a reserve and have their [green] card; but they don't know anything else. I found that a valuable lesson; I said to myself, it is our adults, our parents of today who are going to have children and they no longer know the culture. It is time to recover everything. Especially if they are doing what they love. They love to dance, they love to go out as a group, to eat at McDonald's afterwards; we can profit from the fact that they love dance while, at the same time, [learning/doing] research on dance. [I suggested to them] You could say to them [parents] "when did you do that?" "why does it bring the spirits?" They learned all that themselves because they didn't know it. They had danced when they were little, but they didn't know it. They said, "If we had said that the snake dance was for that, we didn't know it." They didn't know why they danced it. They danced it as if it was equal to a rigaudon. They didn't know the explanation of the dance. . . .

"At a certain moment, I said to myself that this was a good means to preserve the culture in life. The others learn historical information because I talk about Abenaki history when we do performances. Often we give performances with other Indians. They see what others do and they see that others speak their [own] language and they wanted to learn Indian words and so that developed. I found that it was important for the young people, my children, to see the dances of others in order to have a taste for dancing to continue the tradition. I said to myself, if I don't do it, nobody else will. It is important because it takes a lot of energy but I love it. I let myself be carried on, though it is demanding and I find it hard as I said. But even if the troupe didn't exist next year, the path that we made together during the past five years would not be lost. The young now—in the troupe there are two or three who are going to continue to dance, who know the explanations and are ready to show others. . . .

"If they begin that, if they take it, they will develop new creations. That gives the idea to people that the culture isn't anything like it was 200 years ago. It is also today and so we do new things. It's more interesting for ourselves and for the public." (Excerpt from interview conducted by BD with Nicole Obomsawin, transcribed by

Photo 27. The Abenaki dance troupe "Mikwobait" ("Those Who Remember") performing at the annual Fête des abénakis in their own community of Odanak, Quebec, in 1987 (BD 87/1).

Claude Gallant, translated from French to English by BD)

Obviously, concerns about authenticity, whether voiced as concerns about stereotypes, definitions of tradition or expressed in framed performance choices or everyday ways of living and being, are expressed and addressed differently by Native and non-Native people. Equally evident is the need to be sensitive to the power relations accruing to each specific context, the flexibility with which symbols may be created, received and manipulated, as well as the complex interplay of visual image, sound, and process in the creation of musical meaning.

We have explored situations where Native music cultures have been commodified since these contexts often necessitate the selecting of markers of identity, as well as their boundaries and definitions. We have described a variety of creative Native responses to non-Native constructions of "Indian-ness" as well as a number of situations where important community traditions were maintained in diverse contexts. Together, these explorations provide a number of perspectives on concepts of the "real" in relation to non-Native imaging of Native music cultures.

But we heard the label "real" used quite differently by Native elders.

Real-ness and Manufacture

Once, in the context of a discussion about the organization of the instrument documentation in the *Catalogue* (forthcoming on disk), we asked Anishnabe elder Jim Dumont's advice. Since the means by which people categorize the sounds and sound producers in their midst reflects things they value, it was not surprising that Jim's comments about instrument classification encompassed the larger concept of "relationship" discussed in Chapter Two.

Using the example of a "wind" instrument, he explained that whereas the Euro-American might apply this label to an instrument played by someone who produced sound by blowing or using a stream of air (i.e., wind), the Anishnabe connotation for "wind instrument" is multifaceted. Wind connects with breath and voice; hence, the flute might be called a wind instrument because it imitates the sound/voice of the wind. (In an Iroquoian context, on the other hand, it might be described as the voice of birds.) On the other hand, a bull-roarer might also be so categorized by some Innu who believe that it causes the wind to rise (see documentation for CMC III-B-349a with correction in relation to

CMC III-B-611). The connections are physical, aural, and functional.

Extending the logic of Jim's classification, other groups of physically quite disparate objects can be seen as related through their connection with a natural, spiritual force or being. Anishnabe instruments of the thunderers, for example, include a drum with red and blue lightning flashes or horse-hide membrane, a dew claw rattle with a bird head, a similarly carved drumstick, or a disc rattle painted with a thunderbird image. All these instruments represent different aspects of the thunderers (called our grandfathers).

Other criteria for a classification based in natural phenomena emerged during our discussion. Jim explained that some instruments actually *are* the things the Creator has given. Seed pods or gourds become rattles when the seeds are dried, while other instruments might be "manufactured" in imitation of these "real" gifts from the Creator.[12] Still others seem to be in-between the "real/natural" and "real/manufactured," as in the case of the grandfather drum, where (as described earlier) the materials are said to be provided by animals and birds, and the body of the drum carved from a tree trunk. Thus if we wish to apply the label "real" to sound producers, we come a bit closer to Anishnabe/Ongwehonwe/Innu ways of thinking if we connect them with actual sounds and forms of Nature—the wind, insects, birds, trees, and so on. Humans are also, in this sense, "real" sound producers, in speech and in song.[13]

Jim's words resonated with others. Speck recorded the Naskapi phrase *notcimi' umitcu'm* as "forest food, pure food intended for Indians by the Creator" (1935: 249). His gloss "pure" implies something like the natural/manufactured contrast. The forest itself, *nutshimits*, continues to be distinguished from the village on a similar basis by the Labrador Innu who describe the bush as the source of sustenance and positive knowledge given by the Creator to the people. The village, on the other hand, is cast negatively by many Innu since even its location has sometimes been government imposed without regard for the environment which must be heeded for survival.[14] Nature is sometimes described as an Indian equivalent of "books" since one learns to "read" the forest and environment for one's survival. All the teachings intended by the Creator for the people are there.[15]

In the context of Iroquoian communities, fundamental concepts are similar, though nuances differ. Some singers have told us that the turtle, *ha'nowa:*, "gives itself" to be made into a rattle. This opinion varies, since snapping turtles are far from docile creatures and most tend to resist transformation. But an understanding of one's environment is critical for knowing where and when to find turtles best suited for rattles. "Realness" for Haudenosaunee may also be connected to a sense that an instrument is alive. Turtle rattles used during ceremonies or curing contexts gain sensate, cognizant functions. They become alive/real because of their relationship to other beings (such as Hadui, whose hands they represent) and through their experience or use during Longhouse ceremonies.[16]

The Iroquois notion of "realness" is also expressed by the prefix *ongwe-*, which is also sometimes translated as "from here/from this earth/of this place." This prefix can modify "person" as in *Ongwehonwe* ("real people") referring to Native North Americans[17] or words such as "shoes," "tobacco," and "clothes" when referring to traditional Indian clothes or certain objects. The prefix is not incorporated into words for songs or musical instruments, but that does not imply that these are any less "real" or "connected." Concepts of "realness," however defined, resist simple categorization.

"Real" in the sense of "given by the Creator" raises fundamental challenges for the Euro-American-based social sciences. While the issue of ethnocentricity has long been discussed, the matter of anthropo-centricity or human-centredness is rarely considered by the academic community. With this "bias" in mind, some of the questions raised in earlier chapters are viewed in a different light. The "choice" of materials for an instrument is a result of reading and responding to the world around us. Does this concept of the "real" as "that which is given" (or that which was here prior to contact) lead us to a better understanding of the value or power of different instruments? Is it significant that, in some cases, the most natural objects—the gourd or the disc rattle covered with a stomach membrane and filled with the "seeds" expelled from the animal's stomach—are often the most "restricted"? It would be incorrect to generalize about naturalness. The turtle rattle made for sale is not restricted in any way. Instruments such as flutes are still more sensate within an Iroquoian context while "manufactured" instruments (a rattle made from a baking soda tin, for example) serve ceremonial purposes within the Midewiwin lodge. Anishnabe instruments such as the large "dream" drums with painted membranes, or the elaborately tied "little boy" water drum, which are powerful within either private or collective spiritual contexts, may be highly decorated or dressed. Once again it is clear that the instrument and its context (the context of its creation, its keeper, and its use within a community) cannot be separated. Furthermore, the contexts are not always apparent to or consciously controlled by individual instrument makers, keepers, or users. The issues surrounding a definition of "real" as "given by the Creator" intersect with the fourth group of concepts which we are exploring in this chapter: the relationship of the "real" to the tangible, actual, conscious, or intended.

Real Worlds and Others

Wisahkicak was traveling around in the bush and came to a river which he had to cross. He jumped across it but just as he was leaving the ground, spruce partridges flew up from the brush and startled him so that he fell into the river. He waded ashore to the other side but found that his pipe and tobacco pouch had fallen into the river. So he began walking along the bank, looking in the water in order to try and find them. He walked along and finally he thought that he saw his pipe and tobacco bag in the water a few feet from shore. He waded out and leaned over, groping around in the water in order to grab his stuff. He kept doing this for a long time but he couldn't grab onto them. Finally, he happened to look up and saw his pipe and tobacco pouch hanging in a tree where they'd landed when he fell in the river. He had been trying to pick up their reflections in the water. (Story narrated by Henry Linklater, in Brightman 1989: 53)

Photo 28. Wild-rice gathering; reflections in water. Public Archives of Canada (PA 181704).

Many Aboriginal legends and contemporary stories challenge the boundaries of concepts which equate the "real" with the "tangible" and "conscious." Some feature Wisahkicak discovering (or

manipulating) the fallibility and elusiveness of perceptions. Some delight in accidental and coincidental meaning, in unexpected "teachings." Some concern spirit worlds which might be as "tangible" as wind or emotion but without a visual image.

The dual image of the real and the reflected has not preoccupied ethnomusicological study. The dualities of real/unconscious and real/dream are not subjects we understand or discuss easily. As for real/imaginary, we could assume that the division between the two is fundamental to the sanity of any human being. Yet this dividing line has been constructed differently within different social and historical contexts. Where is that dividing line both for ourselves and for those with whom we work? What values are associated, what lessons learned from each side of the boundary? As artists, we place a high value on the "imagination" the "creative" potential of the intangible, the shadow world, the fantasy lands of our minds. On the other hand, there is convincing work by symbolic anthropologists[18] demonstrating that expressive acts, however sharply framed, are, at some level, embedded within the experiential.

We encountered these dualities in many aspects of our research. Images on/of instruments or other objects often reflect something from personal dreams. Some dreams or visions become part of the shared stories and teachings of the people. Hence, the instructions given to Anishnabekwe in Eddie Benton-Benai's Creation story are, in some other versions of the story, conveyed in a dream (see, e.g., "The Vision of Tailfeather Woman," in Vennum 1982: 44-45). Recent Anishnabe practices continue to be shaped by dreams in some cases. The jingle dress dance and outfit, for example, come from a vision of the 1940s.

The visions of Handsome Lake, an eighteenth-century Seneca prophet, form the *Gai'wiio* or Good message, a revision of the traditional Longhouse religion followed by Haudenosaunee. And personal dreams often reveal an Iroquoian individual or community's need for certain curing doings or ceremonies, each requiring specific instruments and music. Since 1989, several multi-community ceremonies have been held to honour Hadui, the wooden-face beings, a need communicated to several people through dreams. Traditional stories also link the origin of certain curing doings (including songs) with dreams. However, few Iroquoian colleagues discuss music revealed in dreams—perhaps new songs are rarely transmitted this way, or perhaps casually discussing such personal and powerful information with non-Native researchers is considered unwise. People from many Aboriginal Nations feel that too much talk about one's dreams weakens their power (see, e.g., Geyshick 1989: 66).

In Innu communities, in particular, however, many individuals speak and write about certain of their personal dreams, the source of songs and instructions of various kinds. Descriptions such as those quoted below reveal that dreams help people stay in touch with beings from whom they are separated, predict hunting success or hardship, or provide direction about some aspect of life (direction which may not be comprehensible for some time after the dream).

The elders could equally predict death or famine. When they took their drum and the words of their songs didn't come to them, that signified that they would be hungry. If they dreamed of fire, if they saw in their dream a fire which lighted with difficulty, which kept going out and which relighted only for a few seconds, that meant that they would kill almost nothing and they would know moments of famine. On the other hand, if in their dream, they saw a good fire and a well travelled road, that meant they wouldn't lack food. However, if the road was obstructed by snow, that was a sign of famine. Others dreamed of Atshen: In their dream, a man would say to them: "Atshen is not far and it is him that you will eat. You will feed off Atshen this winter and you won't be hungry." Others dreamed of a whale which was also a sign of abundance for the winter, indicating that they would kill some caribou. (Innu hunter and author Michel Grégoire 1989: 28)

Fourteen years ago, when I sleep at night, I [was] dreamin' and I see somebody underneath [the] river, you know, and they got to sing [a] song. And then, he said, "I gonna give you it alright—what you want." . . . And then when I got up in [the] morn[ing] you know, I walked] around in the woods, you know, and after that I went to the river, and I see two otter. That's what I [was] dreamin' you know. (Innu hunter Gilbert Rich, in conversation with BD, 1981)

One morning I woke up nearly blinded. I'd been dreaming of that bird, an eagle, and I didn't act on it. I had to go to a fortune teller who helped me figure out who my Indian friend was—this friend put the Eagle Ceremony through for me, and I was all right after that. You have to act on those dreams; you have to figure out what they're telling you. (Iroquois elder Elijah Harris in conversation with MSC, November 1986)

The interaction of dreaming and waking worlds is conveyed in personal dream images on musical instruments and in explanations of mirror images and design symmetries, particularly in Algonquian areas. A classic (i.e., extensively studied) example is the double curve design used widely in Algonquian areas (see Speck 1914, reprinted in Mathews and Jonaitis 1982: 383-428, for drawings of many different variants and for a range of interpretations). Micmac educator Marie Battiste and her husband Sakej Henderson described this symmetrical design as a metaphor for "ways of knowing." They compared it to a Micmac canoe which was reflected in the water.

Fig. 9. From a Montagnais story, "Auass ka mashkut" (The Boy and the Bear).
Illustrated legend prepared as curriculum material by l'Équipe d'Amérindianisation des Services Éducatifs, Betsiamites, Quebec.

Photo 29. Dream-inspired imagery on the personal drum of Montagnais Joseph Kurtness, former Chief of Mashteuiatsh (Pointe Bleue on Lac St. Jean, Quebec). Donated by Edouard Kurtness to the Musée amérindien de Mashteuiatsh (BD 86/3/33).

Photo 30. Fiddleheads, a Maritime delicacy.

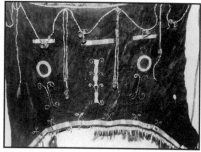

Photo 31. Double curve designs on blankets and clothing. Heye Foundation (FvR 88/52/19).

Photo 32. Micmac woman from New Brunswick (FvR 87/7/9).

Photo 33. Montagnais double disc rattle. Photographed at the Musée des Abénakis (on loan from the Ministère des Affaires Culturelles, Québec) (FvR 85/3/30).

languages of shadow and reflection, which are elaborate tools for dealing with the world. In Chapter Four, we will discuss how certain structural elements and images, particularly on Anishnabe and Innu drums, shakers, and flutes—e.g., the pathways between cardinal directions, or the mirror images of birds, the complementarity of double membranes or halves of a single drum membrane—further reflect both a distinction and intersection of human and spirit worlds, or imply the doubleness of existence. We shall present interpretations of musical instruments which embed notions of transformation—whether between the Innu drum and Tshakabesh's snaring of the sun, between the turtle shell, the lodge and a spoon, or between the Anishnabe imagery of birds and horses. And we shall explore how meaning emerges over time, as events in memory connect with experience. Together with concepts of "reflection" (both in relation to visual design and ceremonial action) and the vital relationship between dreaming and conscious life, these interpretations represent a worldview which values the "real/actual/conscious/tangible" as well as the"imaginary/reflected/dreamed."

"Which is the illusion and which the reality?" This relates to the trickster or Kluskap/Nanabush tales at the heart of Algonquian mythology.

As dreaming reveals, the spiritual environment is part of this world as well as part of another. One visual metaphor for the boundaries of this and other worlds is the hemispheric "sky dome," an Iroquoian interpretation of cosmology. The membrane of an Anishnabe dance drum represents another division between "ordinary" reality and other realms of mind and experience, with sound/vibration resonating from one level of existence to another.

In the next chapter, we will examine concepts in Native

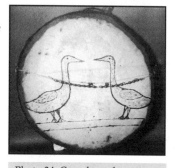

Photo 34. Cree drum from Cross Lake, Manitoba. Collected ca. 1930 by A.I. Hallowell (HEY 17/6820. FvR 88/42/24).

Final Comments

This chapter has explored vastly disparate subjects. It unfolded along a pathway which began with definitions of Indian realities that are most accessible (stereotypes) but problematic representations of "reality." We discussed relationships between stereotypic notions of Indianness and Euro-American concepts of "authenticity," both of which mirror our own identity. We looked at Native responses to and adaptations of these concepts and stressed ways in which they continue, through performance, to be "turned" to positive ends in some contexts. It is not paradoxical that the non-Native images have generally been created and used as gestures of "control." On the other hand, we have tried to think clearly about very different concepts of "real" which elders and consultants have shared with us. These concepts come from different ways of relating to the world, ways which ideally are actively receptive to the teachings of this North American environment. Finally, we began to explore the mirroring of the tangible or visible and the dreamed or illusory; the mirrored and symmetrical images which are sometimes used to represent these "dualities" imply that the doubleness is not oppositional but part of the whole of reality.

This has been our pathway to understand better what the "real" people mean. Speaking from the heart, hearing and seeing with respect and openness. Honouring what is given—in any realm, not just the rational or conscious. Laughing. "Preserving" tradition by doing, recreating, and reinventing, not by objectifying or encasing it. Ojibwe elder Art Solomon's challenge to "Get real or get lost!" is an invitation and a challenge to share in this process.

Notes

1   Issues of representation have also been widely explored in recent ethnomusicology. See, for example, the special volume of the journal, *Ethnomusicology* 34/3 (1990), or Jody Diamond's "There Is No They There" (1990).

2   Non-native writers studying Native culture have also written extensively about issues of "authentic" representation, especially in recent years where these issues have had a front and centre place in virtually all of the social sciences, in some of the humanities (particularly literary criticism) and fine arts disciplines. For a more extended discussion see David Murray's *Forked Tongues: Speech, Writing and Representation in North American Indian Texts* (1991); Linda Griffiths's *The Book of Jessica* (1989); Frederick E. Hoxie's *Indians in American History* (1988); Adam Kuper's *The Invention of Primitive Society* (1988).

3   See Hamm, *Music of the New World* (1983), or McGee, *Music in Canada* (1985).

4   See, e.g., Rhodes, "Acculturation in North American Indian Music" (1952 [reprinted New York: Cooper Square Publications, 1967]), reiterated in reference sources such as "American Indian music" in the most recent edition of the *Harvard Dictionary of Music* 1986: 36.

5   A number of current studies have attempted to take more care in locating the historical moment, examining a wider range of Native musics (including hymns, popular music), and exploring intercultural processes. See, for example, V. Lindsay Levine's "Arzelie Langtry and a Lost Pan-tribal Tradition," in Stephen Blum *et al.*, eds., *Ethnomusicology and Modern Music* (1990); M. Hauser's "Inuit Songs from Southwest Baffin Island in Cross-cultural Context," *Études/Inuit/Studies* 2/1, 1978: 55-83, and 2/2, 1978: 71-105; C. Frisbie's *Navajo Medicine Bundles or Jish: Acquisition, Transmission, and Disposition in the Past and Present* (1987); B. Cavanagh's "Problems in Investigating the History of an Oral Tradition: Reconciling Different Types of Data about Inuit Drum Dance Traditions," *Annuario musical* (1987); or M. Lutz, *Musical Traditions of the Labrador Coast Inuit* (1982).

6   Is it partly in response to this that ethnomusicologists and others have written extensively about pitched instruments, including the relatively few Native string instruments such as the Inuit *tautirut* or the Apache fiddle. See, for example, Arima and Einarsson, "Whence and When the Eskimo Fiddle?" *Folk* (1976) or McAllester, "An Apache Fiddler," *Ethnomusicology Newsletter* (1956). On the other hand, the fantastic timbral variety of the dozens of different types of rattles and drums has frequently been ignored in ethnomusicological as in other academic literature.

7   The extensive holdings of museum collections documented in the *Catalogue* (forthcoming on disk) demonstrate, of course, that in some contexts some of these instruments *were* parted with and sold to museums. Some of the circumstances of these exchanges have been discussed in the *Catalogue*. Here we might note that there were undoubtedly unverifiable instances where a ceremonial instrument "type" was created but without appropriate ceremonial or ritual process.

8   Similarly, a unique instrument type might be constructed for the "museum market" as in the case of wooden hand-shaped rattles made for the Rochester Museum and Science Center as part of a Depression Era craft programme (see RMSC AE7882 and AE2797).

9   Rattles carried by Wooden Face (*Hadui*) maskers are also large, representing the hands of the Hadui spirit being. Such instruments are rarely used by singers, however.

10   The same troupes occasionally used rattles which were adaptations of "traditional" horn and basket types.

11   In her definition, "traditional" dances are choreographed dances. Prior to the mid-1980s, "powwow" in Quebec referred to events that were often church-sponsored and which included folkloric performance, wheels of fortune, etc. Hence her reference clearly relates to a show-type context.

12   This raises the question of the best way to speak of the role of the instrument maker. Is s/he a creator, an inventor? Is s/he a transformer who, like the pipe carrier, can put the parts together to make the power alive (a description of this process is found in Paper 1988: 9-12)? In many cases, a deep knowledge of the process of working with materials is the instrument maker's skill but the dicta for certain structural or

decorative details may emanate from other sources including dreams. On the other hand, many instruments are decorated in accordance with the instrument maker's preference. Within the range of roles which an instrument maker might play, it is evident that respect and gratitude for Creation are in no way a denial of the human capacity for creation.

13   In this regard, we might compare statements by John Cove, based on his work with Northwest Coast people. He urges us to consider "realness" in pan-species terms such that the living and the dead, humans, animals, and spirits are encompassed. "Realness," he suggests, "is more of an additive property, like the prince's stone and like garments, having ordinary-being as its basis" (1987: 81). The hardness of stone, the brightness of skin (clothes, attachments, etc.) are combined in the body. He associates bright, shining clothes with power and suggests they can be taken off to transform power. A similar view has been articulated by dance ethnographer Joanne Kealiinohomoku (paper presented to the Society for Ethnomusicology, Chicago, 1991) who regards the human body as a musical instrument. In her studies of Hopi dance, she describes dancers as instruments which are "played by their paraphernalia" and suggests that all studies of musical instruments should include their "quickening through embodiment."

14   A struggle to relocate the northern Labrador community of Davis Inlet which had been moved as a result of government intervention in the 1960s to an island location remote from hunting grounds, back to Shango Bay, the area of choice of the Innu, was successfully concluded in 1993.

15   There is a striking parallel to the Naskapi village/country complement in Colin Turnbull's representation of the Mbuti pygmy dichotomy between village and forest, one a sort of inversion of the other. Turnbull is exploring Turner's far-reaching theory of "liminality" in relation to his experience in Pygmy society. In his conclusion he makes the perceptive comment that "as long as we insist on taking liminality to imply a transitory in-between state of being, we are far from the truth. In our own terms it would be better seen as a timeless state of being, of 'holiness,' that lies parallel to our 'normal' state of being or is perhaps superimposed upon it, or somehow coincides and coexists with it" (1990: 80). He sees the pygmy forest as this parallel "holy" space and this description is applicable to the Naskapi forest as well. In fact, fruitful comparison could perhaps be made among various cultures which organize their lives in relation to dual physical spaces.

16   Of course, the "gifts" of a being such as the turtle are multiple. It is said to carry the earth on its back, thereby constituting " Turtle Island" which we call North America. It serves Iroquoian social and political structures by giving its identity to a clan.

17   Does this make post contact objects "unreal"? Are Europeans, Asians or Africans "unreal" in the eyes of *Ongwehonwe?* Not necessarily as we understand it. If you are not *Ongwehonwe,* you are simply "not from this place or from among these people."

18   The British school surrounding Victor Turner, and especially the recent anthology *Creativity/Anthropology* (1993) compiled by S. Lavoie *et al.* is one significant branch of this. Research on trance, including Gilbert Rouget's synthesis, *Music and Trance* (1985) as well as dream research (e.g., Barbara Tedlock's *Dreaming* [1987]) are others.

Chapter Four

Languages of Sound

Dialogue

MSC:

I'm struck by the fact that language issues discussed by Native writers, linguists, or speakers are often radically different from the ones we have written about in this chapter.

BD:

Such as?

MSC:

I think that they would speak very passionately about the rich meaning that their language has for them as individuals and their concern about language loss.

One of the things that Iroquoian linguists and faithkeepers often refer to, for example, is a speech which they state that George Washington made. As long as there is fire burning in their Longhouses—that is, as long as the political and religious structures continue—and as long as their language still exists, the American government will acknowledge them as a distinct Nation. Washington cautioned them that "once you lose your language, you're the same as us and you have the same responsibilities and duties, and no more rights." In effect, if they lose their language, they no longer exist.

BD:

Many of the same issues were raised in a widely distributed speech made by Uashat Innu Chief Daniel Vachon. He talked about "invoking the thousands of experiences of a people" (1987: 5) when a language is spoken, when a word of that language is uttered. Many Innu regard language conservation as the most important means of insuring the maintenance of their cultural identity. Impressive curriculum materials, written in local dialects and produced by communities, is an indication of the priority this issue has.

FvR:

In connection with language loss in the Maritimes, Micmac express concerns about how Native languages are taught in schools. English perceptions are influencing Native speech patterns; language is taught as a "subject," using non-Native, English-style grammars and not as a distinctive way of thinking and relating.

When Micmac educator Marie Battiste raises the issue of literacy, she makes clear that any effort to impose non-Native educational systems and methods of language learning on Native youth is just another form of cultural assimilation. She emphasizes that pictographs and petroglyphs as visual symbols and mnemonic aids are part of that long history of cultural expression and identity. Marie's words came to mind when I listened to the non-linear storytelling style of Michael W. Francis. I was reminded of a song scroll or some other mnemonic "text" in which each image would key a larger text.

BD:

But surely the conceptual problems which interest us in this chapter need not be divorced from these important issues.

Naming, for example. An entire worldview is implied in this process. What gets named? How do things get named?

MSC:

Let's clarify our terminology first. I think that "naming," "labelling" and "uttering" have to be distinguished. Naming is partly a process of creating an identity for something. Labelling is a process of identifying or recognizing something which already has a known identity. Uttering or "evoking the name of something" would seem to be quite different, and there are contexts in which we should be talking about uttering rather than naming or labelling with regard to Native languages.

FvR:

We should also bear in mind that naming and labelling are noun-oriented tasks in English but Algonquian languages, at any rate, are verb-oriented. Even objects are sometimes referred to by a verbal phrase.

MSC:
Yes, that seems true for Iroquoian languages as well. The Cayuga word for singer, *hadreno:ta*, translates "he is singing." This is a noun-verb incorporation which suggests habitual action.

On a related but slightly different tack, I am interested in how people receive their own names. Are there fixed lists of personal names for children? Can you create new names? With the Longhouse communities there are specific Indian names associated with different clans. In practice, names from other clans are sometimes borrowed and, occasionally, two people have the same Indian name.

FvR:
There is a difference between what is done and what one can do. I haven't encountered such set rules, but Micmac consultants have told me that certain names would be inappropriate to use since they belong to other geographical areas. I have also been told that certain last names are, in practice, connected to certain clans.

MSC:
But beyond this set list of names relating to clan, there are other ways of receiving names. As a Confederacy Chief, faithkeeper, or clan mother you could be given an additional name associated with this position. You would likely also have an English name. So you could have three or four different names, depending on your responsibilities and connections.

BD:
Because they don't have a formal ceremonial structure comparable to the Longhouse ceremonies, the Innu do not have names associated with official roles or positions to my knowledge. Innu names are often translations of English names into the phonemic system of their language ("Charles" becomes "Tshenish"; "Mary" is "Mani"). An individual often has a familiar name—some might be abbreviations of their publicly known names while others refer to a personal idiosyncracy; the use of the familiar name seems to strengthen relationships within the community.

It occurs to me that we do have an English equivalent for identifying one's lineage in names like "Johnson" for John's son, Robson, Jefferson, etc., but we have almost forgotten that etymology; I rarely think about the history, the recognition of generation upon generation when I hear such English names.

We should also consider when each Iroquoian or Algonquian name would be used.

FvR:
At Elders Conferences, Anishnabe speakers are often careful to identify themselves in several ways, uttering their name, Nation, clan, affiliation in the Midewiwin perhaps.

BD:
The tradition of Elders Conferences in the Maritimes and Ontario was not shared by the Innu of Quebec and Labrador in the 1980s, a period when many public gatherings were focused on opposition to the military testing of low-flying aircraft in their residential and hunting areas. Speakers would identify their name and Nation, certainly, but since they were often addressing non-Native audiences to garner public support for their very survival, they were less concerned about proper intracultural identification in these forums.

MSC:
I think conferences are quite different from ceremonial events. Although they'll often identify their clan, few Iroquoian speakers I've met mention their Indian name at conferences or other social gatherings. Names invite connection, and this can be misused. But in Longhouse ceremonies, people are addressed exclusively by their Indian names whereas their clan is understood—usually known by the community anyway, or else easily determined by recognizing clan seating patterns in the Longhouse.

BD:
Let's talk more about *not* naming. In some contexts—Montagnais myth narration, for example—allusion rather than direct naming is a common mode of referring to something or someone. Certain animals are often described but not named. I think the bear may have the longest list of circumlocutions.

MSC:
Things you cannot utter. Hmm. There are so many things associated with birds that you can't talk about. That flute which you can't mention by name is related to the sound of birds. Oh dear. I just mentioned it.

BD:
We learned that some images of birds, especially those mirror images on drums, were not to be discussed.

MSC:

Things you can't utter . . .

FvR:

But have been given names . . .

MSC:

That have their own names . . .

FvR:

That you can't utter in certain situations . . .

MSC:

That you can *only* utter in certain contexts. . . . Things get difficult here—there are issues and names we can't appropriately discuss in this book.

BD:

We could, however, acknowledge that, in some contexts, restrictions on knowledge about the names of things are more pragmatic. Names for the parts of a Montagnais drum, for example, are better known by men than by women because the men need to know this hunting tool very well.

FvR:

Your example suggests another direction for our dialogue. What kinds of things (or beings) receive names at all? In Micmac and apparently in Iroquoian communities, asking about the names of the parts of a drum was a peculiar academic enterprise. People would make up a polite response— "Well, it's like a shoelace; it's like this or that. What kind of support do I put in a basket? We could give the hoop of a drum that same name."

MSC:

Actually, Iroquoian friends offered very witty and very bawdy responses when I asked about naming parts of instruments, especially when I asked whether parts of a drum or rattle were compared with the human body. Not exactly standard academic terminology!

BD:

My experience in Innu communities was very different from yours. Naming the kinds and parts of things was volunteered as important information by Montagnais consultants. The significance of these specialized vocabularies is also reflected in recent Innu publications. In Sept-Îles one cultural organization has produced a small book[1] with labelled diagrams—kinds of tools, types of tent structures including names for the different tent poles, parts of the drum, the canoe, or various animals, twenty-three kinds of snow, sixteen kinds of wind, and many others—in order to teach young people the detailed vocabulary of the forest. Montagnais names for drum parts often embed references to the physical properties of the world around: sticklike things, skinlike things, stonelike things, waterlike things, and stringlike things. As I understand it, the knowledge of these properties is extended by maintaining the naming practices.

FvR:

This whole discussion of names and labels implies a world in which words and their associated meanings are like building blocks that we string together. But let's not forget that people *use* language creatively and experientially. It seems that in Micmac, at any rate, individual speakers seem to express observed or felt relationships flexibly.

BD:

Polysemy and punning are aspects of this which seem to be especially rich. In some Algonquian languages, the same word might be used for "rainbow" and "ribbon" or for "berry" and "beadwork."

MSC:

What about the connection between "turtle" and "violin" in Iroquoian languages.

BD:

Or "turtle" and "spoon" in Algonquin. All these examples reveal an eye for similarities of shape.

FvR:

Things that curve or take the shape of a path connect to all sorts of things. "Story" and "string" and "fiddle bow" are all related both through their linearity but also through their qualities of flexibility. In Maliseet, the rising action of baking bread or a soufflé relates to the name used for a flute. This is more than a discussion of polysemy; it is often a matter of individuality in creative interpretations of words.

But my original point, here, was more pragmatic. We have all found it challenging to sort out the different understandings that people might have for the same word.

BD:

It's a common problem whenever one learns any new language. But I agree with you: the meaning of an Innu phrase seems to be more context-dependent and often more personal than a phrase in English. I recall working on this very thing with two Innu translators in Davis Inlet, Labrador. One agreed to translate an English passage into the Innu language while the other translated it back again. The domains of their experience, and hence their language, were different. For the snare of the drum, the first translator used the correct name, *nutepin*, but the second translator, who didn't know this word, made connections on the basis of morphemes, parts of the word which mean literally "my skin" and which she translated as "its own sound." Later in the same passage, the buzzing sound of the snare was translated with a word which the second interpreter understood as "the turning thing." At the time, I was really perplexed by these seemingly huge differences in meaning, but, actually, the close relationships between membrane and sound or between sound and motion (such as turning) are, as we came to understand, really fundamental concepts.

FvR:

Your anecdote relates to an area I would like to discuss: newly created words. Some linguists regard these with a certain amount of disapproval, but I find the creative process very interesting. Later in this chapter we present a conversation I had with Michael W. Francis about the word for "radio." He went into the whole thought process of how he develops the word, how he puts it together. He started with "there's this sound; how will I experience that sound?" It's a fascinating process.

BD:

The process ties in with another idea which we explore later: meaning which emerges over time, intersecting with personal experience.

MSC:

But we must be careful that we don't imply Native languages are less specific or more ambiguous than English. Cayuga speakers may feel a bit uncomfortable because they regard English as very vague, while Iroquoian languages allow you to be more specific—you can be very clear as to time, date, place, and participants in an event.

BD:

In Algonquian languages, relationships—who is speaking to whom, whether someone is excluded or included in the conversation—are identified with precision.

MSC:

I would like to take us on to another topic: writing and speaking. Naturally, as non-Native researchers our access to language is often through written texts in dictionaries or grammars. But we have often dis-cussed the differences between oral and written texts and should keep these processes of language distinct in our minds.

FvR:

It also occurs to me that the specificity with which words are used depends on the context of use. As you say, word lists, dictionaries, etc. are very different from speech events. But then, even speech events vary according to who is talking to whom and what degree of interpretation and clarification is necessary.

MSC:

What does it mean to "utter" a word, a name, or a speech in a specific language? And further, what is the appropriate way to give voice to something? When, for example, is song used instead of speech?

BD:

I wonder if we could begin to answer that by looking at how words are altered in songs. I am fascinated by the ways that song words are disguised—I'm not sure if that is the right word—by the addition of extra syllables and by the sound of the drum's snare. I wonder if the snare covering the sound is analogous to layering or clothing/dressing. Some Innu singers suggest that the words need to be masked because they belong to an individual. Montagnais song texts are often too personal to discuss (at least with a non-Native outsider) and they often refer to experiences in the forest which are hard to understand in the village context.

FvR:

Many Micmac songs don't have lexical texts, but when they do, contemporary performers seem to make no effort to disguise them.

MSC:

Certainly, many Iroquoian ceremonial songs have texts. But I sometimes have difficulty understanding "language songs," whether in social dance sets or Great Feather dance cycles, because I find that the drum and rattles obscure the words. I don't think that singers intend to mask the words, but a turtle rattle is very loud. My minimal proficiency in these languages plays a role, too—for people who are familiar with the songs, it's not necessary to hear every word articulated clearly.

Song texts are also filled with metaphors, some familiar to me, some not. I may be able to translate "She is going into the garden," but unless I understand the context, I haven't a clue about what that really means—whether "she" is a woman or a female of some other kind and what's she doing in the garden. Is this song associated with "our life sustainers" (corn, beans, and squash)? Are we talking about spring planting or harvest? What all is implied here? It's this richer level of meaning beyond specific word translation that leaves me gasping.

FvR:

Your comment relates to what I was just saying about the context in which language is used and the degree of clarification that may be needed or desired.

But let me raise another issue. Micmac singers sometimes take a traditional Micmac tune and add different texts to it. In order to make the text and tune fit, they may lengthen certain parts or add things.

MSC:

How often do the added things involve repetition? When are syllables or words or phrases or whole speeches repeated, and why?

BD:

Like *shishikun* (rattle), or *ueuetan* (dressing).

FvR:

Ku-ku-kues (owl). You find lots and lots of repetitions like that. Most seem to be onomatopoeic.

MSC:

Duwisduwi: (killdeer) or *ga:-ka:* (crow).

FvR:

Tam-tam. That's the drum sound itself.

MSC:

The idea of connecting clearly defined, repeated units (again, like those divisions in a Longhouse) to create a "pathway" also interests me in other ways, and visual as well as aural examples come to mind. I've already mentioned the *Ganohonyonk;* it consists of relatively short units with formulaic patterns acknowledging forces from the earth to the Creator. I wonder if there is a similar aesthetic at work in the beaded patterns along the seams or borders of traditional outfits—small, discrete, similar units, sometimes a skydome pattern, each one complete in itself yet part of a whole. Even social music structure fits into this basic structure. Circles, cycles, pathways—I don't know which is the best metaphor, or if they fit together. Paths can be followed back and forth, ascending and descending in a kind of cycle too.

BD:

We could develop the pathway idea further by considering linguistic interaction in various kinds of speech events. Ron Scollon's work on Athabascan communication patterns[2] raises some interesting comparative points for discussion.

He describes the Athabascan propensity for monologue rather than dialogue, or at least, longer segments of speech rather than rapid interchanges among speakers, which he regards as more characteristic of English speakers.

FvR:

The idea of larger speech units seems to hold true in Micmac contexts, but I don't like using the word "monologue" for this. Consider linguistic interaction at gatherings, conferences, and ceremonies where, in my experience, people often sit in a circle and pass the eagle feather or talking stick from one speaker to another. "Monologue" does not draw attention to the relationship between the words of each speaker and the next, nor the relationship of other listeners and potential speakers in the circle. However, in this context, discussion, or back-and-forth exchange, as a means of exploring a subject is not something I have seen very often. It's "Here's my story, here's my point of view; I'll put it out there."

MSC:

The concept of individual perspective is extremely important. When I see people engaging in conversations about ceremonies or speeches or songs, they rarely debate issues; they rarely tell another person that their views are wrong. If they disagree, my friends simply say "Oh!" and drop the subject (which is a strong hint by itself). Or else they'll comment indirectly: "Someone once said that . . . " or "I once heard that. . . ." Everything is qualified.

FvR:

When working with Micmac elders, there are times when they will simply answer a question. But when you just sit and listen, when your consultant runs with an idea he seems to switch to a different mode, a storytelling mode. Aurally and kinaesthetically, the event has been transformed. How is that information, that text, different from the direct answers to questions?

BD:

I believe folklorist Dell Hymes (1981) called what you describe a "breakthrough into performance." What does that mean in relation to the texts we consider? In relation to our text?

Notes

1 *Kuanutin Nutshimiu-Atusseun* (1988).

2 The reference is to *Narrative, Literacy, and Face in Interethnic Communication* (1981).

Languages of Sound

Everybody can say that word *Anish[a]nabe*, that's who we are. That's where I always like to start. According to our tradition, according to our teaching that has come down to us from our ancestors, from the very beginning. . . . I want to go back to this word here and show you how this word reflects our Creation story. When we take that word apart we come up with . . . *anishana*—it's a single word but when you put that together, it asks a question. What does that mean? "Where do you come from?" That's what that word there means. *Anishana.* So we use this term to describe from where do we come. We come from the Creator and our Mother the Earth. *Anishana.*

How? We use this part of it: *inishana*—he was lowered. That means he was lowered. That word was in there. *Nabe[o]*—That last part of it. That means what? Male of the species. That word was the original man. That's what that word means. That Creation story is all in that one word here. That's our Creation story. And there's much more to it than that. That's only a small glimpse of it. That's who we are. And we're all Anishnabek here on this Turtle Island. . . . We are the original people of the island. And I share that message with you.

—Eddie Benton-Benai, Birch Island, 1986

Respect is in the voice. You don't have to add a word for "please."

—Sadie Buck, in conversation with SPINC, 1988

By giving voice to one word, an Anishnabe can find his identity and his history. In its resonance he finds where he came from and who he is.

By speaking in the proper way, an Iroquois woman can offer respect. (Ironically, you are reading both statements on a silent page.)

We selected these two epigrams because Native ways of speaking about language contrast with the "discourse" about language within many familiar academic contexts. Both Eddie Benton-Benai and Sadie Buck speak of language sounded, words spoken. The meaning they find is not just in the definitions of words but in the relationships established when they are uttered—externally by offering respect, internally through the exercise of the imagination which finds words within words and sounds within sounds.

Ethnomusicologists (like linguists, folklorists, sociologists, and others) are also frequently interested in both "language sounded" and "language for sound."[1] The extensive literature on speech acts and on performance theory attests to that.[2] Rarely, however, have we heard the same kinds of connections emphasized. Those we are usually trained to make in the academic world have to do with clearly defining (and often therefore delimiting) information in a specific text rather than being open to its possibilities. Furthermore, we often search for identity, "meaning" and certainly history through webs of text—some verbal, some musical, some pictorial, some gestural, some physical . . . many printed.

Among these searches, an issue to which ethnomusicologists have devoted considerable attention since the early 1970s, are investigations of metaphoric and metonymic domains[3] which relate to the English-language concept of "music." Students of this discipline are aware that, while Euro-American harmony teachers may refer, for example, to pitch relationships using a language of numbers and hierarchical relationships ("dominant seventh," "major or minor third"), a Kaluli might refer to the same sonic distinctions as aspects of a waterfall's motion (see Feld 1982), or a Waiapi to specific bird or animal sounds (see Fuks 1990). While all North American Aboriginal nations engage in expression which English speakers would call "music," none of the languages of the Algonquian and Iroquoian families have an analogous verbal concept. Hence, since we cannot expect to find a monolithic, bounded word or phrase equivalent to "music," the metaphoric domains referenced in relation to sound and sounding of any type are central to our exploration. What realms of experience do people draw upon to talk about song, dance, drumming, or other activities related to our English-language subject?

Our research has led us to question the boundaries between human, verbal languages and sonic communication of other beings, perhaps even between verbal language and "musical" language. The verbal/musical distinction is usually a denotative/connotative one for English speakers. However, our work with elders implied that "connotation" plays a role of a different order in their processes of meaning-making. Further, since their knowledge of denotative aspects of non-verbal sounds was so sophisticated in relation to our own, we had to reconsider our own categories and concepts, especially those which related to the nature and function of "naming," the difference between spoken and written languages, and the nature of "authority" in relation to an aural or visual text.

The Nature of "Naming"

Naming is part of the process which humans use to construct their reality. Lippard calls it "the active tense of identity, the outward aspect of the self-representation process, acknowledging all the circumstances through which it must elbow its way" (Lippard 1990: 19). Names are usually described as human constructions that recognize those aspects of environment and experience that are seen as significant. On a practical level, naming fixes things and helps us remember them. It may do this by classification, a process which in itself gives us a sense that we understand the world around us.[4]

Beyond this, naming permits that which is identified to be shared with others and creates a relationship with the thing named. To be sure, misnaming can often occur, and this may be a painful experience for the misnamed or it may even preclude the possibility of relationship and close the path.

Even if naming is regarded as a completely free creative act, it is clear that sounds are chosen with careful attention to nuances so complex as to almost defy explanation. Consider, for example, the following list compiled by Douglas Hofstadter:

What makes words like "Da-glo" [sic] " Turbomatic," and "Rayon" seem slightly dated? Why is "Quantas" still modern-sounding? What is poor about brand names like "Luggo" and "Flimp"? Why are x's now so popular in brand names? And yet why would "Goxie" be a weak name compared with, say, "Exigo" or "Xigeo"? Why are the ordinary-seeming names that nasal-voiced comedians Bob and Ray come up with—for example, "Wally Ballou," "Hudley Pierce," "Bodin Pardew," and "John W. Norbis"—apt to evoke snickers? How come Norma Jean Baker changed her name to "Marilyn Monroe"? Why would it not do for a movie star to be named "Arnold Wilberforce"? Why is the name " Tiffany" popular today and why was "Lisa" so popular a few years earlier? Is something wrong with "Agnes," "Edna" or " Thelma"? With "Clyde," "Lance," or "Bartholomew"? (1985: 543)

The act of naming, that is, recognizing one's environment and establishing relationships either by conscious convention or by unconscious (sonic) communication, occurs in all languages and cultures. However, the emphasis on each aspect varies, as does the process of naming. Within Native communities, for example, names are used in some contexts to establish a relationship with another being and thus to access their power.

Names give power to people and to those who know the names of others, animal or human. If we call spirits' names, they have to listen or come—good reason for many Indian peoples not to say a spirit's name out loud. Animals and humans may have many names and may

change them according to the events or visions in their lives. **Names may be mocking, given for silly or foolish behavior, but in general, they represent a kind of special power reserved for the person having the name.** (Green 1984: 312)

In other instances, names may be said to be given, not by human agency, but by other parts of the environment. Some people emphasize the importance of naming place. One Micmac elder told Franziska von Rosen that names belong in a place. They are of it. They are it. When new names are created by an individual, the process of using language to name something also helps us understand how our consultants relate to the world around them.

Oral and Written Texts: "If We Call Spirits' Names . . ."

"If we call . . ." says Green in the statement just quoted. Differences between spoken and written texts have been explored extensively[5] and sometimes reductively, as if societies were exclusively reliant on one or the other. Though clearly all contemporary societies emphasize many kinds of text enactment in varied contexts, some fundamental differences between printed and oral forms of communication remain relevant. Walter Ong (1982) has suggested that a spoken word is experienced as something akin to a dramatic event, whereas a written one may be conceptually closer to an object, fixed in place. Fundamental to this, of course, is the fact that a spoken text is received through the ears and a written one by means of the eyes. The sensory experience is different, the effect on memory is different, and so too are the consequences of the experience.[6]

In Native languages, a strong connection between vision, motion and sound—the heard, the seen, the remembered, the imagined—is valued. An example is the uttering of a name: any utterance is the action which makes the words travel. Speech and sound, then, reach across space and through boundaries impermeable to vision.

Furthermore, several consultants stressed the holistic experience of a spoken text. In stark contrast to this, our questions about the meaning of words or phrases were often excised from context and were thus sometimes unanswerable. In the same sense, our written texts and tapes are fragments of experience, isolated from a specific context and performance; yet these may be reinterpreted to become part of a new whole. Indeed, print and recordings can obviously be read/repeated by anyone, anywhere, in any manner.

Authority

The fragmentation of experience accentuated by print is furthermore germane to the issue of authority because print has been invested with great legitimacy throughout contemporary North American history. In our experience, readers sometimes assume that printed texts represent "true," "real," or "expert" perspectives which are widely shared, whereas in reality, of course, both oral and literary texts may represent either an individual's or a group's point of view.

Some oral texts referred to in this study—the Iroquois Thanksgiving Address, for example—might be described as formal since they have "repeatable" elements, spoken in appropriate contexts. Invested with the authority of the group, the speaker of such texts usually has a special culture-given mandate to perform the texts, or the "authority" may lie within the text itself rather than with the individual.[7] In other cases, highly individual "texts"—comments, personal interpretations—were shared with us. They challenged us to explore carefully our "trained" assumptions about "authority." While this kind of critique has become common practice in virtually all the humanities and social sciences, it is still relatively rare to validate "individual" (ergo subjective) texts in academic contexts. This, however, has proven to be an essential task for our understanding of Native expression in both written and oral media and languages.

Sub-Arctic Algonquian: Montagnais (with Some Reference to Ojibwe and Algonquin)[8]

Sometimes it was an Anishnabe elder speaking of the delicate sound of the Creator's thoughts and the low rumbling sound which came before the sound of Creation. Or a Cree hunter explaining and imitating the sounds of geese—the manner in which these sounds change, depending on the height at which the birds fly and the wind direction relative to the flight path and the relative positions of geese and hunter. On another occasion, a Naskapi woman taught the complex vocabulary for the sound of an airplane when it is a long way off, when it is circling, and when it is getting ready to land, and the many descriptive terms for the sound of water—cascading off a cliff, flowing over rocks. Over and over, I was astonished by elders' sensitivity to the nuances of natural sounds, their ability to distinguish and imitate sounds, and sometimes their detailed and rich vocabulary for the acoustic environment. Alongside the word lists, conversation transcripts, and linguistic studies useful in the study of the languaging of song and sound producers, these experiences revealed how fundamentally this sonic relationship with the world—this world-hearing (as well as a worldview)—affects how words are created and used by Anishnabe and Innu speakers.

One example may clarify this. Anishnabek often describe the gourd shaker sound as the "sound of Creation." This intriguing "abstract" image (or so it seemed, initially) is at the same time a physical description: the seeds of the gourd, those elements which permit regeneration and constitute the rattlers in a gourd rattle that has not been opened in any way. But further, the power to create, to regenerate, is *in the sound*, not just in the tangible substance, and not only in the seeds, but in the encompassing of the seeds within a circular form. How does one name something of such fundamental importance? We were told that it gives its name: *shishikun*, onomatopoeically conveying its identity, the *shi-* sound imitating the collision of fine rattlers, their motion already pulsed through repetition.[9] This name for rattle is shared not only among virtually all Algonquian languages—though see the section on Wabanaki below—but across language families as well. Some language may be humanly constructed; some may be given from the environment. Furthermore, "metaphor"—however poetic and elegant—does not necessarily build an analogy to something outside of itself; it may sometimes *be* an imitation of the acoustic experience itself. *Shishikun* might be described, then, as a name that is "given by the Creator," a phrase applied to instruments which are not mediated by humans as we have seen.

Individuals, however, accept responsibility for translating what is "given" in accordance with useful contextual clues, as well as their own abilities and domains of experience. Innu hunters consistently have an extensive language for such things as natural sounds, weather patterns, plant varieties and uses, the life ways and anatomy of animals, or other phenomena useful to them in the bush (*nutshimits*). The detailed naming of such things is valued and deeply respected. One evidence of this is a recent publication (*Kuanutin Nutshimiu atusseun—Work in the Bush*) which records these "special" languages generally on carefully labelled diagrams such as that replicated in Fig. 10. Detailed names for either natural phenomena or parts of objects made for use in the bush are evident in displays in local museums and cultural centres; the Kitigan Zibi Anishnabeg Cultural Education Centre in the

Algonquin community of Maniwaki, for example, displayed, in 1989, snowshoes on which name tags labelled each area of webbing, and each section of the frame. A display of varieties of wood was also exhibited.

Sound Morphemes

Concentration on the smallest units of meaning—the morphemes of language—is consistent with Anishnabe and Innu elders' and hunters' emphases. Some would savour certain syllables by repeating them or uttering them emphatically within a word; others (more familiar with our academic preoccupation with analysis) drew our attention more explicitly to the connotations of specific morphemes relevant to our areas of interest.[10]

Most Anishnabe and some Innu speakers identify a morpheme for sound: *-ue-*. Its sonic structure merits close attention. It has no consonants, nothing to stop the flow of the sound, but rather begins with aspiration, with breath. It is a diphthong, a unit with two vowel sounds in one "syllable"; the change from *u* to *e* embodies "motion," an actual change of pitch—a miniature Doppler effect. In many words denoting sound or some related phenomenon, the syllable is doubled, *-ueue-*. In some dialects, *ueue* (or *wewe* or *wewew* in some orthographies) means goose, nicknamed "wavey." I read it, as I was taught to read *shishikun*, as an imitation of the physical (and acoustic) reality of vibration. Its ability to denote a variety of things, many of which would not be acknowledged by linguists to be morphemically the same, is bracketed by its fundamental sonic form. This suggests that one should be open to relationships among the varied things which might seem disparate and unrelated.

At the most obvious, and uncontroversial level, the *-ue-* morpheme is embedded in the names of musical instruments. In several of the following examples, the association between *-ue-* and "sound" was explained by consultants:[11]

teUEikan—drum (similar word used in Anishnabe and Innu Nations)

shinaUEshikan—hoof rattle (Algonquin, River Desert)

taUEpatsikan—bull-roarer (Naskapi, Davis Inlet)

minuaUEpitsikat—piano (Naskapi, Davis Inlet)

kidoWEYabigahigan—a form of the word for violin found in manuscript sources for Algonquin (cited in the River Desert Education Authority [RDEA] dictionary)

Or it may be used in conjunction with other kinds of sound, including speech, or sound producers:

gashkUEUEman—he urges, exhorts (RDEA)

mistiUE—skin which sounds, used as membrane of drum (Naskapi, Davis Inlet)

Ue- also indicates the physical co-relate of sound, vibration or wavelike motions, such as sweeping, rocking, or balancing:

kiUEtin—North wind (literally, "the wind which returns") (Montagnais, Sept-Îles)

WEWEbasin—to flutter in the wind (RDEA)

WEWEbizon—a swing (RDEA)

UEUEpetnauahu—s/he rocks the baby in the hammock (Mingan, Quebec) (McNulty 1981)

The last word in this list is an interesting dual reference to the motion of rocking and the singing which usually accompanies it.

Connected to other concepts not obviously associated with "sound" by English speakers, *-ue-* has other significant nuances. Here, linguists who read our manuscript argued that we were speculating on connections between distinctively different morphemes. The connotations of the sound structure, itself, however, together with similar associations in other domains (e.g., the physical structuring of instruments, performance usage), lead us to believe that there are *potential* connections among these seemingly disparate concepts.

In some dialects, *ueuetan* is usually glossed as "dressing" or "wrapping" (also "layering" or sometimes "offering"). The same metaphor is used in conjunction with the preparation of Anishnabe drums for performance, the proper assembly of the membrane, or the tying of ropes which hold it, tune it, or form an image on its surface. The ability of sound to surround and envelop (also see reference below to Micmac descriptions of the sound of the *Mi'kmwesu*) may relate the concepts.

A similar reflection of a physical reality is evident in the name for wind instrument in a number of Algonquin languages and dialects. *PU-, the* plosive beginning of all the following words, enacts blowing in the words in which it is incorporated:[12]

POtacikan—wind instrument (Cree, Ellis 1983)

POdajegan—game call (Algonquin, RDEA)

ka-PUtatshigan—flute (Naskapi, Davis Inlet)

The plosive is also evident in the Attikamek word for flute, *papigan* and an Ojibwe term for drumstick, *pagaakokwan*.

Another onomatopoeic syllable occurs in the pan-Algonquian word for drum which begins with *te-, ta-, de-, da-*, described by both Anishnabe and Innu consultants as the sound of the drum itself:[13]

DAbegan (Algonquin, AP)

TAywagan (Attikamek)

TEueikan (Naskapi/Montagnais)

TEwehigan (Algonquin, RDEA)

The same syllable is embedded in the Montagnais word for sound, *peTAkun*, where it may be similarly onomatopoeic.

The connotations of *te-*, like the connotations of *-ue-*, are more far-reaching. Aubin's *Proto-Algonquian Dictionary* (1975), for example, glosses the prefix *te-* as "life." In combination with *wa-* (the morpheme representing a circle), *te:wa* says "he exists." River Desert linguists similarly translate *ta-* or *te-* as "to be, to live, or to exist" but add that the syllable generally denotes a place. But when aspiration is added to the end of the syllable to form *teh-*, the word changes slightly in several Anishnabe dialects to become "heart." Breath or wind (or spirit) effects this subtle but profound change. Interpreters of the dance drum frequently play upon the pun of *te-/teh-*. In the contexts of contemporary powwows, one frequently hears that "the drum is the heartbeat of the Indian Nation." Its third-person, possessive form, *ute*—"his/her/its heart" refers more explicitly in some dialects to drum, *uteikan* (Ojibwe, sometimes spelled *odaegun*), or drum snare, *utepiat* (Montagnais).

When several Montagnais consultants were asked about names for the parts of musical instruments, their patient answers revealed a concern with detailed, accurate terminology. (See two variants of drum terminology in the diagrams below.)

Their explanations of the meanings of these names usually related to the physical properties implicit in a series of morphemes which have also been clearly outlined in linguistic publications. Marguerite McKenzie outlines and gives examples for the following in the dialect spoken around Sheshashit in Labrador:

-aapui—liquid
  miinaapui—jam
  niipiishaapui—tea
  tshimuunaapui—rainwater
  aemieuaapui—holy water
-aashk—sticklike
  mashinaikanaashk—pencil
  utamaikanashk—drumstick
  ashaamaashk—snowshoe frame

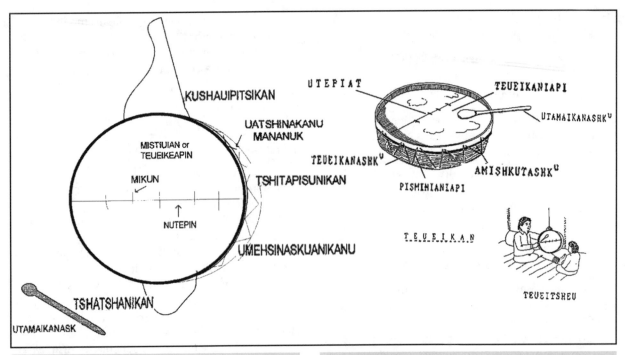

Fig. 10. Parts of the *Teueikan*.
From Davis Inlet, Labrador.

Fig. 11. Parts of the *Teueikan*.
From Sept-Îles, Quebec.

teueikanashk—drum frame
apuaanaashk—roasting stick
-uiaan—hide, fur, sheetlike
mistiue—drum membrane
mashinaikanuiaan—paper
amishkuiaan—beaver skin
atiikuiaan—caribou skin
-aapii—stringlike
teueikaniapi—drum membrane
piishaakanaapii—string, rope
pishimianiapi—drum lacing
ashtishiaapii—mitten string
utepiat—snare
-aapiss—dollar, metal
peikuaapiss—one dollar
nishuaapiss—two dollars

In some dialects, stonelike substances are also designated (*aassii* related to *minaashit*—berry and *assini*—stone, earth).[14]

In Chapter Five we discuss the importance of each of these physical properties of existence as a source of teaching, a different means of relating to the world around one. Embedded in language, the designations for each property draw attention to the multifaceted qualities and potentials of those properties. These qualities and potentials relate, in turn, to the "teachings" of specific objects which embody them. When Anishnabe consultants and elders state that the "drum has all you need to know," we

understand those words to mean that the drum embodies the qualities and potentials of all those physical properties. When Naskapi/Montagnais consultants emphasize the names for the parts of a drum, we think they are teaching us something similar.

Metaphors for Sounds and Sound Producers

The connection of sound (*petakun* in the Innu dialect used in Davis Inlet) to its physical correlation, motion, and the onomatopoeic imitation of natural sounds in language are, as we have seen, reflected in many names for sound-producing instruments. The terminology used in different communities and Nations raises several other issues as well.

First, we might consider the diffusion of names. Is it significant that words for drum and rattle (and flute to a lesser extent) are widespread, while names for other instrument types are highly variable? To some extent, this may reflect historical development, since European-related instruments such as the fiddle or the piano are among the highly variable terms. Additionally, the centrality of the teachings of drum and rattle, embodied in the names as partially illustrated earlier, may help to ensure that the names are more consistent from one region to another.

A second issue concerns translation. Are the English terms used to gloss the Algonquian ones analogous? The blurring of drum and rattle categories in some instances where a disc rattle may be called a "small drum" or the use of *shishigun* as a type-specific name in some instances and a generic category in others suggest that translation should be context-specific wherever possible.

A third issue relates to the creation of new words for sound producers which may be of European origin or recent development. In Montagnais, for instance, "piano" consists of *minu-* (good), *ue-* (sound), and *-sikat* (almost). Hence it is "almost good music." Significantly, a phrase solicited for the fiddle in Davis Inlet was almost the same but had *tshitshe miam* (very good) added to it. This might imply that the fiddle was regarded by this individual more highly than the piano. In other communities, a fiddle was identified by the action of rubbing or brushing; *shishuniku-tauapekeikan* is related to words for brushing teeth, scraping skins, or kneading dough. A tape recorder might be identified by the pattern of its motion: *ka-* (thing), *mistepin* (going, a moving pathway). A similar word is used in Sept-Îles for radio-telephone. In Davis Inlet, on the other hand, radio is referred to simply as *kanatutakanits*, "the thing that you hear."

We did not find many generic distinctions for music. Both Innu and Anishnabek use the same word for "song," spelled variously *nikamun, nakamun, nagamun*. In Innu contexts, it is used for dream songs and for hymns. The same word applies for songs in ceremonial and social contexts. The one repertoire of singing which is not appropriately designated as *nikamun* is the improvised lullaby (called *bebe ataushu* in Davis Inlet).[15] Distinctions among *nikamuna*, however, are often made with modifying adjectives. Hence *aiamieu nikamun* is translated "prayer song" (in Davis Inlet), although the first part of the term literally indicates "words" and may refer to the quantity of text in hymns. Some Innu hunters distinguish songs by an animal or spirit which brought the songs in a dream: *atikw nikamun* is "caribou song," for example. Speck recorded song designations of this type for the following animals: caribou, bear, and otter. The major hunting-related ceremony named among the Naskapi/Montagnais is the *mukusham*—the feast (and dance in some cases) which follows a successful hunt. A very similar sounding term, *makusham*, indicates the steps of the Montagnais dance in which humans are said to recreate the tracks of animals.

While many different song genres can be encompassed by the same term, *nikamun*, spoken genres are distinguished. Differences between two narrative genres usually glossed as "myth" (*atnuhan*) and "story" (*tipatshimun*) are explained in

a number of published sources. Both references to sound and different discourse styles,[16] including singing, in performance, are prominent features of myths. Furthermore, the myth-teller often uses singing at specific points in the narrative, points where the mythic character cannot see the person with whom s/he is communicating. Spoken very emphatically and slowly just prior to a myth song, the phrase *pinetuetimanitshi* serves as a cueing device at many of these points. Myth narrators also imitate bird or animal calls of various kinds. The verb for calls, *ashikueu*, is explicitly linked to singing in one early dictionary: Père Bonaventure Fabre's *Racines Montagnaises . . .* , compiled at Tadoussac, Quebec, before 1695, glosses *achik8an e8* as "chanter, parler haut." The gloss indicates a blurring of the boundaries between speaking, calling, and singing. Some mythical characters may be distinguished by the high or low qualities of their voices. The boy-hero Tshakapesh is sometimes described as having a high or small voice (*nishitashu*) while his adversary Katshenituask has a name which embeds the quality of a "low voice"(*-tshen-*). Algonquins name the "spirit that inhabits waterfalls," *Memegwesi*, with the same root as the word for speaking or singing falsetto: *memegwesikaz-o* (RDEA).

The *atnuhan* or myth is not the only context in which an extensive vocabulary for describing varied sounds and skill in performing the voices of different creatures is evident. In the bush, hunters recognize, verbally identify and imitate with admirable realism subtle distinctions among calls of various natural phenomena. Cree elder James Carpenter could distinguish the height of a goose flying overhead, the wind direction, and the position of the hunter on the basis of sound quality. In his northern Ontario community of Attawapiskat, virtually every boy could do a variety of accurate animal imitations.

Davis Inlet Innu in Northern Labrador helped develop vocabulary lists for detailed sonic distinctions, although they cautioned that long residence in the "country" would be necessary before the complexity of this language domain would be truly understood and appreciated. They distinguished types of animal sounds, often indicating the function of a specific type: e.g., sounds of dogs included *uanu* ("it howls"), and *metshum* ("it barks"), but also *asheku* ("it makes fighting sounds"); a caribou seeking a mate was sonically identifiable (*uishaku*). Airplane sounds were equally nuanced in *innu aimun*: *petuetum* ("the plane is heard in the distance"), *tueu* ("the plane is heard as it lands"), or *natikashipatau* ("the plane motor is heard idling on the dock"). Sometimes beliefs about specific kinds of sound were described. Whistling, for example (*kueskuesku*), is associated with the Northern Lights, which are regarded as spirits dancing in the sky who would approach a whistler and perhaps whisk him/her away.

Innu descriptive phrases about sounds most often relate to high or low pitch, intermittent or continuous quality, clarity, or ringing quality. Several of these aspects also emerged as important metaphoric domains in Micmac and, to some extent, in our work on languages of the entirely different Iroquoian family.

High and low voice contrasts, alluded to above in conjunction with the Tshakapesh myth, are apparent in the following phrases:

kapISHItaukust—high voice (*cf. nISHItashu*, above)

kaTSHENIuitakust—low voice (*cf. TSHENU*—elder, old man)

One Naskapi drummer distinguished between high (*epishitakuats*) and low (*tsheniuitakuats*) sections within a drum song. Some, though by no means all, Naskapi/Montagnais drum songs have two phrases, the former higher in register than the latter.

The continuity of sound—whether steady, trembling, or pulsed—may be described as follows:

nanamueu—a trembling voice (Davis Inlet)

teteuetsheu—a striking, thumping noise (Davis Inlet)

The relative clarity of the sound was described differently in Algonquian languages and dialects:

pagakowe—he speaks clearly, lucidly, coherently (River Desert Algonquin, RDEA)

pagahama-e—he beats the measure or rhythm, as a drummer accompanying a singer (River Desert Algonquin, RDEA)

tatsikauan—loud sound (Davis Inlet)

peukusitakushu—clearly audible (Davis Inlet)

Many dialects have words which are frequently glossed as "bell-like." In Davis Inlet, the church bell is *matuanakut*, and a similar root underlies the label for a waterfall: *matuatshin*. *Matue-* also refers to a ringing sound in some Algonquian dialects: in Maniwaki, a distinction is made between jingling (*shinawe-* as in the name of the ceremonial hoof rattle, *shinaweshikun*) and bell-like or ringing sounds (*madwesin*). Mailhot's *Montagnais Dictionary* (n.d.) of the Sept-Îles dialect defines *matueu* as a "son bizarre," on the other hand. Piggott recorded an Ojibwe distinction between *matwe:we-* ("crackle, make noise") and *matwe:we:ssin* ("ring, sound").

Here, the *-ssin-* morpheme has been associated by Piggott with *assin* ("earth") on the basis of metal contained within it. Hence, he lists *apitwewessin* as a sound which "keeps on ringing." In some Ojibwe dialects, the quality referenced by *madwewe-* is less specific; Vennum (1982: 283) reports the use of *madwewechigan* as a generic Ojibwe term for "musical instrument," usage consistent with that on Manitoulin Island (see Corbière *et al.* n.d.: 39). In Village Huron, Quebec, where many Montagnais and Attikamek words are used (although the Huron language is an Iroquoian rather than an Algonquian language), a rattle is named *mashikun*, using both the onomatopoeic *shi-* and the morpheme denoting ringing, *ma-*.

A somewhat different quality may be implied in some Algonquian dialects by *kishi-* (or *kizi-*). Denoting a squeaking sound, it occurs in Algonquin words in conjunction with the wind or the beating of a bird's wings. In the language of Davis Inlet Innu, the same prefix occurs in the name for "mouth organ," *kishitakuan*. Other Algonquin sound descriptors may not connect to the naming of sound-producing instruments; they include *kaskwe-* ("crackling or dry and snapping") *wimbwewe-* ("a hollow sound, echo, or resonance") and *titawe-* ("noise which is heard coming from an enclosed space").

Actions of creating and receiving sound are described in a manner consistent with the concepts of relationship explored in Chapter Two. Montagnais hunters often describe their use of the drum as *teueikan mistakue tutuanipan*, a phrase which may be translated "he pays attention to the drum." The same phrase is used for performing or listening. Distinct from "s/he hears" (*petam/petueu* in the Davis Inlet dialect), Innu verbs for listening and "going to" (usually referring to a hunter searching for game) are closely related. Like the *-ue-* morpheme, they connect sound and motion:

natutam/natutueu—s/he hears it

natuu—he hunts

natutikueu—he goes to the caribou

The establishing of a relationship by listening is expressed strongly in Algonquin where *nahitawan* ("s/he hears") is glossed as "heed, or obey, to accept someone's words" (RDEA).

A further structural aspect which may be indicative of deep structures of thinking has often been discussed but discounted in relation to Algonquian languages: the division of nouns into animate and inanimate "genders" (paradoxically the male/female distinctions more often referenced

Photo 35."Paying attention" to the drum. Matshias Pone at Lobstick Lake in 1984. Photo by Connie Heimbecker.

Photo 36. Montagnais drummers from Northern Quebec, ca. 1920. Field Museum, Chicago.

as gender with regard to the pronouns and nouns of many languages, including most Romance and Indo-European languages, is not structurally marked in Algonquian languages). The notion that things which English speakers do not regard as animate are so designated in Ojibwe, Cree, Micmac, or Montagnais seems to fascinate English speakers, including ourselves. Linguists have sometimes attempted to relate this distinction to spiritual beliefs in the animateness of particular aspects of the physical world. Linguist Marguerite McKenzie, for example, has commented:

All inanimate nouns refer to non-living things and almost all animate nouns refer to living things. Thus "tree" *mishtikw* would be animate gender but "stick, log," still *mishtikw* would be inanimate. A small group of animate nouns, thirty or forty, refer to non-living things such as a pipe, the sun, the moon, a ball. One hypothesis is that all those non-living animate nouns refer to objects which

have to do with spiritual power. Unfortunately examples such as *astish* "mitten" and *anushkan* "raspberry" which are animate, and *massin* "mocassin" and *utemin* "strawberry" which are inanimate, do not seem to fit this explanation. (n.d.: 242)

Clearly, we must be cautious in attributing consistent spiritual meaning to the animate/inanimate categories. With regard to music terminology, however, there are certain tendencies worth noting. Some Montagnais (but not Attikamek and Algonquin) communities regard traditional musical instruments as animate but those of European origin as inanimate. Beaters or bows are usually the opposite gender of the instrument they activate; hence a beater is inanimate in Montagnais communities such as Maliotenam where the drum is animate. The fiddle bow is animate while the related word for fiddle in Maniwaki is inanimate (there is another word for fiddle which is animate). An inconsistency like those observed by McKenzie is the fact that *nikuman* ("song") is generally inanimate. In contrast, some new technologies are animate, some inanimate. The pattern here may be related to sounds which emanate from an unseen source (animate) or not. Hence, in Mingan, the sound of the foghorn is animate. So too the radio is animate in many communities. The pattern is not entirely consistent, however.[17]

In summary, then, the etymology of words often provides clues about aspects of the underlying cultural values. Connections between sound, motion, and dressing/layering/offering; between drum and heart and existence; between sound and attention; or between sound and each of the physical substances identified with infixes in Algonquian languages—these connections are integral to the world-hearing of the Nations who speak these languages.

Maritime Algonquian: Micmac (with Some Reference to Maliseet)

"What is the word for radio?" I asked.[18] The Micmac elder sitting beside me thought for a moment and said:

MWF:

"Well if it's radio—I guess we got stuck there, 'cause there is no word for radio. Radio is something that just came recently. Well we could make up a word.

"Well if I haven't heard a radio in my life, I'd be astonished at what it is. I would say—well— *meteta'q*—**sound.** *Meteta'q*, **that's sound.** *Meteta'q natkowey* **is something that makes a sound.** *Natuwen* **is someone talking. In that there** *napijek*, *natkowey*, **that** *napijek* **there that I could hear the voices from that—***napijek*. *Natkowey nutum etek*, **it is there.** *Na'kwek etek na'tel wetuwa'q pipukwaqn*, **I hear music; something is there that makes a sound. . . .** *Kesk+mi'sik* **is something like magic, like say that there man that does all that magic tricks. What do you call that man there?"**

FvR:

A magician?

MWF:

"Yeah, a magician. Yeah, it's a magic word. *Kesk+matiket* **is one of those little magicians.** *Kesk+mta'q* **is making a magic sound. Well, you put it together.** *Ala etek natkowey kesk+mta'q. Natuwen pisit etlawo'ket*, **someone in there talking."**

FvR:

Can you say it slowly for me once?

MWF:

"*Natkowey etek na kesk+mta'q. Kesk+mta'q*, **it is a beautiful sound. It jumps from reality.** *Kesk+ma'sik* **means changing from reality to non-reality."** (Michael W. Francis in conversation with Franziska von Rosen 1989)

Photo 37. Michael W. Francis, Big Cove, New Brunswick. Photo by FvR.

"Well, we could make up a word." What does that imply about the process of naming? Does the Micmac language (or any other Native language) simply lack vocabulary, or does it imply that we should approach language, not as something static and frozen on a page, but as an ongoing creative and primarily oral tradition in use? Linguist Robert Leavitt (1989: 12-14) points out the difficulties that Micmac-Maliseet students encounter when they are taught their Aboriginal languages by means of written texts and grammars. The world becomes static—a world of objects (nouns) instead of a world of processes (verbs).

Micmac speakers *do* acknowledge the tremendous loss of language that their communities are experiencing. As the elders pass away so does their knowledge of the language, knowledge which responds creatively to the process of naming and experiencing the world they inhabit.

This creativity is not viewed consistently. Let us look, for example, at two different translations for "lullaby": *nepa'tekemkewey* (MM) rooted in *nepa't-* ("sleep") with *-eke* ("doing/causing"), *-mk-* (indefinite subject ending), and *-ewey* (adjectival ending, i.e., putting to sleep thing). Or *naqnu'semkewey*, literally meaning extinguishing into sleep from the root *nak-* ("extinguish"). I was told, rather disapprovingly, by a Micmac linguist that the first of the two words is "made up," a translation from English which combines the idea of sleep with nighttime and with singing. The second word, he said, is correct Micmac because it is based on the Micmac worldview. In an earlier example, I demonstrated how an elder "made up" a word for radio. His approach was personal and rooted in experience. The differences between these two instances of "making up" a word is based on how each relates to a particular process and location. Naming proceeds from worldview. By severing this connection or establishing a different one, speakers name a different world, as noted by the Micmac linguist.

Traditional creative naming processes, language loss, regional differences, individuals' politeness to researchers who ask endless questions about naming and names—all of these factors and others influence the nature of my language lists. Vocabulary for musical instruments, ways of singing, genres of songs, or ways of speaking about sound varied a great deal depending on the age, location of residence, and language experience of the consultant as well as on the rapport between consultant and researcher.

The same factors also influence the process of translation and interpretation from Micmac to English. Many Micmacs are fluent English speakers and all encounter English in their daily lives. My consultants and teachers, who were not only sources of cultural information but also cultural translators, were often adept at reflecting one culture in terms of the other. The process was also shaped by the ways in which I would ask them to interpret their world for me. So not only vocabulary but also translations reflect a process that is dependent on a wide range of contextual factors.

My work with Micmac linguists was detailed and structural; with a Micmac storyteller, on the other hand, the translations often included lengthy digressions to other stories, stories which might not seem immediately related to the translation. My inquiries about musical instruments, for instance, sparked Micmac storyteller Michael W. Francis to recall childhood experiences and stories from his grandfather.

Vocabulary and classification

Micmac terminology for drums and rattles does not seem to be common knowledge among Micmac speakers. While many consultants said that Micmacs didn't have any drums, and they were not sure about rattles or flutes, others just said that they did not know the appropriate names. The best known name for a traditional Micmac instrument was *ji'kmaqn* (alternate spellings including *chegumagun, jigmagn, tjiigmagun*). The label referred to different things, however.

Manny Metallic of Restigouche relates the word to *jikataq*, a verb whose exact meaning is uncertain to him. His mother used it once in referring to an annoying feedback sound from a loud-speaker (hum, vibrations). I noticed another word, *jikmit*, meaning "he growls." At any rate there appears to be some relation to a sound quality in the root *-jik-*.[19]

Photo 38. The contemporary *ji'kmaqn*. In early sources, the name *ji'kmaqn* was sometimes applied to pieces of folded bark used as a rattle or hit with a stick. Modern examples are made of split ash and are hit against the hand.

The name *ji'kmaqn*, however, also currently describes a rattle: a split-ash stick that is struck against the palm (also called a "slapstick"). This name may reference the nature of the sound it produces. But the split-ash stick was named differently by elder Michael W. Francis, by the process used in constructing/making it: *elaskate'kn*—"he splits off wood into splints."

Ji'kmaqn is also used to name the small (unsplit) stick with which Micmac singers traditionally accompany their singing. The singer creates a steady and rapid beat by striking the stick against the ground or another object. In Big Cove, people also used this word to name the small stick used to accompany singing in the sweatlodge.

But *ji'kmaqn* also names an object struck with another stick, in which case it functions more like a drum than a drumstick or a rattle. Rand's (1888) gloss of *cheegumagun* as both a rattle and an "Indian tambourine" further supports the notion that the boundaries of reference were ambiguous in the nineteenth century; the tambourine itself represents a cross-over between drum and rattle.

A Cape Breton elder described the *ji'kmaqn* as follows:

Photo 39. Tom Paul from Big Cove, New Brunswick made a practice instrument which resembles some early descriptions of the *ji'kmaqn*. Photo by FvR.

"A square thing, you know, made out of wood. It was a cute shape when it was made. It was shaped like a spoon [he hollows his palm]. And when he sings there's a man on the side who starts dancing and repeats 'oh hey ah hey' following the song. He sounds like he's following the song, you know? It's just like when you call [a long way] off, the way the song sounds. You know the caller's sound." (Interview with Simon Marshall 1988)

Marshall recalls that this instrument had no handle, was slightly rough on the bottom, and was struck with a little stick.

Frederick Johnson (1943) describes the *ji'kmaqn* as "a folded piece of birch bark folded once. It is held in the hand and beaten with a stick."

Very few people seemed to know a Micmac word for drum. Some, including a contemporary Micmac drum-maker, told me that the Micmacs never had any drums and suggested that this was why they had no name for it. Those who did know how to name the drum (mainly Micmac linguists and elders) provided the following lexemes. The most frequently spoken name was *pepkwejeteta'q*. This is also the name provided by Rand (1888). Sound is what names this drum:

pepkwek (*bepkwek*; CLK)—it sounds like a drum

pepkwejeteta'q—it sounds thin (as a layer) (RL)

pepkwejete'knatkw—drumstick (-*atkw*—handle)

pepkwet; nuji pepkwet (RND)—a cock partridge or drummer (one who drums as an occupation)

A number of elders suggested that a *pepkwejete'-taqn* is a hand drum because of its thinness. On the

other hand, they named a large drum:

ji'kmaqnte'kn (MWF)—large drum where *ji'kmaqn* is the drumstick

te'kn—something that you hit

It is interesting to speculate that *te'kn* might be a shortened form of *tewegn*, hence relating to Innu and Anishnabe vocabulary.[20]

Elder Michael W. Francis described a heavy birchbark cone covered with earth and pounded with a small stick. Referring to it as a drum that he had seen used when he was a child, he named it *tuknte'kn* ("the place where you get a hollow sound" from *tuknta'q*—"it sounds hollow").

Sound also names the drum onomatopoeically:

"Well you see '*tun-tun, tun-tun*'—Indians say '*tun-tun*.' '*Tun-tun*' is a proper Indian word. '*Juwa tun-tun*' means something that makes a sound like '*tun-tun*.'" (Interview with Michael W. Francis 1989)

Both *tam-tam* and *tun-tun* are used in Restigouche and Big Cove, New Brunswick. The Western Abenaki of Odanak also name the drum *tam-tam*.

The linguistic and conceptual boundary between rattles and bells is also ambiguous. Rand translates rattle as *chegumakun* (*ji'kmaqn* in the Francis/Smith orthography) and bell as *sesuakudaa-gun* (*sesuakuta'kn*) but gives the transitive verb form, "he plays the rattle" as *sesooakadesk* (1988) (*sesuaka-tesk* F/S orthography). Micmac linguist Bernie Francis informed me that *sesuakatesk* refers to the jingling sound of a bell. It is an intermittent sound, something created by back-and-forth motion. According to Francis, the morpheme -*tesk* combined with *alik*- ("to move in different directions") consti-tutes the intransitive verb *aliktesk* ("it vibrates"). Robert Leavitt (personal communication) associates the morpheme -*tesk* with the action of striking, an interpretation which is not inconsistent with Francis's.

In Big Cove, elder Michael W. Francis used the lexeme *sesuwejk* to name rattles and bells. The fol-lowing conversation between us demonstrates the care with which he tried to explain the meanings of words and sounds to me. It also reveals the wide range of meaning that he ascribes to this Micmac word for rattle:

MF:

"*Sesuwejk, sesuwejk* is the rattle. You ever seen those horses' bells? They go '*ti-ling, ti-ling, ti-ling*.' They are called *sesuwejk*. That's the same *sesuwejk*—something that rattles inside."

FvR:

So that describes that there is something inside?

MWF:

"Yeah, as long as it's a rattle, it's *sesuwejk*. Rattling sound."

FvR:

If you had a pail full of nails and you were shaking it . . .

MWF:

"Same principle, rattling nails in a pail, or you [could] have something a little lighter than nails. It is more like [a] tinny sound. *Sesuwejk*, *sesuwejk*—you call it tinkling sound. *Sesuwiskita'q* is more like a little clinkle sound, a more tinny sound. That's what I heard, *sesuwiskita'q*."

FvR:

What about change?

MWF:

"That's *sesuwiskita'q*. There are keys in my pocket. Yeah, same tinkling. *Sesukita'q* means on top of one another."

Motion and sound in space come together in the naming of the rattle. Linguist Robert Leavitt (personal communication) remarked on the interesting parallels between *sesuwetjk* and the following Maliseet lexemes: the prefix *sisse-* would seem to relate further to *shishi-*, described earlier in relation to Innu and Anishnabe languages:

sissihq (RL)—rattlesnake (Maliseet)

sisse- (RL)—prefix meaning scattering in different directions (Maliseet)

Sounds of objects scattering, tinkling, or clinking against one another in different directions in an enclosed space: this is the physical phenomenon which names the rattle and the bell.

As we examine Micmac and Maliseet approaches to naming flutes and whistles we again discover multiple associations and relationships. *Pipukwaqn*[21] was a word familiar to most Micmacs, but their translations ranged from a specific wind instrument—particularly a flute—to a generic term for all musical instruments, to a music box (including a radio or phonograph). Contemporary usage seems to favour the latter, but there seem to be etymological associations between *pipukwaqn* and blowing or breath, as well as motion and shape, which facilitate multiple associations:

pipukwaqn—flute (in general use in Big Cove, New Brunswick, and elsewhere by Micmac speakers; said to be related to *pipnaqn*—bread, something that rises)

pipukwey (*pepoogwa*; CLK)—I play on a wind instrument; now applies to any instrument

wisqwi pipokwaqn (*wiskwe pepogwokun*; RND)—bagpipe[22]

pipukwes (*pipugwes*; DBL)—a chicken hawk (screamer)

pipiqe (RL)—he plays a flute (Maliseet)

pipiqat (RL)—something that flutes, that plays using wind (Maliseet)

putuw- (RL)—to blow (with the mouth)

putu's—person who relays important messages (political position next to the Grand Chief of the Micmacs)

putuwatmn—sending something out with a breath of air (Micmac, general use in Big Cove)

putuwakon (RL)—whistle; something blown— raised bread (cf. Maliseet *putawehtikon*)

putuwe (RL)—s/he blows, s/he puffs

One Micmac elder and storyteller translated flute/whistle as *jibaskw* in connection with a story about the *Mi'kmwesu*, a trickster spirit of the forest (Fig. 12). The *Mi'kmwesu* is a flute player and the elder associated the sound of the flute with the "weird" sound made by tree branches when they rub against each other. The association led him to name the instrument *jibaskw*:

jibaskw (MWF)—whistle

jip- (RL)—prefix indicating startling, fearsome, frightful, perhaps as strong as terrifying

-askw—suffix used for a tree root or bark; also found in *kikwesuaskw* (muskrat root—DBL) or *pilaskw*—new bark

People tell numerous stories about the power of this sound. They always describe how they were drawn into the woods and then encircled by the sound. This sensitivity to sound, particularly sound which is heard but not seen, is also associated with a particular plant called *meteteskawey*—rattling plant. I was told that the prefix *mete-* is difficult to translate but that it describes a sound "heard through the ears." Others suggested that *mete-* means hearing but not seeing, an interpretation that coincides with the mysterious *meteteskawey* plant that can occasionally be heard but very seldom found. The word also embeds *-tesk-*, a tapping or

Legend of the Mi'kmwesu

A lot of young kids
get lost in the woods,
a lot of people get
lost in the woods, right,
Indians are PRoud
no Indian ever gets lost in the woods.

So, so, now, put it this way
MI'Kmwesu got him
they never return;
if he does return he might return as a
bird, maybe crow, as an animal
said Mi'kmwesu will CHAnge you
into the, into the form, what he WAnts
to be.
He'll play music
the music will DRAw you
to him music so
beautiful music.

So this young fella,
young boy or girl go up there,
look for music;
he see Mi'kmwesu,
see, see the spirit.
"Now young child
what do you wish to BE?"
"O-oh, I wish I was a squi-irrel
I wish I was a de-er
I wish I was a bi-rd, maybe cro-w
maybe raven
I wish I could be a
an
EAgle."

"Well
you pick what you wish my child.
I'll play you music
while I'm PLAying it
you shall be, you shall be a bird
you shall be a _____."

While he is listening
he will tra-nsform
into a deer, or maybe bird,
what she wish.
He doesn't go back to his village
anymore.
He'll go back
won't be RECognized
because Mi'kmwesu
has captured his so-ul
and changed him to a de-er
see
maybe rabbit or chickadee or bi-ird.
One day
old lady there
"your brother's go-one
Mi'kmwesu got him
probably comes back as a crow
maybe raven."

Fig. 12. Michael W. Francis's drawings and narration of the Mi'kmwesu legend.

A—h, A—h
"my chi-ild your brother is ba-ck
you see up there, crowing
that's your BROther."
So the young fella call up there
"HI BROther."
So they communicate together
the crow will know that it's his
brother to-o,
they will join and fly together.
That's mi'kmWEssu.

And that MUsic
is a tree
it's a tree
you can hear tree it goes
eeeeeeeee
en————ng
that's still playing.
That tree will make noise
even today
flute
that tree rubbing, sounds like a flute
eeeeeeee.
You go in the woods
even toDAy
you can hear Mi'kmwesu
and tree, will
make noise.

That's still playing,
even today still playing flute
that tree rubbing, sounds like a flute
eeeeeee, eeee.
That's where music comes from
cause tree make a lot of music.
THAt's what INDians call MI'Kmwesu
when it comes right down when it
boils right down
that's how legends come from
from the trees

from natural resources
water dropping
leaves rattling
whhhhhhhh——h, natural sound
leaves rattling,
and that's whispering
SPirits
PIne, piwiwiwiwiw.

intermittent rattling sound. In *Penobscot Man* (1970 [1940]: 241), Frank Speck discussed the *mete-* preverb, interpreting it as "the sound drumming" or as a "drum sound person" but also relating it to other sounds, including talking, walking, or dancing.[23]

Singing is sometimes expressed by a polysemous term whose meaning may or may not be related:

elte'm—knocking it over *that* way (where "that" is a gesture)

elte'm—I am voicing it thus

Singing is often described, however, in a verbal phrase conveying two actions simultaneously, one of which is often motion related:

pemintoq—s/he is walking and singing at the same time

wapintoq—s/he is singing until dawn

wejkwintoq—s/he is coming along, singing as s/he comes

pemtokse (CLK)—I make a rustling sound as I go along

In describing sound qualities, distinctions between continuous and interrupted sound are important:

metakutesk (*medakuadesk*; CLK)—it jingles, rattles

meta'qtesteket—usher (the "jingler" referring to the sound of money collecting in the basket)

-tesk—jerky motion, striking, tapping

metuta'q—a sound hard to make out

-ta'q—smooth, continuous sound

As with the other languages considered here, Micmac embeds the perception and experience of a complex sound universe. Continuous sounds, intermittent sounds, smooth sounds, sounds hard to describe are all given expression, and that expression reflects a particular relationship and connection to the environment. Sound, motion, and space frequently converge in the processes of identification and naming.

Iroquoian: Cayuga (with Some Reference to Seneca and Mohawk)

HB:

"You're the what-do-you-call-it, 'musician' and anthropologist, Sam. So analysis, I guess that's up to you—that's your *profession*."

MSC:

But Hubert—*hadreno:ta*, you're a singer too.

HB:

"Oh no! But I live it. That's a little bit different." (Six Nations Notes, Hubert Buck and MSC 1989)

Iroquoian languages are said to "come up from the ground." They are a living part of *ongweowe:ka* (the "Indian" way of being), part of one's identity, part of the emotional, physical, and spiritual environment of this landscape. They help you connect. As a Longhouse speaker said, **"When I hear *Ganohonyonk* (Thanksgiving Address), I think of all these images. I feel, I see everything that's being said; I'm part of it all."**

There are six related Iroquoian languages, one for each nation in the Confederacy.[24] Most have basic grammatic principles and at least some vocabulary in common. Seneca is spoken at Longhouse events at Allegany Reservation, in southwestern New York, while at Six Nations, Ontario, the linguists I worked with favour Cayuga. Both Mohawk and Cayuga are taught at immersion schools at this reserve, and Onondaga is used in another Six Nations Longhouse. English is spoken in every community.

As with all living things, Iroquoian languages respond organically, adapting as necessary to their surroundings. Quite naturally, they reflect changing technologies. A radio? In Cayuga, it is usually called *wadrenota'* ("something that sounds/it sings"), a general term applied to most non-Native instruments and audio equipment. Tools of my profession include *gawenaye:nahs* (Cayuga "it catches the voice")—tape recorders (or recording devices such as wax cylinders, as used by researchers at Six Nations since the 1890s) and *gaya'daha:* (Seneca), camera or movie. It is also possible to talk about a telephone (*odwenoda:tha'*, Cayuga for "one uses it to put one's voice in" [RH]). Dishwasher, computer, or microwave ovens—all these expressions are "made up" in the sense that they—like these technologies—are comparatively new; yet each fits comfortably within traditional descriptive vocabularies, filled with images of movement, shape, function, and relationship.

For Haudenosaunee, music heals and entertains. It is connected with everything around us; *Ganohonyonk* explains that even the birds have a responsibility to sing in order to ease our minds. People share this gift—they sing, they dance in order to celebrate life; this is considered our responsibility to the Creator. Not everyone can lead a song, not everyone is a skilled dancer, but everyone can participate in some way.

Learning music and language involves this same principle of mutual participation and responsibility.

Ideally, teachers create an environment in which you learn through shared experience rather than didactic instruction. Context is everything—you need a "clear mind" to acquire understanding; you should practise traditional songs or speeches with someone early in the day; and above all, you should learn these things in order to benefit the community.

Context is holistic. As we worked on word lists and narratives, friends showed me how to make rattles and water drums, they shared concerns about the lack of fluency in the community, and they reminisced about singers they once knew. Each vocabulary list, each instrument we discussed encouraged more stories—this vivid personal level of association is an essential part of learning. Very rarely, however, did linguists or singers talk abstractly or metaphorically *about* singing or sound in general. Once when he was younger, Cayuga linguist Reg Henry had heard a word describing the sound of wind; he couldn't quite remember it though and no one really used it any more. Then he laughed, saying "I could make something up for you, if you're really keen on it!"

For some time I was preoccupied with this apparent "lack" of discourse about sound and music which are, for the most part, only briefly included in dictionaries. And description of specific kinds of sound seemed strained in conversations with Longhouse linguists. Of course, there are narratives telling the origins of several ceremonial and curing songs, and there are names for each instrument. But I was not hearing the same rich discussion of metaphors for "creating and receiving sound" that Bev and Franziska were. Given that sound/music/song/dance/speech/motion are basic to Iroquoian culture, surely they must be "languaged." Was I asking the right questions? Could every linguist everywhere have "lost" this knowledge? Was information restricted, or was I simply not hearing what was being said?

Vocabularies for Sound

HD:

"The Seneca word for sound? Let's see, let's look that one up." (She checks her dictionary—Chafe 1967):

kaistowa:neh—loud/big (*gowa:*—"noise"; *kaista'*—"metal")
'okgae'ni:h—it's noisy
okgaeas—it makes a noise
wa'oeo'taka:eh—the gun sounded
kihka:e'—I'm making a noise, shouting

ostowe'sae:ka:h—the rattle is sounding
'o'watekae'nis—it made a noise.

"That's it. I can't think of anything else right now. In the middle of the night you might say 'I hear something!' 'It made a noise!'; that 'something' depends on the context. But you know, that translation is not quite right—'noise'—it really means sound." (Conversation with Dr. Hazel Dean, Allegany 1993)

Mohawk linguist David Maracle adds other dimensions. The verb phrase *iora:kahre* translates as "it is noisy, it resounds and it is loud." Closely related words include:

teia'onhahrha' (DM)—it makes noise (rumbles)
ioterihstakahrehraston (DM)—it is ringing (*karihstatsi*—"metal")
ketshe'takahrehrahsta' (DM)—I ring a small bell (*katshe'*—a small bell, bottle, container)
katkwirakahrehrashsta' (DM)—crack a whip (*o'kwire*—"rod, sapling"). (Maracle 1985: 151)

Sound therefore is characterized by clarity and volume; some sounds are continuous (rumbling), some abrupt (cracking). Sound implies media or material—metal, particularly, has a loud ringing quality. Significantly, metal is not used in Longhouse instruments. Handsome Lake, a Seneca prophet who helped restructure the Longhouse religion, rejected metal (especially stringed) instruments for Haudenosaunee; he felt that fiddle-playing and alcohol were too closely linked. Traditionally, dancers also wear deer-toe garters rather than powwow-style bell garters in the Longhouse; the latter are too loud for this enclosed place, drowning out the singers' voices.

Sound has a quality of movement. It echoes, it resounds, ringing throughout a given space. It serves to draw attention (for example, gunshots sounded at the beginning of some Longhouse ceremonies, the crack of the turtle rattle which shakes the earth, or the ringing of bells, possibly associated with Christian worship). Above all, it is contextually determined; if you understand a story or environment, you can identify the sound. According to David Maracle, it seems that sound, like colour, is rarely described in traditional narratives unless it is unusual (as perhaps is metal). It is up to listeners to fill in these details for themselves. Thus, a rattle simply "sounds"—it shakes, it makes a noise. If for some reason a rattle rang like a bell, *then* it would be the subject of further conversation.

Names and Naming

MSC:

I've heard Ojibwe elders say that thunder has different voices—some are loud, some sound like bells. . . . How do people talk about thunder? Have you ever heard people describe how thunder sounds?

RH:

"Oh, thunder, that's our Grandfathers. No—I guess not, I guess I never heard anybody talk about the *sound* of thunderers. Of course, the name says a lot." (Conversation with Reginald Henry, MSC 1989)

Some words are onomatopoeic. The names for birds, especially, or certain insects suggest their sound; many of these names are built through repetition:

jilik jilik (Cayuga) or *taraktarak* (Mohawk, DM)—cricket

duwisduwi: (Cayuga)—killdeer

o'o:wa:' (Seneca)—owl

ga'ga:' (Seneca)—crow

ho:nga:k (Seneca) or *kahon'k* (Mohawk, DM)—(wild) goose

Some words describe action or connection; the name is what they are, what they do, what they resemble. A singer, *hadreno:ta* (Cayuga) literally is one (he) who habitually "stands up" a song. The morphemes *en/wen/ren* are associated with "word, voice, language, tone, tongue, and articulation":

owe:na' (Seneca)—voice

gae:na' (Seneca)—song

jo:yaik tode:no:t (Seneca)—a robin is singing

karen:na' (Mohawk)—song, tune, hymn

tewenniak'ke: (Mohawk)—goose (*tekia'ks*—to break, cut in half : DM)

agadreno:ni' (Cayuga)—I make songs

hadiwenodagye's (Cayuga)—thunderers (they howl their voices along)

Another infix, *-o:t*, denotes the act of standing something upright. This motion is associated with constructions, as in *tkanohso:t* (Cayuga; RH—"standing house") or *khniotha'* (Mohawk; DM—"I erect, set up, stand upright"; with natural phenomena—*iotsha:tote* (Mohawk; DM—"the fog is lifting"); or with drawing attention/putting an object, song or event into the foreground. At Condolence ceremonies, new

hereditary chiefs are said to be "raised up" as they are installed into office.

Not every utterance is so designated, however. In Cayuga, a Longhouse speaker is known as *hatha:ha* ("he speaks"; Foster 1974: 30) and the expression *oto:wisahs* ("she sings female chant"; Cayuga; RH) refers to women's individual chants associated with planting and harvest.

Sound-producing instruments are called *odren-odahkwa*, "something you sing with." Names of each instrument are widely known, but identifying them involves much more than simple translation. In Cayuga, *odrenodahkwa* include:

gana'tso—small water drum

oghiwe: ganahgwa—Feast of the Dead drum/keg—large water drum

ehwa'esta'—drumstick (literally "something you hit with")

gaksaga:nye—chipmunk sticks—wooden rasps

onaga: gahsda'wedra'—(cow) horn rattle

osno gahsda'wedra'—bark rattle

onyosa' gasda'wedra'—gourd rattle

gano:wa—snapping turtle rattle

ganya:de: gano:wa—snapping turtle rattle

ganya:hde gasda'wedra'—snapping turtle rattle

ganyahde: ohsida gasda'wedra'—turtle foot rattle

othowesa'ta' gasda'wedra'—box turtle rattle (for women's chant)

Reg Henry distinguished these from *wadrenota'*— it sings—a category of non-Native equipment and instruments; and *deyo:tgwa:ta'*—dancing things—such as *dyotgwa:ta' ojia:ne:da'*—deer hoof clackers/garters worn by men. He did not find it necessary to classify gunshots or sounds produced by blowing a conch shell, *jidro:we*. Both are used to announce Longhouse events.

Certain instruments, however, cannot be named. Those associated with curing doings are often sensate beings. By naming them, you communicate directly with them, you bring yourself into their consciousness. Native linguists and singers cautioned me against speaking about (let alone identifying) a particular flute, primarily for my own well-being since I did not have the knowledge or means to protect myself from its unwanted attention. Not to name, then, is seen both as a matter of respect and common sense.

Linguistic analysis clarifies relationships among instruments and other objects. For example, an infix in the verb phrase *ha:nyehs* (he rubs it) links playing techniques for chipmunk sticks (*gaksaga:nye*) with violins (*ha'nowa ga:nyehs*—he is a fiddler). You rub both the rasp and the strings of a violin. Reg also suggested a potential connection between the word "horn," *ona'ga:* (Cayuga) and "he is whistling," *hana'ga*, though these have slightly different structures. An example in Seneca (Chafe 1967: 72) may illustrate this:

kanao'keotashae'—horn war club

kanökaeos'—it whistles, whistling frog

A number of Longhouse faithkeepers associate whistling with curing doings and spirit beings, and so it is not casually discussed.

Ehwa'esta' can refer either to a drumstick or baseball bat (something you hit with). Similarly, the basic shape and perhaps sound of a bell in Cayuga (*ojihweda*—possibly including sleigh bells) and deer dewclaw garter (*okia:ne:da'*) are related. And the general term for snapping turtle rattle, *gano:wa*, may be used in other contexts to mean violin, banjo, guitar, or padlock—the same word acknowledges their common shape. Not surprisingly, naming gives rise to puns and word play—though perhaps it only seems like I drum with a baseball bat rather than a drumstick.

In Cayuga, there are several ways to describe voiced and instrumental sounds: the pitch may be high or low, and the beat either hard/loud or gentle/soft/slow. For example:

sgeno:oh drodadoh—he's shaking (the rattle) gently/slowly

sgeno:oh honajowetra'e—he's hitting (the drum) slowly

Implicit in an Iroquoian concept of "having a voice" is an ability to create different pitch levels. Rattles might "sound" loudly or softly, but like the human voice, drums may be either high or low pitched. If you turn a water drum over to wet the drum head, its voice changes:

he'tgeh gyewenade'—she (singer) is high voiced

he'tgeh tawenade'—he (singer) is high voiced

he'tgeh tgawenade'—it (drum) is high voiced

There are several other ways to assess performance; occasionally, someone might say *hejoih do:hoh* (Cayuga; RH)—"he hasn't got the beat/he's hitting here and there"—or *e:neken ieskerennenha's* (Mohawk; DM)—"I regain a higher note after singing out of tune/losing the tune." However, critiquing singers is usually considered inappropriate, since you are criticizing the ability that the Creator

chose to give them. It is linguistically possible but culturally unacceptable to say "that song is better or worse than any other" or "she/he/it has a worse/better voice."

Certain Iroquoian phrases express a sonic relationship with the Haudenosaunee environment— the voices of birds, for example, sounding in their names. Yet quantitatively, there seem to be far fewer metaphors expressing a sensitivity to sound as compared with Algonquian languages. I have rarely heard songs structurally analyzed, although singers do identify the mid-point of *eskanye* (women's shuffle dance), for example. Here the drummer/head singer "straightens out the beat," returning to a regular rhythm after playing a tremolo pattern; the melody also repeats at this juncture. I am not familiar with any other analytical terminology for the more than forty other Iroquoian song cycles. Nor have I heard names for or any discussion of the six distinct vocal styles characterising ceremonial and curing sets, or the several unique rhythmic patterns associated with this music.

Possibly I haven't asked the right questions, or heard their answers. Perhaps the subtleties of Iroquoian languages have been lost in the "exuberances and deficiencies" of translation. Or perhaps, as Hubert Buck, Sr. and so many other singers have suggested, a deep understanding of music also exists in non-verbal domains of experience and association—there may be no need to analyze these musics in a manner that separates them from performance. David Maracle explained,

"It's hard to talk about karen:na' without singing karen:na'. There has to be a reason, some kind of separation to create an explanation. Our communities are small enough that we all can hear this music; we can take part.

"Knowledge comes to you actively. Wahaneiente'hta'ne'—'he learned; the manner of it came to him.' It comes to you through direct experience. Truth, reality, understanding has to do with the experience of something. A story is only true because you have had that experience, and it is true only for you." (Notes, MSC 1993)

Another teacher observed, **"*Hadui-geha*— that's the wooden face songs. Everybody knows what *hadui* sound like: honh, honh, honh, honh. We know *gano:wa*. Why do we need to describe them?"** And indeed, for whom would they be describing them?

HD:

Well, these are the only words I know. Oh, but Sam, there are so *many* sounds.
There are all the different sound patterns in Seneca, glottal stops and nasal tones that make up our language, where you place your tongue, how you shape your mouth.
So many *different* sounds.
There are sounds when you're cooking,
sounds of people laughing,
sounds infants make,
sounds when babies are being born.
There are sounds you hear when
ashwood is being pounded to make splint baskets.
There's the sound when people are dancing on those hardwood floors in the Longhouse.
Sounds of birds
sounds of the trees,
so *many* sounds. . . . (Allegany Notes, MSC 1993)

Other Languages—The "Sounds" of Instruments

Thus far, we have discussed verbal languages, that is, denotative expressive systems given voice by humans. At this point, we turn from language *about* sound and sound producers to the language *of* those sound producers. How is the former (verbal language) related to the acoustical variety of the latter (instrument "language")?

In a 1968 article, "Redundancy and Coding," which appeared in a volume on animal communication, anthropologist Gregory Bateson argued that the "iconic" codes of humans (that is, the nonverbal means of communicating through gesture, eye contact, paralinguistics) related closely to the language systems of other animals. However, he stated "categorically that man's verbal system is not derived in any simple way from these preponderantly iconic codes" (1972: 411). Although research on animal communication systems has advanced in the intervening decades, we suspect that many people would agree with his basic premise. With regard to the sound-producing instruments of Algonquian and Iroquoian Nations, however, the close relationship between environmental sounds and naming, through onomatopoeia, leads us to question whether some parts of these verbal domains are not more like "iconic" codes than Bateson suspected.

The sounds of drums and rattles may reflect natural sounds and, in turn, be reflected by the imitative sounds of their verbal names and descriptors. The fundamental question concerns how the metaphors for sound, explored thus far in this chapter, relate to the variety of instrument voices we actually encountered.

Our reflections and observations only begin to answer this question, and a "beginning" is all that is possible and appropriate, since we regard all instruments as worthy of respect rather than dissection and analysis. Every instrument (but particularly the closed vessel of a rattle or drum) has an invisible world inside: rattlers differing in number, material, size, hardness, weight, and shape; snares; offerings. Many instruments have not one but multiple sonic components, some louder, some softer: an Iroquois drumstick with one or two moving wooden balls clicking gently inside the handle (CMC III-I-1232); a loud rattle vessel sound plus a softer tinkling sound produced by hoof segments or metal cones attached (e.g., HEY 18/2002); a vibrating drum membrane plus buzzing snare, with clicking rattlers bouncing on the membrane's surface (virtually all Naskapi and Montagnais drums as well as most Cree); a rattle which sounds loud or soft, clear or muffled when held upright or upside-down (GLE AP1456). It is significant that not all materials inside a shaker are sound-producing; some, such as cloth or wood, are rather sound-reducing (ROM 33088, ROM 12435, HEY 24/2277). The cloth or wood material may serve to mask the sound or to fulfill a requirement for a specific material or colour. The material which encloses the rattle or drum vessel, whether the soft woven ash splints of a basket rattle or the hard shell of a turtle's carapace, the thick hide of a moose or the paper-thin skin of a rabbit or bird, shapes its voice. We paid attention to these "individual" voices but we were not, of course, privy to the private worlds which determined them. How did each instrument get its voice? Who controls the voice of an instrument?

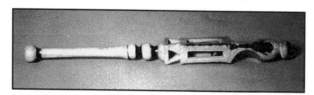

Photo 40. A Mohawk water drumstick made by Frank Thomas, Akwesasne Reserve. Collected by Gordon Day (CMC III-I-1232. FvR 88/3/7).

How Do Instruments Get their Voices?

Again, there is no single answer. An instrument may be "given by the Creator" or elaborately crafted by skilled instrument makers. In the former category are such instruments as seed pods or gourds whose dried seeds constitute rattlers; or, as described by a Cree consultant, a bird's ejected stomach lining in which the small stones or seeds similarly provided rattling materials without human mediation (except that the membrane was often stretched with a circular wooden frame). In the case of most instruments, the physical environment is drawn upon for the materials which provide the instrument's voice. Corn kernels, beans, or cherry pits are widely used for certain Iroquoian or Abenaki shakers, but these seeds are not available for the more northerly Innu who use pebbles or beads more frequently. The choice of skins, bark and wood, stone and metal, or lacing material is often a way of indicating relationship with the natural environment. In some cases, to an outsider, this relationship may seem to be a cultural construction, but often its basis lies in a very close observation of environmental forces and sounds. A case in point might be the Anishnabe association of quill materials and/or bells with the Thunderbirds. While the quill is a logical connection, the reason for choosing bells eluded us until we were told that a certain type of thunder which one might hear on a clear day has, under the more obvious "boom," a ringing, bell-like sound. Even where a manufactured material (e.g., lead shot, beads, a tobacco tin, baking soda containers, plastic drain pipe, or Pepsi can) is preferred, it is often a natural *sound* ideal which influenced the choice of material. The human voice is, of course, part of this "natural" sound world, and its natural pitch level may influence the structure or preparation of a drum or rattle; an Iroquoian water drum, for example, may be tuned to sound good with the pitch of a specific singer, although there is not a consistent interval between drum and initial or central vocal pitches.[25]

In some cases, an instrument's voice results from factors which many non-Indian people regard as extra-musical: a personal dream indicating the materials a rattle "needs" (e.g., GLE AP1456, CMC III-G-663). On the other hand, instrument makers sometimes have very precise control of the sound of an instrument. In an Iroquois instrument-making workshop, the instructor explained that, for cowhorn rattles, "twenty-five bee-bees are the right sound." This particular rattle needs to ring, and a good craftsman knows the appropriate thickness of the vessel walls as well. Precise control of the instrument's voice was also evident in the structure of certain Anishnabe gourd rattles; many of these instruments in museum collections have loose handles, a factor we attributed to disrepair, but we were told that the loose handles could be turned to each of the four directions, creating different sound qualities at each cardinal point.

Who Controls the Voice of an Instrument?

In many contexts, human agency (whether that of the instrument maker, owner, or player), the "living" instrument and the intended receiver are closely linked. This is clear in the case of animal calls, which constitute the most direct examples of onomatopoeic instrument language. Cone-shaped, birch-bark moose calls, made extensively in Algonquin and Attikamek areas but used elsewhere as well, are the most familiar type. Others, for which we have little documentation, include double-barrelled aerophones (MCC 929.6, MCC 929.7) and a Maliseet reed whistle (PEAS E25706) described by Speck as a muskrat call. Small whistles associated with bird calls are found in many areas (CMC III-B-474, CMC III-B-493), although they were infrequently collected by museums.

Photo 41. Cree whistles used as bird calls (CMC III-D-547 and 548. FvR 88/18/2).

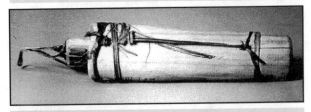

Photo 42. An Iroquois whistle from Six Nations, Ontario. John Jamieson told collector F.W. Waugh that it was a "whistle for suspension in fields to scare birds away" (CMC III-I-605. FvR 88/4/37).

Other instruments for which the intended "recipient" is known are buzzers and bull-roarers, which, in the Northeast, are used to make the wind rise to harden the snow surfaces and facilitate travel. The serrated edges on these instruments both produce wind through the whirling motion required to play them and imitate the wind's howl with their sound (CMC III-B-322, CMC III-B-349a).

Photo 43. A sound producer identified as a game call from the "East" in the collection of the McCord Museum, Montreal (MCC ME929.7. BD 88/4/1).

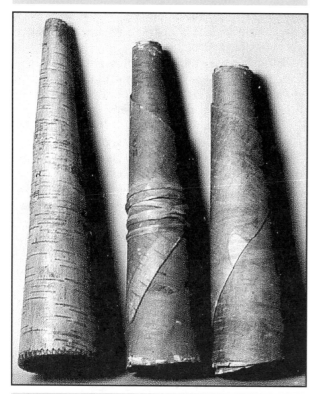

Photo 44. Micmac and Maliseet moose calls (CMC III-F-2, E-1, and E-2. FvR 88/9/34).

"To begin with, moose or deer hunting which is begun at evening or late afternoon is called *wlu'k'what*. . . . After midnight, about two o'clock, several long, loud, and tremulous calls are given on the moose-call, or 'horn' as it is called, *muswi'kwi.m'ət*, consisting of a sheet of birch bark rolled into the shape of a megaphone, and fastened either with a couple of wooden pins, or by sewing if the horn is a permanent possession, or sometimes merely wrapped around with a strip of root, splint, or a moccasin string. The Penobscot birch-bark moose-calls are about fourteen inches long with the opening wide enough to admit the palm of the hand. Some of the hunters prize their horns and have them ornamented.

"The first long call, lasting sometimes nearly half a minute, is to signal the district. During this call the horn is revolved several times in the air in a circle, then the call is

brought to a close, mouth downward. If a bull is within hearing he will proceed to answer and approach. When an answer is received, a luring call is again given, after which all is kept quiet until a few hours before sunrise. The bull is, during this time, approaching cautiously from a point possibly several miles away. Just before daybreak, about four o'clock, another encouraging call may be given, with the horn held straight out, and then turned down. About daybreak the final trial is made to bring the bull within range. The delay is made purposely until enough light comes to see to aim. Between the periods of calling the hunters sometimes enjoy a nap. In making the last calls, the operator spreads out a little flat space on the dead leaves and holds his call within six or eight inches of it, the mouth pointing directly downward. More of a speakng tone is incorporated into these calls, representing moose-passion, to hurry the bull's approach. By this time he may be heard trampling down the bushes and thrashing the thickets with his antlers in impassioned rage. The hunters make ready, and a few whispered words of warning precede the last call, which is meant to bring the bull into sight. When his huge form appears in the dim light, he is shot." (Speck's description of Penobscot moose-calling, 1940: 39-41)

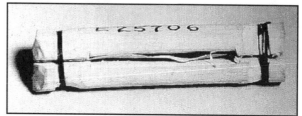

Photo 45. A Maliseet muskrat call, collected by Frank Speck (PEAS E25706. FvR 87/10/11).
"Blowing through this produces a resonant buzzing which resembles the call of the muskrat. The instrument is called *made'kwe'zudi*, calling tube. The same sound can be produced by drawing the lips tightly and sucking through one corner in short jerks." (Speck 1940: 46)

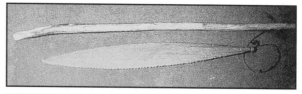

Photo 46. A bull-roarer collected around the turn of the century and similar to Montagnais and Attikamek instruments which are used to make the wind rise so that the snow will pack hard enough for travel (HEY 2/9224. FvR 88/44/18).

In a few instances, instruments in museum collections were described as spirit instruments. Certain Anishnabe shakers with no rattlers were said to be audible only to spirits (not damaged and incomplete as we originally thought). Small frame drums from Innu and Anishnabe communities have no handles, hanging loops, or other means of visible support; they were similarly described by consultants as intended for spirit use (CMC III-G-1109).

Some instruments such as the Anishnabe flute have a voice which is "mediated" by the animal-shaped external block. Who controls the voice of the flute?[26]

Photo 47. Ojibwe flute (MCQ E326. BD 88/8/16).

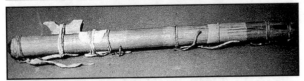

Photo 48. Ojibwe flute (HEY 2/1072. FvR 88/45/7). The Ojibwe flute is constructed so that air passes from one chamber through an external block which is often animal-shaped, into another chamber.

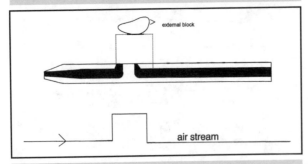

Fig. 13. Who controls the voice of the flute?

Sounds of Shakers

The consistent Native use of the English word "shaker" for what we have often called "rattle" in this book is, in itself, an important metaphor. "Shaker" makes a connection to motion and to the consequences of sound; "rattle" to the quality of the acoustic event. Beyond this general metaphor, we are aware of specific verbal descriptions of the sound of some but not all types of shakers. We did not learn specific descriptors for the gentle sound of dried peas or beans in an Abenaki woven splint rattle, for example, or for the loud but hollow sound of similar seed types (but often fewer seeds) in an Iroquoian hickory bark rattle. Neither Innu nor Anishnabe disc rattles—diverse with regard to rattler material, number of rattlers, and consequent sound—were specifically described in a particular way. On the other hand, verbal phrases such as "the

sound of the Creator's thoughts," sounds "to shake the earth," or "ringing" and "jingling" sounds were used often in association with particular rattle types or materials.

Sounds of Shakers: The Sound of Creation

In both Iroquoian and Anishnabe teachings, the gourd rattle is described as the sound of Creation.[27] The Anishnabe migration stories tell of the first sound, a shimmering sound, which went out in all directions; this was the sound of "the Creator's thoughts." As mentioned earlier, the seeds of the gourd constitute both the voice and the metaphor, since they *are* the source of newly created life. The sound of this instrument with its own seeds as rattlers is gentle and ringing.

Human-made Anishnabe gourd rattles, however, are the sites of the greatest sonic diversity (a product of many different types of rattler material, often in varied combinations) of any rattle types that we documented. The notion of "creation," then, may be linked to "re-creation" in several senses; when mediated by human instrument makers, the gourd's sound is recreated in accordance with instructions received by means of dreams or other authority. The diverse materials contained in gourd rattles could not be scrutinized in most cases but we could observe that contrasts between soft and hard materials were characteristic of some shakers, that the size and shape of rattlers was variable (see specific *Catalogue* descriptions for CMC III-G-910, CMC III-I-445, CMC III-I-69, CMC III-J-68 for examples). One damaged rattle contained megis shells, undoubtedly associating it with the Midewiwin. Different gourd types or vessels such as coconuts were other factors affecting the sound.

Sounds of Shakers: To Shake the Earth

This metaphor is often used in Iroquoian communities to describe the purpose of the turtle rattle. The phrase is apt for the loudest sound producer among the "singing tools" in the Longhouse. The sharp sound of the turtle's shell hit against the edge of a wooden bench, and the noise of large rattler materials (cherry pips, corn, wood chips, stones, or wampum) are evoked.[28]

Sounds of Shakers: Ringing and Jingling Sounds

References to "ringing" and "jingling" sounds occurred in relation to specific materials rather than specific shaker types. A distinction between the two qualities was not always clear. Both horn/bone and metal materials were described as "ringing." Iroquoian instrument makers often valued this sound quality in a cowhorn rattle—usually one that had a thin vessel wall and the appropriate type and number of rattlers. Hubert Buck, Sr. used a similar distinction to indicate his preference for cowhorn rattles with wooden handles rather than handles cut from the horn itself (CMC III-I-822); the latter were duller sounding because the hand held the vibrating material directly.

With reference to the Anishnabe Midewiwin, "ringing" sounds produced especially by copper were associated with women (see HEY 2/7997, GLE AP3214). We were told that tin can rattles might be used when copper was unavailable but note that Reagan suggested that in the early twentieth century, can rattles were a later replacement for gourd rattles (see CMC III-G-15). The care with which certain ringing sounds in the environment were mirrored is evident. Anishnabe elder Jim Dumont explained that, at one period, Pepsi cans had a metal alloy which produced the ringing sound like that heard in a specific thunder sound; hence, they were preferred for can rattles. When the metal alloy was changed, the cans were no longer used. Museum evidence suggests that small tobacco tins, baking soda cans, or bullet tins were favoured in the early twentieth century (see, e.g., CMC III-G-368) although other factors such as colour may have been operative. The ringing sounds of can rattles is also a product of the hard rattler materials—stones or lead shot in most cases (e.g., HEY 2/7997, CMC III-G-15, CMC III-G-611). See also Colour Plates 8 and 9.

Photo 49. Ojibwe tin can rattle covered with rawhide collected around 1912 in Rainy River, Ontario (HEY 2/7997. FvR 88/37/24).
"This could be used in the Midewiwin lodge. Copper is the best but a tin can will do. It is the sound as well as the material that is important. A ringing, bell-like sound is especially important for women's rattles." (Jim Dumont)

Photo 50. Ojibwe jingle cone rattle, collected in Northeastern Minnesota by Fred Blessing in the 1950s (GLE AP3214. FvR 88/22/4).
"The sound of copper is really ringing." (Jim Dumont)

Other shaker types with bone materials were sometimes described as ringing: deer-hoof rattles, for example. The association of this rattle type with thunderbird imagery (carved zigzags on the wooden handle or the hoof segments which serve as rattlers, carved bird heads at the distal end) confirms a relationship between thunder and ringing sounds.

Reference to the "ringing" quality of horn rattles was also made by Wabanaki consultants. In Western Abenaki communities, the gender nuancing of this sound quality reverses the pattern observed earlier for Anishnabek: horn rattles are used only by Abenaki men, drums often by women (see MAB—SPINC ID:III.J.3006.d).

"Voices" of Drums

Iroquois musicians describe drums but not shakers as having "voices" because they may be tuned; pitch, then, is regarded as an important attribute of "voice." The amount of water added to a water drum or the wetness of the hide affects both pitch and timbre. Singers choose/make drums which can be pitched to blend with their voices. The air pressure inside the drum vessel is also described as a factor relating to the brightness or dullness of the sound.

The metaphor of "voice" was not used in the same way in Innu or Anishnabe contexts. Innu consultants, however, used "voice" in reference to snare sounds, described as "spirit voices." The choice of snare material for Innu (and some Anishnabe) drums is relatively consistent within specific historical periods. In the Naskapi/Montagnais area, feather quill and bone rattlers were preferred in earlier periods; small carved wooden pieces—usually with slightly enlarged ends painted red—are used on most contemporary drums. Stone rattlers, lead weights, or a combination of wood and stone (e.g., HEY 17/6820) occur on certain types of Cree frame drums, but we don't know the reason for this preference.

"Voice" was used by several Anishnabe consultants with reference to the caribou, an animal

Photo 51. Anishnabe "little boy" water drum.
Identified in its caption as a Shawnee water drum and drum-stick, the latter tied in a manner which indicates that it belongs to the Thawikila division or White Turkey band of Absentee Shawnees, this was identified by an Anishnabe consultant as the only published photograph of the "little boy" which he had ever seen.

Photo 52. Cayuga water drum (CMC III-I-463. FvR 88/7/36). This Cayuga water drum was collected by Marius Barbeau in Oklahoma in 1912. It looked, to our eyes, like the "little boy" and we wondered if the identification was incorrect:

"This is not tied like the little boy. For the little boy there used to be a pickling jar that was exactly the right shape—no barrel effect. There is also one for women." (Jim Dumont)

"This is something like the peyote drum in that marbles are tied in the skin. The wooden stick is twisted and the drummer steps on the rope to tune the drum." (Sadie Buck)

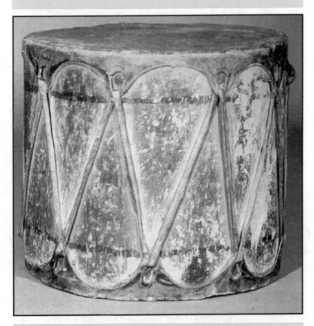

Photo 53. Plains Cree drum acquired by John Hellson from Dan Ochapewis, Ochapowace, Saskatchewan (GLE AP2545. FvR 88/26/19).
"If this was a little boy, the stones would be tied in the middle of the arches formed by the lacing points. The drum is the leader of that way of tying. With the little boy, the drum is tied in seven different ways for seven ceremonies and parts of ceremonies. Tying creates different patterns on the bottom of the drum." (Jim Dumont)

described as having a good voice since its hide sounds good on a drum. The plug hole on Anishnabe water drums (and an unplugged hole on a Wabanaki drum) were described as the "mouth" of the drum into which one had to breathe life (GLE AP3215, PAS—SPINC ID:III.F.3004.d), but the effect of this action on the sound quality was not specified. More complex factors affecting the sound of a drum such as the Anishnabe "little boy" are the variations in tying this drum. A rope ties seven round stones—said to be left by lightning—into the hide of the membrane. In the process of "dressing" the drum, the rope is then drawn under the drum in one of forty-nine (seven times seven) different patterns, each creating a symbolic image with specific uses. The "feather" tie which represented "standing in truth, straight like the shaft of an arrow" was demonstrated at the 1988 Elder's Conference at the Native Canadian Centre in Toronto. A pronged deer horn is used to tighten the lacing on the "little boy."

The "dry" frame drums of the Innu (Naskapi, Montagnais, Attikamek) and Anishnabe (Cree and Algonquin) may also be tuned by means of a rope tie which can be twisted to tighten the lacing securing the rims which hold the membrane in place (HEY 13/7014). Innu consultants related this directly to sound quality. Other differences in lacing style were described as regional variants or time-saving practices rather than acoustic modifications.

Photo 54. Tuning an Innu drum (HEY 13/7014. FvR 88/44/32).
"The extra rope wound around the stitching might be to tune the drum. Gilbert has seen drummers twist the lacing to tighten the drum head." (Vollant family)

Materials for both snare and membrane are other obvious factors affecting sound quality. Preferences again vary. Naskapi-Montagnais instrument makers choose caribou over moose hide while Maritime Ojibwe drum-maker Eddie Kabatay found caribou hide to be too thin. The medicinal value of certain materials influences some choices. Fish-skin disc rattles (MCQ 966-46-II, ROM 968.61.4) are used for specific healing ceremonies. The value of fish skin may also relate to the images which can be read in the scale patterns. One Innu consultant described seeing Christian imagery in the shape and patterning of a fish; Podolinsky (ms. in Quebec, Musée de la Civilisation) documents similar Algonquin practices.

Innu drumsticks are currently virtually all carved from lightweight wood such as birch. L-shaped bone sticks or ball-headed bone femurs reinforced with wood are extant in museum collections and described as earlier types. Small disc rattles also serve as drumsticks, in which case the additional rattle sound adds to the complex frequencies of membrane and snare (an example is a contemporary Cree drum and rattle made by John Kawapit, MCQ 83-5. See Photo 5).

The striking end of Anishnabe drumsticks varies in shape and hardness. L-shaped or bird-shaped sticks used for the "grandfather" are occasionally painted but not wrapped. Other Midewiwin-related drumsticks are unwrapped; a carved wooden straight stick with a spherical end

(HEY 16/9204) is an example. On the other hand, dance drumsticks are usually straight with leather-wrapped or cloth-covered striking ends. A small number of ring-shaped strikers on sticks made of root material were documented most often in association with Cree frame drums (CMC III-D-717, CMC III-D-717). The shape of these ring-ended sticks is imitated in some Cree drumsticks carved out of wood (e.g., CMC III-D-64) and was said to relate to the shape of the lacrosse stick.

Voices of Drums: The Thunderers

For Anishnabe consultants, the choice of drum-membrane material could point both to the kind of voice and to associations with spirit beings. Horse hide is used for "thunderer" drums (privately owned, SPINC ID:III.G.66.d and PEAH 41-72/24397) since it is regarded as a symbolic extension of the association between thunderbirds and horses and since it is said to create a voice which sounds a long way. Other sounds associated with the thunderers are made by bells and quills, both of which may sound together on a frame drum snare (HEY 9976 on which the diagonal placement of the snares is distinctive).

Voices of Drums: Continuous and Intermittent

The distinctions made in Algonquian languages between continuous and intermittent sounds, the latter implying pulse and also embodying nuances of clarity, are applied more often to environmental sounds than to music, in our experience. The distinction is often embodied in performance practice rather than described in language.

The contrast between continuous/intermittent may be juxtaposed within a performance. An Innu drummer, for example, usually precedes and accompanies some songs with a gentle, rapid striking motion producing a continuous vibration of the snares. He changes to a pulsed, triple-metre dance rhythm when, in the descriptions of some consultants, the hunter can "see" the game he seeks or when he remembers a dream. When struck with a disc rattle, the *teueikan* has a residual sound—almost continuous—together with the intermittent drum sound.

Cree honour songs may begin with a tremolo drum-beat and then move into pulsation. Anishnabe Midewiwin songs may start with four slow drum and rattle beats but may have "tremolo" cadences.

In Iroquois *eskanye* songs, the steady beat of the water drum used by the lead singer is reinforced by cowhorn rattles played by the rest of the group; the rattle players change to a tremolo pattern at the end of each song section, "straightening out the beat" when the co-ordinated pulsed pattern resumes.

Final Comments

Discourse about sound and sound producers is, of course, highly variable, but that variation seems to be patterned in certain ways. While Iroquoian speakers employ precise verbal descriptors for speech events, many distinctions about such things as singing styles are not articulated in language. Algonquian speakers use a rich vocabulary relating to natural sounds, a vocabulary evident in their mythology and in the less formal "texts" explored in our study. While some ways of describing sound, sound producers, and sound events rely on "relational" discourse, others employ words which characterize the fundamental physical aspects of the phenomenon described. Again, this distinction seemed to map onto an Iroquoian/Algonquian division. While many names in Innu or Anishnabe languages are onomatopoeic, names in Iroquoian languages seem less concerned with mirroring non-verbal sounds. While some language is common to Aboriginal speakers from widely separated areas—a phenomenon which may suggest a long history of usage—language for recent sounds (guitars, pianos) and technologies is often the result of highly personal creative processes which result in individual or localized usage.

In light of these substantial differences in how consultants spoke about sound and sound producers, several common themes surfaced. Of all the expressive modes available to living beings, sound is regarded as one of the strongest ways of establishing connections, since it moves through space, permeates visual and physical barriers, and conveys information from the unseen forces in the universe. Hence, sound is, by definition, a means of "relationship" as well as a "transformation" of energy. The link between sound and motion is emphasized—though in different ways by different Nations or groups within them—in many First Nations languages and discourses. This is evident in descriptive phrases ("to shake the earth") and in naming practices (for example, using the physical vibration of the diphthong *-ue-* or connecting to concepts of blowing or breath through *-pu-* in Algonquian languages).

In this chapter, we have explored in tandem various kinds of sound which are often separated: sounds of verbal languages and non-verbal expressive media such as song. Sounds of humans and animals, birds or other living beings, such as musical instruments or spirits. While undoubtedly the differences between human and animal communication are profound, we have juxtaposed these subjects because, as we understand it, First Nations languages and thinking recognize a large realm of overlap among them through their mutual reflection of environmental sounds.

Notes

1   At this point, a large number of ethnomusicological studies have revealed that "sound" which might be described as musical sound is defined in many different ways cross-culturally and connects to a wide range of other domains. Among the classics in this regard are Zemp (1978 and 1979), and Feld (1982). Within Native studies, important explorations of metaphor relevant to musical sound include Powers (1980), Parthun (1978), Witherspoon (1977), and Tedlock (1984). Also see studies of vocables, especially Frisbie (1980).

2   Among the studies which influenced our work are several of these, including: Hymes (1981), Tedlock (1982), Toelken (1976), and Diamond Cavanagh (1985).

3   The distinction here is Jakobson's (1962) between condensing/collapsing meanings or transferring/displacing them. This distinction, itself, however, may be drawn differently or even eliminated by speakers of different languages.

4   Linguists Kress and Hodge go so far as to suggest that our reality is reduced by the limitations of the names we construct. "Language fixes a world that is so much more stable and coherent than what we actually see that it takes its place in our consciousness and becomes what we think we have seen. And since normal perception works by constant feedback, the gap between the real world and the socially constructed world is constantly being reduced, so that what we do 'see' tends to become what we can say" (1978: 5).

5   See Ong (1982), for example.

6   The dichotomy of "orality" and "literacy" which Ong (1982) has defined as a fundamental criterion of difference among cultures has been used as a means of categorizing the organization and activities of social groups who engage in music-making (Guilbault 1987). It is not our intent, however, to categorize cultures and subcultures as oral and literate but to acknowledge the aspects and contexts of both qualities in each modern society.

7   Terminology suggested by Halliday and Hassan (1989) and quoted in Poynton (1989: 8-10) may be useful here. "Register" includes three sub-compo-

nents: the "field" or "institutional context of the discourse," the "tenor" or relationship between the speaker and addressee" and the "mode" or "channel being used to communicate" (e.g., written or spoken). "Genre" is defined as "structured or staged ways of getting things done by means of language in a particular culture." They are kinds of structures for speech (e.g., telephone conversation, essay, meeting). "Ideology" includes the beliefs, attitudes, and values which underly a particular utterance. While Halliday and Hassan subsume the "mode" of a text (oral or written) under "register," we have discussed this particular issue at greater length because of the significance it has for our work and because it relates to the issue of authority which is a central concern.

8   The many languages of the Anishnabe and Innu are, like Micmac and Maliseet, part of the Algonquian language family. Most differ substantially from one community to another, and the extent of mutual comprehensibility is not always clear. Neither Anishnabe nor Innu speakers understand Micmac or Maliseet, for example. My community-based study—in Davis Inlet, Labrador, in 1981 and 1983, and in Maliotenam and Uashat in the summers of 1985-89—involved the Innu only. Nevertheless, Anishnabe consultants in Ontario often made reference to related topics or aspects of language, and these enabled us to speak, at times, about common elements.

9   Individuals describe this as the sound of the tail of the rattlesnake, even in areas where there are no rattlesnakes. The snake, however, is powerful as a mythical figure in these same areas.

10 These specialized domains are not to be confused with specialized linguistic research which our competence precludes. While we are grateful for the advice of linguists about the interpretations offered in this chapter, we must accept responsibility for a number of metaphoric connections which linguists regard as speculative.

11 We did not have an opportunity to work with Algonquin speakers or linguists. Examples are taken from the River Desert Education Authority dictionary (1987). Orthographies differ from one source to another. Other published sources are abbreviated as follows:
Ellis—C. Douglas Ellis. (1983). *Spoken Cree.* Edmonton: Pica Pica Press.
JM—José Mailhot et Kateri Lescop. (n.d.). *Lexique Montagnais-Français,*MS.
McN—Gerry E. McNulty and Marie-Jeanne Basile. (1981). *Lexique Montagnais-Français du Parler de Mingan.* Quebec: Centres d'études nordiques, Université Laval.

12 Note that these are essentially the same words in different orthographies.

13 Another name described by Native musicians as onomatopoeically representing the sound of the drum is *tam-tam,* used in Huron and Wabanaki areas.

14 Related infixes exist in Wabanaki languages. Leavitt (1989: 47) presents a chart of "the Description of Shapes in Maliseet" where the following are in-

cluded: *-apsk-* (lumplike); *-ek-* (sheetlike); *-anok-* (layerlike), *-ahq-/-aq-* (sticklike); *-atok-/-tok-* (stringlike—also applicable to a story); *-alok-* (holelike, hollow).

15 For more about the reasons for this categorization, see Diamond Cavanagh (1989).

16 For an analysis of these, see Diamond Cavanagh (1988).

17 Other concepts relevant to our study are equally complex. Images, for example, are variable. Photographs are consistently animate, while cameras are inanimate. Designs can be one or the other.

18 We are grateful to Robert Leavitt for his detailed comments and corrections to this section of this chapter. Abbreviations for language sources used in this section include the following references to published dictionaries and wordlists: RND—Rand (1888), CLK—Clark (1902), DBL—DeBlois and Metallic (1983), RL—Leavitt (1989) except where indicated as personal communication. Names of consultants are also abbreviated as follows: MWF—Michael W. Francis, Big Cove; MM—Mildred Milliea.

19 This morpheme is also found in words meaning "listen" and "be silent" in Maliseet (spelled *cik-*) and Micmac. Personal communication from Robert Leavitt, University of New Brunswick, 1989.

20 Leavitt agrees that this connection is possible since, in Maliseet, the root is something like *-htihikon* (*o* = *schwa*)—"strike" plus "instrument for"; in Micmac, the *htVhV-* is reduced to *-te'-*a common type of correspondence found between Maliseet and Micmac words.

21 Leavitt compares the Maliseet *pipiqat,* a transitive verb participle—"that which s/he makes music by blowing."

22 Pacifique (1939) gives *wisqui* as "surprising."

23 Apparently distinct is *metuta'q* ("it makes a difficult to hear sound") which consists of *metu-* ("difficult"; a preverb distinct from *mete-*) and *-ta'q* ("it makes a sound"). DeBlois and Metallic (1983) list a further word which may be related: *metetogsit* ("heard calling").

24 The orthographies used in this section were developed by Seneca Longhouse head-speaker Reginald Henry from Six Nations, Ontario; linguist and Wolf Clan mother Dr. Hazel Dean, Allegany, New York; and linguist David Maracle, from Tyendinaga, Ontario. We value their patient wisdom and humour.

25 There is a parallel here with Iroquoian singing groups. Sadie Buck, leader of the Six Nations Women Singers, the oldest and most experienced *eskanye* singing society for women, explains that the group experimented with seating arrangements until they found one that best facilitated the blend of individual members' voice qualities. A strong singer sits opposite her for balance. A different quality voice blends with one person but not another. Unlike the Euro-American choir tradition where singers are sometimes told to adjust vocal qualities in order to blend, the Iroquoian sound ideal cherished the individuality of voices but effected a resonant, choral

sound by experimenting with the spatial arrangement and the relationships between different singers' voices.

26 In response to this paragraph, one SPINC member queried why we wanted to know this. Did it connect us with the controlling force or enable us to have control? Another member of the group responded that it seemed to call into question human agency; the human player could not be thought of as the controlling force but as part of a chain of connected beings who, together, constituted the flute's voice.

27 As a point of comparison it is interesting to note that Paula Gunn Allen, writing from a Laguna Pueblo/

Sioux perspective, implies that thought preceded sound (1986: 11, 16). The northern Ojibwe migration stories state at the outset that the "sound" of creation was preceded by a deep rumbling sound and, before that, another sound, the sound of the Creator's thoughts, which travelled faster than any sound.

28 Other playing techniques are described in Conklin and Sturtevant (1953: 268-69) who label the different playing styles as the "Roll," "Scrape-roll," "Snap," "Contact Snap," and "Crash."

Chapter Five
Languages of Image, Design, and Structure

Dialogue

FvR:

The other day, Sam asked a couple of very big questions which relate in many fundamental ways to design. "What draws attention?" "What is the meaning of drawing attention by using an image?" To begin to answer these, we may have to ask a few more questions. When is it appropriate to draw attention at all? Some things are left unadorned while others may be visually commanding. Why these differences?

MSC:

Which objects are selected for decoration? Traditional Iroquoian outfits have beautiful bead and ribbon work, and silver brooches. Ceremonial wooden food dishes and stirrers are carved; pipes have incised human or animal images which face you; tobacco baskets are decorated with multi-coloured ribbons; hair combs (associated with wakes, used to comb the living spouse's hair) have designs indicating clan animals, sometimes with identical images facing each other. But generally musical instruments are *not* highly decorated. I would have thought that turtle rattles would be elaborately painted (thinking in a hierarchical way, I suppose) signifying their special connection with Turtle Island/North America and clan symbols and their use in ceremonies. But rattles are not comparably "flashy"—they're usually painted black, an earth colour, and lacquered to make them shiny and durable. Very practical. The only exceptions I've seen are in museum collections.

BD:

Museum collectors have also been drawn to the spectacularly painted Naskapi coats or painted skins which were formerly used in ceremonies at daybreak. Today, many Montagnais women continue to make and wear traditional red and black-sectored hats with elaborately beaded bottom edge bands and double curves. Clothing. Skins. They seem often to be selected by the Innu for decoration.

But objects selected for decoration are not necessarily the same as objects which draw attention.

Montagnais drummers may not "decorate" a drum but that hide is full of images—from their dreams and experience.

FvR:

What objects draw attention? For the Micmac, musical instruments don't. Clothing often has design added. Micmac ceremonial dress with borders of double-curve motifs comes to mind. There are many fancy baskets decorated with elaborate quill-work. But musical instruments are often left in their natural state. A case in point is the folded birch bark, mentioned in early ethnographies as a type of drum to accompany singing.

But we should also ask "To what is attention drawn?" Sometimes an unadorned instrument is preferred because the singer does not want to draw attention to himself. On the other hand, design may draw attention to something unexpected. A hand drum with an eagle design on it was interpreted as indicating that the singer had a high voice. Thunderers' drums are made of horse hide because, according to one drum-maker, it produces a higher pitch which can be heard a long way, like thunder. The connection between visual designs and "voices" is an especially relevant one for us.

MSC:

This brings up the question of *whose* attention is drawn to what? There will always be different perspectives.

BD:

Differences between "traditionalist" and Catholic, for example, sometimes mapped onto differences between emphases on the aesthetic or symbolic dimensions of their work.

FvR:

But then, again, there are some interesting blends of traditionalist and Catholic imagery in the design of objects or events. At the Ojibwe community of West Bay, Ontario, for example, the Mass involves four-direction symbolism and the burning of sweetgrass. New Brunswick traditionalists occasionally ask a

Catholic elder to open their gatherings with a prayer.

BD:

Sam's last question may imply something other than differences in perspective. I'm thinking of occasions when we were looking at a visually commanding element while a consultant paid more attention to something less obvious.

FvR:

Like the hand drum with a prominent tree design shown in Photo 56; an Ojibwe consultant spent almost fifteen minutes examining what may have been a faint outline of a figure at the foot of the tree. Did we even see it, or was our attention so focused on the obvious—the large, central design—that we missed it? In Micmac legends it is also frequently the seemingly insignificant that proves to be most powerful. A tiny snail is able to transform into a powerful, giant, horned serpent.

BD:

It's not unlike the skill of reading images in the natural textures and colour gradations of a rawhide membrane. Sometimes an Innu hunter might stitch around an area or even burn holes in the hide apparently to mark or enhance patterns.

MSC:

Implicit in this is the idea that the instrument has some agency. This is analogous to a conversation I had about *hadui* masks studying us while they are warehoused in museum collections. Some colleagues have suggested that the masks will return to Iroquoian communities when they are ready, bringing back their understanding of non-Native culture. And what do they learn about us in those contexts?

We often fail to see this two-way relationship with sacred objects as equal partners. An Iroquoian friend says that when he puts on his *hadui* mask, the mask puts on him. *He* is the enhancement, the complement added to the mask.

In a way, I think this relates to the way we talk about "attention," "images," "designs," "decoration." They're all nouns. How do we talk about processes of *doing* design? How have we heard these processes explained in Native communities? How have we seen them done?

BD:

And why? What function does decoration serve? Does a decorated thing enhance power? Point to change? Represent identity?

MSC:

Your questions closely relate to issues of individuality and relationship again—so many of these ideas overlap! Let's consider drumsticks, for example—each unique, beautifully balanced and probably the most highly (and idiosyncratically) decorated among Iroquoian instruments. They are made from wood, and thus once alive. At the same time, they are something you hold, something which connects the drum to the player. So, does the decoration exist because of the medium (wood)? Does it connect singer with sound, or does it bring the instrument maker into the performance event when it's used?

FvR:

Both words and images are sometimes described as re-creating something that exists elsewhere. Perhaps the design creates a bond with whatever can be "heard but not seen" a phrase conveyed efficiently in both Micmac and Naskapi languages.

BD:

Are you saying that the design of a moose on a moose call helps bring the moose?

MSC:

In the case of an instrument used in Iroquois curing ceremonies or "doings," even the name draws the attention of that instrument.

FvR:

But let's not overlook obvious things. We know that many elders use images to draw attention to teachings. We might also note the connection between designs and teachings such as those represented by the wampum belts, designs and records of "oral" history, designs as mnemonics (on Ojibwe song scrolls, for example).

BD:

So far, we seem to have avoided using words like beauty. Can we turn our attention to aesthetic concepts?

FvR:

I am struck by the variety of patterns and colours of the traditional Micmac design—quillwork for example. The Micmac and Maliseet words for decorating, embroidering, whittling, (even dancing) all contain the morpheme -*amal*- which implies variety of patterns and/or colours. The preference for calico, or other cloth that has a variety of colours could also point to this.

MSC:

Barbara Tedlock's work on Zuni aesthetics comes to mind here; the Zuni preference for a variety of colours may be somewhat similar.

BD:

Tedlock pointed not just to variety, as I recall, but to one or more "things" (colour, texture, costume, song phrase, dance movement, etc.) which broke the symmetry of a visual or aural form. Whether this is different from the Micmac *-amal-* concept might be worth further exploration.

Franziska's comment on calico, however, may have a slightly different Naskapi/Montagnais parallel. Older women in the communities I have visited prefer dark plaids for clothing. The notion of patterns which are not quite symmetrical is there. I'm speculating though. I've never heard anyone discuss reasons for their plaid preference.

On the other hand, words like "beauty" seem, in Innu usage, to be applied often to European things including music—the piano is the "thing which sounds beautiful"; hymns are described as beautiful. Traditional *nikumana* may be useful or effective, but I have not heard them described as "beautiful."

MSC:

With regard to the concept of "beauty," I keep coming back to the importance of relationship and interaction. I remember hearing about a White Dog ceremony at Six Nations which took place in the 1930s (that particular breed of dog no longer exists). The ceremony, which included a ritual strangling of the dog, was extremely moving—people wept because of the beauty and power of this experience. Everyone was connected—the people, the dog taking their message on to the Creator—everything in creation was said to be focused on this event.

BD:

"Let our minds be as one . . . " a familiar phrase in opening ceremonies at Elders Conferences and other gatherings.

FvR:

This resonates with a Micmac friend's use of the word "beautiful" when the A.I.M. song was sung at an evening social at Trent University. More than a hundred people were standing in a tight circle around the drum singing. The moment was right; the focus was as one. "Beautiful."

Languages of Image, Design, and Structure[1]

Photo 55. Islands in the St. Lawrence River near the Montagnais community of Mingan, Quebec. Photo by BD.

What Does it Mean to Draw Attention?

A visual image draws attention.

In itself, this statement can be applied cross-culturally. More culturally dependent, however, are the acceptable ways and appropriate contexts for drawing attention.[2] Dancing might be encouraged at a rock concert but not condoned in the middle of a theatrical performance. Painting one's face is appropriate for women in some cultures, more so for men in others. There may, of course, be occasions where we overthrow the rules, although ritual theorists have taught us that these very "reversals" in extraordinary contexts serve to clarify what is normal and appropriate in "ordinary" life. In very obvious, well-known ways, drawing attention by our choice of dress, speech, or behaviour is contingent on many things: our ethnicity, class, gender, age, personality, and the context of the specific event, to name a few.

There are fundamentally different attitudes across cultures as to what draws the eye. Mainstream North American media often assume that what we define as important should have attention drawn to it. Hence, an art gallery might place its most valuable painting in the best light or the central position. Advertisers use big print, catchy songs, or cute children to convey the most vital parts of their message, and newspapers use bigger bolder titles for the most dramatic stories of the day.

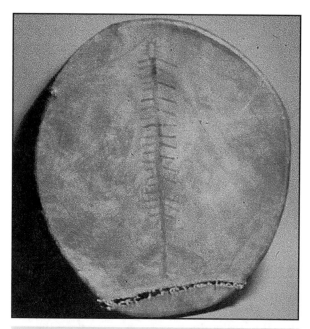

Photo 56. Plains Ojibwe frame drum collected by Frank Speck (PEAS E28136. FvR 87/8/29).

In this study, on the other hand, Native consultants were often drawn to what seemed to us to be obscured or irregular details. Things which didn't fit, in our eyes, were sometimes regarded as engaging. Comments were made about the small red smudge at the bottom of a drum membrane (GLE AP815) rather than the dominant image of the tree; the tinkling sound in certain kinds of thunder was observed rather than the "boom"; the thin red line on top of a densely painted black sector was the clue to the perspective on a drum (HEY 9976); the small piece of copper wire looped around the handle was "needed." We were reminded of an experience related by Alanson Skinner whose Menominee consultants told him, with regard to ribbon or silk appliqué, that the primary colour was strictly decorative while the secondary colour[3] had ceremonial significance (Skinner 1921: 268). Similarly, filmmaker Sol Worth observed that Navajo filmmakers were sometimes fascinated with accidental shots; he relates a story, for example, in which a camera was "carelessly" pointed at the grass:

The camera movements were, to our minds, random, meaningless, and chaotic. Nothing was level and parts of the movement were so fast that we couldn't make anything out. When we (the investigators) looked at it several times, we could see that it was earth and grass that we were looking at. But whereas we "knew" that we were not supposed to see anything—that the footage was only leader—the Navajo saw it as the most interesting shot in the roll. They told us that they knew there was something

there because of the way "it" moved. "It" was either the grass or the camera—both movements seemed to count, not only individually but in relation to one another. They laughed at our puzzled looks, and when we explained that we hadn't "meant to make anything like that," that it was an accident, they still insisted that they could use the shot to show a thing moving in the grass. (1972: 94-95)

Similarly, Mary Black has observed from her work in Ojibwe communities that while

there is *general* agreement about a core of entities that are *most likely* to have great power, there is always the possibility that a *seemingly* powerless one may at some time exert the very ability to perform some special good or harm. This is dogma and leads back to the other dogma, the unreliability of outward appearance or of "face-value" interpretation of sense data. (Black 1977: 101)

In each of these cases, "accidental" or "coincidental" moments in life, rather than merely the aspects we think are humanly controlled, are regarded as important.

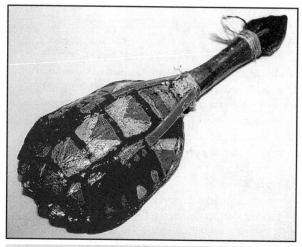

Photo 57. An elaborately decorated Iroquois turtle rattle dating back to the War of 1812 according to catalogue information (ROM 975X73.18. MSC 86/1/13 and 2).
It had been used at Six Nations for *Ostowagowah*. Sam showed Elijah Harris the photos, wondering how he would react to the elaborate decoration, the geometric designs of yellow, red, and black.
Lige looked briefly at the slide and gave it back to Sam.
"It's so sad, Sam."
"Sad? Why is it sad?"
"I guess it doesn't want to be there." (Conversation between Sam Cronk and Elijah Harris, March 1987, Six Nations)

In Native performance contexts, visually drawing attention can alternatively serve a practical function. An Iroquoian cowhorn rattle, especially the handle, will probably be painted so that a singer can easily identify and gather together his instruments at the end of a "sing" or social. The horn itself is rarely painted, although it is often glossily varnished. On the other hand, turtle rattles are more often left natural, painted black, or given a coat of high-gloss urethane. Earth colours are retained in this way, and attention is *not* drawn to an inappropriately painted rattle. Furthermore, since only two turtle rattles, at most, are used at a ceremony, they are less likely to be separated from their owners than are cowhorn rattles.

On the other hand, a powwow fancy dancer—flamboyantly clad in feather bustle, reflective materials, and face paint—might be the visualization of a spirit animal which, in everyday life, is invisible. By attending to that which is hard to see or to find, but which, in one way or another, draws attention by a quality of unusualness, the spectacular power of that thing can be represented in the appropriate performance context.

Experiences such as these led us to design questions which continue to fascinate us: what is the relationship between images and "power"?[4] Does the addition of a visual image add or detract from the power of the instrument (i.e., is power considered inherent or applied)?

In Chapter Three, we related Jim Dumont's comments about the power of a seed pod shaker in its unadorned, natural, dried state. Gourd shakers, highly respected in both Anishnabe and Iroquoian communities, tend to be left natural (although both paint and incised designs decorate a number of these). Are those sound producers given by the Creator and least adorned by humans the most powerful?

Some scholars of northern Algonquian cultures suggest the opposite, arguing that the main function of decoration was to *enhance* power. Concerning the Naskapi, for example, Speck relates pictorial representation to control.

The pictorial or symbolic representation of the plant or animal whose aid is to be secured, or has been secured, is equivalent to the creature or object itself. Hence, we may say, to put it roughly, that there is an analogy in far northern Algonkian philosophy between symbol or picture and control-power, in bringing the objects portrayed under the dominance of the individual human spirit for the accomplishment of its needs. . . . (1935: 197)

He comments, further, that "animals prefer to be killed by hunters whose clothing is decorated with designs" and that the "souls of the hunters also like to see them dressed and decorated in colours" (ibid.: 199). He then elaborates on a concept which he glosses "satisfaction":

When a man dreams . . . the animal of the dream asks the hunter for something . . . to satisfy . . . some article of apparel or use, [is] decorated with design to bring about

this form of satisfaction, *nahe'itoem* (Mistassini). At Lake St. John the corresponding term is *mi'lowe'ltoem* "good thought." (Ibid.: 199)

In a different publication (1985: 16) he speaks of the beaver as the message-bearer regarding the location of game and comments that he [the beaver] "also wants his meat pan to look pretty." Hence, the valuing of the natural does not preclude the powerful motivation to decorate those objects which are made to imitate or reflect the sounds or perceptions or potentialities of nature.

Whose Attention?

There were many ironies relating to attention-getting in the course of our research. Through museum collections, we had physical access to instruments that would otherwise have been kept out of general view except for specific contexts. The artificiality of this, the conceptual basis of it—that images are somehow neutral and available equally—struck us quite forcibly. We were not the intended recipients of these images. Who was/is supposed to see the bear at the bottom of a water drum (e.g., GLE AP3116) the painted interior of a frame, the underside of a turtle rattle? Why were these images placed in a specific location? They were clearly not intended to get the attention of people other than the maker and user of the instrument. The primacy of individual knowledge about (and legitimate access to) images such as these was stressed by virtually all consultants. Paradoxically, the importance of individuality is thwarted in most public museum displays where photographs might appear with generalized labels identifying Nation or culture area rather than individuals.

Photo 58. The inset bottom of an Ojibwe "grandfather" water drum (GLE AP3116. FvR 88/23/15).
"The bear is often associated with the underwater panther. In fact, they are like two forms of the same creature. The line down the centre of the bear indicates that it is a spirit." (Jim Dumont)

Photo 59. The inset bottom of an Ojibwe "grandfather" water drum from Mole Lake, Wisconsin, probably dating from the late nineteenth century. Collected in the 1940s by Mr. and Mrs. John Shalloch from John Pete (CMC III-G-743. FvR 88/5/22).

The images which were hidden from a human public, however, could be oriented to other beings. Does the figure on the bottom of a water drum "call" or indeed speak to creatures below the earth? Is an image distinct from the creature itself? Such questions further accentuated the ironies of decontextualization.

How Do Images Communicate "Meaning"?

"What do you see?" asked Cree elder James Carpenter, as he prepared to explain the musical instruments on one slide after another to a group of young people in Attawapiskat, Ontario. He asked us each to stretch our individual powers of observation, to make our own attempt to observe with care before he offered an explanation to the eager group.

In our feedback interviews with elders and consultants, as we were honoured with interpretive comments of various kinds about image and design, it was clear that individuals "see" differently from one another and that such differences are respected as individual, not discounted as wrong. Here are three cases in point.

Situation 1

In an extended interpretation of a beautiful nineteenth-century Ojibwe drum from the area north of Lake Superior (HEY 9976), Jim Dumont shared the following comments, carefully indicating that he spoke from an Anishnabe, Midewiwin perspective: The membrane of this drum/rattle, he explained, shows a sectoring of earth and sky realms with the red line on the surface of the black sector possibly indicating the earth level. The concentric arcs at East and West may be the reverberations of thunder. Similarly, the figure associated with the Midewiwin embodies the four universes above the surface of the earth in Anishnabe cosmology: hemisphere, triangular body, head, and wavy lines. The other membrane of this drum was described as possibly a long-range view of the earth seen from the vantage point of the sky if the central figure could be a buffalo or, conversely, sun and crescent moon. He presents alternative possibilities, by acknowledging his perspective, and by reading the flat surfaces as three-dimensional space, space which, furthermore, can be macrocosmic or microcosmic, close-up or wide-angle, representing the individual or the whole (Colour Plate 10).

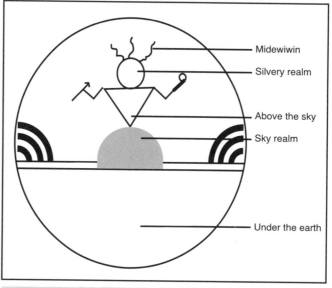

Fig. 14. Interpretation of the images on the Anishnabe drum, HEY 9976 (see Colour Plate 10):
"This is the sky side. The figure might be a thunderbird spirit. The black bottom has a red earth line on top. This might be a view seen through many different levels [suggested by the alternating red and black arcs]. Or the arcs could be the reverberations of thunder. The arrow suggests the shooting part of the Mide ritual. Or this is a human figure and the buffalo [on the other side] an underwater spirit. The bells inside make the sound that you can hear in a certain type of thunder on a clear day." (Jim Dumont)

Situation 2

In other instances, different individuals interpreted the same pattern in a variety of ways.[5] The familiar red dots on Montagnais and Algonquin membranes and frames, described to Frank Speck as the symbolic representation of sunlight rays filtering through the trees which help direct hunters to game (1935: 193), were described on different occasions as "stars." Another interpreter saw the array of red dots as the four or eight directions; to still another, the same pattern was "the one and the all." They were thought to relate to a dream for one hunter; for yet another respected consultant, the dots had no symbolic connotations but were "just for the beauty."

Situation 3

In other cases, interpreters seemed to enjoy the ambiguity of certain complex images. Shapes might be composites of different creatures, perhaps something like visual puns. Do you see birds' or horses' heads in these drumsticks: CMC III-G-404b, AMNH 178379, GLE AP3217, GLE AP3239, GLE AP312b, HEY 15/5558.

"The drumstick head is supposed to be a bird but at some point they started making horse-shaped ones. The bird/horse ones are always used in the Mide lodge." (Jim Dumont. See HEY 24/2179.)

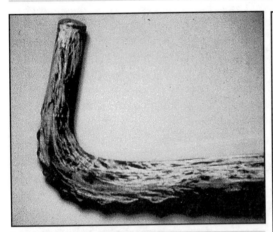

Photo 60 (above). Ojibwe bird/horse drumstick, pre-1929, collected by D. Jenness at Parry Island, Ontario (CMC III-G-404b. FvR 88/2/1).

Photo 61 (left). Possibly Ojibwe, mid-nineteenth century, collected by Peter Jones at New Credit, Ontario. American Museum of Natural History (178379).

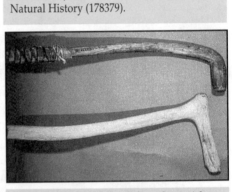

Photo 63 (above). Plains Ojibwe drumsticks (collected by Fred Blessing and Hugh Dempsey respectively in the 1950s) (GLE AP3239 and AP312b. FvR 88/22/1).

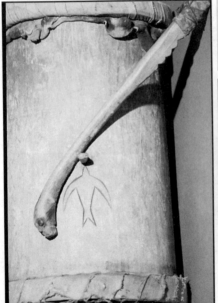

Photo 62 (left). Ojibwe drumstick collected at Mille Lacs, Minnesota by Fred Blessing in the 1950s (GLE AP3217. FvR 88/20).

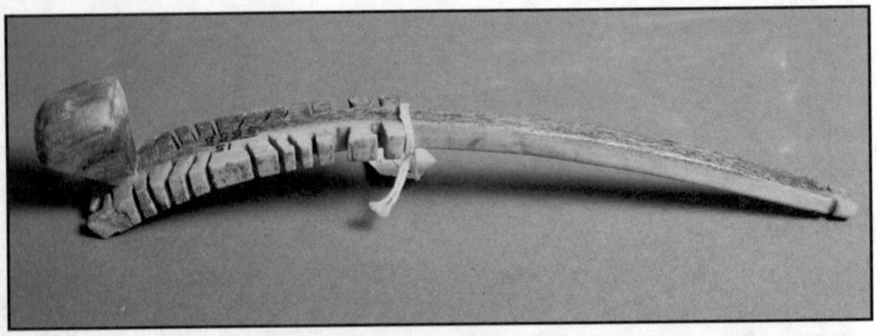

Photo 64 (above). Naskapi bone drumstick which resembles the "horse-shaped" Anishnabe drumsticks (HEY 15/5558. FvR 88/45/13).

Emergent Meaning

Examples such as these have often been considered problematic from the viewpoint of Euro-American scholars who have been taught that meanings which are culturally shared are somehow more important than ones which are individual. Many of us were taught to query how the data might be "verified," or substantiated by multiple sources. The traditional ethnographic frames of reference with their stress on sensory, tangible observation, which is often claimed to be objective and verifiable, are not helpful in arriving at a less ethnocentric understanding of the *processes* of creating meaning in the three situations we described. Varied individual interpretations, meaning that may change if the perspective is one thing or another, forms which may be seen as *x* or as *y*—these styles of "percept ambiguity" (to use the terminology of Black 1977) have challenged the scientific biases of ethnologists. Recent ethnography tends to be cautious about individual interpretations, acknowledging but sometimes simultaneously discounting them. The figure below illustrates what we might describe as a "cautious" response to earlier published interpretations through its careful referencing of personal experience. By setting up a dichotomy between the "conventional" (implicitly, the shared) and the "esoteric" (knowledge derived from personal religious experience) and by parenthetically labelling much of the information in the referenced source as "dubious," however, the caption on this drawing goes beyond caution to disparage slightly the validity of individual interpretations.

A number of factors further complicate our interpretive process. The ideology or system of beliefs which underlies the perspective of an interpreter may govern the style or substance of the interpretation. As we have just seen, some Indian people regard the sound-producing instruments that we have scrutinized as reflections of rich levels of meaning, symbolic concepts of cosmogeny and identity which are at the heart of Anishnabe and Haudenosaunee cultures. Other people, however, suggest that design and decoration are connotative rather than denotative. A design might be said to enhance the beauty of the object through its proper proportioning or skillful patterning.

Montagnais artisan Thomas Simeon eloquently articulates the latter perspective in writing about the process of making birch-bark baskets:

Précisons, en tout premier lieu, qu'il n'est pas d'usage que les motifs représentés soient de nature religieuse, magique ou autres. Non, pour bien dire, chacun employait les dessins qu'ils jugeait être les plus "beaux" et encore aujourd'hui, il en demeure ainsi.

Mais, bien que les motifs les plus souvent retrouvés et employés représentent, soit une fleur sauvage, une feuille ou un feuillage et même parfois un arbre ou un animal sauvage, la préférence va à ceux qui reproduisent des choses de dimension égale ou quasi à celle du casseau; raison d'esthétique. (1979: 4)

Several other Montagnais artisans asserted, similarly, that designs, colours, or attachments on musical instruments are for the sake of beauty, not religious (or other) symbolism.

While, for the most part, the former group—those who describe meaning in symbolic terms—has many "traditionalists" while the latter group has a larger proportion of Christians, it would be inaccurate to draw a sharp boundary between the two. It would be a still greater injustice to dismiss the latter perspective as "acculturated" and describe it simplistically as a loss of meaning rather than as an aesthetic shift. Each perspective warrants respect and serious consideration.

In some cases, varied interpretations of images (or indeed of any "sign") rely on different sign-types available to the interpreter. Here the field of semiotics has developed terminology useful in making some distinctions. We refer to the system of Thomas Pierce, for example, and his threefold distinction among "icon," "index," and "symbol." An

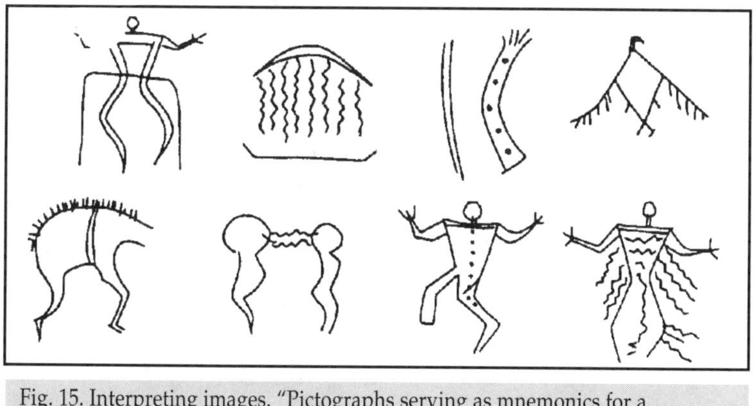

Fig. 15. Interpreting images. "Pictographs serving as mnemonics for a Midewiwin song, incised on a birchbark scroll. While some Chippewa pictographs used for songs and other texts have conventional meanings (the fifth and sixth from the left represent a thunderbird and a bear, and the double bar in the third position indicates a rest period) songs are often specific to an individual and the interpretation of their mnemonic pictographs requires esoteric knowledge derived from personal religious experience (much of the interpretation of this scroll obtained by Hoffman 1891: 218-19 is dubious). Length 39 cm; collected at Red Lake, Minnesota, 1887-89."

Dept. of Anthropology, Smithsonian: 153136, from Trigger 1978: 755.

image of a bird, for instance, might be interpreted iconically as a "thunderbird" sign, indexically as something that pointed to the "jingling" sound of the instrument, or symbolically as an indicator of the owner's membership in the Midewiwin, or in Eagle or Thunderbird clans. Or, in the case of the aforementioned example of red dots, we find that symbolic interpretations predominate (dots as stars, as four directions, or as "the one and the all") but that indexical ones (a key to the physical perspective on the sky which the drum represents) are also among them.

But there are at least two problems with semiotic models. One has already been raised in relation to "whose attention?" An image that is received as a "representation" and one that is received as a "transformation" of a being are not the same. The imposition of Piercian categories may impose the rules of "representation" on a system that is fundamentally more fluid. Secondly, the naming of sign-types draws our attention to the end product rather than to the *process* of creating or observing meaning. It is this process which is perhaps the most consistent and distinctive aspect underlying the many interpretations which we heard.

A number of consultants phrased their explanations of design cautiously: it "could be seen as" or "might be considered." In the paraphrases of their interpretations presented earlier, we took care to preserve these phrases, since it would clearly be wrong to suggest that such explanations were shared by all members of a culture. But are we just talking about polysemy here—multiple meanings for any cultural text—or are we actually talking about a different *locus* for the meaning?

So far, we assumed that the source of meaning rested with the "teacher," the "doer," or perhaps with the cultural "object." But there are suggestions in Native explanations that there are multiple "events" in the creation of meaning. For example, a pathway to game might be "read" by a Montagnais hunter in the natural shading of a membrane but only when the sound of the drum helped him see images in that shading and enabled him to recall his dream. The locus of meaning is the coming together of the dream, the membrane pattern, and the sound of the drum/song. Visually, we might see no evidence of any of this or perhaps the general area of such images might be marked with stitched outlines (e.g., CMC III-B-584). Sometimes an image might be drawn on a membrane (see an Anishnabe response to the Winnebago drum GLE R1824.99) for a particular ceremonial context. Such an image may not be intended to be seen beyond the temporal bounds of

the event, nor by anyone other than an individual drummer/hunter. In other cases, more permanent "dream" images might be painted on a drum membrane, but without the other experiential elements, without the performance, the loci of meaning do not become one.

Photo 65. Drum membrane (GLE AP1635. FvR 88/31/25).

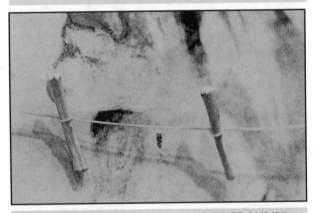

Photo 66. Membrane—Kurtness drum (MAPB. BD 86/3/31).

Photo 67. Cree disc rattle collected in 1966 by Michel Brochu in Chisasibi, Quebec (MCQ 966-46-II. BD 88/5/9).
"You can see the Virgin Mary in the shape of a fish." (Innu consultant)
"Some disc rattles were used in the shaking tent. Is the skin fish skin?" (Jim Dumont)

As discussed in the previous chapter, there may also be multiple "roles" in the creation of meaning. Many First Nations maintain repertoires which are not regarded as conscious human creations but products of dreams. For the Innu, virtually all songs respected as *nikumana* originate in this manner. In such cases, intermediaries rather than composers receive rather than invent new songs. Similarly, instrument makers may create an instrument in accordance with someone's dream even when they do not know the meaning of the constructional details they are creating. That such instruments may reflect or indeed "perform" a message which is individual and private is not the end-point, however. The structures and designs become active players with "potential" meanings for others. These potential meanings may be read in a variety of ways. The locus of renewed or new meaning, then, becomes the coincidence of a particular design and an observer or user with the experience or perhaps an appropriate mindset to actively receive or interpret the particular design. This sense of meaning is consistent with non-interventionist forms of social interaction.[6] A story may be "put out there" and people will learn from it what they are ready to learn from it. Not only does this result in polysemy but in a never static, always contextually dependent way of experiencing and interpreting the world.

As mentioned earlier, Mary Black has presented a related discussion based on Ojibwe teaching. She comments that her Ojibwe teachers classified what they perceived

on the basis of such attributes as the ability to change form, the power to appear to someone in a dream or vision, the ability to cause things to happen from a distance, or to control weather events or illness events or life and death. These are important discriminators throughout the domain of living things. . . . They are not, however, immediately perceivable attributes. . . . (1977: 101)

She goes on to describe the very personal meaning of certain experiences (an encounter with a *memengwesi*, for example) emphasizing that the validation for such an encounter is often "not expected to be known until some later moment" (ibid.: 103). In the case of some things which we have explored, it seems as if the images on a sound-producing instrument may *be* that validation of the encounter, a sort of visual re-enactment of what may finally be known. But at another level, the images become encounters for each contemporary viewer, some of whom may see in them potential messages which may or may not be validated at a future point.

The implications of cross-cultural differences in defining the locus of meaning are considerable when one considers a written document such as this book. Print fixes meaning. Even where we note that such and such a person said such and such a symbol meant such and such a thing at such and such a time, we have still frozen what is, in reality, a system in motion. A second implication for writing about design and meaning is to consider the roles of author and reader in the process. We are both active respondents to the images and sounds depicted in this book. A real understanding of Native meaning derives not merely from writing or reading the interpretations of others but also from understanding the creative process in the manner appropriate for the culture.

"What do you see?" asked the Cree elder.

"It's individual," said Lige, **"individual, Sam."**

The Individuality of Instrument Design and Elements of Meaning

The meaning of "individual" is hard to sort out on the basis of the external forms and designs of sound producers. On one hand, there were widely distributed instrument "types," types which crossed the lines of language family, or which related to shared stories and traditions. Among the former were disc rattles found in Algonquian communities from Labrador to the Prairies, but also in the Nations of other language families. Like turtle rattles which are used in Wabanaki, Iroquoian, and Anishnabe communities, these are similar in form, though associated with different ceremonial and social practices. There were types such as the dance drum associated with a more formal spiritual tradition, or the similar powwow drum. Similarly there were "types" such as the grandfather and little boy water drums, gourd rattles, and metal rattles in particular, associated with the Midewiwin. In relation to these instrument types, an instrument maker can, of course, express personal identity through an individualized style, the carving of his or her name (see, e.g., SPINC ID:III.I.7019.r, CMC III-I-822, or HEY 21/9593) or the representation of experiences. He/she could express shared identity as a member of a clan or Nation.

Photo 68. Iroquois cowhorn rattle, personalized (HEY 2/9593. FvR 88/39/1).

On the other hand, there were instruments which were either one of a kind or rare. Some of them, such as the large, wooden, hand-shaped rattles made for the Rochester Museum's Indian Arts Project in the 1930s (see RMSC AE2797 and AE7882) may have been intended as a good joke; to play them, one shakes the wooden hand! Others, such as a Cree fiddle made from sinew strung across a caribou shoulder blade (described by Attiwapiskat elder James Carpenter) may have been ingenious adaptations of materials at hand. This may also be an explanation for an Iroquois sound-producing garter[7] which has silver spoon bowls strung on a blue cloth (HEY 22/4534). According to museum documentation, other unusual types such as the Naskapi shoulder blade rattle (HEY 23/6638 and CMC III-B-485, both collected in the 1960s) may have been used for ceremonial purposes; the former is described by the collector as a sweat lodge rattle. Their relative rarity in museum collections may parallel that of other widely used forms such as the Anishnabe "little boy" water drum which was rarely allowed into the hands of collectors. Some types with which we were unfamiliar were probably brought into Northeastern Woodlands communities from areas outside the geographic boundaries of our project; the Delaware half-globe shaker, SI 409072, is a case in point. Some may imitate European instrument types (a possible explanation for an Iroquois "tambourine":

ROM 958.131.742). Others seem to use the form and materials of one instrument type to construct a different type, thus creating a physical analogy for percept ambiguity; see, for example, a Seneca cowhorn flute (HEY 20/7292), a small gourd ocarina (PEAS E27864), and a pre-1920s Micmac conical birch-bark rattle, rolled like a moose call but with a distal plug (ROM 16997). Certain types of animal calls are also rare in museum collections; these include forms such as a double-barrelled (two-pitched) game call with duct "eyes" (MCC ME929.7 for which the catalogue documentation vaguely specifies "East"). In still other cases, we cannot posit even a speculative explanation for unusual instrument types. Two hemispheric Mohawk drums from Kahnawake, Quebec, donated to the McCord Museum in the 1930s, are among the mysteries (MCC M18207 and Colour Plate 11). So too is a pair of concentric "rims" with a layer of deer hoofs suspended between them (HEY 2/79990), a Micmac disc rattle with two exterior strikers (PAS—SPINC ID:III.F?.3002.r) or a flat wooden rattle with a leather top (ROM 43338, no identification). These unusual types of sound producers may be examples of completely individualized forms, rather than individualized realizations of more widely used forms. As such, they may merit more attention than we have paid them in this study. Their very individuality, however, makes them extraordinarily difficult to research.

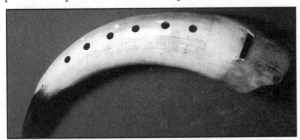

Photo 69. Seneca cowhorn flute (HEY 20/7292. FvR 88/39/2).

Photo 70. Spoon rattle or garter (HEY 22/4534. FvR 88/41/6).

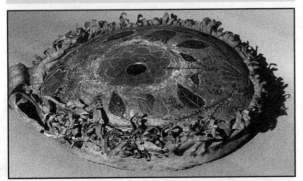

Photo 71. Mohawk hemispheric drum from Kahnawake, Quebec, resting on flat, membrane-covered side. Collected in the 1930s by the Molson family (MCC M18457. BD 88/2/7). Also see Colour Plate 11.

Photo 72. Micmac rattle "used in the Serpent Dance" according to museum catalogue. Pre-1920 (ROM 16997. MSC 86/11/2).

The sections to follow explore design/construction practices and interpretations—some shared, some individual, many a coincidental product of acquired knowledge and personal experience. The specificity of each example is clearly significant (although many details of documentation are not possible given the lacunae in archival documenta-

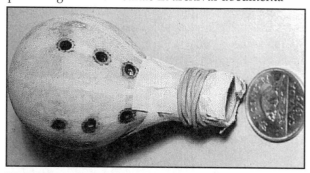

Photo 73. Gourd ocarina collected by Frank Speck (unidentified further but kept with his Iroquois collection) (PEAS E27864. FvR 87/10/14).

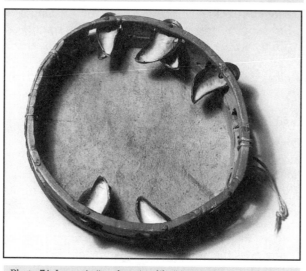

Photo 74. Iroquois "tambourine-like" instrument (ROM 958.131.742). Photo by MSC.

Photo 75. Huron goat-horn rattle with incised pattern on distal end (CMC III-I-629. FvR 88/5/9-10).

Photo 76. Unidentified Woodlands rattle (ROM 43338. MSC 89/2/8).

tion). For this reason, reference to the *Catalogue* (forthcoming on disk) will be useful.

Materials

An intimate and detailed knowledge of natural materials and processes for "handling" or transforming materials enables a deep relationship to one's environment. For urban dwellers, such knowledge often seems formidable. We had little experience of the several layers of bark about which some consultants spoke. We did not know about the parts of a root, or the number of shell divisions on a turtle's back; nor could we recognize many different feathers, or the processes which could be used to tan a hide in order to produce colour variation. It was perhaps in relation to materials, and thus to the natural environment, that our domains of knowl-

edge as "musicians" were vastly different from those of the Aboriginal "musicians" who worked patiently with us on this project.

Photo 77. A demonstration at the Fête des abénakis of the technique for splitting ash splints. Photo by BD.

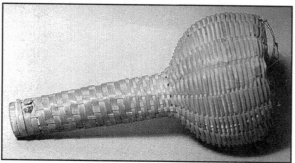

Photo 78. An Abenaki baby's rattle made ca. 1900 from fine woven ash splints and sweetgrass, and filled with dried peas (PEAS 25848. FvR 87/8/17).
"It is an interesting question whether this rattle type was introduced by Europeans. It is given to the baby to learn to hear and play rhythms and to protect him/her from harm." (Jim Dumont)

Language structures remind us of the importance of "material" as a source of teaching. Earlier, we described infixes in Algonquian languages which convey the nature or shape of material and draw our attention to fundamental physical attributes of "substances" in the world: waterlike, stonelike, skinlike, stringlike, and sticklike. What qualities are evoked when one of these infixes is embedded in a word?

Consider the attributes of sheet- or skinlike materials, for example. Their qualities of delicacy, their flexibility and stretchability may constitute aspects of their "teachings." Many sheet- or skinlike materials are absorbent; hence, they may form a special sort of relationship to waterlike substances. Functionally, they may also share attributes. Human skin, for instance, protects, containing within it the elements of life which it keeps safe. It covers, perhaps even "hides" things so that they are not accessible or visible. But in itself, it is highly visible and can be a marker of identity through its colour or other attributes which may be applied (make-up, tattoos, attachments). It binds things and serves as a divider between "inside" and "outside" worlds. It is also vulnerable in that it may be scratched or torn quite easily. Hence, it demands care. Clothes, similarly, protect, cover, and hide, while also marking identity. A tablecloth, a curtain, a canvas tent, a piece of bark—all share certain functions and attributes.

Sometimes these attributes are foregrounded in ceremonies. A cloth curtain, used only in the Longhouse during condolence ceremonies, temporarily separates participants as the dead chief is being mourned and a new hereditary chief installed. In the Labrador forest, Christian Innu pray facing the walls of their tent, regarding it as a division between human and spirit worlds.

On a drum, skins become voice—the sound producers—transmitting vibrations not only of drummers but of the world around. The double-headed Anishnabe dance drum is said to reflect sound back in all four directions. On certain Innu frame drums, the skin serves to divide the earthly and spirit worlds. The skin hides and protects; hence drumsticks and rattle handles may be wrapped with multiple layers of cloth so that the point of human contact—the hand—is buffered by sheetlike objects. The attributes and functions of skinlike materials help us understand the way in which musical instruments may embody teachings about the natural world and one's relationship to it. Individual experiences may differ, of course, so that each person's reflection on any one of these qualities will vary.

As we understand it, this is part of what is meant when an elder suggests that certain drums have "all you need to know." The explanation of the Anishnabe grandfather drum (in Chapter Two), describes how the elements come together. Certain other drums also embody different materials. The Anishnabe "little boy" has a sticklike vessel, skinlike membrane, liquid (water inside), stringlike rope ties, and seven stones tied into the membrane. The Innu *teueikan* similarly has parallel elements in the frame and membrane; its snare (and perhaps rims) and lacing are stringlike; the snare rattlers may be bone in some cases, as may be the drum beater.

Furthermore, some instruments bring all the elements together just before performance. Innu hunter Thomas Noah advised that the *teueikan* be disassembled when not in use. In many instances, a final element or action is needed in order to give the drum its voice. Water is added both to Iroquoian and Anishnabe water drums as well as to the membrane of the Innu *teueikan*. Wabanaki drums are heated until the membrane is taut. The Anishnabe "little boy" is dressed. The dance drum is smudged with tobacco. Only when all elements are brought together in the right way do many instruments' voices sound as they should.[8]

Teachings in Construction Processes

There are instances when a sound producer is needed quickly. In the bush, a birch-bark moose call may be made in ten minutes, or a cast-off bone (MCQ 75-282) may serve as a drum beater. Such natural sound producers may require little or no process of manufacture.

In other cases, however, every detail of construction is the product of long hours of work, careful attention to visual, aural, and tactile qualities, as well as highly sophisticated knowledge and skill. How does one acquire knowledge of the various processes required?

There is no single answer to this question. In some cases, a person may be "chosen" (in a sense) to become an instrument maker. One Innu drummaker explained that three dreams of a drum must precede the making of one. (We have read analogous requirements in relation to Cree canoe-making; see Taylor 1980.) For other artisans, this was not a necessary pre-condition. An Anishnabe drummaker began his craft on the instruction of an old woman in his community who designated that he continue the tradition.

All Iroquoian children are encouraged to develop instrument-making skills if they show an inclination and skill to do so, although most of the active contemporary instrument makers are men. In other cases, a particular family might hold specialized knowledge or a skilled artisan might be asked to make an instrument based on instructions given in another's dream. At the present time, courses in instrument making, open to all, are offered on several reserves.

Photo 79. Hubert Buck, Sr. making a turtle rattle at Six Nations, Ontario (MSC 87/4/3).

In many cases, traditional construction processes are collaborative, seeming to reinforce one or more aspects of reciprocity. In the case of the Iroquoian turtle rattle, for example, the turtle is said to give itself to become a rattle. The flesh of the turtle is cleaned out by insects and wind as the turtle is hung in the open air. Hence, the preparation is a collaborative process between people and other beings in the natural world. For other instruments, men and women are each responsible for the preparation of some kinds of materials. Skins for drum or disc rattle membranes are often prepared by Innu women, for example, while the wooden frames or rims are made by men. Innu couples often collaborate in the same way in the construction of snowshoes: men make the frames and women, the lacing.

Iroquois and Abenaki men and women often collaborate similarly for basket making: men may cut and pound the ash but women weave the splints.

Complementarity is also evident on a larger scale. Because specific plants and animals live together in an area, a knowledge of certain materials may come to be associated with a place or community: ash splint work with the Abenaki and Iroquois Nations, for example, or birch bark with the Algonquin and Attikamek; naturally tanned skins with the northern Cree and Naskapi-Montagnais. In a sense, the instruments made from specific materials also complement one another, different types embodying specific locales and environments within the total sound of Creation.

In the construction of a sound-producing instrument, furthermore, the maker establishes a temporal relationship with the materials s/he is using. An instrument's manufacture sometimes not only takes time but embodies time (with materials of different ages perhaps) and reflects an awareness of proper conduct within the cycling of time (perhaps by the choice of material at the right time of day or the right moment of maturity as we discussed in our dialogue). Similarly, the instrument is a dynamic, living entity which requires ongoing care. It must be renewed and respected. This might be a simple process such as changing a drum head when it is dirty (with reference to HEY 13/3098, an Innu drum-maker contrasted the dirty and uncared for membrane of a museum instrument with those in the bush where membranes were kept clean and replaced when damaged), or a more complex, ceremonial one. Design, or attachments, might be added at a later time to reflect new relationships (e.g., tobacco ties attached to instruments or masks used in Longhouse curing doings or ceremonies). Some of these aspects are explored further in Chapter Six.

The processing of materials in the construction of an instrument may also bear a resemblance to metaphors explored earlier. Cycles of a repeated sequence of actions remind us of successive dance circuits or song repetitions. When Micmac instrument maker René Martin of Restigouche, Quebec, created a drum (so that Franziska could record the whole process photographically), we noted that he alternated use of electric and hand tools—a chainsaw for first cuts but a hand chisel to remove wood, layer by layer, from the vessel interior as well as a hatchet to cut away exterior bark at the top and then the bottom of the drum vessel.

At an Anishnabe drum-making workshop in Birch Island, Ontario, in 1986, the cycling of layers of yarn and contact cement to form the properly

Photo 80. Micmac drum-maker, René Martin, from Restigouche, Quebec. Photos by FvR.

Photo 81. Micmac drum-maker, René Martin.

Photo 82. Drummer Tom Paul with Micmac drum-maker, René Martin.

shaped ends of Northern-style drumsticks, was explained as shown in Figure 16.

The treatment of skins may require similar cycles. The alternation of scraping, stretching, washing, and applying paste are described in field notes made by Frank Speck in Temagami:

A caribou skin is first "scraped on [the] flesh side with [the] vertical leg bone (tibia) or iron bladed scraper; [it is then] stretched on [a] frame or laid on [the] ground. [It is] worked over [with a] fleshing stick stuck into [the] ground to remove fat and grease." Second, the instrument maker tries "to remove hair[;] hair [is] scraped off, with the grain not against it, on [a] slanting round log set in [the] ground with [a] *pɔckwuteigɔn*, [a] leg-bone (radius) spokeshave for two hands. ([It is] often soaked previously in brine.) . . . [The] skin (either with hair or without) [is] washed in water and hung to dry in shade." Third, the "skin [is] rubbed on [the] flesh side with [a] paste of caribou brains, marrow, fat (and flour) rubbed on [the] outside, while spread on [the] ground. [The] skin [is] washed again and allowed to dry partly. [It is] rubbed with powdered clay, chalk or burned bone or flour to absorb fatty matter." Fourth, the "skin [is] pulled and stretched by several persons and dried gradually by the friction. The skin [is] wrung by twisting with a tourniquet (or two) held in [the] hands or suspended from a tree." Fifth, the "skin [is] washed and smeared with brains again, then pulled, wrung and slowly dried by friction again if [the] first operations do not soften it enough, as in [the] case of thick skin. Repeat if necessary, three to five times." Sixth, if white skin is desired, the "skin is stretched on [a] frame and left for days exposed to frost drying to whiten it. In this condition it is not washable, but dries stiff after being wet." On the other hand, "smoking [is used] for brown or reddish skin. [It is] sewed into [the] form of [a] funnel bag, with [a] canvas neck and smoked (time according to judgement, generally several hours). It is then washable and dries soft after being wet. [It is] smoked with chips ([in] Ungava with fungus)."[9]

Process is integrally linked to the appropriate care of the instrument and the achievement of the right sound in the explanations of instrument makers. The aforementioned Anishnabe drumstick direction sheet contrasted the softer sound of Northern drumsticks from the "Southern style."

In a set of directions for the Iroquois water drum by Cayuga Confederacy Chief Deskaheh (also known as Levi General),[10] the proper balance of both air and water are described as complements of the right sound:

Indian Drum—directions for care and tuning it Right[.]
First: If the tub and leather is in a state of dryness, place
the tub and leather in water long enough to soak it
through or just pour some water in the tub and place
the leather in there to soak, then take the leather out,

Fig. 16. From the Birch Island Drum-making Workshop, 1986.

Northern Style Drum sticks are usually shorter and have more whip than Southern Style. They also usually have furs for their head, making a softer drum sound. The style and method shown here have been worked out with the help of Great Lakes area singers and is tried and tested over several years.

Materials:
1 Fiber Glass rod cut to 19"
1 Quantity of Yarn
1 Pc. imitation fur (Optional - Icelandic Sheep or Short Sheep fur
1 03. Contact Cement
1 Bobbin Size F Nylon thread
1 Glovers Needle
1 Pc. Buckskin

Steps:
1

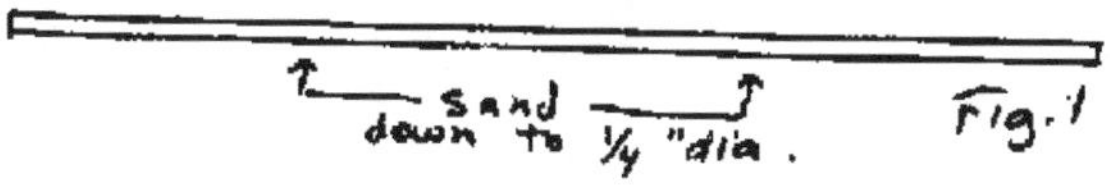

Sand down to 1/4 "dia.   Fig. 1

2. Apply glue to 5½" at top of rod. Begin winding yarn over the 5½" area. After one layer is applied, cover yarn with Contact Cement. Continue to add layers of yarn and Cement until desired Shape and Size is attained.

Fig. 2

3. Apply glue over last layer and let dry.

4. Cut fur for head as shown in Figure 3.

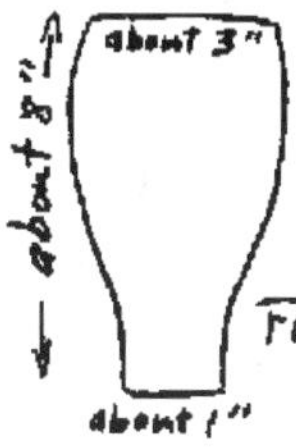

about 3"
about 8"
Fig. 3
about 1"

5. Hold fur in place on head and fold over the Top 1½ inches. Draw edges Together and sew for a tight fit using a baseball stitch, from the Top of the head To the bottom. (Trim excess off Fur piece as you go if necessary)

thread
Fold over top.
Fig. 4

6. Apply Glue and yarn To handle in the desired Shape as in Steps 2 & 3

Fig. 5

7. Custom fit the buckskin cover on the handle Like a baseball cover. Starting at the bottom of the stick, Sew using a baseball stitch towards the Center of the drum stick. Use small, Carefully spaced Stitches.

Fig. 6
Buckskin
Cover
Shape

drain some of the water but leave enough to cover the bottom of the tub, now place the leather over on rough side out, then slip the hoop down but not too tight at first until the leather is stretched, by using the split stick, how to make the stick, get a hickory stick green about half inch diameter in length 12 inches or any kind of wood in same limpness—split this stick in the center about eight inches of the whole length, then place the leather end between the split stick, then grip the split end with your hand this will hold fast of leather then give it some turn in order to get more purchase on leather. Then press it downwards by portion of your weight repeat this all around the tub where ever you can get ahold of ends of leather then tighten the hoop to hold the leather in position, you can now beat the drum to test the sound, now the water which you left in the drum becomes necessary when in use (the beating of drum), leather is subject to drying so just by shaking the drum [at] intervals the leather is kept moist, and that is too much air in the drum and to relieve just take the pluck [plug] out then replace it again, you will notice the difference. (F.G. Speck Papers, Box N7, Freeman MS no. 553; letter from Deskaheh, ca. 1910-20, Six Nations Reserve)

Other construction differences may relate to regional preferences, specific usage, or experiential elements which dictated the needs of the drum. Lacing styles are a case in point. Montagnais consultants related different procedures to community preferences; the rawhide was wound around rims in two westernmost communities but laced through drilled holes around Uashat and Maliotenam. We are uncertain that the contrasts in Anishnabe lacing styles, on the other hand, are simply regional differences.

Many processes in the construction of an instrument result in a transformation. Some, such as the application of paint/dye/varnish, the carving, incising, or burning of design, or the addition of

Photo 84. "X-lacing" with a fur-covered perimeter. Ojibwe frame drum collected by Dennis Walsh in Minnesota (CMC III-G-900).

Photo 85. "Triple" lacing. Plains Cree frame drum, made by Big Knife from Star Blanket Reserve, Saskatchewan. Elders recently shared the following information with the Glenbow Museum: **Big Knife made the drum in about 1925. His father, Ohoo, or Owl, taught him how to make the drum. There was no special ceremony or dance associated with it; it could be used any time a drum was needed.** (GLE AP445. FvR 88/24/14).

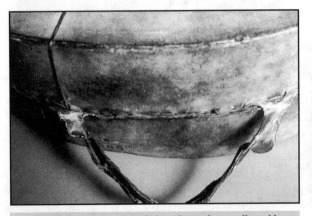

Photo 83. "Running" stitch. Ojibwe frame drum collected by Frederick Johnson at Parry Island, Ontario, in 1928 (HEY 16/2589. FvR 88/41/2).

Photo 86. Innu lacing style: through angled holes in frame and rim. American Museum of Natural History (MSC).

Colour Plate 1. The Birch Creek Singers (left) and "Micmac Dancers" from Eskasoni (right) perform inter-tribal and local music and dance at the Nova Scotia Summer Games (Cambridge, NS). They have both shared and separate repertoires. Sarah Denny accompanies the Micmac Dancers on a hand drum for some dances. Photo by FvR.

Colour Plate 2. Ojibwe "grandfather" water drum (GLE R1792.9a, b, and d. FvR 88/28/31).

Colour Plate 3. Ojibwe "grandfather" water drum from Mille Lacs, Minnesota, collected by D. Walsh (CMC III-G-893. FvR 88/6/27).

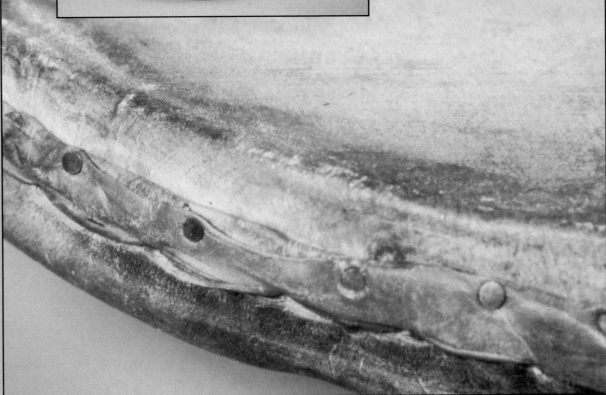

Colour Plate 4. "Sky" (blue on bottom edge) and "earth" worlds (red on top) meet. Ojibwe frame drum/rattle acquired from dealer Jonathan Holstein. Museum documentation describes this as a Midewiwin drum (CMC III-G-1109. FvR 88/11/9).

Colour Plate 5. Ojibwe dance drum stand probably made in the late nineteenth century. Each of the four curved posts is decorated with beads and bells (HEY 11/5864. FvR 88/40/25).

Colour Plate 6. Ojibwe dance drum probably made in the late nineteenth century. The frame is covered with red and navy wool, fastened with brass tacks. A heavy, wooden ball-ended drumstick painted red with a yellow ring around the handle accompanies the drum (HEY 11/5864. FvR 88/40/37).
"The red and blue exterior sometimes separates the male and female halves." (Jim Dumont)

Colour Plate 7. Miniature medicine drum, possibly Ojibwe. Collected in the late nineteenth century by James Mclaughlin and housed formerly in the Old South Church (PEAH 30-69/K58. FvR 87/11/1).

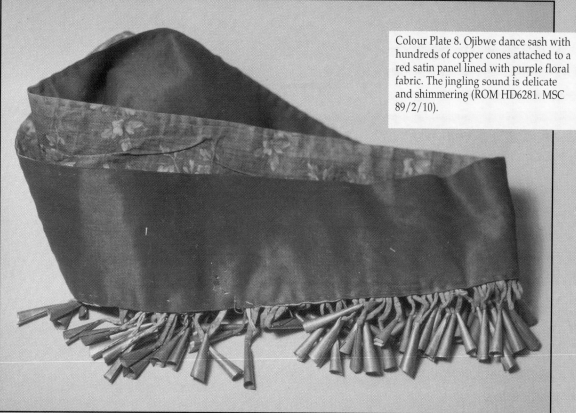

Colour Plate 8. Ojibwe dance sash with hundreds of copper cones attached to a red satin panel lined with purple floral fabric. The jingling sound is delicate and shimmering (ROM HD6281. MSC 89/2/10).

Colour Plate 9. Ojibwe drum. Isaacs/Innuit Gallery, Toronto. Photo by A. Isaacs.

Colour Plate 10. Ojibwe frame drum collected north of Lake Superior ca. 1830 by Robert Shackleton. See Fig. 14 for an interpretation of the image (HEY 9976. FvR 88/40).

Colour Plate 11.
Mohawk hemispheric
drum from
Kahnawake, Quebec.
Collected in the 1930s
(MCC M18207.
BD 88/2/5).

Colour Plate 12.
A large (58 cm
diameter) Cree
drum from
Deer Lake,
Ontario (CMC
III-D-63. FvR
88/8/19).

Colour Plate 13. Maliseet horn rattle with elaborately carved and painted images. The rattle was made by George Frederick Paul of St. Mary's, New Brunswick, in the 1970s and is privately owned (FvR 85/2/5).

Colour Plate 14. Eddie Kabatay with the "thunderer's" drum he made ca. 1975. He explained that it was given to him by an old woman at Seine River, Ontario, so that he would keep the tradition going (FvR 85/2/20).

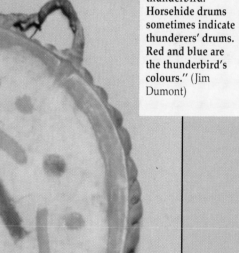

Colour Plates 15 and 16. Ojibwe frame drum made by Gekay at Sagawamick. Collected by David Bushnell around 1900 (PEAH 41-72/24397. FvR 87/12/13). **"The horse is associated with the thunderbird. Horsehide drums sometimes indicate thunderers' drums. Red and blue are the thunderbird's colours."** (Jim Dumont)

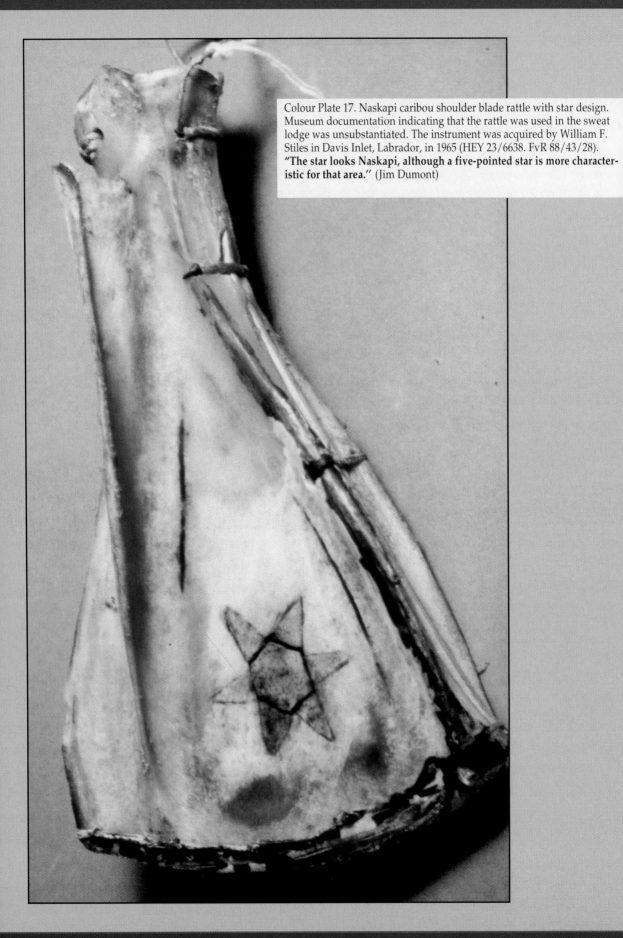

Colour Plate 17. Naskapi caribou shoulder blade rattle with star design. Museum documentation indicating that the rattle was used in the sweat lodge was unsubstantiated. The instrument was acquired by William F. Stiles in Davis Inlet, Labrador, in 1965 (HEY 23/6638. FvR 88/43/28). **"The star looks Naskapi, although a five-pointed star is more characteristic for that area."** (Jim Dumont)

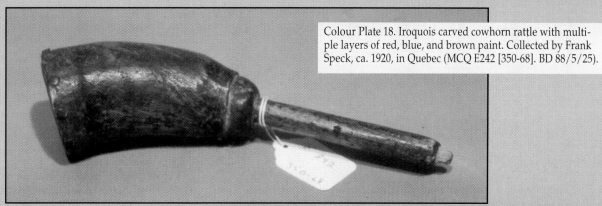

Colour Plate 18. Iroquois carved cowhorn rattle with multiple layers of red, blue, and brown paint. Collected by Frank Speck, ca. 1920, in Quebec (MCQ E242 [350-68]. BD 88/5/25).

Colour Plate 19. Cree disc rattle with a shiny, transparent membrane. Collected in Chisasibi, Quebec, by Michel Brochu in the 1960s (MCQ 966-45-II. BD 88/5/7). **"Some disc rattles were made from the ejected stomach lining of birds. A wooden frame was inserted to create a cavity and the rattlers were the seeds in the bird's stomach."** (Bertha Mathat)

Colour Plate 20. Potawatomi water drums with inversely related blue and red painted vessels and membranes. Collected by M.R. Harrington in 1912 (HEY 2/7601 and 2/7602. FvR 88/42/10). **"The colour order may indicate male and female."** (Jim Dumont)

Colour Plate 21. Iroquois turtle rattle, collected around the turn of the century. This instrument type is usually painted black or left a natural dark colour, but is painted, in this instance, with bright flowers and variegated dots outlining the shell's thirteen segments (HEY 9153. FvR 88/41/15).

Colour Plate 22. Green Ojibwe gourd rattle, collected by D. Walsh in Minnesota (CMC III-G-910. FvR 88/18/7). **"Green is the woman's colour."** (Jim Dumont)

Colour Plate 23. Anishnabe frame drum with a green sector on one membrane. A blue ring around the circumference and along the top of the green sector may separate earth and sky. Collected by Densmore in Minnesota (SI 278116. MSC 87/3).

Colour Plate 24.
Grass dancer, Odawa
powwow, 1987.
Photo by FvR.

Colour Plate 25. Early twentieth-century Montagnais drum of Chief Joseph Kurtness of Pointe Bleue, Quebec. The realistically styled imagery covers both membranes, each of which has a babiche snare with five bone rattlers (MAPB. BD 86/3/26-33).

Colour Plate 26. Early twentieth-century Naskapi carved antler drumstick, collected by Frank Speck in northern Labrador. The wedge-shaped distal end has notches of different shapes along the perimeter. The front face is naturally half grey and half ivory coloured and this division extends the length of the stick. Rings are incised around the handle (HEY 15/5558. FvR 88/45/10-18). **"At an earlier period, things were more individualized. Now, even from one community to another, they are more uniform."** (Alexandre Michel) ˇ

Colour Plate 27. Lige, all ears, in 1985. Photo by MSC.

Photo 87. Innu frame drum with lacing wound around outer rims. Teueikan from Betsiamites, 1892 (PEAH 94-38/62489. FvR 87/11/15).
"The lacing style is from further West [than Sept-Îles]. . . . **It probably saves time since you don't have to drill holes for the lacing."** (Alexandre Michel)

"attachments" function in an individual manner and may indicate a change in the relationships of the owner/user (see description of III-I-465 in Chapter Six). Others are fundamental transformations which give a new voice to the materials. A four-legged creature becomes a good drum voice. A segment of a tree trunk or a cowhorn has the ability to "ring" because its walls are made thin. A gourd dries so that its seeds become delicate "shimmering" rattlers. Obviously, the effectiveness of the instrument's voice is dependent on the care and skill with which the processes are carried out. Less obvious, perhaps, is the sense that each cyclical repetition in the construction process may be experienced in a manner analogous to the circuits of a social dance or the successive strophes of a song as a strengthening of the voice of the instrument.

Virtually every process teaches patience.

Shape and Pattern

In our discussions with elders, and in our language studies, we were struck by the frequency with which pattern and shape were mentioned. As we discussed in Chapter Two, an object might be seen as a visual metaphor for other similarly shaped phenomena in the universe. Certain shapes—the circle, the turtle's shell, the lodge, the Iroquoian tree of peace and skydome—embody fundamental philosophical principles. It seems appropriate to consider such fundamental shapes first, since these are some of the foundations on which other patterns are superimposed or within which other patterns are emphasized or highlighted.

Circle Imagery

By far the most prevalent shape for musical instruments is the circle, or its three-dimensional form, the globe. Regarded as the most basic shape in nature—the shape and path of the earth, sun, moon, and stars; the trees' rings; the footprint of a tipi, the motion of a sound wave or a ripple produced when a stone is thrown in the water, the limbs of the body as well as the head (to name some instances)—circularity is a basic tenet of Anishnabe and Innu thinking and living as described in Chapter Two.[11] A central icon for Haudenosaunee is the symbol of a circle of chiefs, holding hands, encircling the tree of peace—an image made tangible by the chiefs' wampum, a circle of shells which represents the confederacy of the Six Nations.

Many types of sound producers replicate the circle, of course, either in two dimensions (as with the frame drum or disc rattle, or with certain types of Anishnabe drumsticks which have disc-shaped striking ends associated by some with the shape of the lacrosse stick) or three dimensions (as with the distal end of many drumstick types as well as the gourd or globe rattles, the latter more common among Plains peoples but also found in the westernmost communities of the area usually designated "Eastern Woodlands"). Iroquois and Anishnabe water drums as well as Innu frame drums have circle-upon-circle: rim over round vessel or frame.

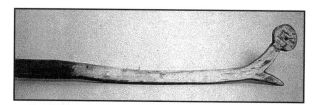

Photo 88. Cree ceremonial drumstick collected by C.H. Brown in 1952 in Pekangekum [*sic*], Ontario (CMC III-D-64. FvR 88/19/23).

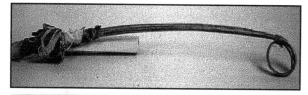

Photo 89. Plains Cree drumstick made from tree roots. Made by Nathan Gavain from the Red Earth Reserve, Saskatchewan, for use in the Rain Dance (CMC III-D-717b. FvR 88/19/11).
Compare CMC III-D-63b about which Anishnabe consultant Jim Dumont remarked: **"The shape of this drumstick, the lacrosse stick, and disc rattle are all related."**

Some rarer types such as the hemispheric drum shapes of Mohawk and Micmac cultures are segments of spheres.[12]

Photo 90. Workshop on drumstick-making, Birch Island, Ontario, 1986.

Sometimes associations with the circle are pragmatic. Iroquoian water drums, made from cylindrical tree trunks, have drum heads secured, of necessity, by round rims. Sometimes the symbolic associations of the circular are made explicit. The Innu *teueikan* (frequently with red outer rims) is depicted as the sun or fire in some contemporary artists' work. This association may have roots in the Tshakapesh myth, wherein the hero tries to snare the sun, or in the experience of hunters who sometimes see "fire" in the drum.[13] The painted membrane designs on other frame drums were sometimes interpreted as sun symbols (SPINC ID:III.?.1004.d, HUR). The latter image resembles symbols described as "sun motifs" by Ruth Phillips (1987: 58-59). Yarn loops, or ribbon in some areas (see CMC III-C-318), around the circumference of some disc rattles (e.g., HEY 13/3224) were sometimes also related to the sun's rays.

Fig. 17. Michael W. Francis's drawings and explanation of the construction of a Micmac hemispheric drum.

"Now the paper was cut, right, that birchbark. We make the centre here, then we cut it there, then you fold that.

"Like an ice cream cone. The cone, it is sewn together. Now what you do, you put mud, clay, mud, mud, and you go to work and leave this open. This is going to be set down on the ground; you just set it down flat on the ground, smooth it on the bottom. You put it on [the ground] just like a saucer. . . . Then you go to work to pile your mud, corner first, just like that, against the birchbark. You wet it down so the mud will stick to the ground. Then after it is done, pile the mud all around it. Smooth it down. Thick mud. About an inch and a half thick mud. The whole thing. This is all solid. Be sure to put little rocks all [around] to show that nobody steps on it."Then *ji'kmaqn* goes up here. Tap, tap tap, that sound. This sounds hollow—the bark inside—tun tun tun. This was the sound it make.

"Be sure to water it down. Take all the grass away and pack it with clay. Let it dry and then put loose dirt on top and let it dry for several days. A little grass grow on it.

"The sound will echo through the ground. The ground brings out the sound. It will transmit the sound outside. . . . The sound will just carry, the same as waves in water. You hit that water—waves. Now this one is same principle, like a pulsation going out from it. The sound will carry for quite a ways. . . . It is amazing all the sounds you can get. Only certain people, they meditate. Her son played it. He played it and then she played it and the son played the rattle. It is something about the vibration of the ground. She said 'ke keuk,' 'let me call an earthquake.' "

Fig. 18. The logo of the Innu Nikamu festival held each August in Maliotenam, Quebec.

Photo 91. Naskapi disc rattle (SPINC ID:III.B.54.r. FvR 88/43. Compare SPINC ID:III.C.3002.r).
"From an Abenaki perspective [note that the rattle is Naskapi], **this type can be used by women. The symbolism is that the yarn represents rays of the sun.''** (Nicole Obomsawin)

For some Anishnabe interpreters, painted circles can also indicate a perspective on other spheres. These designs frequently involve not just a single circle but a pattern of concentric circles. Published studies associate the pattern with elements of the sky world: Mallery (1972: 695) depicts four concentric circles as a sun symbol; Densmore suggested that Mide drawings use a double circle to represent "the sky, in which the moon is seen" (1972: 16). Some Anishnabek with whom we worked, on the other hand, saw painted rings as indicators of perspective, rather than "representations" of other spheres.

Hence, a red ring might indicate a view into the sky world as described in "Situation 1" (p. 99).[14]

A mythological basis for this interpretation may be found in the story of Cingibis, a Temagami version of which was narrated as follows:[15]

CINGIBIS:

"There were people camping, same as here. In winter time bush band wigwams. That time all animals could talk together and two girls were sleeping out of doors, made their bed there. They were red (real?) like rest of people. They were foolish, talk foolish. That's another foolish [thing?] to sleep outside in winter. One of those girls asked other. What star you like to sleep with, the white or red? Other says I like to sleep with red star. Oh that's all right. Other says I like s[leep] with white star; that's the y[oungest]. The red is oldest. Then they slept. When wake up they saw there was there two girls, two stars. The white star was very old, gray bearded, the youngest was red here that was red star. They were disappointed. They found themselves in another world, the star world. They stayed long time. The one who had white star was very sorry her man was so old.

"There was old w[oman] there who sat over hole. When she moved a little she showed them hole and said 'That's where you came from.' They looked thro[ugh] and saw people playing down below. The girls were sorry, they homesick. One evening near sunset o[ld] w[oman] moved a little way from hole.

"The hole is seven stars in circle. This was the first MITEWIN lodge and seven poles are necessary. Unless seven are used conjurer's tent will not rock. She [tempts?] (old woman) the Mitewin. When she moves [?] from hole there is sure to be mitewin somewhere here below. The stars form rim of hole through which she helps the y[oung] girls.

"The y[oung] girls heard the noise of MITEWIN down below. When pretty near daylight again o[ld] w[oman] sat on hole again and noise of mitewin stopped. It was her spirit."

Anishnabe and Innu disc rattles (and handleless drum/rattles) are especially relevant for the discussion of concentric circles, since a number of variants of the basic design occur in this instrument type. In some instances, the exterior (stitched area) of the rattle is the painted "ring" and a central circle often painted on each membrane is the "one" (CMC III-B-536). Here, the rings are in different planes. In other instances, the concentric images are in one dimension, but possibly distinguished by different colours (CMC III-B-356; CMC III-D-716). In other cases, a central, more realistic image is encircled by a blue- or red-ringed border (GLE AP3102). Some Plains Ojibwe rattles are doughnut shaped (i.e., the central "circle" is an actual hole as in GLE AP2850).

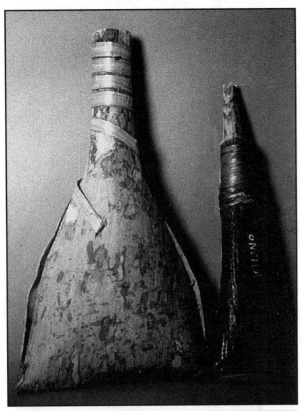

Photo 92. Layers: Iroquoian bark rattles made from an interior and exterior layer of bark, respectively. CMC III-I-1158, made by A. Jamieson, Six Nations Reserve and collected by McFeat and Twarecki in 1965, and CMC III-I-1405, provenance unknown but obtained by the museum from Saul Hendler ca. 1976 (FvR 88/8:31).

Photo 93. Layers: Attikamek and Algonquin moose calls as well as a tiny "pipe" made like a moose call. The largest is described in the museum's catalogue as an Attikamek moose call although it was made "for sale" by Wallace Molson from the predominantly Algonquin community of Winneway, Ontario, where it was collected by A. Webber in 1975. Note the seven birchbark bands of different circumferences, each with a distinctive arrow-shaped join (MCQ 75-183. BD 88/8/37).

Rings on Anishnabe grandfather water drums may be painted at different positions around the drum vessel. We were told that, in some contexts, these could be clan indicators, in others they might emanate from a personal dream, while in others, they could designate a male or female drum (see CMC III-G-893).[16] Concentric rings might also be painted on drum membranes where they may be associated with higher degrees of the Midewewin lodge (see Winnebago drums, HEY 2/7601 and 7602, Colour Plate 20). Of course, the top rim securing the membrane and often also a bottom hoop constitute other concentric rings with the drum vessel or membrane itself as the inner circle.

Four-direction Imagery

In other Anishnabe instances, circular designs were associated with direction, the four cardinal points on the axes which defined the circle, or Medicine Wheel. For Anishnabek, the four directions symbolize concepts which are fundamental to spirituality. They take many forms, sometimes emphasizing the sectoring of the circle (SPINC ID:III.D.1000.d, at HUR), sometimes the directions themselves or those in-between the cardinal points (Amherst; HEY 2088; MCC ME967x.45; CMC III-I-229), and sometimes representing floral petals, hearts, or elements of the natural world (SPINC ID:III.B.3003.r and 3004.r at MAB) to cite only a few examples. Occasionally, the four directions merge with other symbols (HEY 24/2275 with arcs which were interpreted as mountains). Obviously, such descriptions are reductive; each teaching of the Medicine Wheel, for example, and its many elements requires far greater space and time to be more fully understood. Even after these several years of conversation, we realize that we understand only the most basic principles, those which can be appropriately discussed with non-Native people during limited time frames of interviews and conferences. During such stages of learning, what is most easily accessible to us are the lists of different components and interpretations; what is likely more important within this holistic framework are the connections and relationships among these components, all existing simultaneously, layer upon layer.

Within Anishnabe music, the symbolism of directions is represented not just in instrument design and decoration but also in some of the processes of construction and use. The Creation story of Eddie Benton-Benai presented some aspects of this in Chapter Two. He described the four curved wooden posts, each placed at a cardinal point, and cross-lacing, especially on frame drums (see close-up photo of Maliseet drum, SPINC ID:III.F.6.d).

Photo 94. Ojibwe drumstick for a grandfather drum collected by A.B. Reagan in Bois Forts, Minnesota, in 1912 (CMC III-G-33. FvR 88/1/1).

With reference to sticks of this design, Anishnabe consultant Jim Dumont said: **"Sticks made in the cross shape are more recent than the bird/horse-shaped ones. The one direction is longer."**

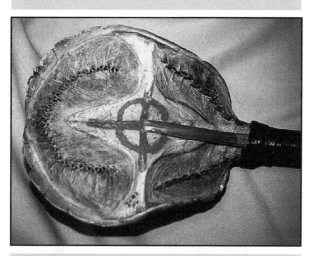

Photo 95. Painted design enhancing the natural divisions of the turtle's belly. Iroquois rattle, provenance unknown (RMSC AE2876. MSC 87/10/29).

Photo 97. Incised wooden plug in a Seneca cowhorn rattle made by Jackson Jamieson at the request of C.M. Barbeau in 1911. Jamieson was originally from Six Nations but living in Oklahoma (CMC III-I-229. FvR 88/4/7).

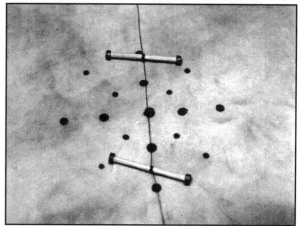

Photo 98. Painted design (dots) on Montagnais frame drum (MCQ 87-3654.1. BD 88/8/9).

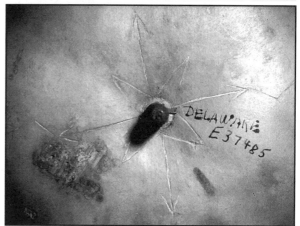

Photo 99. An incised pattern on the distal end of a Delaware gourd rattle, collected by Mrs. Sterling Pool (PEAS E37485. FvR 87/10/5).

Photo 96. Four-dimensional lacing on a Passamaquoddy drum played by Donna Newell. Privately owned (FvR 88/35/2).

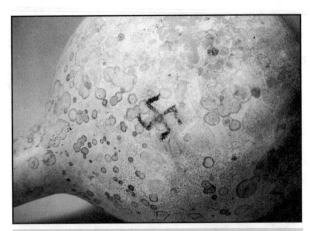

Photo 100. Four directions in motion. Iroquois gourd rattle, purchased ca. 1944 by Ernest Dodge from Alexander General (PEAS E24984. FvR 87/8/20).

"The symbol is the life symbol, the sun symbol, the four directions in motion. People say that when Hitler used the swastika, he put this ancient symbol on its side and the negative aspect emerged." (Jim Dumont)

While the Medicine Wheel and its four-direction symbolism has been widely discussed at Elders Conferences, and in both scholarly and "popular" publications by both Native and non-Native writers, two aspects rarely mentioned are the *motion* of the wheel and instances when the directions are *unequal*.

For Anishnabek, there are patterns which visually represent the four directions in motion (PEAS E2984, HEY 24/2275). In some cases, however, this aspect is represented by the fact that the directional axes in design are not quite aligned with the cardinal points. Jim Dumont explained to us that the force of the cardinal directions may be so great that ceremonial gestures (within the pipe ceremony, for example) may be performed a little to the side of North, South, East, or West. By analogy, the alignment of patterns on the membrane of a drum or the position of a snare may be slightly off-axis. The subject of motion will be developed further in the final chapter of this book.

In the non-judgemental ideal of Native discourse, we have most often heard that the different peoples around the circle are not hierarchically arranged, nor are different stages in the cycle of life. Each is valued and necessary. There are, however, some contexts in which the directions are not equal. Drumsticks which are made from two pieces of wood at right angles may represent one direction as longer and more powerful than the other three (CMC III-G-33).

On the Montagnais *teueikan*, the E/W snare is on top and the N/S is on the underside of the membrane. On a Passamaquoddy drum design the N/S axis is painted with a yellow, wavy line, the E/W with a straight blue line. Some Anishnabe inter-

preters see the former as the spirit pathway, the latter as the human. Although this symbolism was not explicitly articulated by Innu consultants, their practice may be implicitly the same, since the invisible snare below the membrane, the sound of which was often described as spirit voices, is the N/S snare. Other arrangements of snares are used in other contexts, of course. Cree frame drums usually have parallel snares (often two or three) from N to S on either side of the membrane (e.g., see CMC III-D-63 and Colour Plate 12). Certain archival instruments (particularly double-membrane Anishnabe frame drums of the type sometimes designated *wabeno*, or medicine, drums) had interior snares only; one such instrument (HEY 9976) had snares from W to S and N to E, an unusual variation from the axes at right angles. From different perspectives, then, the significance may vary.

Among the Haudenosaunee, the concept of directionality has both practical and philosophical implications. One dances counter-clockwise (only during biannual *Oghiwe*, or Feast of the Dead, do you travel in the clockwise direction of dead spirits); it is not advised to sleep with your head facing west (again, because of a physical connection with the dead); the metaphoric Longhouse representing the Iroquoian Confederacy has both eastern and western "doors" (represented by the Mohawk and Seneca Nations respectively); and the roots of the symbolic tree of peace extend to the four directions, thus inviting all of humanity to join the Confederacy. While the cardinal points are occasionally represented (RMSC AE2876; PEAH 03-32/62613), they appear only infrequently on musical instruments. Sometimes the natural segmentation into four quarters on the underside of the turtle may be emphasized by a variety of painted designs (examples are described below). However, it is important to remember that, although certain designs appear cross-culturally, they may be interpreted very differently. Perhaps more significant than comparing design elements is recognizing philosophical parallels. Certainly, Longhouse communities also acknowledge the many directions of the wind, the cycle of seasons, sacred plants, ideal moral qualities, and the diverse races of humanity, but the Medicine Wheel is not their teaching, and thus its specific imagery is infrequently used.

Realistic: Earth and Water Realms

An important category of design moves us from the stylized to the realistic. In basketry, beadwork, appliqué, and weaving, as well as on musical instruments, the creation of floral or animal designs may play several roles. Some "realistic" patterns are mnemonic, although these are not generally associated with musical instruments as much as with Iroquois condolence canes, Anishnabe song/speech practice boards/books, or Midewiwin song scrolls. Many naturalistic forms relate to identity: an Iroquoian tree of peace, for example, might indicate your Nation; a small turtle rattle, your clan; specific berries or leaves, your environs. Art historian David Penney has suggested that some Nations may use floral imagery to mediate between cultures.

Through the discourse of exchange and marketplace, floral images came to represent an Indian identity that could be marketed to whites by the Huron. . . . [T]housands of articles decorated with floral patterns were sold to Euro-Americans up through the twentieth century, as evidenced by their abundance in museum collections. (1991: 63)

He regards floral styles as an ethnic signifier which also functions as "a subversion of mission-taught embroidery" (ibid.: 71).

A wide range of style in naturalistic representations is evident in the collections which we documented. In some instances, a figure may be represented by a mere outline, while in others, fine detail such as the texture of fur is conveyed (e.g., compare the caribou images on the Algonquin birch-bark moose call, MCQ 80 24.5.7 3, and a Micmac one, MCC M103). By some, gradations of colour (e.g., CMC III-G-742) may be preferred, while others choose to create bold, contrasted figures (e.g., MCQ 75-281; see also Colour Plate 13).

Photo 102. The same late nineteenth-century Ojibwe drum (bottom). The top and bottom membranes exhibit dramatically different styles of painted design.

Photo 103. Iroquois rattle made from a coconut with painted "sunburst" imagery (HEY 1/2826. FvR 88/33/26 and 28).

Photo 101. Late nineteenth-century Ojibwe drum (top) belonged to John Pete from Mole Lake, Wisconsin, where it was collected by Mr. and Mrs. John Shalloch in the 1940s (CMC III-G-742. FvR 88/3/2).

Photo 104. Attikamek moose calls purchased in the 1960s in Manouane, Quebec. The alternation of positive and negative layers, each with a different style of imagery, represents a "layered" universe (MCQ 69-71. BD 88/8/5).

Photo 105. Iroquois water drum. Photo by M.S. Cronk (SINM).

Photo 108.

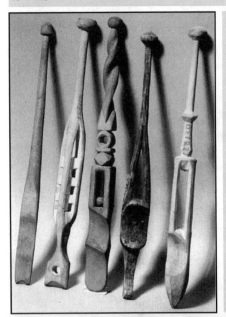

Photo 106. Iroquois water drum-sticks from the Peabody-Salem collection (FvR 87/9/14).

Photo 107. Different styles on top and bottom (Photo 108) membranes of a single Ojibwe drum. Isaacs/Innuit Gallery, Toronto. Photo by A. Isaacs.

The turtle, which represents North America (Turtle Island) and is a clan animal, is obviously an important part of both Iroquoian and Algonquian worlds. On or as a sound producer, it may appear in either stylized or realistic forms. In the Anishnabe Midewiwin, the turtle appears sometimes as a rattle, or it may be associated with the "grandfather" drum as the being that swims up from below the earth to plug the bottom of the drum with its shell; hence, its image may be found on that bottom (see CMC III-G-743). MCQ 965-19A, an Iroquois water drum with an ambiguous figure which may be a turtle, is a rare example outside of Anishnabe contexts. The membrane for some Anishnabe drums may be cut in the shape of a turtle, perhaps reversing the orientation of the drum with regard to earth and sky worlds. Turtle images are occasionally painted on Anishnabe drum or drum/rattle membranes, although some examples of such an image are ambiguous composites, as mentioned earlier.

In museums, we encountered dozens of Iroquoian turtle rattles,[17] instruments important in several Longhouse ceremonial contexts (used by singers during the Great Feather Dance and by members of the Wooden Face Society). Both snapping and box turtles are used as rattles, the latter associated solely with the women's *Towisas* (which celebrates certain plants, "Our Life Supporters"). Naturally, Iroquoian and Anishnabe perspectives of the turtle differ—the shell is not described by Haudenosaunee as a pathway of life, nor are the divisions of the shell interpreted as stages of life, as some Ojibwe consultants discussed. However, snapping turtle shell segments are sometimes described as a calendar for the Iroquoian year. Significantly, Iroquoian turtle rattle-makers sometimes enhance natural features such as shell divisions or, more frequently, the edges of the shell (see HEY 9153 and Colour Plate 21, an unusually elaborate rattle with red and yellow/green dots outlining shell partitions as well as floral designs; RMSC 70.89.24; and CMC III-I-1105 which draws attention to the natural segments in a different manner, by means of a small red circle on each). Yet with or without decoration, this naturally patterned rim with its hemisphere-like repetitions resembles the sky-dome edging common in Iroquoian design on instruments (HEY 9153; CMC III-I-1201a; or ROM 17023), clothing, *gustoweh* (headdresses) and beadwork. The two parallel back splints which form a pathway down the centre of the shell are also often varnished or painted where they emerge from under the handle wrapping (e.g., RMSC AE2876).

When the turtle is turned over, the plastron (the natural quadrant division) of the underside is apparent; these natural patterns may be enhanced with paint in a number of different ways. Red paint on the quadrant divisions is the most frequent (HEY 9152, HEY 25/452, WICEC 975.6.51). Other instruments have green (AGE M69-34) or black quadrant division (see HEY 7/3606), sometimes with red edges in the centre of each quadrant (RMSC AE7107A11.341 or RMSC 70.89.25). Less usual are incised designs forming a cross or triangular pattern (ROM HD12709). The eyes of a turtle may also be filled or painted (see HEY 7/3606, BRA/SPINC ID:III.I.3022.r and BRA 972.13.33 which have wax-filled eyes; WICEC 978.49.1 which has blue beads inset in the eyes; RMSC E13.1.354, one of many rattles with a cord through the eyes). Nevertheless, many turtle rattles are left in their natural state or painted their own colour (the shell may be painted black, for example; see CMC III-I-118, CMC III-I-180, SI 253672, WICEC 978.56.3, 978.56.6). A brightly coloured Iroquoian rattle such as ROM 975.X7318 is

Photo 109. Frame of an early twentieth-century Ojibwe Midewiwin lodge in Northern Ontario. Public Archives of Canada (PA 131709). Photo by F. Waugh.

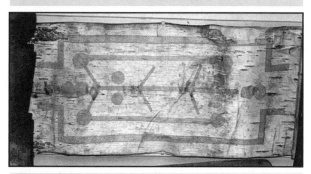

Photo 110. Ojibwe bark design. Heye Foundation display (FvR 88/45).

Photo 111. Iroquois *towisa* rattles (CMC III-I-1060 and III-I-144. FvR 88/13/7).

Photo 112. Micmac or Maliseet rattle. Department of Indian Affairs, Amherst, Nova Scotia. Photo by FvR.

"From an Anishnabe, Midewiwin perspective, the shell is the Mide lodge. The three images represent the three fires. The middle image is a tree. The handle insertion is the path of a bear who comes to the Eastern doorway and looks West. The Western doorway is the doorway of the Thunderbird." (Jim Dumont)

"The turtle rattle was important [for the Maliseet people] in the past. They used the shell only with a stick inserted. The turtle shell rattle was used in sweats." (Alma Brooks)

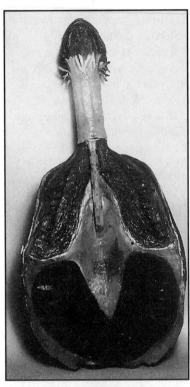

Photo 113. Turtle rattle (bottom) from Six Nations, Ontario. Collected by Chief John A. Gibson ca. 1911 (HEY 7/3606. FvR 88/41/10).

Photo 114. Turtle rattle (top) from Six Nations, Ontario (HEY 7/3606. FvR 88/41/9).

rattles, some resembling a turtle only in basic shape, some with intricately incised shell and plastron, are described by Iroquoian singers as "practice" instruments (CMC III-I-657, ROM HD15413, ROM HD15431), although those in museum collections appear minimally used. Both Iroquoian and Wabanaki turtle foot rattles are also occasionally found in collections (privately owned, SPINC ID:III.E.2.r), though such rattles are never used in the Iroquois Longhouse.

Other under-earth/underwater beings are also represented on sound producers. The powerful families of snakes, panthers, and horned beings may be painted or incised on Algonquian instruments. Anishnabe stories name the snake in conjunction with the rim of the grandfather drum, as in the description in Chapter Two. The rag-wrap coils about the hard core, as does the string overlay on many drums. By its ability to change shape—to become a circle in this instance—as well as its ability to transform through the shedding of its skin (the rag-wrap can be removed or replaced on the rim) the grandfather drum resembles the snake, which embodies similar characteristics (see earlier reference to comments by Black re percept ambiguity). Painted images of snakes are sometimes stylized (e.g., the Menominee border design which Skinner learned was a snake representation, 1921: 263):

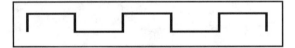

Underwater beings, such as a long-tailed panther, may be either painted or incised on Midewiwin drums (e.g., see the mid-nineteenth-century Plains Ojibwe water drum, BM 2223 with two panther figures facing one another, as well as its accompanying song board, depicted in J.C.H. King 1982: 62; or see GLE RY110). The same figure is found on pictographs north of Sault Ste. Marie, Ontario. The long tail is characteristic and was described by one of Skinner's Menominee consultants as "the panther road" (1921: 263). Hence, for both snake and panther, the notion of a pathway is relevant, but one which flexibly adapts to different shapes.

Closely associated with the panther is the bear, which is sometimes represented on the inset bottom of grandfather drums with a line through its middle to indicate that it is a spirit figure (GLE AP3116). Like the turtle, the bear appears in variants of the origin story of the grandfather drum (see, for example, James Redsky's version in *Great Leader of the Ojibway*: *Mis-quona-quab*, [1972]: 103-104) as the

an unusual exception, both in museum collections and in ceremonial use. (The resemblance of this particular rattle to the water drum, ROM 22265, raises the possibility that these two instruments may have been paired, although they were acquired by the museum at different times.) Carved wooden turtle creature who pushed the drum up through the earth. Several Ojibwe instruments (BM 2223 or GLE AP412), generally from Plains areas, are painted, in accordance with this story, half black or green (the portion which remained below the earth) and half red (above the earth).

For the Wabanaki, the snake is regarded positively. On a Micmac stick (SPINC ID:III.f.3006.d) the carved form of a snake affirms the clan membership of the instrument maker. (Similar snake designs may be found on Wabanaki pipes.) Abenaki consultants described the snake dance performed in a ceremony for adolescent boys. The horned headdress appropriate for this ceremony is sometimes worn at community festivals (see Photo 119).

Although the snake figures prominently in Wendat (Huron) myths and dances, it is rarely represented on musical instruments. At the Village Huron outside of Quebec, a giant snake is said to reside under the waterfall near the community (see story in Appendix A) and the snake dance is performed at community socials.

Images of snakes or horned serpents, or underwater beings are rare on Iroquoian instruments; Haudenosaunee view such creatures as negative and destructive forces. The Thunderers, our Grandfathers, are said to hurl lightning at them to destroy them. One turtle rattle documented by the Glenbow Museum as Iroquoian (GLE AG62) has added horse hair "whiskers" which, to our eyes, look like incipient horns; but the concept of "horned" snapping turtles (fierce enough in their own right) amused Iroquoian consultants. Snakes were found on carved drumsticks only in one collection (see HEY 23/7856 where the snake spirals toward the proximal end, which has a carved human head on it). The image brings to mind an Iroquoian story recorded by Parker of a pretty little snake brought home by a young boy; it grew in size and appetite, finally consuming the entire village. Interpretations of this story may identify the snake with non-Indians.[18]

Unlike snakes, the symbol of "horns" (or antlers) is as important in Iroquoian as in Algonquian cultures. Traditional Haudenosaunee Confederacy Chiefs have deer antlers on their *gustoweh* (or headdress) signifying their status and their connection to the peaceful strength of such animals. Some Iroquoian colleagues also link antlers to "antennae" signifying the ability of the chiefs to detect movement and oncoming danger. A cowhorn rattle made by Hubert Buck, Sr., now used by the Six Nations Women's Singing Society, has this incised design encircling the distal end. Although the pattern may

resemble the double curve motif, it clearly refers, in this context, to Hubert's role in the community.

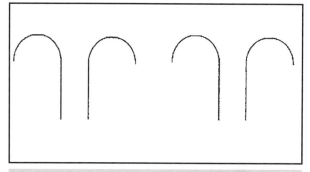

Fig. 19. Antler design incised on a cowhorn rattle made by Hubert Buck, Sr.

In Anishnabe culture, both the image and material of horn is regarded as powerful. We were told that the medicine of horn or bone material is not appropriate for the Midewiwin, although it serves in other healing contexts. Horn-shaped bones are sometimes added to a frame drum (e.g., CMC III-G-730) or even embedded in the wood of a grandfather water drum (Chicago Field Museum collection). Painted horns often resemble the crescent moon or the horns of the buffalo (see HEY 9976).

Photo 115. Ojibwe frame drum handle bone attachments. Acquired in the 1940s from the Shalloch family in Mole Lake, Wisconsin (CMC III-G-730. FvR 88/4/28).

Photo 116. Huron cowhorn rattle made by Ovide Sioui of Lorette, Quebec. Collected by C.M. Barbeau in 1911 (CMC III-H-40. FvR 88/5/2).

Photo 117. Iroquois turtle rattle with horsehair "horns" collected from M.D. Vernon in 1965 (GLE AP62. FvR 88/22/16).

Photo 119. Local attendee at the Fête des abénakis, 1988, wearing a replication of the ceremonial headdress described by Thérèse Obomsawin. Photo by BD.

Whole cowhorns are commonly used as rattles in Micmac, Abenaki, and Huron cultures. Iroquoian people truncate the horns and insert a wooden handle. A number of musicians and instrument makers say that the current type was preceded by a type using buffalo horns; we speculate that the horns from the wood buffalo which once inhabited New York State might have been used. We did see rare instances of horn shakers from the early twentieth century which used carved vessels, thicker than contemporary types (MCQ E242). The shapes and colours of horns selected for rattles seem to vary regionally. Abenaki and many Maliseet rattles are often dark, olive, or brown. Huron rattles, on the other hand, are most frequently light coloured with a black tip (CMC III-H-40 and CMC III-H-41).[19]

Photo 118. Micmac and Maliseet rattles in the collection of the Canadian Museum of Civilization. CMC III-F-120, collected by Gabe Paul in Old Town, Maine; III-E-25, collected by Mechling in New Brunswick in 1910; III-F-121, collected by Gabe Paul in Old Town, Maine (FvR 88/9/23).

As Jim Dumont's interpretive comments for HEY 9976 suggested, the crescent shape is polysemic, connoting horned creatures such as the panther or the buffalo. Furthermore, some consultants noted that the crescent moon has a similar shape, although the orientation of the figure is different. The connotation of "turning" (discussed further in Chapter Six) may be relevant here. Certainly, the moon and the earth/under-earth creatures have different associations although some scholars have suggested that both are, in some contexts, associated with female spirituality (Jordan Paper, MS 1989).

Realistic: Sky Realms

Frequently represented on Algonquian instruments are aspects of the sky worlds. Birds are presented in varied forms. Reference was made earlier to bird figures carved with various degrees of abstraction as Anishnabe water drumsticks. While the origin story of the grandfather drum presented in Chapter Two associates these with the loon, they are sometimes related to the thunderbirds by contemporary interpreters. This association may be reinforced by their ability to "transform"; in particular, the horse may be regarded as a thunderbird transformation (see AMNH 178379, a mid-nineteenth-century drumstick from New Credit, Ontario; HEY 2/7601b, Potawatomi, pre-1912; HEY 24/1727, 1728, and 2179, all Kansas Potawatomi; HEY 8/2990,

Wisconsin Menominee, pre-1912; GLE AP3217; CMC III-G-4046; CMC III-G-207; GLE AP3239; GLE AP3126). The manelike protrusion at the top of these sticks suggests a horse to some, but a bird's crest might also be seen. The colours blue (or black) and/or red are also associated with the thunderbird/horse; these colours are often applied only to the distal end (see HEY 2/7601b, HEY 16/2623, CMC III-G-781, ROM 958.131.45, ROM 958.131.19).

While Innu consultants do not recognize the thunderbird as part of their tradition, or use a water drum, the form of early bone drumsticks often resembles the horse-head shapes of Anishnabe L-shaped sticks. HEY 15/5558 (Colour Plate 26) is an elaborate case in point; the natural coloration of the bone clearly divides into white and grey halves; the edges are notched, possible representations of a horse's mane; the striking end is squared like the snoutlike ends of some Anishnabe sticks. Also see CMC III-B-82 on which traces of blue paint are visible, or ROM 958.131.19, a carved and incised wooden stick with the distinctive pipe/horse shape.

As Anishnabe painted designs, thunderbirds take various forms—some stylized to the point of being a geometric representation: GLE AP2593 has both a stylized and a more realistic thunderbird; also see CMC III-G-898 and CMC III-G-899, the latter with red "power lines" emanating from the blue thunderbird figure. More "realistic" bird images, some eaglelike, are also commonplace (GLE R1792.11 has a thunderbird on one side and two birds described as "prairie chickens" on the other). The powerful imagery of PEAH 41-72/24397 depicts combined features of horse and bird. In two instances, a thunderbird is incised on a grandfather water drum (one is GLE AP3215) just below the bung hole, which was described as the "mouth." Occasionally, a horselike image is also the form of a carved external block—made of stone like many other thunderbird-associated instruments—on an Ojibwe flute (MCQ E-326), an instrument which also incorporates the thunderer's colours (red and blue/black) in its design. A thunderer's instrument may also be indicated by means of horse hair (PEAH 30-69/K58) or horse hide (Kabatay's drum, SPINC ID:III.G.66.d; Colour Plates 14-16). As we discussed earlier, sometimes it is the power attributes of a being rather than its form which are essential to its identity. In the case of the thunderbirds, who are said to shoot lightning from their eyes, a jagged edge or zigzag design down the length of a hoof rattle stick, along the edge of its rattlers (CMC III-G-395) or down a drumstick (AMNH 178379 depicted earlier) is sometimes used to represent their power.[20]

Hoof rattles may have both a zigzag and a bird-head (see Potawatomi rattles HEY 16/2618 and 2619). Wavy lines emanating from the heads of spirit figures, often described in the literature as "spirit" or "power" lines[21] are related to representations of lightning. Thunder, on the other hand, is sometimes imaged with concentric circles said to depict the sound going out (HEY 9976). Instruments may combine several of these features, as we saw in the case of HEY 9976. In Chapter Four, aural analogues for these visual patterns, the use of bells or quill rattlers for the thunderbirds, for example, were discussed.

Photo 120. Potawatomi hoof rattle (HEY 16/2619. FvR 88/35/31).

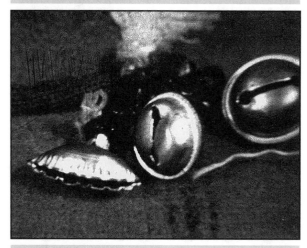

Photo 121. Bells (FvR 88/29/30).
"Bells and quills are the sounds associated with the thunderbird." (Jim Dumont)

Thunderbird representations are part of the imagery of the Anishnabe Midewiwin. Specific instruments (a photo of Midewiwin instruments from Densmore is reproduced in Vennum 1982: 36), designs, and construction techniques are associated with each of the "degrees" within the lodge. Although both the grandfather and little boy water drums are central to Midewiwin ceremonies, the little boy is curiously absent among the artifacts in museum collections which we documented (museum documentation such as that indicating GLE AP1206 was a "young boy" was regarded as erroneous by Anishnabe consultants). Jim Dumont showed us a photograph of a Shawnee instrument from the Heye collection, identifying it as the only known published photo of the "little boy" currently used in Northeastern Ojibwe communities. The imagery of the little boy is integrally linked to its use; the patterns created on the bottom of the drum through the tying and holding of its rope in seven-times-seven different ways constitute an elaborate but impermanent form of image created only when it is prepared for a ceremony.

The many grandfather drums in museum collections, on the other hand, permitted more extensive exploration. We received fragmentary information about several aspects: the use of different styles of drumstick and rim construction for different degrees, the use of painted hides in higher degrees. In a few cases, a grandfather drum was paired with either a song scroll (BM 2223) or can-shaped rattle made of either bark or tin (GLE AP412 and 413). In many other cases we do not know enough about specific instruments such as gourd rattles, tin can rattles, or instruments with copper, a material whose sound is "needed" within ceremonies and is particularly associated with women's instruments, to identify for certain whether they were used within the Midewiwin. A group of frame drums, on the other hand, painted with triangular/circular designs, usually black/blue and red, were identified specifically as Midewiwin designs. Similar images have been described in King (1982: 62) and Phillips (1987: 64-65).

While the Montagnais and Cree east of James Bay do not recognize the thunderbird as part of their tradition, they do associate spiritual power with bird figures on drums. A frequently used image, particularly on Cree instruments, is a mirror representation of birds which sometimes resemble geese (HEY 17/6820). Ojibwe instruments also have similar imagery in some instances (CFM 84434, HEY 19/567; see also Chapter Three). In Naskapi, Montagnais, and eastern Cree myths, humans often transform into birds.[22] There is a further connection sometimes made between the spirits of the dead and birds; the Milky Way is named in either fashion. On one hand, it is described as the path of migrating birds; on the other it translates as the road which souls must travel to get to the other world. As described in Chapter Four, the snares of the Innu *teueikan* are sometimes made of quills, and snare rattlers are also described by some consultants as spirit voices.

Bird images appear on Attikamek and Algonquin moose calls. On pre-1970 instruments, a layering of positive and negative bands also indicates, for some interpreters, the multiple layers of the earth and sky worlds (MCQ 69-71). Birds in the Iroquoian cosmos may be associated with the flute.

Photo 122. Algonquin ensemble with traditional drum and fiddles, Maniwaki, Quebec. Kitigan Zibi Anishinabeg Cultural Education Centre.

Other sky-world phenomena may be painted on instrument frames or membranes. Several Algonquin drums (MCQ 75-281, see also drums in archival photographs such as the one above) have frames painted with stars, sometimes in association with the crescent moon or a Y in a circle. The location of the image between the lacing points corresponds to the location of red dots which sometimes decorate Montagnais *teueikana*, a location suggesting a correspondence with interpretations, cited earlier in this chapter, of red dots as stars (HEY 22/4137). The forms of stars may be used to identify a specific Nation: the Naskapi are usually associated with the five-pointed star, the Cree with a six-pointed one. If this association is consistent, one might query the museum identification of the shoulder blade rattle, HEY 23/6638 (Colour Plate 17), which has a six-pointed star as a Naskapi instrument. Although the majority of people in Davis Inlet where this instrument was collected are Naskapi, a number of families are Cree. Stars also appear on Plains Cree instruments, GLE AP2650 and HEY 18/5867. One Ojibwe "dream" drum had a large blue star with red background painted on the bottom membrane, possibly in a reversal of "earth/sky" sides (CMC III-G-742, Photo 102). It may be significant to note that among the collections which we documented, Attikamek and Algonquin moose calls depict sky universes with birds or clouds but without stars (Colour Plate 15).

Abstract

A final category of "shapes" is more abstract. Some of the most difficult for us to understand are simple patterns such as single lines. One such instrument is the (Plains) Ojibwe frame drum GLE AP815a with short yellow vertical lines all over one membrane. Is this denotative? Rain, for example? On the song scrolls, lines sometimes indicate the number of songs, or, conversely, they may imply a pause in the ceremony. Does this meaning also occur on musical instruments? Some such designs have been interpreted by ethnographers and travellers of earlier periods. Kohl, for example, reports that groups of three short horizontal lines were, for the Ojibwe, a representation of the North Wind (1860: 150-51, cited in Phillips 1987: 58). Speck recorded a group of geometric forms used by 1920s Attikamek (called Têtes de Boules in his writing) basket makers:

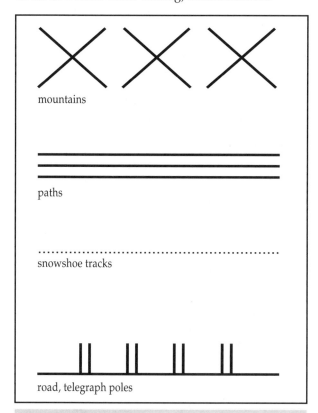

Fig. 20. Attikamek patterns.

Rows or edges of linked patterns are prevalent images. Some Micmac interpreters linked triangles to representations of peaceful relations among Nations. Such triangular patterns occur on musical instruments of a number of different Nations (MCQ 69-71, ROM 975X73.18, ROM 22265). Linked patterns on wampum records of many Eastern Nations use similar designs to consolidate alliances; Iroquoian wampum belts use squares or diamonds to confirm alliances.

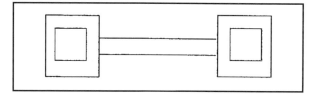

Fig. 21. Wampum belt pattern depicting the open pathway/alliance between Iroquois and Ojibwe nations.

Hemispheric "skydomes" may be painted on Iroquoian instruments (CMC III-I-1201a); they also occur in the natural scallops along the edge of the turtle's shell.

The elaborate carving of small water drumsticks by Iroquois craftsmen combine abstract geometric design with an exquisite sense of balance, both visual and physical, as illustrated in the photo of groups of sticks from the Peabody Salem collection (Photo 106). Smooth and lightly varnished, each is carved to suit an individual singer. Some drumsticks are intended as jokes, such as WICEC 973.103.58, with a carved nude female form. Another impressive style involves openwork carving with a freely moving wooden ball carved into the interior of the openwork (HEY 22/4289); this, of course, creates an additional "sound" for the instrument but one masked by the sounds of water drum and cowhorn rattles. This style is more commonly found among older singers at Six Nations, Ontario, than elsewhere.

Placement

Are designs central or peripheral? Are they placed on certain parts of the instruments and not on others? Are they isolated or combined? If the latter, how are they combined?

Among the Algonquian instruments that we studied, borders, circumferences, and joins are an "area" of the physical form that is often decorated. In some cases, this is described as a way of "dressing" the instrument: encompassing and protecting the whole object. Moose hoof rattles often have leather bands (MCQ 75-279 or MCQ 75-280) over the area where they attach to each other and to the handle. Disc rattles often have paint or small bits of cloth around the stitched circumference (CMC III-B-93; CMC III-C-318). Dance drums (and some disc rattles, especially the Attikamek variety where the membranes are separated to reveal the lacing pattern) are "dressed" over the lacing (HEY 22/2021). Rattles may have a beaded or fringed leather band at the point where the handle inserts into the vessel (SPINC ID:III.H.1000.r. MAR).[23] The quality of encompassing or protecting seems related both to skinlike wrappings and to paint. Do the skins "hide" power, we wondered, in the way that, according to some Anishnabek, the Thunderers hide behind the clouds, so that their power is not so strong as to destroy? This may (and the analogy is drawn by the authors) explain the propensity for border designs and especially for "covers" of areas which are joins. As we understand it, surfaces which represent a meeting point between worlds—heaven and earth, head and tail—need special attention.

Furthermore, areas which touch the ground or the hand are also paid special attention. We have

Photo 125. Attikamek disc rattle made with a drum-style "skirt" covering the lacing, in the style characteristic of that area (HEY 22/2021. FvR 88/46/13).
"Stitching under the dressing makes it look like a drum." (Jim Dumont)

already seen ways in which the point of contact between the Anishnabe grandfather drum and the earth may be painted or decorated with design. The peace drum, and some medicine drums, on the other hand, do not touch the earth. Ceremonial drums are suspended from four stakes, as described earlier. Modern powwow drums are often placed on a blanket so that they do not touch the ground.

Border designs and the decoration of joins are also characteristic of some Iroquoian instruments. Some, such as water drum ROM 22265 or horn rattle CMC III-I-388, are covered with designs, but an attention to edging seems particularly important. Significantly, it is the borders of traditional Iroquoian clothing that are most elaborately beaded and edged with ribbon, the rims of pottery that are most highly incised. Although this connection might be overstated, it is perhaps also significant that many spirit beings are said to dwell at the borders and rims of the earth and skydome; indeed, Iroquoian communities are described as clearings with boundaries marked by the woods' edge.

Certain images may be placed variably. Red dots may occur on the top or bottom membrane of a *teueikan*, or disc rattle, or they may be painted on the exterior or interior of the frame (This is a tendency which seems to cross the boundaries of different Innu Nations: see Algonquin drum CMC III-L-203, Attikamek rattle HEY 22/2088, and Montagnais drums HEY 22/4137, MCQ 87-3654.1 and .2, MSI, or ROM 9a64.140.31A. A solid rim of red paint, on the other hand, always encircles the exterior edges of the outer/upper rim. The centring of these dots, mid-point on a membrane or between the lacing points, seems to be a consistent aesthetic criterion.

Somewhat related to the placement of design is the distribution of pattern on an object and the rela-

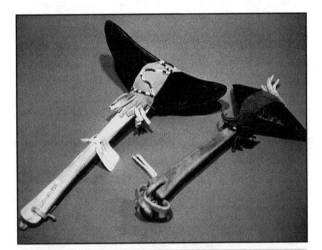

Photo 123. Two Algonquin *shinaueshigans* with zigzag beadwork covering the hoof join. Made by John Rat. Collected in Rapid Lake, Ontario, by Alika Webber (MCQ 75-279 and 75-280. BD 88/5/28).

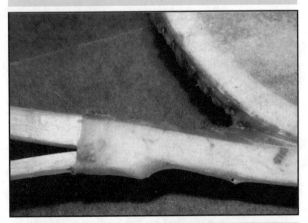

Photo 124. Membrane-covered handle extension on an Attikamek disc rattle, collected by W.F. Stiles, probably in Obedjiwan, Quebec, in 1953 (FvR 85/4/17).

tionship of this to aesthetic preference. Proportion was cited earlier as an aspect of Montagnais Thomas Simeon's stated preference. Similarly, the natural patina and "feel" of an Iroquois instrument is often judged paramount. On the other hand, we referred earlier to the Wabanaki concept of *-amal* or variety and this may be reflected in the combination of decorative techniques (paint as well as carving; see, for example, the elaborately painted horn rattle owned by Margaret Paul, Colour Plate 13), or the variety of imagery on a single instrument. Art historians have observed the frequency with which asymmetrical design distribution occurs in Anishnabe design. Ruth Phillips notes that "the front and back or upper and under surfaces of containers and utensils and the left and right sides of garments display different motifs or colours" (1987: 89). She suggests that "the tendency towards asymmetry in visual art may be related to the spatial structuring that was a fundamental aspect of Woodlands cosmologies. The division of the universe into upper and lower realms, the central vertical axis—the great World Tree [of Peace] of Iroquoian mythology—that joined the layers of the cosmos, and the quartering of the earth's surface by the cardinal directions, established clear spatial zones vital to an individual's sense of orientation" (ibid.). The examples presented in Chapter Two in relation to instruments and "twinness" are relevant to her analysis.

Colour

We describe colours as either signifiers (symbols) or perspective indicators (indices). To understand aspects of both we might start with colour names. Among Iroquoian languages, specific names relate to trees or to wood in various stages. "Green," for example, is the colour of leaves; "brown" the colour of wood or rotten wood; "gray" the colour of ashes (important in curing ceremonies and Stirring Ashes, part of the Midwinter ceremony of acknowledgement and renewal) and "black" the colour of charcoal.[24] Red is often related to the colour of blood, another symbol of life, while purple is connected to the pokeweed.

Generally, however, the colour of an animal or plant is rarely mentioned in conversation or traditional Longhouse stories unless it is unusual. There are abundant narratives, for example, about albino animals; hunters avoid killing these since they are considered bad luck (as are certain creatures such as blue otters and white buffalo which live under the earth). It is not the colour (white) which is suspect

but, rather, their unnaturalness which sets these beings apart.

In Iroquoian languages, verb stems are added to colour names to distinguish shades of light from dark (as in Seneca, *ge:et* and *aji:h* respectively; see Chafe 1963: 40).[25] George Hamell observes that for Haudenosaunee, "light sources," and naturally occurring bright and white colours are tangible metaphors "for life itself, for . . . physical, social and spiritual wellbeing" (1992: 455). This seems partly true: the background for most wampum belts is made from white quahog shell and the symbolic covenant chain, a treaty established with British governments, was forged in silver, a white metal which must be polished frequently—thus renewing the treaty—to remain bright (Hamell 1992: 462). But within Iroquoian aesthetics, light/bright/white/shiny materials are often paired with darker, non-reflective colours. Perhaps a better metaphor "for life itself " is found in contrast or complement, in the differing layers of colour and texture. Wampum belts have purple designs on white shells; dark cloth leggings of traditional outfits are edged with light-coloured beadwork; contrasting ribbonwork and silver brooches decorate women's calico overdresses. As Mohawk linguist David Maracle comments, even the night sky has its contrast with the brightness of the stars and moon.

Haudenosaunee painted instruments are rarely one solid colour—bright red water drums, for example, have calico cloth wrapping around the drumhead rims; a line of yellow or red paint around a rattle handle contrasts with the natural colour of wood or horn. Even gourd rattles, left unpainted and unvarnished, are naturally mottled. Similarly, dark colours are often associated with layered colours. A rare example of this in the Iroquoian context is a remarkable carved horn rattle, MCQ E-242 (Colour Plate 18), collected by Speck. Dark blue covers a red paint layer, as evident in the mottled surface of the rattle. Traces of brown or black paint seem to underlie the blue and red layers. In this instance the handle and vessel plugs are also painted dark colours). (See also AGE C-73.)

Like Iroquoian languages, Algonquian languages such as *innu aimun* often relate colours to natural phenomena: red to blood, green to the ocean, or brown to tobacco.[26] Different dialects sometimes make different associations; orange, for example, is associated with fire in one community but with the fruit of the same name/colour in another. Shades of black are connected to the variations in light between day and night; *ka kashteuat* (black) has connotations of hiding while *ka uapanuat* (grey) indicates that "it is becoming day; it is getting brighter." For the study of musical instruments, a particularly important association relates to things which are white or bright in colour. The -*ua*- morpheme which indicates these qualities of whiteness and brightness occurs in words for white objects such as rabbit, the rising of the sun, or vision.[27] In Montagnais, colours such as grey (*uapanuat* in the Sept-Îles dialect—"the coming of the light of day,") or blue (*uasheshkunat*—"getting clear") embed this infix.

Whiteness or brightness seem to be important properties of some musical instruments. The skins of some Montagnais *teueikana* seem to be whitened, and some are chalky (MAB. SPINC ID:III.C.3003.d; also note a frame drum which has a white *paper* membrane: ROM 958.131.177). No *teueikana* have the gold or brown membranes of Cree drums (MCC ME984X.86.1 or HEY 7/1063). Occasionally white membranes, but more often white rag-wraps are found on Anishnabe and (to a lesser extent) Iroquoian water drums. White "additions" (a feather collar, a tie, or rattlers such as fruit pips, beans, or even the megis shell in Midewiwin sound producers such as CMC III-G-775ab) are sometimes used, apparently to bring this colour to an instrument. White paint may also be used; white vessel plugs occur on some Iroquois horn rattles (e.g., WICEC 973.103.80) and inside or on the bottom of some Ojibwe water drums (e.g., GLE AP1407 for a Plains example).

A quality of translucence, exclusive of colour, on the other hand, is characteristic of a limited number of double membrane frame drums (e.g., GLE AP97-1e, a sun dance drum which also has a white rope with it), and Cree fish skin disc rattles (e.g., MCQ 966-45-II (Colour Plate 19) or ROM 966.73.11). Translucence also seemed to characterize certain types of natural dye, especially red ochre (see, e.g., MCC M12538, MCC ME967x.45, CMC III-G-728, or ROM 958.131.361; see also Colour Plate 17). Virtually all of these instruments were also documented as "ceremonial."

A shiny quality is characteristic of some Anishnabe instruments and instrument types. Metal sound producers are, of course, shiny (except where they have been allowed to oxidize in museum archives or other circumstances). An extraordinary can rattle is HEY 2/7997 (see Photo 49) where the very shiny strip of tin is evident only between the edges of a rawhide skirt which dresses it. In this case, as in a number of other extraordinary instances where aging does not seem to be evident, there seems to be no indication of oxidation, although the instrument pre-dates 1912. The addition of copper,

often just a wire wound around a rattle handle also brought the quality of shininess and the properties of that metal to an instrument. Metal jingle cones adorn dresses of contemporary powwow dancers, rattles similar in form to hoof rattles (HEY 16/4762; GLE AP3214 which has copper jingle cones), dance belts (ROM HD6281), bandoleer bags, or even a dog whip (ROM 959.50.170).

Certain older Iroquois water drums, especially those made from wooden kegs, have shiny metal hoops at the lower edge (ROM 970.279b, or WICEC 973.103.51). Iroquois horn rattles, deer toe garters, and some turtle rattles (ROM 975x73.18, CMC III-I-1423, CMC III-I-1204, or SINM 83-0016-00-05) are also finished with lacquer or a high-gloss varnish (or less frequently, gloss paint); instrument makers prefer this to a matte finish because it "catches the eye" without completely altering the natural colour. Such instruments embody the opposite (or complementary) qualities of brightness and darkness, with varnish applied to naturally dark materials such as shell, hoof, and horn.

As signifiers, colours may be pragmatic choices, indications of personal aesthetics, or they may convey various levels of meaning about identity. Red is the most prevalent colour among Innu. Some consultants relate it to the colour of blood (and hence life) as well as fire (also associated with instigating life), and sometimes extend these associations to identify red as a symbol of First Nations generally or, more often, to the Innu Nation, especially with reference to red external rims or dots on *teueikana* of Labrador and Northern Quebec. Many consultants, however, do not regard these same features as denotative, stating that they are "just for the beauty."

Innu interpreters sometimes relate colours to natural phenomena; the red, white, and green yarn ties on snowshoes or disc rattles, like green and white paint on a frame drum, may be connected to the sun, the snow, and the grass. Speck reports that coloured cloth or ribbon (such as that attached to the circumference of disc rattles) on Innu ceremonial game-carrying straps had analogs in types of game— in some instances, red was associated with small game, green with large (1935: 213) while, in others, the colour associations varied so that, for example, another hunter might associate both red and green with beaver, pink with caribou or lynx, blue with bear, and yellow with fox (1935: 217). Such associations, however, are not part of a shared symbolism.

In Iroquoian contexts, some colours have shared symbolism. A wooden face mask, for example, is usually painted red and/or black, denoting the time of day it was carved. Certain colours are contextually appropriate or inappropriate; people are discouraged from wearing red clothing at funerals or wakes. But for the most part, colours on Iroquoian instruments are more idiosyncratic. Red, for example, is a favourite colour of Hubert Buck, Sr.; his cow-horn rattles are often identifiable by their red handle segments (CMC III-I-1423). How one chooses to interpret this is individual—whether, for example, he related this to colours of blood or fire, or whether as he often suggested, this colour simply "caught a singer's eye," or whether high-gloss red paint is relatively accessible and economical. Among Iroquoian people, purple is possibly a more "popular" colour (even if less evident on instruments); it is directly associated with the colours of shells on Iroquoian wampum belts, and has become a favourite for T-shirts, baseball caps, and embroidered jackets worn by Longhouse singing societies.

On the other hand, Anishnabe interpretations more often relate to a widely shared symbolic system. The prevalent combination of red with blue or black, as we have already seen, sometimes indicates the Thunderbird, and many Anishnabe Midewiwin instruments are marked in this way (HEY 9976, MCC ME984X.91, CMC III-D-717a, CMC III-G-898; see Colour Plate 14). One Midewiwin instrument uses red and green, colours described as indications of a woman's instrument (CMC III-G-1109; see also Colour Plate 22). The desirability of materials which combined certain sounds (a ringing metallic quality, for example) with the colours red and black may have contributed to the selection of certain types of manufactured cans (Hunt's Baking Powder for CMC III-G-15, or Imperial Tobacco for CMC III-G-368).

Although the Midewiwin has not been historically documented, nor is it currently established, in Innu areas, similar colour choices are evident in their musical instruments, although we did not hear similar explanations for a preference for the red/black combination found, for example, on rattles made from Dominion Cartridges tins (HEY 2/8900). Many other Naskapi-Montagnais instruments use the red/blue combination (Colour Plate 20; see HEY 15/5478, HEY 16/2590, HEY 18/1575, CMC III-B-356, CMC III-B-536, ROM 958.131.540, for example), a contrast sometimes acknowledged as symbolic of the twinness of earth and sky but described currently by most of our consultants as an aesthetic preference, rather than a symbolic choice. Blue alone also occurs on Naskapi-Montagnais instruments (HEY 2/8961 or CMC III-B-485; also note the blue bows on an Attikamek frame drum, HEY 14/2079). Blue/green, and yellow are sometimes said to symbolize the Cree Nation (CMC 79-42-76; CMC III-D-63a).

Photo 126. Naskapi disc rattle with ribbon. Heye Foundation 11565 (HEY 13/3224. Also shown HEY 14/3025).

Anishnabe clan affiliation may also be implied by colour. Loon clan members may carry an instrument with the colour green. Most Anishnabe clans, however, have more than one colour, frequently painted in rings on the grandfather water drum (CMC III-G-893; clan may be indicated by rings on other drums such as HEY 8/2990, GLE AP3116, or GLE R1824.98). We were also told that gender may be indicated by a switching of the order of the colours. See Colour Plates 22 and 23.

At least in Anishnabe contexts where teachings of the Medicine Wheel are respected, colours may indicate the cardinal directions. Elders from different regions teach variable aspects of this rich image's "teachings." But while four-direction symbols are prevalent on Algonquian musical instruments (see Photos 94-99), they rarely embody the four symbolic colours. Rather, two contrasting colours may be alternated at 90 or 180° on the drum stands of dance or dream drums or on the painted images on frame drums, for example. Red and blue, red and black, or red and green are the most frequent combinations in the collections we documented. Two colours may sometimes be related to another directional axis—the sky and earth worlds, as indicated (see Colour Plates 4 and 23).

The most varied use of colour in designs occurs on particular instrument types. Iroquois water drums are occasionally highly painted (ROM 22265, CMC III-I-1201), although plain brown drums are also commonplace. The skirts of Anishnabe dance drums may be elaborately beaded. Wabanaki horn rattles are occasionally elaborately painted. Dream drum images are sometimes complex paintings (CMC III-G-742). Although dream images are closely associated with the Naskapi-Montagnais teueikan, they are rarely painted on drums; a notable exception, however, is the Kurtness drum displayed at the Musée amérindien de Mashteuiatsh, Quebec (Colour Plate 25).

This discussion of colour would be misleading without indicating that colour changes also occur for a variety of reasons. Differences between our observations of colours and those of museum documentors who examined the same artifact at an earlier point are indicative of fading caused by light/ heat in storage or on display as well as colour transformations relating to chemical changes caused by "conservation" methods.[28] Of course, colour does change with natural cycles though perhaps in a more predictable way than that caused by museum insecticides and display techniques. We know that each season is dominated by familiar colours, and that many natural phenomena such as the leaves on trees undergo vivid and dramatic transformations. Perhaps this explains why colour may be interpreted in a variable manner with regard to many cyclical elements. Other natural colour changes in instruments function as indicators of age and the passage of time. Thus instruments, like other living entities, are situated in time and the potential to transform exists on several levels.

Number

Numeric symbolism is part of a traditionally accepted worldview for Native communities. This symbolism is fundamental to many of the classic philosophical, historical, and spiritual bases of both Iroquoian and Algonquian societies. The profound import of the Iroquoian Great Law of Peace or the Anishnabe Midewiwin migration stories is related more fully in translations and interpretations published elsewhere. The brevity of our references to these texts must not be mistaken for an explication of their significance but rather as an indication that metaphors such as the Iroquoian image of the roots of peace extending in the four directions, or the seven fires of the Anishnabek, underlie the design of musical instruments just as they underpin other aspects of Iroquoian or Algonquian cultures.[29]

Other numerical symbolism, on the other hand, has individual import. One drum-maker told us of a rattle which he had made in accordance with a person's dream; it had a specific number of rattlers, but he did not know why it had to be done in that manner. Hoof rattles, in particular, are extraordinarily variable with regard to the number of rattlers on them. One artifact which we saw had only one (hence it could not rattle effectively); others had upwards of 150.

As we discussed in the previous chapter, numbers can also relate to the aesthetics of sounds. A precise definition is evident in statements quoted

such as "twenty-five bee-bees is about the right sound" (for a cowhorn rattle) or "there must be 365 jingles on a jingle dress." Often the numerical references relate to several dimensions of experience. Using 365 jingle cones not only makes the right sound, but is also an indication of process; some explain that it is ideally supposed to take a year to make a dress with one cone added per day. There are many such examples of the precision which goes into the creation of an instrument's "voice." Hence, numbers are rarely arbitrary, although their meaning may not be transparent or widely shared.

Size

The relative sizes of museum instruments have often been meticulously measured by scholars (including ourselves) in search of accurate, verifiable data. Such data, like other dimensions of design, however, are necessarily interpreted in relation to culturally embedded assumptions. A case in point are smaller than normal musical instruments which are often designated as children's instruments in museum catalogues. In some cases, the attribution combines with a negative value judgement, something to the effect that the instrument was formerly used for ceremonial purposes but has now "degenerated" to the status of a toy used by children (see, e.g., CMC III-D-770). While indeed there may be instances of small instruments used as toys, our data reveal a somewhat different profile, one consistent with the traditions of several of

Photo 127. Iroquois cowhorn rattles in the collection of the Canadian Museum of Civilization (FvR 88/3/31).

the Nations consulted for our project, many of whom regard a newborn baby as close to the spirit world and consequently both vulnerable and powerful. An Innu disc rattle serves as a medium of protection according to some individuals. The little boy water drum of the Anishnabek is, in a sense, the stronger of the Midewiwin pair, whereby the grandfather is the earthly realization of the boy in the spirit realm. Each creature has the capacity for growth and, in the case of the powerful spirit creatures such as the bear, snake, eagle, or thunderbird, a giant of the species is recognized and often named. On the other hand, the tiniest creatures (the snail with it miniscule horns, little people in the stories of most Nations, or insects which are categorized as spirit creatures in many Algonquian languages) are often especially powerful. Small instruments such as the Ojibwe "medicine drum" (PEAH 30-69/K58), or the smallest Anishnabe and Innu rattles (HEY 18/1575, MCC ME984X.91, ROM 968.61.4) were described as having strong medicine.

The Interplay of Meaningful Elements

When elders describe the meaning of a drum or perhaps tell a myth, they sometimes use the phrase "nothing is forgotten." The Creator forgot nothing and hence the complement of elements produces balance and harmony. On the other hand, the words above present components, not wholes.

Our structuralist organization of the "elements" of design is not without uses: it may assist those who are unfamiliar with artifacts such as the ones we discuss to see details which they might otherwise overlook; effectively, we look at visual metaphor which connects somewhat differently in each of the historically situated traditions concerned in this study. The structuralist approach, however, is undoubtedly more appropriate for outsiders who seek meaning necessarily using the familiar tools at hand. And yet it lacks sound and motion, as well as the myriad of connections which draw us to these instruments and these musics.

Notes

1 The words in this title were chosen with care but compromise. With "image" we hoped to avoid the inappropriate connotations of "decoration" which suggest an ornamentality which is extraneous in some way to the structure of the object. On the other hand, the division between image and structure is a somewhat artificial one, since the creation of "pattern" is part of the process of structuring just as it is

part of the process of imaging. There is pattern in the cutting or assembling of materials, in the processing of hides, in the dream which inspired a painted image or the things tied to the instrument. There is pattern realized only in performance or use. There is pattern in the choice of natural materials with which to work. Our intent is to understand how meaning may be derived from the interplay of elements.

2 Whether in anthropological studies of expressive culture or guides to proper etiquette, structures for appropriateness, with regard to attention-getting, are often explored with regard to human societies but rarely with regard to "material" objects. In Native contexts, however, where consciousness is acknowledged in some so-called "material" objects, where an instrument may be regarded as the human body or the cosmos, where connectedness and relationship are primary, the same questions about the structures for appropriateness can be extended beyond the human realm.

3 Skinner's use of "primary" and "secondary" is ambiguous for several reasons. Are primary sounds or images those connected with human intentionality? Does our own categorization replicate the ambiguity where, for instance, it is not clear that leg bell rhythms are classed as more obvious than fringe rhythms on the basis of an assumed hierarchy of the senses (the aural over the visual), the actions (dance steps over knee bends and body motion) or simply volume (loud over soft)? This also begs the question of "importance"; just because an elder paid more attention or time to an aspect of an instrument which seemed less obvious or significant to us, that aspect was not necessarily marked as more important.

4 The discourse about "power" has often been shaped by non-Native concepts for which there may be no equivalent in Native languages. Whether in musical, spiritual, or political realms, the notion of "power over" something, for example, differs from the Algonquian *manitu*, usually glossed as "spirit." Chafe (1963: 59) lists a Seneca word, *ka'hastesha*, for natural or supernatural power/strength.

5 There are many other documented instances of similar interpretive pluralism. In Dorothy Burnham's study (1992) of Innu and Anishnabe caribou-skin coats, for example, she states that "motifs undoubtedly had specific meaning for the man who dreamed them, but that significance was not always recognized and agreed upon by others. For example, a motif might be interpreted as a flower by one person, a celestial body by another, and a 'soul' or 'heart' by a third" (1992: 59).

6 Rupert Ross (1992: 12-28) discusses this as "the ethic of non-interference," a phrase he quotes from Mohawk psychiatrist Clare Brant. A subsequent section in the same book, subtitled "The Notion that the Time Must Be Right" (ibid.: 38-49) resonates with our representation of the locus of meaning and "meaning as emergent."

7 Catalogue information describes this as a "rattle" rather than a garter.

8 Of course there are forms in nature which are self-sufficient sound producers, as we mentioned earlier—whole gourds with dried seeds, or other seed pods—as well as some instruments such as the turtle rattle which are virtually self-sufficient (on turtle rattles where the lacing is the skin of the turtle, itself, only the wood splints, handle wrapping, and rattlers may be extraneous). As well, there may be substitutions of materials, often with careful attention to preserving the desirable sound quality. Hence a Pepsi can was, at one time, a preferred vessel for tin can rattles because the metal alloy used at that time produced the desired ringing quality. Some materials have been used less frequently in recent time periods. The Innu, for example, used bone more widely for earlier instruments but frequently substitute wood at present. Bone (together with quills) more often served as the rattlers on frame drum snares; elaborately carved bone drumsticks were prized; bone rattles such as the Naskapi caribou shoulder blade rattles—CMC III-B-485 and HEY 23/6638—the latter of which was said to be used in the sweat lodge, were also used.

9 Speck Papers, American Philosophical Society, Microfilm 2964/Box 2.

10 For information about his political achievements see Wright (1992: 320-27).

11 Many Nations have individuals such as the *heyoka* who reinforce, by reversing, the circular norms, by doing such things as squaring up dinner plates. Such actions demonstrate the folly of the non-round in their contradictory way.

12 Our *Catalogue* documents only two hemispheric Mohawk drums, MCC M18207 and MCC M18457, both collected at Kahnawake prior to 1935 when they were acquired by the McCord Museum from the Molson family; we have not seen a hemispheric Micmac drum at all but have only heard it described and seen it drawn by Michael W. Francis.

13 See transcripts of "Alexandre McKenzie," videotape in the Culture Amerindienne series, Quebec: IQRC, n.d.; also note that fire may be used to burn a drum membrane in special circumstances as in the case of SPINC ID:III.B.3002.d.

14 Other interpretations relate to other things. On drawings of song scrolls recorded by Hoffman, concentric circles were said to indicate the heart (see Mallery 1972: 233) or the place of sleep (ibid.: 234). We have been told that a circle within a ring could indicate "the one among the all" (see HEY 2/9537).

15 Transcribed in Frank Speck's papers, American Philosophical Society, Microfilm 2964/Box 2; also see Freeman MS no. 369.

16 An interesting analogy within Cree and Attikamek tradition is the practice of painting rings on trees in which the emblems of the hunt—especially the skull of the bear—are hung in a gesture of respect to the animals.

17 The *Catalogue* (forthcoming on disk) documents over sixty of these.

18 Note that snake dances have different forms and connotations in other areas. In the context of Iroquoian social dancing it is relatively meaningless, although the floor pattern of stomp dances is sometimes related to snakelike movement. At a powwow, however, a snake dance may sometimes be performed in which the dancers jump over a stick "into the next life." The Maritime Algonquian Nations and Western Abenaki have a snake dance; in fact, Fewkes's recording of a Passamaquoddy snake dance—though he conflated the ethnography with information from the Hopi—is well known as the earliest recording of any Native music.

19 A number of Algonquin, Attikamek, and Montagnais influences are evident in Huron language and culture. Speculating about such an influence, one might posit that a possible symbolic rationale for the Huron choice of black-tipped horns may relate to the dualism of the worlds of sky and earth and their analogies in the body: head and tail. Horns are clearly associated with the head, but are usually also associated with creatures below the earth (the horned panther, the horned snakes, horned hairy beings). Their position is, hence, interpretable in two ways. CMC III-H-40 has a crown of feathers at its distal end; might this indicate the head of the rattle thus completing the symbolic reversal? It is interesting to note that eagle tail feathers have a similar colouration to the horns which are often chosen as rattles.

20 In relation to Naskapi, Montagnais, and Cree caribou-skin coat design, Burnham (1992: 100) concluded that zigzags were rarely used after the middle of the nineteenth century. They occur frequently on musical instruments collected at a much later date, however.

21 See, for example, the explanations of Ojibwe song scrolls in Mallery (1972 [1888-89]: 231-50) for a very old instance and Phillips (1987: 64) for a recent one.

22 See e.g., Aiashiu, or Summer Birds. Translations of the former have been published in Basile and McNulty (1971) and Savard (1979: 12-14); a Cree version appears in Brightman (1989: 105-12); translations of the latter appear in Speck (1935: 62-65).

23 Skinner (1921: 352) mentions the same practice.

24 None of these references are negative; it is important to recall that the ceremony of Stirring Ashes at New Year's is seen as rejuvenating, giving life.

25 According to George R. Hamell (who has worked extensively with Dr. Hazel Dean) "Seneca language colour terms are comprised of the verb root meaning 'to be the colour of ' and a noun root referencing some physical entity of which that specific colour is a salient physical attribute." He describes the dyad of white/black and the triad of white/black/red as the central historic colour schemes (1992: 465).

26 In the Sept-Îles dialect these are *ka mikuat* (red), *ka shipekut* (green), and *ka tshishtemauaput* (brown). These associations are both pragmatic and symbolic, since natural materials were often dye sources. While colour sources and painting methods were often unclear and undocumented for the musical instru-

ments that we studied, contemporaneous research in this area suggests probable methods. Dorothy Burnham has summarized some of these with regard to painted skins. Yellow, generally produced from fish roe, was, according to Burnham (who cites Lucien Turner), the easiest colour source. Yellow is often found on Cree but not on other Algonquian musical instruments. Several reds are apparent, however. Burnham cites vermilion, as well as earth pigments, lead, and iron ore as sources. She speculates that charcoal was the source for black and she distinguishes two shades of blue, one a trade product, the other a lighter shade produced by laundry blue (1992: 37-38). The reliance on trade products as dye sources is, we suspect, an incomplete explanation.

27 Ruth Phillips (1987: 89) has commented on the importance of light and luminosity within a Northern Woodlands aesthetic. She mentions the sun as the "ultimate source of light," and reflective materials as indicative of supernatural beings, citing both the Naskapi word for mirror "which translates as 'see soul metal' and the Iroquoian word for glass bead which is also the word for eye."

28 For examples, note descrepancies between catalogue descriptions and contemporary descriptions for GLE AP1718, or GLE AP3220. The Glenbow collection facilitates comparison because their catalogue descriptions offer detailed comments about colour.

29 The Iroquoian Institute has published the Great Law of Peace (Thomas n.d.) and a contemporary interpretation of the Seventh Fire Anishnabe has been written by Eddie Benton-Benai (1987).

Chapter Six
Motion, Cycles, and Renewal

Dialogue

BD:

When I think of "motion," I recall that, in the relatively early days of the SPINC project, we philosophized after lunch one day about what it means, personally, to move our knowledge ahead. We created drawings that would recur in subsequent discussions.

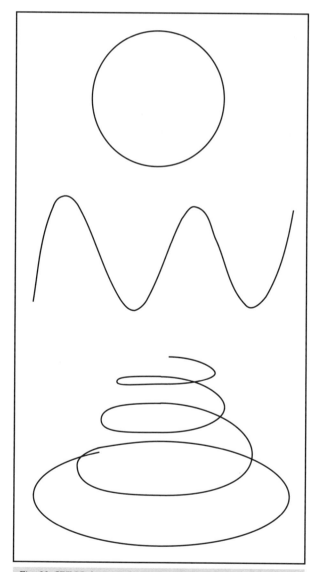

Fig. 22. SPINC drawing for motion dialogue.

Franziska drew a circle, emphasizing the cyclical. Mine was a waveform. Sam's was a sort of spiral, a combination of circle and wave—an image showing that the circle wasn't static. Subsequently we spoke about natural images which bring together circle and wave: the circles of energy which radiate outward when you throw a stone in a still pool of water, for example.

I wonder if we could talk about the relationship of these images to the work that we did in the intervening years. How *did* we move our knowledge ahead? How did we come to understand our metaphors of motion in relation to ones our consultants created?

FvR:

Your question, as well as the images which combine circle and wave form, confronts us with the distinction between "experience" and "image." Looking at the pool of water from the point where you throw a stone, you see concentric circles. But if you are a particle in the water, you experience the motion quite differently: it feels like a wave. And then, if you draw a picture of concentric circles, perhaps you become more preoccupied with boundaries or visual stopping points for each wave rather than a sense of motion.

MSC:

The image of water takes us back to a subject raised in our "Languages of Sound" dialogue. I mentioned the idea of reverberation as similar to the formal structure of a speech; short phrases are spoken to thank the Creator which may be repeated in slightly altered form, something like the ripples going out in a water pool. I have been thinking about other visual forms or physical structures which are perhaps like the radiating energy of a water pool and the folding back of waves.

Several stories come to mind . . .

In Iroquoian communities, people are encouraged to consider the implications of their actions seven generations ahead, and they understand that decisions made seven generations ago still reverberate. What the community does now echoes in both the past and the future. Time overlaps in that way.

Reg Henry's perspective on Iroquoian history (which he has kindly permitted us to use) relates to this. He described periods of calm and ensuing unrest; the Creator provided *Ongwehonwe* over time with the ideas needed for survival—the clan system, the Confederacy, certain ceremonies, and finally the *Gai'wiio* (Good Message of Handsome Lake), all gifts to the Haudenosaunee to resolve crises. At the heart of each of these gifts is the essential message of respect for life and for each other. Each message took a different form but each expanded on earlier teachings.

On a different scale, I also think of a conversation which flowed from an Allegany friend's recent sighting of Northern Lights, an unusual occurrence in Salamanca, New York. We discussed negative connotations of these reddish lights—a suggestion that perhaps they predict hostility in the community over the current lease negotiations for the city of Salamanca (the land is owned by the Seneca Nation but occupied predominantly by non-Indians). Conversation then shifted to earlier sightings—before World Wars I and II, and other events associated with witchcraft or impending disaster, and to future anticipated sightings in inappropriate seasons and locales. Stories overlap; time overlaps. You add your personal recollections; you listen to future predictions. The circle doesn't always expand outwards. But there is a sense of repetition, connection, movement.

BD:

Anishnabe elders use images of reverberation in their migration story. They describe how the races of man went out from the Creator, and how Anishnabe also went out. When Anishnabe had gone so far, he turned around to look back toward the Creator. The motion involved a folding back like a wave. The "seven fires," or stopping places in the course of their migration, are not unlike the phases of history described by Reg; each fire expanded earlier teachings.

FvR:

Neither sound nor stories go out into oblivion. There is a call and response. The rattle and the drum may be paired in this way. Midewiwin songs start with the shimmering sound of the rattle, like that first sound that was sent out. We've been told that the drum then responds to the sound of the Creator, that gourd rattle.

MSC:

When Iroquoian people discuss "sending out a sound," they mention loud, sharp reports such as rifle shots, blowing on a conch shell, using the turtle rattle to "shake the earth." All these sounds attract attention, signalling the start of a ceremony, notifying the community, drawing the Creator's participation. In the Great Feather Dance, when the singer strikes the bench with the turtle rattle, I've been told that "the earth stops to listen," everything pays attention, the focus is drawn to that event. This attention forms the pulsation, the response.

BD:

This image is something like the one an Innu hunter evokes when he says he "pays attention to" the drum.

FvR:

An interview that I had with Simon Marshall of Cape Breton comes to mind when we talk about "sending out" a sound or a message. Simon was the *putu's* or Deputy Grand Chief of the Micmacs. *Put'wutmn*, he says, means to send something with a breath of wind and it indicates his responsibility to spread the news or relay messages when important events take place.

BD:

It's interesting that movement is integrated into the concepts underlying political structures. Quite a contrast with hierarchical terms like "Premier" or "Prime Minister."

MSC:

I'm not sure that expanding circles are the only or best way to represent Iroquoian concepts, although the *deyodyohgwao:hasto'* (Cayuga), a wampum belt which literally translates as "the binding of the people in a circle," in the Confederacy structure may be similar. But there is another concept based in Iroquoian diplomacy known as "extending the rafters" which is extremely relevant. When another Nation or an individual is "adopted" they become the "children" (usually of the Cayuga Nation). The framework of the Confederacy, which is represented as a conceptualized Longhouse, remains unchanged. The Mohawk Nation remains Keeper of the Eastern Door, the Seneca, Keepers of the Western Door—yet internally, the structure (and thus the Confederacy) expands. I am dazzled by the possibility of connections among processes of Iroquoian diplomacy, storytelling, music, and even archeological studies of Longhouse structure, all suggesting a similar pattern of internal expansion.

I've been thinking about Longhouse speeches such as the *Ganohonyonk* (or "Thanksgiving Address") which vary in length according to performance context. Here's an example: every version of Ganohonyonk acknowledges spirit forces ranging from those on earth to the cosmos. In shorter versions, there is always some brief reference to strawberries, which thus come to represent all berries. At a spring or summer ceremony, a longer version might mention elderberries, raspberries, gooseberries, and the like. The syntax is unchanged; the patterns and phrases which begin and end each segment of the speech are unchanged—but the internal content is extended or expanded. I'm working through similar ideas of expanding/contracting structures in social dance music as well.

On the other hand, I wonder if powwow songs could be represented visually through concentric circles. There's a pulse, an initial melodic idea, and four or more slightly varied repetitions, expanding out from the centre. I seem to be transferring my image of the singers, grouped in a circle around the drum, on to the musical structure.

FvR:

Micmac storytellers lengthen or shorten their stories in different contexts by controlling the amount of detailed description that they provide. Beginnings and endings remain the same, but they are always in a sense "incomplete." There is always "more to it than that." Then there are the stories embedded in stories embedded in other stories—more circles within circles. In the end have we come back to the same place, or is this story just another beginning at a different place and time?

BD:

The repetition of short musical phrases in an Innu *nikamun* is something like radiation. Depending on the context, the intensity of the moment, even how big a breath the singer takes, the phrases will be repeated more or less often. Some singers will repeat a phrase as long as they have breath left. Within the span of a breath, each repetition is like a pulsation, or perhaps better, a small wave. And each new breath is like a larger wave.

MSC:

As I understand it, the idea of concentric circles with something radiating from the centre is not exactly an Iroquoian image, but it's similar. For example, the image of the Tree of Peace, the basis of the Confederacy, is described as having a circle of Chiefs surrounding it and a circle of Chiefs sur-

rounding them. Each circle is different, connected, enclosing, but not exactly "radiating" outward in endless waves. Similarly, the Longhouse is not simply the "heart" of ceremonies, as the Anishnabe drum is the "heart" of a powwow; instead, it also encloses people. Iroquoian friends may have a different take on this, however.

FvR:

Now we seem to be talking about boundaries, particularly the boundaries we put on motion in time and space. There are times where the boundaries seem to be very important in the context of Native events. Completion of a pathway is part of this. When a Micmac friend was recording some songs for me, it was important for him that we fill the tape, that we "complete" what we had begun. In the context of Elders Conferences, I have also often heard people emphasize the importance of "completing what we set out to do." During opening ceremonies, a "path" is laid out, and at closing ceremonies the path that has been travelled is reviewed and declared completed for that place and time.

MSC:

But wave motion does that too. It folds in back on itself.

Some boundaries *are* certainly fixed by cyclical events. Longhouse ceremonies are an obvious case in point. After the first thunder of the year one must burn tobacco. The strawberry ceremony is held in June. These are natural, practical frameworks in which the boundaries of seasons or positions of the stars or moon determine an appropriate time to begin or cease hunting, planting, or ceremonial activity.

There is also an Iroquoian interest in geographic boundaries, particularly expressed in the condolence ceremony which begins with a greeting called "At the Wood's Edge" where one group meets another group of chiefs "coming along the road."

BD:

This sort of cyclical bounding has a lot of relevance for the process of making the musical instruments discussed in this book, of course. Birch bark has colour-contrasted layers in winter. Roots must be taken when the sun is on the right side of the tree, since they should never be taken in shadow.

MSC:

Turtle rattles are made during the spring or fall because snapping turtle shells are hardest then.

FvR:

On the other hand, I am thinking of Micmac story-teller Michael W. Francis who often tells the ending of a story first. He says you have to know the "why" and then the story explains that "why." There is always an extra explanation after the story is over. The video we made collaboratively began with the sunset, at his request, when I had thought the sunrise would be more logical—especially since the Wabanaki are the people of the rising sun.

BD:

So the boundaries can overlap just like Franziska's stories within stories. But is the overlap always the point of return in a cycle?

MSC:

Do you mean the "starting point"? I think connections cut across time and there are probably multiple overlaps. I don't hear a strong Iroquoian concern with "first" things—the invention of this or that, the absolutely authentic original source. "Firsts" are a big issue in Euro-American culture, as we know. Primal primacy?

BD:

Yes, we certainly honour "inventors" and "authors"—the innovators, and the originators of things—in a very big way. We also do the opposite. In the mid-twentieth-century in particular, we tended to damn artists and musicians who were "derivative," for example. This seems to take us back to issues of authenticity which we discussed in an earlier chapter but without saying much about how concepts of authenticity are linked to concepts of history.

Photo 128. Montagnais women with hats. Glenbow Archives.

Both Euro-Americans and First Nations sometimes look backward in time to label something as an "authentic" symbol of who they are, but their explanations of the authenticity of that symbol can be quite different. An anecdote will illustrate what I mean. An Innu consultant and I were discussing the black and red-sectored Montagnais hat which dates to the nineteenth century but continues to be typical dress for many Innu women. I assumed the hat was valued because it was old and I wanted to find out more about why it had been regarded as an important symbol of this Nation for over a century. My Innu friend explained neither the history of this type of hat nor its meaning for the group but rather, the personal history embodied in each specific hat. Each ring of beadwork on the headband portion of the hat reflects a successful hunting season, she explained; she regarded the hat as "Montagnais" because it conveyed something about her family's experience, the annual cycles of their lives. The difference in our approaches makes me question how we have related "age" to ideas about cultural "purity."

MSC:

Why do we freeze time by declaring certain moments as more "authentic" than others? Is time a succession of static images for us?

FvR:

Perhaps we can come closer to answering your questions if we consider an aspect of motion which relates to "authenticity" in a number of Anishnabe stories—that is the motion of turning. When things turn, they often become something else. Hence, they are no longer what they were, no longer "authentic" in relation to their former identity. The sun symbol, or four directions in motion, becomes the swastika if it faces the wrong direction. The military bass drum becomes a powwow drum if it is turned on its side. The power changes. In each case there is a shift of power involved.

MSC:

Are you saying that the powwow drum is the opposite/good twin/authentic of the bass drum? Or that looking at the same thing from another way creates new possibilities?

FvR:

I think that varies. Everything has a certain order, a pathway, but turning creates new possibilities that have the potential to be positive or negative. I remember an occasion when I was invited to sit at the drum with an all-male drum. Afterwards an elder explained that by inviting a woman to sit with the drum the men had "turned" the drum and made it a "family" drum. Was it less authentic?

BD:

Another aspect of turning which we have learned about in conversations with Anishnabe elders is a slight turning in order to diffuse the strength of something. When the pipe-keeper points to the cardinal directions and moves a little off axis, or when the drum has a design or a snare that is not quite E/W or N/S, we were told that this was done in order to lessen the force of the four directions. So turning can be something other than a complete reversal.

FvR:

But some things *are* reversals, as with dancing one way and then dancing the other way in an Iroquoian round dance, for example.

MSC:

It depends where you are located. Haudenosaunee dance in a counter-clockwise direction, a direction associated with the living. Yet at a ceremony such as *Oghiwe*, the Feast for the Dead, you move clockwise. There is a reversal in direction among the living and the dead.

And what is the turning/opposite/changing of motion itself? Stasis! Is anything living static?

Is there ever a wave going out into oblivion? As Franziska said, they seem to come back, to rebound at some point.

Photo 129. Wave going out.

Motion, Cycles, and Renewal

. . . nous repérons ce que nos ancêtres ont appris à voir. Nous sommes donc "conditionnés" par la vision du monde de nos ancêtres.

—Daniel Vachon 1987

As people of the First Nations of Canada we have a vision of the sort of country we want to live in and to build in collaboration with other Canadians. It is certainly not the sort of country we have now, one in which our people have been relegated to the lowest rung on the ladder of Canadian society; suffer the worst conditions of life, the lowest incomes, the poorest education and health; and can envision only the most depressing of futures for our children.

We do believe, however, that our situation can be turned around. We believe not only that we can rescue ourselves from these depressing conditions, but that, in the process, we can contribute enormously to the health, effectiveness, and decency of Canada, benefiting every person who lives in this country."

—George Erasmus 1989

Although historians are becoming more interested in native history and culture, the history of Canada as it relates to people who have come to North America—largely from Europe—since the sixteenth century continues to be viewed as fundamentally different from that involving native peoples. In universities, the study of Canadian prehistory and of contemporary native peoples has traditionally been the subject matter of anthropology, while history departments have concentrated on understanding the activities of Canadians of European origin within the broader context of European history.

—Bruce Trigger 1985

In the English language, the word "motion" is used with reference to several domains. Motion can occur in either space or time. In both dimensions, aspects such as direction, pattern, or speed may be described, though the vocabulary relating to these aspects may be space- or time-specific as is the case with "East/West" or "past/present." The concept of motion is also employed in relation to changes which take place in thinking/feeling: we may say, for example, that we are emotionally "moved" by a person, an idea, or a piece of music. When English speakers/ thinkers use "motion" with reference to thought or feeling, they often convey the sense that this motion is "out of time" or "space."

In Algonquian and Iroquoian oral and visual languages, there are also concepts relating to the three English-language meanings—motion in space, in time and in thinking/feeling—many of which have been discussed in earlier chapters. As those earlier discussions revealed, many metaphors, stories, and images did not separate time and space in the same way that English concepts do; nor did they divorce changes in thinking/feeling from their situation in time and space. The Anishnabe Medicine Wheel is a case in point, since it uses a spatial configuration—the axes of the four cardinal directions—to image both temporal motion (the pathway of a life, for instance) and emotional/intellectual motion (the passage from vision to experience, to knowledge, to action, for example). Yet there are other important concepts related to sound and motion, many connecting motion both in time and space/place to processes of renewal.

Renewal and the fundamental importance of cycles and return underlie Vachon's and Erasmus's words. The first quotation, from a speech made when Vachon was Chief of the Montagnais community of Uashat/Maliotenam, Quebec, describes history in terms of the "vision" which is passed from one generation to another. Our dialogue refers to a similar perspective often voiced in Iroquoian communities: that our actions today relate to decisions made seven generations in the past, which will reverberate seven generations into the future. The truth of this is especially poignant in relation to George Erasmus's observation of the wide repercussions of injustice toward First Nations people. But Erasmus asserts the possibility of "turning," moving around the circle, or swinging the pendulum back to complete the vibration.

In the third excerpt, anthropologist and historian Bruce Trigger challenges the Euro-American academic tradition which has often represented Native cultures as static. The history/anthropology division which has paralleled a European/Other dichotomy is especially outdated and misleading in the Native context where the very definition of identity depends on respect for the people who came before, on a link with the vision of those ancestors which remains active in the lives of the living, and on a sense that each generation remakes the original teachings of the culture in their own way, for their own time and place. Only in the 1980s and 1990s have histories begun to appear which reflect Native perspectives on the unfolding of events and interactions.[1]

The academic study of music has often perpetuated sub-disciplinary divisions similar to those described by Trigger. Within the study of European music, motion in time—history—has often been regarded as so important that it constitutes a widely used framework for study. Some studies of non-European music have, on the other hand, privileged motion in space—diffusion, transmission processes; a recent emphasis on historical studies in "ethnomusicology" has changed this disciplinary imbalance somewhat.[2] Paradoxically, the fantastic ability of music to "move" us emotionally is discussed more often in conversation than in the scholarly discourse of musicologists although that, too, is changing in the 1990s.[3]

Reviewing Metaphors of Sound/Motion

Sound and motion are integrally related in many Aboriginal language and performance structures. As we have mentioned, the circle is one of the most pervasive metaphors of sound/motion, as evident in the natural world as in expressive culture. This fundamental image appears in the visual design of instruments and in the dance circle, in which motion (clockwise for Anishnabek and Innu; counter-clockwise for almost every Iroquoian dance) replicates the direction in which living things are said to travel. It serves as a metaphor for

Photo 130. Spider web.

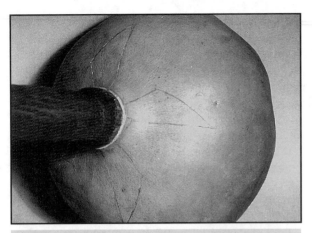

Photo 131. Potawatomi gourd rattle donated to the museum by Mrs. Sterling Pool ca. 1961 (PEAS E37485. FvR 87/10/7).

the "pathways" of human lives and the cycles of history. It is reflected in the cycle of ceremonies which are linked with seasonal cycles of growth, harvest, and new growth (especially apparent in the annual cycle of the Iroquois Longhouse tradition).

Anishnabe elders speak of the circle of life and refer to the "lodge" of life (also metaphorically the Midewiwin lodge) in ways which seem to be homologous. We have seen that a similar metaphor in Iroquoian political theory and social philosophy—the conceptual Longhouse—embodies slightly different images of motion through processes such as "extending the rafters,"[4] processes which also relate to the performance of the Thanksgiving Address which may be expanded or contracted within the structural framework of acknowledging each major element in the cosmos.[5]

Among the verbal metaphors which connect sound and motion are references to their physical indivisibility: vibration. In Algonquian languages, the close connection between sound and motion is evident in the -ue- morpheme, a diphthong which embodies motion in the vowel shift itself and which brings connotations of oscillation, or waving, to many words in which it is embedded. The Micmac infix -tesk- implies vibration and is embedded in some names for rattles. Other verbal concepts connecting sound and motion include the Innu *natu-tau/natutueu* ("s/he listens") implying "motion toward" or "searching."

Related in concept though not marked linguistically in the same way, Iroquoian narratives express pulse, heartbeat, rhythm, and movement. Instruments such as the *ha'nowa* (turtle rattle) or gourd rattles are considered to be animate, sensate, conscious, capable of reaction. Gourd rattles let a singer know when they will be needed for curing "doings" by shaking themselves. Turtle rattles and their com-

panions, *hadui* (wooden face) masks, are said to be able to "jump down from the walls" (fall off the hangers or supports) in an effort to leave houses or museum displays where they are being used inappropriately.

Some conceptual sense of motion or action seems implicit in music and in sound-producing instruments through the Iroquoian suffix *-ot*, which suggests "standing upright" (as in *wa'ë:no:d*, "post stands upright" in Seneca, and *ohonro:ta'*, "pipe/conduit" in Mohawk). To sing, then, is literally to "stand up a song" (similarly, *wa:dënogod* translates as "he held/stood up a ceremony"). According to linguists Reg Henry, Hazel Dean, and David Maracle, the act of "standing up" suggests "calling attention to," "bringing to the fore," "raising up/lifting up/putting into effect." Singers do not literally stand or dance for many songs. Possibly, this concept of motion/putting into play may be connected with *deyohkwa'*, "it lifts up/it throbs, pulses" as translated by Chafe (1967: 54).

We also explored a conceptual relationship between sound and wind/breath/spirit. The Algonquian prefix *pu-* implies a sending out on the breath both when it names a sound producer such as the flute, or a government official such as the Micmac Deputy Grand Chief or *Putu's* ("one who blows the message forth").[6] Some Algonquian instruments are associated with the wind, not just because their sound is activated by blowing, but also because they sound like wind or have the power to cause the wind to rise, as is the case with bull-roarers in Cree and Montagnais tradition (see CMC III-D-162, or HEY 2/9224). Certain Anishnabe instruments have "mouths" through which one breathes to give life (see GLE AP3215, HEY 10/372 or PAS SPINC ID:III.F.3004.d) to the instrument before it is used.

Perhaps the most obvious manifestation of the connection between sound and motion is the indivisibility of song and dance in virtually all Native traditions. The soundscape of an Iroquoian social, for example, would be hard to imagine without the sound of the dancers' feet, marking drum and rattle patterns, or the sound of the singers themselves, stomping as they sing; some singers say that it would be almost impossible to sing with the legs and body still.

Similarly, an Innu *makoshan* combines the drum and dance rhythms as well as the "spirit voices" within the sound of the buzzing snare with its jiggling rattlers. Or, at a powwow, the dance rhythms, accentuated by bells or jingle cones which are part of the dance outfit, are an integral aspect of the experience. Male traditional and fancy dancers wear knee bells; the newest category for men, the grass dancers, on the other hand, do not wear audible sound producers, although the long and colourful yarn fringes sway and swirl around their motions almost as if this "vibration" is too soft for human ears to hear (see Colour Plate 24). With women's dance categories, the "dynamics" of the outfits are reversed. Traditional and fancy dances are silent, while the newest type, the "jingle dress" dancers, are the loudest as a result of the dozens of shimmering metal cones in motion on the surface of the dress.[7]

How can these concepts of motion be used to shape our exploration of sound-producing instruments, both individual instruments and generic types? To answer this, we attempt to look at historical issues, not as exclusively linear phenomena, but as cyclical and renewable.

The One . . .

Individual instruments in themselves may represent a human pathway or constitute one in their own

right. Yet in only a very few instances can we know something about the relationship between a specific instrument we examined and the life of the individual to whom it belonged. There are a few instruments which record images of a personal narrative. Consider, for example, a horn rattle collected by Marius Barbeau on the Seneca Reservation in Oklahoma: CMC III-I-465. The documentation at the Canadian Museum of Civilization tells us that the elaborate engravings on this rattle were made by Chief Bigbone, who "was Christianized in school at Carlisle, Pennsylvania." The rattle perhaps records the narrative of his conversion or reflects a synchronization of the spiritual dimensions of his life. His pre-Christian period is represented by a seven-pointed star and vertical zigzag lines which may indicate lightning—all possibly depict natural forces embodying spiritual power. This particular star design reminded one of our Iroquoian consultants of the pattern of ropes on the bottom of the Peyote drum. Her association may suggest an additional religious affiliation (the Native American Church) denoted in his narrative. The opposite face of the

Photo 132. Traditional dancer, Odawa powwow, 1987. Photo by FvR.

Photo 133. Jingle dress dancer (foreground), Moose Factory, 1987. Photo by K. Hamlin.

horn shows a heart, a cross with an arch over it and the words "JESUS ONEM TO PRAY" (catalogue information transcribes this as "Jesus Only to Pray"). While this might indicate a move away from traditional spirituality to Christianity, it is significant that contemporary Iroquois interpreters described the design as "ecumenical." The adoption of Christianity was regarded as a spiritual increment, not a substitution (and thus blended, rather than exclusive).[8]

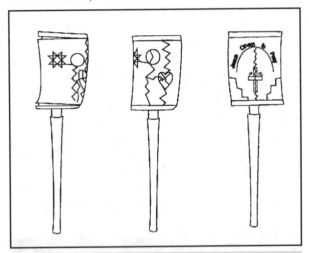

Fig. 23. Images on Chief Bigbone's rattle (CMC III-I-465).

It is likely that other instruments, especially ones with a series of diverse images, represent personal histories, although documentation is non-existent. Another horn rattle, CMC III-I-388, depicts a series of images which may connect in a narrative of some sort. Here the images include a hunter with bow and arrow, a caribou, plants (including a strawberry motif), tree, animals, tent, horn, and diamond-shaped band. In other cases, multiple types of paint on a single instrument or variation in the style of different images suggest that such images may have been added at different points in time, possibly to record new experiences (e.g., CMC III-G-899). Instruments with dream images (e.g., see MAPB) may also "key" narratives, memories, and stories for their owners. These instruments, then, represent a human pathway.

Instruments, however, may have their own pathway, or be part of a larger motion involving other parts of Creation. Elders frequently remind us that a consideration of life cycles draws us, not merely to the human makers/owners/users of sound producers, but to the instruments themselves. In the following statement, for example, Mohawk Confederacy sub-Chief and Longhouse

speaker from Akwesasne, Tom Porter, comments on such a teaching by an elder from his community:

He says that drum, he says it's living. The drum, he says, is just like you, really he said. That drum is a human being too, he said. If you understand what he means, it is living, that drum. Cause the Creator gave that to our people when the earth was new. He said, it's the same thing when the Creator put the people on the earth here. (Video *The Drum*, Ojibwe-Cree Cultural Centre, n.d.)

First Nations contexts are among many others in which instruments are regarded as alive. In fact, the prevalence of such beliefs has led one ethnomusicologist, Sue Carole DeVale, to construct a framework for studying the life cycle of musical instruments. In "Musical Instruments and Ritual: A Systematic Approach" (1990: 128) she charts twelve stages of an instrument's life, acknowledging its spiritual life, its birth, and death, as illustrated in Fig. 24. She recognizes that the construction and use of an instrument is not merely a physical process but one which requires psychological and spiritual preparation.

Similar issues have been described in relation to First Nations instruments. Tom Porter spoke about the necessary spiritual preparation to use a drum:

One time this older man . . . he says you must not just pick up the drum and start playing with it. He said, "Don't do that." And I says, "How come?" . . . " That means you're gonna scare the drum; you are gonna scare the one that is in the drum if you just pick up the drum and start hitting it. By rights what we are supposed to do before we touch the drum," he said, "you should have a good head and a good mind before you go next to that drum, even touch the drum. You should fix things between the Creator and yourself. (Tom Porter, in video, *The Drum*)

Several Anishnabe and Wabanaki drummers made reference to the gestation and birthing of a drum. At an education workshop, a Micmac drum-maker explained that this process began after he had fasted and received a vision which gave him the drum. He described the fast as reciprocal; since a four-legged brother sacrifices his life so that there is a hide for the drum, the drum-maker must give something of himself in return.

"During that time when I was learning about [the] drum, it took me nine months to learn it. I had to learn everything about the drum before I put it together. For that drum is just like a child being conceived. If anybody wants to make a drum they have to learn about it and it takes nine months to learn. And patience and time you have

to put into it to learn. It's just like a commitment. And I am really grateful that drum has been born and brought back to me. And grew important. And during that nine months the name of the drum group came along with it. . . . For the next nine months I travelled, everywhere I wanted to. I talked with singers, drummers, drum keepers. I talked to them. They taught me everything I knew about the drum. And it took me nine months before it was born. I tanned the hide. . . . I had to learn, I had to teach myself to do that. I didn't go up to anybody and ask them, how do you tan a hide? I had to do it myself." (Henry Augustine, workshop presentation at Conne River, Newfoundland, October 1987)

The end of an instrument's life cycle may also be marked. A Maliseet/Passamaquoddy drum was returned to the woods when its sound was no longer "alive." Anishnabe Midewiwin water drums, sometimes with song boards or can rattles, were occasionally buried with their owner (see, e.g., BM 222312) suggesting that the life of the instrument was linked to that of the human who used it. Several other Anishnabe instruments were "collected" from their resting places in the woods where they had been placed after their human users had passed away (e.g., GLE AP339).

Certain Iroquoian instruments, chipmunk sticks, for example, used for wakes or curing doings at Six Nations, must be destroyed after use because of their function.[9] In general, however, Iroquoian instrument makers did not speak of instruments dying, although they may be regarded as cognizant or sentient. When Hubert Buck, Sr. was asked what happens if a gourd rattle breaks and he can no longer repair it, his reply was practical and sensible: "I throw it away and make a new one."

During an instrument's lifetime, respect can be shown in various ways. The big drum, the dance drum, used intertribally, must rest on a blanket or be suspended on a specially constructed and decorated stand; it is covered when not in use. It is smudged with tobacco before use, and the players show respect by abstaining from the use of alcohol or drugs; they may burn sweetgrass to purify their bodies and their thoughts. Some drums have their own songs which must be sung before other repertoire is performed.

Each tradition is somewhat different of course. For example, Innu drummers did not speak of the "birthing" of instruments, although instances were cited, in the previous chapter, of other connections made between a drum and the human body. Some Innu drum-makers say that their dreams provided

Photo 134. Innu disc rattle collected by Frank Speck in Sept-Îles, Quebec, in 1924 (HEY 13/3098. FvR 88/43/19). **"The membrane is dirty and uncared for, not like in the bush where care would be taken to keep the membrane clean and to replace it if it was damaged. . . . Museums lack respect for these things."** (Alexandre Michel)

Photo 135. Potawatomi gourd rattle (GLE R301.47. FvR 88/28/12). **"The membrane is an ingenious way of repairing a damaged gourd."** (Jim Dumont)

instructions to make a drum;[10] others, however, do not regard dreaming as a prerequisite for drum-making.

Like Anishnabek, Innu consultants emphasize the importance of showing respect to musical instruments. Innu drummers sometimes disassemble their drum when not in use and regularly repair or replace a damaged skin.[11] Before use, the drum-maker speaks privately to the drum, and the skin is sprinkled with water until the tautness is right.

DeVale's chart for the lifetime of an instrument provides a useful format for considering these examples. In this context, however, it might be appropriate to focus, not just on the artifact, but on the life of the natural materials from which it is constructed. Consider, for a moment, a drum membrane. Ojibwe teachers explained that the caribou "has a good voice"—the animal skin will sound well when it is made into a drum. The qualities of the animal itself are embodied in its new form.[12] But, perhaps, the skin has not one but several different uses. As mentioned earlier, a Cree elder referred to an artifact as "not yet a drum" (see GLE 999). Hence, while DeVale's model incorporates a single circle of use during the lifetime of the instrument, perhaps a chart oriented toward First Nations instruments should have a series of circles relating to the multiple uses of the natural materials used in the construction of the instrument. The idea of renewal, of the recycling of materials, is thus relevant in yet another way.[13]

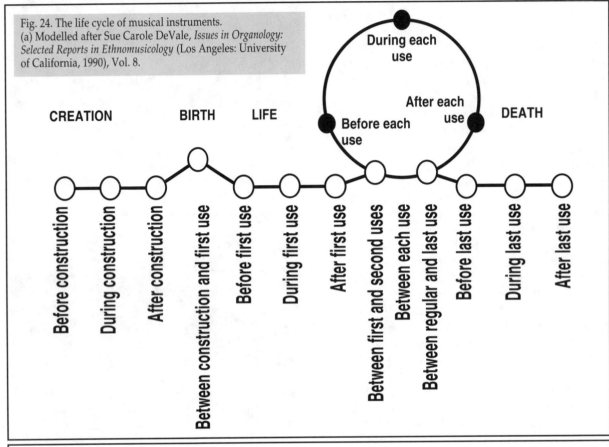

Fig. 24. The life cycle of musical instruments.
(a) Modelled after Sue Carole DeVale, *Issues in Organology: Selected Reports in Ethnomusicology* (Los Angeles: University of California, 1990), Vol. 8.

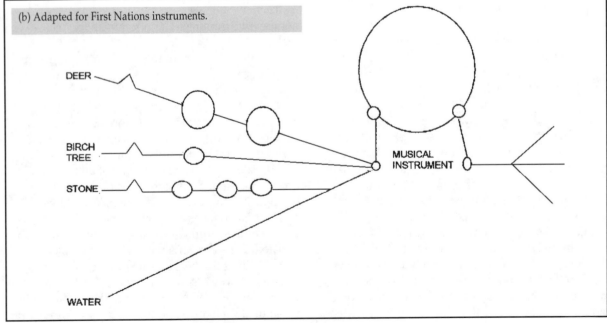

(b) Adapted for First Nations instruments.

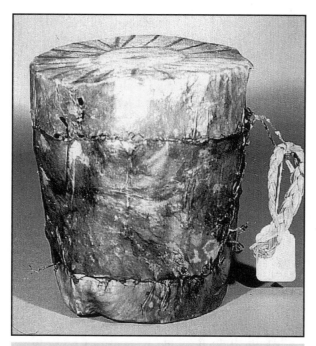

Photo 136. Plains Cree artifact identified as a water bucket which was "not yet a drum" by a Northern Ontario elder. Saskatchewan elders have recently shared the following information with the Glenbow Museum: **The drum belonged to Annie [Blue Eyes'] father, Old Blue Eyes, who was from Fishing Lake [Saskatchewan] and who died in 1957, aged 92 years. It was used in the Sah-puh-too-wan Ceremony. John Skeeboss, of Poorman Reserve, says that this is a Medicine Transfer Ceremony of the Saulteaux Indians** (GLE AP999. FvR 88/25/27).

And the All

Individuals, of course, constitute the components or actors within larger frameworks of history. As we turn to questions about the processes of interaction and the motions which are larger than a single life-time, several factors must be considered.

First, the information available in museum settings contains many well-known discontinuities. "Artifacts," in themselves a sort of Native discourse, are often accompanied by "documentation" which is predominantly non-Native, incorporating variable styles of Eurocentric strategies for naming and interpreting information either shared by Native consultants or simply observed. Information about the human creators/users/owners or about instrument use is often particularly scant; hence the separation of artifact and social context is especially problematic. The interpretations of our consultants are, in relation to museum artifacts, also separated by time and place. Hence, our history is based on three linked but separate sorts of information: the physical forms of sound producers primarily in museum collections, documentation of those forms

and related ones, and contemporary explanations and interpretations of them.

A second issue relates to the interlocking "rhythms" of motion in time and space. Clearly, it is important to situate the historical period for which we have information in relation to the whole pathway of Native history. In fact, the extant artifacts come from a small sector of that pathway, beginning in the early nineteenth century and extending to the present day. The rhythm of such data, particularly the evidence of changing patterns observable in museum collections, may be very different from the rhythm of change in the collective and individual experience of these Nations.

This suggests a third issue: how do different ways of framing questions about historical process influence the resultant "story"? We might, for instance, rely on an "organic" model in which new events are viewed in a cause-and-effect relationship with those which precede or follow. Alternatively, we might construct what Michel Foucault (1972) calls a "genealogy" which explores the multiple and complex factors that create discontinuities, disruptive change, and new directions. The latter approach would be less concerned with change and development within a group, but would focus rather more intensively on interaction between or among groups. In the case of First Nations history, interaction exists, of course, both between Native and European as well as among different First Nations. Exploring multiple responses to actions or events—as well as their repercussions, interpretations, and reinterpretations—enables a better understanding of the dialogue among Nations in North America.

In relation to these rather abstract statements about how we frame "history," consider one historical interpretation by Cayuga linguist Reginald Henry. His "Spiritual Evolution of the Iroquois" describes three religious reforms "in the Iroquois course of time." Each of these represents a new direction—an intellectual, social and political gift from the Creator—taken in reponse to social circumstances and often shaped by the influence of a powerful individual, usually working in consort with others. Hence, like Foucault, Henry represents the abrupt turns in the historical process. Unlike Foucault, however, he emphasizes that each of them are expansions of fundamental cultural principles, which existed a priori.

Prior to the reforms described in this passage, he explains that the religio-political system "was more of a Thanksgiving Ceremony of Mother Earth's creations, of which we benefited almost entirely for survival." He then describes this way of living in a passage quoted in Chapter Two. The article continues:

"Some few thousand years later, the first religious reform enters the Iroquois cultural structure, after tribes were formed and split into different directions. Then came sin with disastrous results. Killings, scalping of each others' people, the plundering of each others' villages, for whatever reason is not clear; it seems it may be the power to rule larger domains for hunting purposes. It brought misery to the women and children. Peace was a thing of the past.

"Then the Creator gave us a man of wisdom, a man with unusual powers, the divine power to survive many attempts on his life, to curtail his purpose of life, to bring peace amongst the Five Nations of the Iroquois. A Five Nation Confederacy that would govern the Iroquois in a unique peace format that would be called the Great Law.

"It was a God-given political structure that would be of religious significance which makes it unique in every sense of the word. Which in itself is hard to believe by non-Natives. The Five Nation Confederacy would consist of the Onondagas, Senecas, Mohawks, Cayugas and Oneidas. In the course of his peace mission, he was to recruit a helper to accomplish this peace mission. After many trying years it was finally accepted by all Five Nations. Much later, the Tuscaroras and Tutelos were accepted into the Confederacy. This peace mission did bring peace to the Five Nations, restored its formal ways of life to a favourable degree. There were no more killings and scalpings. There was peace between the Five Nations. This also was the beginning of the Five Nations political strict structured format.

"The Creator again sent someone from his heavenly domain to restore peace and love amongst his Native people. This was the coming of the fatherless man; this was the second religious reform amongst us Iroquois.

"To restore peace he made the Natives more aware of our Creator; he taught them to appreciate most everything that was created for us, in a more specific way—through ceremonies that mostly consisted of dancing, as dancing is the highlight of any happy event. These ceremonies were continuous from when the air warmed in spring until the air grew cold in the fall from the frost. It was a continuous event of thanksgiving dancing from the first awakening of summer, the running of sap of the maple tree until harvest time in the fall.

"The biggest events amongst the Iroquois are the Green Corn Dance and the Midwinter Dance.

The Green Corn Dance is a three-day ceremony when the Creator and all of our sustenance are given thanks through speeches and dancing. Our main sustenance are corn, beans and squash but the many additional forms are also included. The coming of the fatherless man seems to coincide with the fact that the Natives already had agricultural skills to supplement their natural sources of survival.

"The other big event I spoke of is the Midwinter Ceremony which lasts for eight days at Six Nations. This ceremonial time varies in the different Iroquoian areas. In some areas the ceremony is shorter or longer. Aside from these two big events, there are approximately eighteen events in between. To follow this new religious format closely, there would be little time for killing as the songs and speeches of these ceremonies are also long and require a good deal of time to master.

"At this time, most of the games we know of today were introduced by the fatherless man. Still at this time, there were only Natives on this North American continent.

"The fatherless man's effort was successful and still exists today with the first and second reforms combined. This was life some two thousand years ago.

"Then came the third and last religious reform amongst the Iroquois. This was some 181 years ago, when sin again ravaged Native villages, but this time on a larger scale. Several times over what it was in the past thousand years. This time the Creator transferred his feelings and wants through a medium of this new era, Handsome Lake.

"Handsome Lake declared alcohol the greatest source of sin. Alcohol was bad for the Natives; it changed the mind; it made people capable of sins that they would not commit under normal conditions (sobriety). Alcohol was the biggest force of sin in changing the lives of Native people. The introduction of a new people, a new culture, changed their whole outlook on life. In short, us Natives could not handle what this new culture had to offer; it was new, it was tempting, [and] we became so immersed with this new culture that we lost many of our ways, a culture that was meant only for us Natives. This new culture brought many sins that were unknown in the past.

"Handsome Lake brought this message from the Creator to the Native people and because we were not wholly to blame for the sins, he gave us this wonderful thing of repentance. We could repent for sins we committed, repent to the

Creator. Handsome Lake spent the remaining years of his life preaching this new religious reform amongst Iroquois villages.

"This still exists today. But for how long?

"Handsome Lake predicted, as he did so many other things in our remaining years, that this new culture will introduce their language which in time will completely erase our own Native language from our minds.

"This will be the last of the Natives as a people."

The breadth of Reginald Henry's vision of Iroquoian history, its integration of political and spiritual elements, and its fundamental assumptions about processes of change merit careful consideration with regard to an adequate or appropriate way to write about the history of Iroquoian sound-producing instruments. Similar issues arise

with regard to Anishnabe and Innu instruments. Because questions of "origin" and "agency" may be framed quite differently from different cultural perspectives, histories may vary accordingly.

Musical Instruments: A Linear Approach

A stark contrast to styles of Native discourse about historical process would be a "scientific" assessment by means of quantifiable data. Because of the breadth of our research, as well as our documentation of large numbers of instruments, such an approach is not unwarranted, especially with regard to "museum artifacts." Statistics about these sound producers, however, are the products of such a complex array of factors that one must read their significance with care. The chart in Fig. 25, for example,

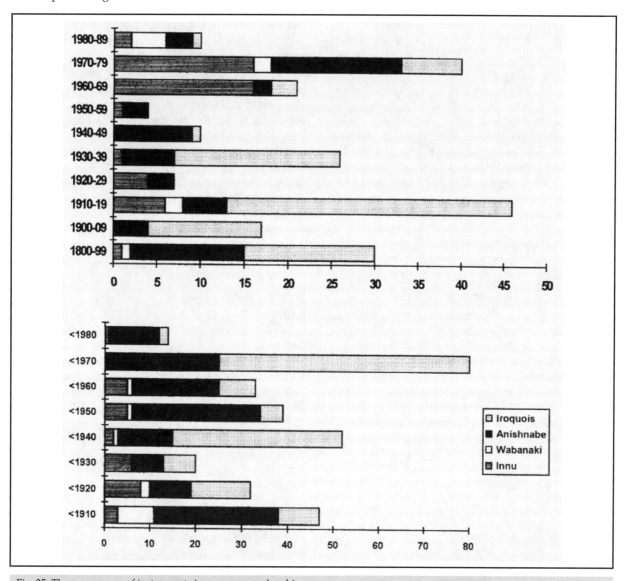

Fig. 25. The provenance of instruments in museums and archives.

165

summarizes information about provenance. The very consistency of collecting indicates a continuing vital instrument-making tradition. For approximately two-thirds of the instruments examined, a construction date can be delimited in some way. Some instruments in museum collections and many in private use have dates inscribed on them; in fact, this design factor continues to have importance for instrument makers themselves. Many can be dated before a certain time (at best with reference to the time when they were collected or, at worst, before the date when they were acquired by a museum). Their history up to that date is unknown to us. Were they made yesterday or used for many generations? Is the documentary information reliable? Are dates incised by owners or users always indicative of construction period, or could they reference other events such as the transfer of ownership? Is any chronological information meaningful unless accompanied by careful documentation of instrument usage such as that recently undertaken by the Glenbow Museum (see *Catalogue*)?

The chart does indicate a modest amount about collection practices. Extensive activity in the first two decades of the twentieth century reflects, in part, the economic interests of private collectors such as D.R. McCord and George Heye. A surge in the numbers for the 1960s and 1970s, on the other hand, is indicative of the rise of regional and local museums/archives in Native communities at that point. Unevenness in the representation of specific Nations and communities, on the other hand, relates to specific collectors' interests or research location. The large number of Naskapi-Montagnais instruments in the 1960s and Algonquin in the 1970s are, for example, both the result of Alika Podolinsky Webber's work and Iroquois instruments of the nineteenth century are largely part of the Lewis Henry Morgan collections. Hence, the chart does indicate certain points within the history of non-Native research interaction with Native communities where an interest in expressive culture is most evident.

A closer examination of specific instrument types reveals some patterns of change which may be more significant, although the meaning of these patterns generally remains a mystery to us. Conclusions must be drawn with care since, as we have described elsewhere, instrument structure and design is individual. In particular with regard to symbolic design elements, meaning may relate to an individual dream, to a group's social or spiritual tradition, to the identity of a Nation, or to an even larger intertribal tradition. Other variables which

are hard to disentangle are regionally rather than temporally based. Assessing change, then, from one geographic area to another or one time period to another, may risk the inappropriate conflation of these varied levels of meaning. The examples below will illustrate.

Iroquoian Instruments

Probably because of the relative ease of travelling among Iroquoian communities and because most of the instrument types remain in current usage at social dances, and "sings," or in Longhouse ceremonies, there are many consistencies in the construction and use of specific Iroquoian instruments. There are some slight regional or chronological differences in preferred shape or size (Allegany rattles tend to be smaller and slightly thicker than those from Six Nations, for example) but these are rarely the things that Iroquoian musicians or instrument makers choose to talk about with us.

Whether or not changes in instrument design relate in any way to changes in dance style is a question discussed by Iroquoian consultants and one meriting further research. Six Nations musicians described significant increases in the tempi of social dance songs; Amos Key suggested that dance tempi changed in the 1930s, a time before which dancers were said to be able to create beautiful, slow patterns with their feet as they moved across the Longhouse floor.

Singers and instrument makers emphasize that instruments are "individual." This was demonstrated in a variety of ways: for example, singers could identify the colour preference of a particular instrument maker when they saw slides of museum artifacts, and they often stressed practicality when asked about the significance of specific design features.

Nevertheless, some regional patterns and historical changes are observable. As mentioned earlier, horn rattles vary in size and shape among contemporary communities. In particular, Allegany rattles from the 1920s and 1930s were recognizable for their smaller size and distinctive shapes. Painting of the horn is now rare, although lacquer or varnish is often used. A few instruments collected in the 1920s, however, were painted in layers. An unusually shaped horn rattle (MCQ E242, collected by Frank Speck, Colour Plate 18) with layers of blue and red paint (and possibly other colours underneath) is a case in point. This particular rattle, which is different in size, shape, and texture from any other Iroquoian horn rattles documented during the course of our work, brings a question about intercultural contact into sharp focus. Is the contemporary cowhorn rattle a post-contact instrument, or a modern substitute for horns from the wood bison, known to have lived in what is now southern Ontario in earlier centuries? This would be consistent with aspects of Reginald Henry's historical discourse which viewed reforms not as replacements of but expansions upon traditional structures.

Water drums similarly reflect individual styles and specific functions (see Conklin and Sturtevant 1953). These small hand-held instruments are used for ceremonies and social dances; larger water drums ("Carry out the Kettle") are used only during *oghiwe*, or Feasts for the Dead. A singer with an especially high voice might otherwise choose a particular drum size or shape to best suit his or her voice. (Vessel size, thickness and dimensions of the inset bottom, membrane tautness, and, of course, the amount of water it contains are the co-determinants of this; however, the interval between the specific pitch of the drum and that of the singer's initial note varies on an individual basis.)

Some differences among the water drums documented, however, seem to relate to historical change. One aspect noted by Native consultants in this regard was shape. A member of the curatorial staff at the Woodland Cultural Centre could accurately recognize pre-and post-1940 drums in this manner. A shift from a nearly cylindrical or inverted, slightly conical vessel to one with a smaller top and larger bottom diameter is partially supported by our documentation. There are exceptions to the pattern, however, suggesting that our measuring tools are insufficient criteria. Our consultant's assessment undoubtedly was subtly influenced by other factors we have not recognized.

Photo 137. Seneca water drum with the date "1805" on the inset bottom. Metal rims are scraped to reveal silver. The drum was collected by Joseph Keppler ca. 1912 (HEY 2/9538. FvR 88/39/13).

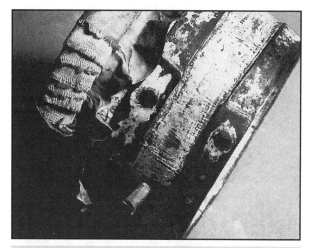

Photo 138. Iroquois water drum (HEY 2/9538. FvR 88/39/14).

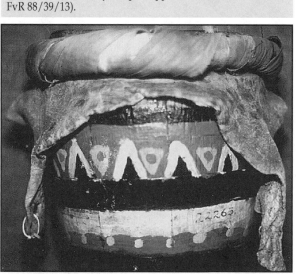

Photo 139. A vividly painted Iroquois water drum with "1812" painted on the inset bottom (ROM 22265. MSC video).

Photo 140. Seneca water drum from Cattaraugus, New York. Acquired by the Heye Foundation in the 1940s as part of the Gyantwaka Collection. Collected by Joseph Keppler whose work in Iroquoian communities was primarily in the first decade of the twentieth century (HEY 20/6707. FvR 88/39/17).

Photo 141. An Iroquois water drum with an unusual inset bottom. Collected before 1920 (HEY 10/4022. FvR 88/39/20).

Photo 142. Red inset bottom of the same drum.

Photo 143. A water drum collected by Guy Spittal at Six Nations in the 1960s (MCQ 965-19. BD 88/8/6).

Photo 144. A water drum from Six Nations with an unusual padded drumstick. Collected before 1930 (AGE C-73. FvR 88/53/1). Concerning a similar water drum, Hubert Buck, Sr. told us that he once lowered the pitch by making a padded stick. See CMC III-I-1201b.

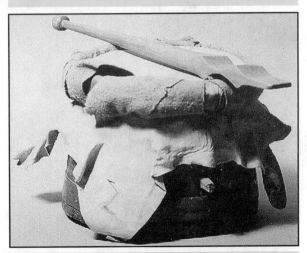

Photo 145. A water drum acquired from "Little Bear" by Frank Speck before 1944 (PEAS E25216. FvR 87/9/8 and 9).

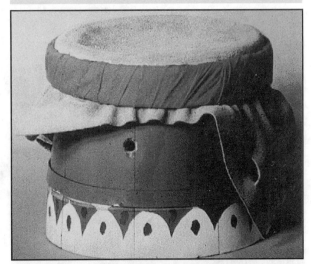

Photo 146. A water drum belonging to Harold Thomas of Akwesasne. Probably dating to the 1950s or 1960s (CMC III-I-1201. FvR 88/1/19).
"You know by the shape that it is post-1940s." (Sadie Buck)

Photo 147. A large Seneca water drum from Tonawanda, New York. Collected by Keppler prior to 1912 (HEY 2/9537. FvR 88/39/31).

Photo 148. Hubert Buck, Sr. drumming at a "Social" at Queen's University (BD 88/1/2).

Overall, there are clear historical changes in construction materials, yet differences in the rate of deterioration of specific organic substances (wood and water-soaked hide do not last long; turtle shells, however, do) sometimes mean that certain parts of an instrument have been replaced. Thus a drum may be a composite of materials and moments. Maple syrup buckets and small sugar barrels used during the nineteenth century were less frequently used for water drums collected after 1930, although their overall form was retained. The return to a "traditional" use of burned-out sections of logs to form the drum frame seems to be a comparatively recent, post-1975 phenomenon in museum collections. Few contemporary instrument makers employ this technique. More recently, plastic pvc tubing has been employed very successfully, with a hardwood inset glued in the base of the drum. Significantly, this essential determinant of the sound quality is carefully selected according to kind of wood and dimension, in the traditional fashion. Drums with plastic frames are used on social occasions in the Longhouse, and less frequently at ceremonies, although singers appreciate their tone quality; they seem minimally attractive to museum collectors, however.

Aspects of decoration also vary historically, to some extent. While external decoration is found on relatively recent water drums, most, but not all, interior designs or painted inset bottoms date from the pre-1940 period (an exception is MCQ 965-19-A).

The elaborateness of carved drumsticks varies throughout the historical period represented in the collections documented. The two with carved snakes are pre-1920. While no post-1940 drumsticks with moving parts were documented in archives, several elaborate sticks with moving parts continue to be used by contemporary singers. Unlike drum vessels, many drumsticks are left unfinished, although brown, black, and/or red paint was used on some artifacts, especially in earlier periods.

A possible preference for more decoration in earlier time periods is supported very slightly in the turtle and horn rattle collections. Turtle shells were less often painted than other instruments, but those with shell division outlines or designs often date from the turn of the century (see, e.g., HEY 9152 as well as the bold floral painting on HEY 9153; Colour Plate 21). One turtle rattle with an unusual stitching pattern, ROM HD7818, is an early nineteenth-century instrument but it is not known whether this stitching style was widely used. Apparent decorative patterns must be interpreted with care. The Brant County Museum and Heye Foundation collection have many black-painted turtle shells among their earliest artifacts, while others such as the Peabody collections contain more "natural" turtle shell rattles. Probably collector or museum preference, rather than an Iroquoian aesthetic, is a factor here. At any rate, we reiterate that contemporary Iroquois instrument makers emphasize individual choice.

While the extent of our documentation enables us to locate certain aesthetic patterns in time and, within a limited historical period, to trace certain changes in construction or design, it is important to state that these are not the sorts of issues which Iroquoian people stress when discussing drums or shakers. Every turtle is unique, caught at a different location, and prepared in a different way.

Significant, too, is the absence of certain materials in collections. There are comparatively few box turtle rattles (although these were and are used in specific Longhouse ceremonies), notched "chipmunk" sticks and drumsticks used at wakes and generally burned at the end of these events, and deer-toe garters (rare at least in relation to the large number of male dancers who likely wore them at Longhouse events). It would be easy to oversimplify or overemphasize change or consistency in design in museum artifacts (and thus our documentation) unless we remember that collections are fragmentary.

Algonquian Instruments

In the Maritime area, as we noted earlier, the variability of terminology and the loss, by the twentieth century, of certain elements of traditional culture complicate attempts at historical reconstruction. Controversy over the existence of pre-contact drums in this region is discussed in Appendix A as are certain shifts in the usage of terminology such as *jikmaq'n*. Furthermore, both historical and contemporary instrument descriptions indicate more diversity than museum collections (which contain only cowhorn rattles and moose calls from this region). Western Abenaki basket rattles seem to have developed concurrently with the splint-basket industry in the nineteenth century although, like the Iroquois cowhorn rattles, they may have been modelled on some earlier form; drums in contemporary collections are all made within the past few decades. The introduction of western traditions seems to have accelerated since the 1940s as families such as that of Ontario-born Anishnabe Eddie Kabatay moved east. The traditionalist movement associated with the big drum began in the 1980s; western teachings are welcomed by some individuals but regarded by others as "not theirs." Change occurred rapidly in the

1980s, however, so that, the number of traditional drums active in the Maritimes expanded from one to at least fifteen by 1990. Many young Micmac boys began to carry drumsticks tucked into their belts, and set up the drum in the schoolyard between classes. Furthermore, Catholics and traditionalists speak of mutual respect and have met together in ceremonies since the early 1990s. The instances of ecumenism reaching across ethnocultural boundaries have also increased; for example, the Micmac and Acadian communities of Canada's smallest province, Prince Edward Island, celebrated the Feast of Ste. Anne together for the first time in 1993.

In Innu and Anishnabe areas, on the other hand, a few tentative historical and regional variations may be observed, although, in every case, data are not uniform or consistent. There are some indications that musical instruments are now decorated or embellished less than in pre-1940 periods.[14] There is more evidence, however, for changes in the style of imagery. Among the extraordinarily varied Midewiwin grandfather water drums of various Nations, half red/half blue drums as well as instruments with incised panther designs were mostly collected for museums in early periods (GLE AP412 is an exception) and from western regions. Like the bird/horse-shaped sticks used with the grandfather drum, it may be that older instruments stay closer to the mythic origins in which creatures such as the loon gave itself to be the drumstick or in which the drum is sometimes said to have been pushed up through the earth until half was above ground and half below ground. Colour rings, indicative of clan in some cases, are not specific to a region or time period. On the other hand, while there are many grandfather drums in archival collections, it is likely that the "rhythm" in design/structural change is slower than that represented by those instruments described in this study.

This asynchronization between the rhythm of the data and the rhythm of historical change is clearly evident in Anishnabe drumsticks. Elders explained that bird/horse-shaped sticks pre-date the cross type made from two separate pieces of wood (see CMC III-G-33). All three of the cross-type sticks described in our documentation, however, are pre-1920 (BM Am1982 A2811 is mid-nineteenth century; HEY 2/7995 and CMC III-G-33 are from the 1910-1920s decade). Hence, the limited chronological range of museum artifacts implies a sequence which runs counter to the larger patterns of history referenced by elders.

In Innu communities, a reduction in decoration over the course of the twentieth century is evident in the museum artifacts and is described by a contemporary Montagnais drum-maker, who observed the uniformity of present-day instruments as compared to earlier periods, when instrument designs were more individualized. Such an individualized drum is the turn-of-the-century Kurtness drum (MAPB; Colour Plate 25), which represents a dream narrative in paintings on each of its two sides (according to the Musée amérindien de Mashteuiatsh, to which the family has entrusted this instrument). Drums with red and blue dots or with rims of various colours have, for the most part, given way to the red-rimmed style most prevalent in contemporary north-shore communities in the 1980s.

Photo 149. Alexandre Michel of Sept-Îles, Quebec with a drum which he made in 1989. Photo by BD.

Visually striking are the intricate carved designs of nineteenth- and early twentieth-century bone drumsticks, particularly those from Naskapi communities (e.g., HEY 15/5558, Colour Plate 26). These resemble Anishnabe wooden sticks with horse features (square snout, mane) associated with the grandfather water drum. The current type of whittled wood stick as well as a form with bone reinforced by wood (HEY 22/5476) appear to be later styles.

Shifts in snare materials are also observable, although there are regional as well as chronological distinctions in this regard. All Naskapi *teueikana* documented in our catalogue have quill snares. Two drums with bone snares are widely separated in time (PEAH 94-38/62489 dates from the 1890s, while MAPB may be as recent as the 1950s). While consultants describe wood snares as more recent than either bone or quill, drums with wood snare rattlers from the 1920s are among those documented in museum collections. A currently popular style of wooden rattler with red painted ends was already established at that time. The earliest wooden rattlers in collections are from the more westerly Montagnais and Attikamek communities. Some Cree and Algonquin drums (see, e.g., ROM 969.323.1a, possibly dating from the 1960s and CMC III-L-203, from the 1940s) have similar snare styles with red-tipped wood rattlers. Other Cree drums from different decades have distinctive parallel snare configurations (see HEY 7/1063, CMC 79-42-76, or CMC III-D-63) or single snares with stone rattles (e.g., HEY 17/6820). Again, however, we emphasize that conclusions are premature, since regional and historical variations are sometimes hard to distinguish.

Algonquian disc rattles, widely used in both Innu and Anishnabe communities, depict functional as well as both regional and historical diversity. Distinctive shapes are sometimes specific to a community or region. Long, relatively straight handles were made in communities west of Quebec, while convex curved or looped handles are the norm in Northern Quebec and Labrador (compare Cree or Ojibwe straight-handled rattles—CMC III-G-446, CMC III-D-121, 525, or 770—with Naskapi-Montagnais curved handles—HEY 13/3098, CMC III-B-93, or ROM 958.131.361; HEY 13/3224 is an exception, a straight-handled Montagnais rattle). Attikamek rattles use a wider "frame" (called internal structural support in the catalogue) over which the membrane edges are separated and sometimes covered with an additional membrane. In the collections documented, Cree instruments had the widest range of membrane material, including bird skin, fish skin, and bird stomach lining—each with specific medicinal value.

Although our documentation was quite extensive, it is not possible to speculate about the loss of instrument types or the development of new ones.

In many cases (e.g., in the case of the Midewiwin little boy drum), ceremonial instruments were not collected, or disassembled instruments were not recognized. Some instrument types are more prevalent among those from early decades; Iroquoian gourd rattles were more widely collected pre-1930 (although a number of later ones are found in the Peabody-Salem collection, mostly donated by a single instrument maker). It is likely that these valued, sensate instruments were kept out of the hands of collectors in later decades. The same explanation may be true for the handleless rattle/drums which also date from earlier periods. Some instruments described by elders (e.g., a Cree fiddle made from a caribou shoulder blade, a Micmac hemispheric drum) appear in none of the collections we saw.

It should be reiterated, in conclusion, that the rhythms of historic change and continuity are often not the same as the apparent historical shifts in form and design evident from the documentation of museum artifacts. What shifts we are able to observe may stimulate further research, but, in themselves, are not to be regarded as significant unless reinforced by other factors. Comments by elders about changes in function or social practice are much more reliable indications of significant changes in instrument usage or meaning. Furthermore, the very emphasis on change rather than continuity constitutes, in itself, a Euro-American bias.

Music, Motion, and Interaction

What are the implications of the contrasts between the approaches to history demonstrated thus far in this chapter for a (re)vision of the history of First Nations music culture? How can one write a history with respect for the fundamental concepts which underlie Native "texts" (some of which are musical instruments) representing a oneness of motion in time, space, and thought/feeling? How can we approach the subject of interaction within and among human societies without discounting or losing sight either of the importance of individuality, on one hand, or, on the other, the incredibly large rhythms of Aboriginal history, rhythms which may not be reflected in the segments of "data" available in archives and museums? Is the very concept of "sequential history" compatible with the fundamental First Nations metaphors of circles, cycles, turning, and renewal? We do not presume to have profound answers to these difficult questions. Rather, we regard this final section not only as a completion of the circle of our study but, at the same time, as

the beginning of a new circuit. Here we offer only a few examples of some directions such a circuit might take.

First, we might return to Reg Henry's assertion that all spiritual and ceremonial developments are gifts of the Creator. Consistent with this belief is the fact that for certain Iroquois ceremonies, especially for *Ostowagowah* (Great Feather Dance) and curing society "doings," no new songs or instruments are created. These *odrenodahkwa*/musical instruments and song cycles are considered to be already complete—they are gifts from the Creator, and as such, do not require radical innovation. Their repeated performance, in the right sequence and the right way, establish and strengthen relationships. In the Iroquoian worldview, retelling stories and re-experiencing ceremonies does not connote a static (ergo lifeless) tradition. It seems that Iroquoian and other First Nations communities perceive these traditions as fundamentally re-creative, establishing anew a system of universal relationships. Like the changing seasons, each ceremony, each instrument is unique but is part of a sequenced pattern of existence. This philosophy is similar to that described by Anishnabek with reference to the Midewiwin or by Innu with regard to the classic myths known as *atnukana*.

Traditional genres may find new venues and media: the ever-burgeoning repertoire of Iroquois *eskanye*, women's social dance, considered to be one of the oldest cycles of social music, existing since the earth itself began. New repertoire often incorporates text and melodies borrowed from other music. Songs may be performed for community social events and after ceremonies, or even at conferences and lectures. During the past three decades, biannual "sings" have been introduced, where individuals from all Iroquois communities gather for a joyous day of music-making. Surrounded by tape recorders of every colour and size, *eskanye* groups renew and refresh a tradition enjoyed by countless generations of *ha:drenota'*.

The Innu *mokoshan* is similarly multifunctional; although still associated with hunting practices, an association described by singers when they bring the *nikumana* ("songs/hunting tools") into a contemporary concert or festival setting, the same "repertoire" is sometimes used for a social dance concluding wedding festivities, for example. A huge repertoire of Innu myths, told within family circles especially during the long, dark winter months, are also renewed in theatrical performances or even puppet productions.

There are, however, further musical implications to the fact that motion is often related to

Changing Innu Performance Contexts

Photo 150. "Nascapee (*sic*) dance at Seven Islands." Photo by Frank Speck, 1924 (HEY neg. 12063).

Photo 152. The Innu Nikamu festival at Maliotenam, Quebec, in 1988. Drummer is Joseph McKenzie from Schefferville, Quebec (BD 86/5/20).

Photo 151. A procession led by a *teueiganask*. Archives Obedjiwan.

natural processes. Wabanaki Simon Marshall (who was, at the time of our interview, the Deputy Grand Chief of the Micmac) implies an answer as he describes changes in the music of his community of Eskasoni, Cape Breton. Traditional Micmac songs were retained in memory in Maritime Micmac communities even though they lost many of their earlier functions and these repertoires are now being retaught. He refers to several of the important tradition-bearers and teachers: Michael Paul (father of one of our primary consultants), a respected singer, and Sarah Denny, who formed the first Micmac dance group in Cape Breton and who performs in a wide variety of contemporary contexts ranging from the Canada Games to concerts with two widely acclaimed colleagues, the poet Rita Joe and the fiddler Lee Cremo:

Renewal

An 1860 description of performances before the Prince of Wales:

"His Royal Highness then rode off the review ground in the midst of the most enthusiastic cheering from the multitude surrounding the reserved space, and under a salute from the Volunteer Artillery.In the course of the afternoon he rode out to the Common again, in plain dress, and witnessed the rural sports there going forward; the racing and the Indian war-dance, performed by the remnant of the Mic Mac tribe, in particular attracted his attention." (Kinahan Cornwallis, *Royalty in the New World; or the Prince of Wales in America* [New York: Doolady, 1860])

Photo 153. "Micmac War Dance of 1914." The photographer (possibly by Mechling) documents the event as follows: "Of course in Warfare and in the war dances therein, the kilt was the only clothing—the shirts and stockings herein shown are concessions to modern ideas of propriety." McCord Museum.

Photo 154. A 1986 performance of a Micmac social dance, by dancers from Cape Breton, directed by Sarah Denny. The dancers' costumes are re-creations of nineteenth-century clothing styles. Photo by MSC.

"[Michael Paul] he sang good songs; they sounded like the circle [at Chapel Island, an important site for annual Micmac gatherings as well as the place Micmacs go each year to celebrate Ste. Anne's Day]. When he started singing it filled right up, you know. It was good the way he sang it, you know. And he sang the dancing songs different, like he was playing the fiddle. And if you heard him singing—even if you didn't know the step—you could dance to it. Do you know what I mean? There were those who knew how to dance to it. I know how to step-dance, you know. I'm not saying that I'm a champion but I could dance to it because I understand it. . . .

"On the island. That was a long time ago, on the island. Nobody else sang after that, just like him. . . . Sarah, she changes them [the songs] you know. The air changes, that's how the air happens." (Simon Marshall, Sr., in an interview with Franziska von Rosen and Tom Paul, 1988)

Without regretting the loss of a singer such as Michael Paul and the loss of the tradition of singing in a way which inspired dance, without denying that the contemporary performances of a dance ensemble are somehow different in style, Simon Marshall celebrates change with analogy to the essential nature of motion in nature. "Air changes" if life is to be sustained.

Related to this explanation is his easy move from a description of traditional Micmac singing to fiddle music and step-dancing. By resisting a rigid distinction between genres, he demonstrates what Todd has recently stated: "when we articulate the dichotomy of the traditional versus the contemporary, we are referencing the centre, acknowledging the authority of the ethnographer, the anthropologist, the art historian, the cultural critic, the art collector" (Todd 1992: 75).

The prime function of song—to heal, to inspire good feelings and joyous actions such as dance—is fundamental; new repertoires are developed and used within this basic paradigm. The same attitude is evident in many other situations and statements. The use of new materials for musical instruments (whether Pepsi cans for Anishnabe rattles or plastic water pipe for Iroquois water drums) does not represent disruptive change if the right sound and right connection to the natural and social environment are maintained. The celebration of contemporary songwriting by Innu musicians "Kashtin," staging of contemporary theatre by Huron playright Yves Sioui-Durand, or performances of fiddle music and step-dancing by Attikamek youth from Obedjiwan at the annual Innu Nikamu ("the Indian sings") fes-

tival in Maliotenam, Quebec, are seen not as threats to tradition but as opportunities to renew the language and the traditional values of Aboriginal people. The same is true when the word "traditional" is applied to newly created dances by the Abenaki dance troupe, "Mikwobait" ("those who remember") from Odanak, Quebec, or to new songs brought to the Micmac drum of Big Cove by musician/elder George Paul.

Just as it would be naïve to assert that the motion of "air" was always life-affirming and never destructive, it is necessary to consider instances where cultural change was, perhaps, not so passively available. Music associated with the Christian church, the introduction of the fiddle by seventeenth- and eighteenth-century Celtic and French fur traders, or the regimental and civilian bands of the British had variable impact on the musical traditions of different communities and Nations. The complexity of the interaction, and the diverse responses of Native and non-Native peoples to the music of the other communities has, as yet, been researched relatively little.

That music censorship was in some cases part of the widespread oppression of Native people is undeniably true. In some areas, such as the James Bay coastal communities, aggressive repression of traditional ceremonies, language, and other practices included music (see Whidden and Preston in RAQ 18/4, 1985/86). Drums were destroyed or their use not permitted. Some Native consultants think that such suppression also accounts for the absence of drums in Maritime Algonquian cultures in the nineteenth and twentieth centuries. In communities such as those of the Innu of Labrador and northern Quebec, however, drumming continued even though Christianity was generally adopted. Possibly the fact that the drum was described as a "hunting tool" and often used away from the village context made it less problematic in the eyes of missionaries. Early twentieth-century photographs depicting drums in the context of religious processions, however, reveal that drums were integrated into Christian events in some Northeastern Woodlands village contexts.

Native responses to the music of the Christian church were first represented by the authors of the Jesuit *Relations*. Their particular interests in convincing European superiors of the success of their conversion efforts shaped the style and substance of those representations. Only recently have descriptions of hymn-singing in Native (rather than missionary) performance contexts emerged (see Cavanagh 1988 [1992]; Grant 1984; Powers 1987).

The Uncertain History of Micmac Drums

Photo 155. A contemporary Abenaki drum made by Monsieur de Gonzague, Odanak, Quebec (MAB. FvR 85/1).

Photo 156. Micmac or Malecite drum collected in New Brunswick, ca. 1913, by Mechling. Canadian Museum of Civilization. See CMC III-F-213 a and b.

The historical position of drums among the Micmac is a subject of contention.

In the late seventeenth century, Father Le Clercq observed Micmacs accompanying their singing by "striking with a stick upon a bark plate or upon a kettle" (1910: 292).

In the eighteenth century, Dièreville describes the instrument with which the Micmacs accompany their singing as "a little stick about a foot long, which an Indian who is not dancing, strikes against a tree, or some object, according to the place in which they happen to be . . ." (1935: 173-74 [1710]). Father Maillard describes a Micmac feast at which "girls and women come in, with the oldest at the head of them, who carries in her left hand a great piece of birch-bark of the hardest, upon which she strikes as if it were a drum . . ." (1758: 4-10).

In the nineteenth and early twentieth centuries, references to Passamaquoddy and Penobscot drums appear. Prince published a transcription which he labels "The Song of the Drum." Speck states that the "drum has never been used in dance performances within memory [at Penobscot]" (1940: 271) but he suggests that the drum has disappeared due to Christianization (ibid.). He witnessed dancing accompanied by the cowhorn rattle or, in the case of a dance he calls "The Micmac Dance," a baton struck on the floor (ibid.).

Contemporary Micmac describe several instruments:

"Over here in the Eastern part, North-eastern part of Canada, along the coast, among the Micmac people we didn't have such a drum as that [big drum]. We had birch-bark hand drums and blocks of wood that we used to use, and rattles. Rattles were made out of the cloth of the deer and moose. And rattles were also made out of black spruce bark, alder bark, and horns. Our culture is related to only [the] hand drum." (George Paul, speaking at a cultural workshop for Micmac children at Conne River, Newfoundland, in 1987)

The birch-bark hand drum, described by George Paul may have looked like this single-membrane frame drum (Photo 156). It has a bleached rawhide which completely covers a wide frame and is "button-hole stitched" to the lower edge of the frame. Double-membraned frame drums like those of the Penobscot (see Photo 157) and several other types are currently used in Micmac and other Wabanaki communities.

These accounts reveal a wide range of active creative responses by Native communities to Christianity. It is clear (as we saw in conjunction with Chief Bigbone's rattle) that Christianity was, for some people, an addition rather than a substitution within their beliefs. Just as traditional ceremonies were not necessarily abandoned with the acceptance of some aspects of missionary teaching, so too were Christian practices sometimes borrowed and adapted to traditional contexts.

Musical instruments were sometimes integral to this renewal process. For example, around the turn of the century, the Saulteaux around Lake Winnipeg fused the fiddle with the vision quest, according to accounts by Jack Steinbring.

This fusion comes about in the requirement that during a four-day fast, the male initiate must learn to play the fiddle. An old man completely departed from the norm of Ojibwa stoicism when he wept in relating his failure to accomplish this feat. He had taken his fiddle to a deep, interior location on Black Island, a sacred place. For four days, he tried his best. At the end of the period his fingers were torn and bleeding, and he could not play tunes. It was his greatest personal disaster. He later became a strong advocate of Christianity. (Helm 1981: 251)

Such syntheses between one tradition and a new, borrowed activity, however commonplace in other human societies, have been little acknowledged in First Nations contexts until recently. Sharing and borrowing of traditions was seen as a one-way road in which Europeans might adopt the toboggan or snowshoe without risk to their identity, but Indians who played a fiddle or wore a cross have been pictured as acculturated or assimilated in scholarly texts as well as popular culture.

In other instances, descriptions of cultural synthesis exist but in a way which undermines the

Photo 157. Penobscot drum (CMC III-K-52. FvR 88/9/16).

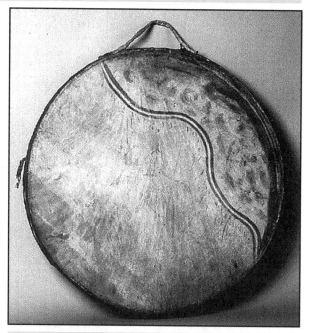

Photo 158. Ojibwe drum associated with the moccasin game (two sides) (CMC III-G-1110. FvR 88/11/19).

Photo 159. Other side of drum shown in Photo 158 above.

"They accompany their songs with drums. I asked the origin of this drum, and the old man told me that perhaps some one had dreamed that it was a good thing to have, and thus it had come into use. . . .

"As to this drum, it is the size of a tambourine, and is composed of a circle three or four finger-lengths in diametre, and of two skins stretched tightly over it on both sides; they put inside some little pebbles or stones, in order to make more noise; the diametre of the largest drums is the size of two palms or thereabout; they call it *chichigouan*, and the verb *nipagahiman* means, 'I make this drum sound.' They do not strike it, as do our Europeans; but they turn and shake it, to make the stones rattle inside; they strike it upon the ground, sometimes its edge and sometimes its face, while the sorcerer plays a thousand apish tricks with this instrument. Often the spectators have sticks in their hands and all strike at once upon pieces of wood, or upon their *ouragans*; that is to say, upon their bark plates turned upside down. To this din they add their songs and their cries, I might indeed say their howls, so much do they exert themselves at times; I leave you to imagine this beautiful music.

"They use these songs, this drum and the noises in their cures. . . . Sometimes this man enters like a fury, singing, crying, howling, making his drum sound with all his might; and the others also cry and make a terrible din with their sticks, hitting them on whatever is in front of them; they make the young children dance, and then the girls, and then the women. They kiss the earth, blow on the drum and then toward the fire; they whistle like a snake, and take the drum without the stick, shaking and turning it; they strike the earth with all their force and turn him [the patient] on his stomach; they close his mouth with one hand and with the other, you would think they wanted to break the drum, they strike it so hard against the ground. They move, turning from one side to another, circling the fire several times, then leaving the cabin still crying and making noise." (Le Jeune, 1634)

"authenticity" of traditional religion. The ethnography of the Anishnabe Midewiwin is a case in point. The origin of this institution is disputed in different sources. Historians such as Hickerson (1970) believe that it is post-contact and influenced by Christianity. His reasons may be rooted in the lacunae in existing writings—the absence of references to the Midewiwin in the earliest European accounts such as the Jesuit *Relations*—lacunae which could also be explained as self-interested masking of the vitality of competing religious beliefs. The hypothesis has led to interpretations of symbols such as the cross or crescent as Christian (see Hickerson 1970: 62). Contemporary Midewiwin members, on the other hand, observe that such ethnographies have ignored the pre-Christian usage of the same symbols.

While there has been relatively little writing to date about the musical responses of Native people to Christian traditions, there has been even less about non-traditional indigenous music which functions in First Nations "social" settings including weddings, church socials, legion concerts, square dances, and house parties. The ubiquitous fiddle and button accordion were especially popular in areas of northern Ontario and Quebec. In the community of Maniwaki, we were told that virtually every adult owned and played a fiddle a generation ago. In the Attikamek community of Obedjiwan, a step-dance ensemble for children is supported by the community. In the Maritimes, the fiddle was equally valued. The well-known Micmac fiddler Lee Cremo regards his fiddle as a vital personal possession; he explained that his father told him: **"You don't lend your wife away and you don't share your fiddle; it's something real special in other words"** (*The Sound of the Drum* 1990: 60). In addition to "old time" square or step-dancing, western swing and country music were popular with Native audiences from the 1940s. As with other repertoires, new genres often complement (rather than replace) older ones; hence a Cree dance may alternate rock, country, and fiddle tunes.

Some traditions functioned under the auspices of European institutions or Native imitations of them. In the first half of the twentieth century, instruction was often provided on violin, lute, or mandolin, as well as in keyboard and vocal music within the residential school system. Stories about the traumatic experiences of Native children in these schools, which often separated them from parents and community and denied them the right to use their language, are beginning to emerge in mainstream media. Whether music instruction was part of the oppression or part of the rare happier moments in these contexts merits further attention.

Both regimental and civilian "Indian Bands" flourished in northeastern Woodlands communities from the mid-1800s until the 1960s. Community-based bands performed in traditional-style outfits, attracting both Native and non-Native audiences at parades, fairs, and exhibitions. A separate phenom-

enon emerged at the turn of the twentieth century when entrepreneurs, capitalizing on the popularity of travelling 'Wild West' shows, organized international tours of Native musicians. A few of these bands still flourish; the Oneida marching bands, for example, are among local groups that take part in the Indian Border Crossing Days celebrated each July between Ontario and New York State.

Native musicians endeavouring to establish professional careers in Canada have encountered unique challenges. Until a revision in 1951 to the Indian Act, for example, it was illegal for Native people to enter or perform in restaurants or bars licensed to sell liquor, although such regulations were occasionally overlooked. Musicians challenging such barriers earlier this century included baritone soloist Os-Ke-Non-Ton (Louie Deer, 1890-1950) from Kahnawake, Quebec, and jazz pianist Robert Jamieson (1877-1966) from Six Nations Reserve, Ontario. In the 1920s and 1930s, Os-Ke-Non-Ton performed in Toronto and New York, later touring in Great Britain and Europe. From the 1930s through the 1960s, Jamieson was in demand in nightclubs in southern Ontario and New York State; his performance style was strongly influenced by Fats Waller, Count Basie, and Stan Getz. He served with the US army in the 1940s, later returning to Six Nations where he continued to play at local dances and legion concerts.

From the mid-1960s through the 1970s, a new wave of folksingers began to voice Aboriginal issues in music which developed an urban, cross-cultural audience.[15] From the communities involved in this study came Cree singer Morley Loon, Algonquian/Mohawk performer Willy Mitchell, and Abenaki filmmaker/singer Alanis Obomsawin among others. Some artists such as Winston Wuttunee oriented many of their songs specifically to children and youth in their own communities. Initiated by Montagnais singer/guitarist Philippe McKenzie, an increasing number of Native performers in Quebec, in particular, composed songs in their own languages and often incorporated traditional stylistic elements. The new style, called "folk Innu" was supported at local festivals and the large-scale, annual "Innu Nikamu" festival in Maliotenam, Quebec (since 1985). The extraordinary success of the Montagnais duo, Kashtin, whose first album with songs exclusively in their own language sold over 200,000 copies in Eastern Canada, lends additional impetus to this movement at the present time.

Contemporary non-traditional music resists simple categorization, reflecting the diverse audiences in urban and reserve contexts as well as the

Photo 160. Odanak music class. Musée des Abénakis.

Photo 161 Members of North American Indian band. Glenbow Archives.

Photo 162. "L'Harmonie Abénakise," 1914. Musée des Abénakis.

Photo 163. Teaching Micmac dance. Conne River, Newfoundland. Photo by FvR.

various musical influences and cultural traditions which shape it.[16] In the 1980s and early 1990s, blues seems especially popular, represented by performers such as Murray Porter from Six Nations, Ontario, Ben Simon from Big Cove, New Brunswick, and Leonard Martin from Moose Factory, Ontario. Reggae is among the styles created by the eclectic group, 7th Fire (formerly known as Thom E. Hawk and the Pine Needles) based in Ottawa. Using humour as an effective means for social commentary in songs such as " The Death of John Wayne" and "High Tech Teepee Trauma Mama" they succeed in expressing emotionally charged issues in a way that is accessible to all audiences. Rock bands have thrived in virtually every reserve community since the 1970s. The James Bay Cree band Harrapashires is among those achieving regional success and reflecting a broad range of contemporary issues, among them world events as in the song "Tiananmen Square." Many bands are now reaching beyond the boundaries of community and country, often relating the need to take Native teachings to other parts of the world to environmental issues; the Micmac band, Eagle Feather, for example, prepared a programme of traditional and country/rock music for a European tour in 1993. Perhaps the most consistently popular genre in Native communities is country music. A few performers have acquired a profile beyond their own community, among them Mark Laforme of New Credit, Ontario, Eagle Feather from Big Cove, New Brunswick, or the C-Weed Band, led by the singer Errol Ranville, from Winnipeg, Manitoba.

Within the diversity of styles, what emerges as "shared" is the emphasis which Native musicians place on the emotional quality of the pop music they perform, the continuing close connections between music and dance, the humour and strength with which Native perspectives and values are affirmed and, in some cases, the uses of music as vehicles for social change. Statements about these qualities enable us to begin to understand the importance of new genres as forces for renewal and, at times, resistance.[17] In some cases, these statements could hold true in a variety of cultural contexts. Algonquian singers Clifford and Joan Tenasco from Maniwaki, Quebec, for example, explain:

"Country music is like an international language. It's part of everybody's life, because it sings about lost loves, it sings about heartaches, good times, what people go through. . . . There's always a memory or a connection that you make with it."

In other cases, statements reflect a desire to be recognized as culturally different. As Gilles Chaumel stated in *Rencontre* (February 1989):

"The new aboriginal music is precisely about building an identity. This new music is alive because it is constantly changing. It reflects aboriginal society . . . which itself is being transformed."

It is clear that the perspectives of non-Native observers have shaped the historical picture of Native music in several ways: by ignoring the identity of individual Native participants in music-making, by privileging Euro-American elements in certain traditions which were adopted within Native contexts, or by failing to regard instruments themselves within the framework of "all my relations." The emphases suggested by consultants in this study, on the other hand, would cast a different history. The sharing and borrowing of traditions would be seen as culture enrichment, not culture loss. The "authenticity" of ceremonies would not preclude identification of Christian or European influences. The possibility of dual/plural religious affiliation would be entertained. And the extent of Native achievements in other musical/artistic domains would be acknowledged. Perhaps, most fundamentally, the capacity for renewal, a capacity which is amply being demonstrated in North American society in the 1980s and 1990s, would be adequately recognized.

The treatment of historical questions is, of course, consistent with the treatment of other domains—the study of language, image, or process. In all cases, the challenge of respecting and responding to a fundamentally separate pathway has been the issue, whatever the "subject" of study.

Final Comments

Like every other abstraction explored in this book, "motion" can mean various things within different languages or cultures. This chapter describes different "rhythms" in historical descriptions, and considers how concepts such as renewal or "expanding the rafters" might help to frame a history which respects the approaches of Anishnabe, Haudenosaunee, Wabanaki, and Innu consultants. We have shifted the lens from one section to the next, focusing on the physical forms of artifacts, and then on the way in which these artifacts lead us to stories about the development of institutions within Native societies or the interaction among Aboriginal and European people. These shifts are not arbitrary, in our view, but reflect a belief that patterns and meanings may be played out at different levels and in different ways.[18] As we understand it, this belief is consistent with some of the ways of "knowing" which many patient Native consultants and musicians have tried to teach us in the course of this project.

In this regard, we are reminded of a statement by John Cove referring to the Northwest Coast Tshimshian culture: "each domain [natural, cultural, supernatural] provides metaphors for the others, and . . . the overall system cannot be reduced to any one of them without distorting the underlying understanding" (1987: 50). While the area about which he writes is geographically and linguistically remote from the ones in which we have been learning, his description of the manner in which metaphors are mapped from one "system" to another is consistent with what we have learned in the course of this study.

With Cove, we believe that "history is emergent"; its shape and meaning changes as events, images, and texts intersect with new experiences. Further, we have argued that "meaning is emergent" at the same nexus. This is a difficult argument

Photo 164. Drum. Photo by MSC.

to make in print, since written words are more often regarded as objectified, not performative. In reading print, one risks the loss of these qualities of coincidence, emergence, and ambiguity which we explored in relation to sound/sound producers and the discourses of both language and visual design that relate to them. In many cases, meaning has not yet emerged in this study; we make no apology for this. One elder suggested to us that this book would serve to "light fires." By this, we understand that he had faith that further meaning would emerge, further stories would be shared, and further energy generated in the future if information that has often not been easily available to Native communities was put forward openly and if problems of understanding that information were discussed honestly.

Fundamental to our attempt to do this is our belief that we should not discount the range of individual interpretations which may be true for a time, a place, or a person. Furthermore, we reflected on our individual ways of responding to these interpretations. Western scholars sometimes criticize this way of knowing as solipsistic, arguing that it is fallacious to believe that the self is all that can be known. We argue instead that the self is where we start and where we return. We affirm the importance of acknowledging the *range* of individual experiences. In its diversity, this range constitutes the larger-than-self, larger-than-history processes of knowing which may be shared by many individuals or even many Nations. We believe that this direction may enable us to see ourselves—as the double-row wampum belt suggests—as fundamentally separate, fundamentally equal, *and* fundamentally connected. In this framework, we think we may arrive at a better answer for a question which we were frequently asked in the course of our research: Why do you want to know this?

Notes

1 Dickason (1992) or Wright (1992), for example.
2 The term "historical ethnomusicology" may first have been used by Kay K. Shelemay (1980). For an overview of scholarly work see Widdess (1992). With regard to North American Aboriginal music, several articles in Blum *et al.* (1990) are of particular importance.
3 Several areas of study which regard the social grounding of music have arisen since the late 1980s. Among these are works influenced by reception theory (e.g., Leppert and McClary 1987), and feminism (McClary 1991, Solie 1993, and Subotnik 1991).
4 For a detailed discussion of this process with regard to the Thanksgiving address, see Foster (1984).

5 For a translation and interpretation of this text, see Foster (1974).

6 The holder of this title at the time of the interview, Simon Marshall, Sr., explained the term to Franziska as follows: **"Putu's, I'm a deputy Grand Chief. Like 'putu's,' 'put'wutmn' [sending something with a breath of wind]. Send a letter to [address] whatever is going on. If anybody died [in] my place [or jurisdiction], I send [a] counsellor at his reserve or call him and send the [word to] spread this [news]. And [I am] looking after [the] Grand Chief. If he goes away I take over myself."**

7 We have wondered if this reversal relates to statements by one elder in 1990 that women's medicine must be used at this point in history.

8 This is consistent with a number of other accounts of dual or multiple religious affiliation in other Native communities. See, for example, William K. Powers, "Dual Religious Participation: Stratagems of Conversion among the Lakota," in *Beyond the Vision: Essays on American Indian Culture* (1987): 94-125, or John Webster Grant, "A Yes That Means No," in *Moon of Wintertime* (1984): especially 249-50.

9 The life of the "being" used in the making of a sound producer also raises a question about the "age" of specific instruments. A single instrument might embody materials of different ages just as the poles of certain lodges are from trees of different ages. Some of our group photos of turtle rattles, for example, look remarkably like a "family." In other cases, an instrument which is very old by human standards (e.g., HEY 9976, an early nineteenth-century frame drum) exhibits no signs of aging. These fragmentary examples suggest that this might be a fruitful area for future research.

10 In a widely toured photo exhibit by Innu artist Serge Jauvin, instrument maker Mathieu Mark is quoted as saying that a hunter must dream three times of a drum before he could "know the drum well" (see Jauvin 1992: 120).

11 The following archival instruments illustrate several repair techniques: GLE R301.47, a damaged gourd rattle covered with a thin membrane; HEY 22/5544, a drum with double membrane layer as reinforcement.

12 On the other hand, this connection between voice and skin preference should not be generalized.

Iroquoian drummers often express a preference for the readily available skin of the woodchuck—an animal not distinguished as a "singer."

13 Conversely, it is interesting to note that certain industrial processes are viewed as the opposite of this renewal of life in a new form; the Iron Ore Company in Schefferville was called "Nakanau"—something that is stopped in its movement.

14 Fred Blessing concluded the opposite in relation to his 1950s study of Midewiwin medicine bags; see Blessing (1977).

15 Much of the following information about contemporary popular music by Native musicians was compiled by Sam Cronk for the *Encyclopedia of Music in Canada* where it appears in a somewhat different form (Kallmann *et al.* 1992: 931-33).

16 A major achievement for Aboriginal musicians was the acceptance of this argument by the Canadian musical establishment with the founding of a separate Juno award for the best recording of Native music, awarded for the first time in 1994.

17 For a representation of the variety of Native musicians' experience, see the interviews in *The Sound of the Drum*, a publication which accompanied a conference of the same title hosted by the Woodland Cultural Centre at which traditionalists shared the stage with hymners, and pop bands.

18 To others, all this shifting may have perhaps more of a quality of restlessness than real motion. We are reminded of a story told to us first by a Native professor and borne out in our own experience at many gatherings. In his university classes involving both Native and non-Native students, he described how non-Native students always wave their arms eagerly with the first insistent questions. Native students, he suggested, were more careful to appraise the situation, live with the information received, understand all the angles, and *then* be ready to move. He related these perspectives to the Anishnabe Medicine Wheel: unlike the Anishnabe pathway described in Chapter One, the Euro-American one started in the West, acquiring knowledge quickly and then moving immediately (perhaps achieving a vision and experience after the fact!).

Appendix A
All the Nations

Historical Contexts

The presentation of an accurate summary of significant events and historical developments shaping the First Nations communities which concern us in this study is fraught with many difficulties. The documentary record is problematic; to a large extent, it consists of written materials created mostly by Europeans who did not understand the language or even the names of the people they met in the Americas; though oral histories exist and are becoming more accessible[1] they are partial visions, variably detailed, depending on their contexts and uses (chronological precision, for example, may not be necessary for the functions which a story may serve in peoples' lives though it may be useful for the historian). The biases of many published studies, the stereotyping which influenced the historical record, the lack of clarity with regard to the historical usage of indigenous names for communities or groups,[2] and the complexity of the negotiations among Nations are all further challenging factors.

The Native history which has remained in our memories from childhood was a mere appendage to that of Europeans in North America. Indians were either fighting or fur trading. Few of them had names. The Algonquins and Hurons were allied with the French, the Iroquoians with the English. Such reductionist childhood memories would seem irrelevant to serious academic study were it not for the fact that the same biases appear in a large amount of the academic history as well. The excessive emphasis on warfare—little on intergovernmental negotiation, little on mutually beneficial alliance, little on peace-making—is perhaps the most striking.

A much needed "re-visioning" of North American history has already clarified the record of Native-European/American relationships in the Northeast in a number of ways.[3] Two-way intercultural interaction has been foregrounded by recent Native and non-Native historians, among them Olive Dickason, Georges E. Sioui Wendayete, Peter Schmaltz, Bruce Trigger, J.R. Miller, Kenneth Morrison, and Sylvie van Kirk. They emphasize "aspirations at variance"[4] and acknowledge the generosity and grace of Indian leaders in their tolerance of European objectives even in the face of encroach-

ments on their land and their way of life.[5] At the same time, local and community histories are emerging on a possibly unprecedented scale.[6]

The aforementioned studies by Trigger, Morrison, and Miller demonstrate that Indian Nations often worked hard to maintain a neutral position in conflicts between European Nations or between the British and Americans, although they were often drawn into battle to defend their own lands or protect their own people. The Iroquois Confederacy, long depicted as the most "aggressive" and "war-like," particularly in the seventeenth century where their successive defeats of the nations around them look like a systematic consolidation of power, is now being reconsidered; Doxtator (1990), for example, has examined contrasting notions of alliance and their relationship to structures of kinship and government. Posluns (1990) has described how differences in the relationship to the land influence the historical record. To the present day, the different perspectives on individual "ownership" of the land (the European perspective) in which trade, acquisition, and title are negotiable or "extinguishable," and collective "trusteeship" of the land (the Native perspective), which is non-negotiable, are a source of misunderstanding.

Contemporary histories are also beginning to sort out the differing motivations of the English and French. The contrasting histories of the Iroquoian and Algonquian Nations are, in themselves, probably more indicative of European rather than Aboriginal narratives. Morrison has explained these differences in light of traumatic events in Europe following the Reformation and Counter-Reformation.

The two peoples thought about the world in radically different terms. While Protestants came to reject the secular world as debased, Catholics increasingly embraced a moderate tradition of reform. These religious dissensions profoundly affected Indian-white relations. French Catholics' acceptance of folk religious practices gave them a far more tolerant perspective on American Indian cultures. The tremendous cultural and linguistic diversity within France may also have fostered cultural relativism. English and French may have agreed on their Christian mission to American Indians, but they were preconditioned to quarrel about the task. (1984: 46)

Morrison reads a symbolic interpretation of the environment into these preconditioned differences:

New England's symbolic reaction to the wilderness and to the Indians who inhabited it forms a haunting theme in the region's historical consciousness. Influential colonials believed that angry Indians reflected the disorder of English social and spiritual life. "God is not among us," Cotton Mather declared to the General Court in 1689. It seemed to the English that wilderness overwhelmed their communities. (1984: 144)

While there are, no doubt, exceptions to the pattern, Morrison's depiction of the English narratives of "wilderness" (perhaps most vividly drawn in Richardson's novel *Wacousta*), as opposed to his description of greater tolerance and a spirit of reform among the French, is consistent with other historical accounts. The antithetical stereotyping of Indians as "pesky redskins" or "noble savages" is related to this historical response, and the way in which it became incorporated into an American "mythology" has been studied by a number of scholars writing from both Native and non-Native perspectives.[7]

The historical account is surely most instructive where it looks, not merely at the causes of war and alliances on the battlefield, but at the consequences within communities of the disrupted balance in their lives. The devastating consequences of the American Revolutionary wars and the War of 1812, as well as subsequent policies of assimilation and, in the US, removal to lands west of the settlement frontier (the Mississippi River) evoked various creative strategies for cultural and physical survival in different areas. The rise of religions such as the Handsome Lake religion following the American Revolutionary wars, or the Native American Church following WWI, the quiet underground continuation of traditional ceremonies during periods such as the Canadian ban of the Sun Dance and potlatch (although neither are central to the area of this book) or the formation of stronger Native political institutions in Canada such as the Native Indian Brotherhood (later the Assembly of First Nations) at the very point when the federal government would reaffirm a commitment to the assimilationist policies of the nineteenth century (as in the Canadian White Paper of 1969) are not coincidental.

Introduction to the Historical Background and Musical Traditions of Specific Nations

The Beothuk

Resident in Newfoundland, the Beothuk of the pre-contact period are known to have had friendly rela-

tions with both the Micmac and Montagnais prior to the seventeenth century.[8] The scant historical record after that time, however, focuses on their defeat and supposed extermination by the French and Micmac allies who were offered a reward for Beothuk heads. Shanawdithit, who died in 1829, has been romanticized as the last Beothuk (e.g., see Howley 1915), but descendants of Beothuk, progeny of earlier intermarriage perhaps, were contacted by Speck in 1911 and by contemporary scholars, including von Rosen.

Information about the Beothuk way of life is scant. Debate continues about whether their language was separate from or related to the Algonquian language family. Working from archeological data, a moderate amount of reconstruction has been attempted, although this is bound to be incomplete.

There are few references to music-making. Using evidence from archeological investigation at Port au Choix, Tuck (1976) presents photos of three bird bone whistles, made from a swan or goose ulna. Measuring 10 to 14.8 cm in length with one or two finger "perforations," they produced a "shrill high pitched sound." Four artifacts which he tentatively identifies as flutes were also found at this site. He also posits that small pebbles found at grave sites may indicate the use of rattles, the wood or bark of which has disintegrated.

The Wabanaki: Abenaki, Micmac, Maliseet, Passamaquoddy, and Penobscot

Prior to the seventeenth century, these Nations stretched along much of the Maritime seaboard. Because of their strategic maritime position and their control of waterways such as the Hudson and St. John rivers, they were courted by both French and English during the colonial period. They formed a Confederacy during the mid-eighteenth century, the great fire of which was located at Kahnawake where they met regularly until the mid-nineteenth century. Extensive contact with the Mohawk (both military struggle at times in the sixteenth and seventeenth centuries and friendly association) has marked their history. Following the historic conversion of Micmac Chief Membertou in 1610, many became Catholic.

Morrison (1984) has shown that the Abenaki were particularly torn as a buffer; they traded with the Dutch and English but were allied militarily with the French in the seventeenth century. Beginning in 1662, and again, during the Seven Years War, 1756-63 (called the French-Indian War in

US history textbooks), a number moved to Canada (the Montreal and Trois-Rivières areas as well as the St. Francis River). This "western Abenaki" group consolidated on the St. Francis following the American Revolutionary wars. Alliances were split during this period. The movement of Loyalists affected their land base in the nineteenth century. Eastern Abenaki, on the other hand, also moved north following land cessions (in North Carolina, New Hampshire, and Maine) in the late eighteenth and early nineteenth centuries. A splint-basket industry developed in the second half of the nineteenth century.

At least since the mid-eighteenth century, Maliseet and Passamaquoddy lived relatively separately, the former on the inland rivers in New Brunswick and Maine, the latter on the sea coast. A major settlement was located at Meductic, but people were relocated to Aukpaque in the late eighteenth century and finally displaced by Loyalists in 1794 (when Massachusetts allocated reservations west of the St. Croix River). In the early nineteenth century, several families went to Viger, Quebec, others to the Woodstock reserve in New Brunswick (established 1851). Consolidation into central reserves caused further upheavals in the mid-twentieth century. At this point, many moved to the formerly Penobscot community at Old Town, Maine.

The Micmac are often described as the most powerful, militarily, of the Maritime Nations. Histories often cite their defeat of the Beothuk, as mentioned above, their defence of the Gaspé from Iroquois encroachment, and their conflicts with the Maliseet and Penobscot nations who moved into New Brunswick in the eighteenth century. Like the western Abenaki, as Whitehead has explained, they were buffers in French-English conflict, "suffering both the indifference and political machinations of their French co-religionists and the campaigns of the English, who loosed their Mohawk allies against them and commanded that they be exterminated" (1991: 77). From the eighteenth century on, their head district was located in Cape Breton. Like other eastern Nations, their land base was eroded after the 1755 expulsion of the Acadians by the British who made land grants to settlers, a process which accelerated as Loyalists entered the area after 1780.

During the nineteenth century, a turn to farming was thwarted by the potato blight of 1844, as well as subsequent drought. Illness, especially tuberculosis, ravaged their numbers. Late in the century, reserve lands began to be set aside and some social services were put in place. In the 1940s, government centralization programmes forced relo-

cation to larger reserves such as those at Shubenacadie and Eskasoni.

Relative to the sub-Arctic Algonquian Nations, a greater degree of loss of traditional music has occurred among the Micmac and Maliseet. The historical records are often contradictory and confusing. Nevertheless, such sources as the recorded collection of Mechling (1911) and transcriptions in ethnographies (e.g., Speck's *Penobscot Man*, 1940) facilitate a certain amount of reconstruction by contemporary scholars and performers.

Historical accounts describe ceremonial music associated with weddings (e.g., Mechling 1958-59: 37), with funeral and mourning rites (e.g., Wallis and Wallis 1957: 24), as well as social dances including a snake dance, greeting dance, and trading dance (see transcription in Burlin 1907: 16). Speck writes that the Penobscot distinguished a Maliseet "peddlar's dance" (1940: 295) and he describes "the Micmac dance" which was "distinct in motions and tempo" from those of the Maliseet, Passamaquoddy, and Penobscot (ibid.: 296ff.). Chief-making ceremonies (Prince 1897) included singing.

There are very few Micmac or Maliseet drums, rattles, or other instruments in museums and archival collections. (Woven ash-splint baskets, fancy quill-work boxes, and colourful beaded clothing or bags are the material items most frequently representing the Wabanaki Nations in these institutions.) The historical position of drums among the Micmac is a subject of contention. Seventeenth- and eighteenth-century sources describe the use of a stick striking a sheet of birch bark, a tree, or a kettle in song accompaniment. Hoffman (1955: 677-86) quotes LeClerq, Dièreville, and Maillard, the latter in the context of a Micmac feast at which "girls and women come in, with the oldest at the head of them, who carries in her left hand a great piece of birchbark of the hardest, upon which she strikes as if it were a drum" (after 1758: 4-10). Late nineteenth- and early twentieth-century records document the use of drums by the Passamaquoddy and Penobscot, close neighbours and allies of the Micmac. Prince (1901) makes reference to a "shaman's drum" in the text of a "Passamaquoddy Witch Song," and Speck also describes a snare-strung frame drum used by a Penobscot shaman (1919: 242). In early twentieth-century archival collections, the double-headed Penobscot drum as well as several distinctive single-membrane frame drums, one of which is attributed to the Micmac, are extant. The latter has a bleached rawhide skin completely covering and "button-hole" stitched to the lower edge of the wide frame.

At the present time, Micmacs and Maliseets as well as Abenaki use hand drums, Iroquois water drums on occasion, various sizes of double-membrane drums, or large intertribal style drums. The latter are used by "traditionalists," people identifying with an intertribal revival of spiritual teachings and ceremonies. In the Maritimes, the "traditional" drum groups often make their own drums and have them ceremonially purified and blessed. Iroquoian social dances are sometimes also sung using the big drum.

Contemporary dance troupes, on the other hand, frequently use hand drums, often played by women, to accompany social dances which are historical reconstructions in many cases. Such reconstructions function in the life of communities in the late twentieth century. In the western Abenaki community of Odanak where, since the 1970s, a Native-operated museum occupies the former residential school, young dancers and singers learn and perform social dances at the spring ceremonies and Indian corn feast held for the community as well as in concerts and festivals oriented to broader audiences such as the annual Fête des abénakis or folklore festivals in Quebec, Montreal, and Drummondville. The same is true in the Maritimes, where a troupe such as the Micmac Dancers directed by Sarah Denny at Eskasoni, Cape Breton, perform such dances as the Welcome Dance, the Feather Dance, the Snake Dance, and the "Native" Dance within the community, at larger gatherings such as the Nova Scotia Summer Games, and for intercultural audiences.

Historical accounts of rattles include reference to dew-claw (Le Clercq 1910 [1610]: 220-23), and moose horn (Parsons 1925: 83) types, as well as a bell owned by the trickster-transformer Kluskap.The unique Micmac *ji'kmaq'n*, its present form an ash stick split into several layers at one end and beaten against the hand, is also named in historical sources although descriptions are highly variable: Rand (1894: 115), for example, images it as "a sort of tambourine beaten upon with a stick" but translates the name as "rattle." Museum collections include, mainly, the full cowhorn rattle, some intricately carved. Other types of rattles are splint-woven basket rattles, used as baby rattles (especially by the Abenaki), turtle rattles, rawhide globe rattles, and gourd rattles.

The flute (*pipukwaqn*) is widely mentioned in Micmac mythology in association with the Mi'kmwesu spirit where sound is used as the means of transforming the listener.

Traditional hymn repertoires in Micmac and Maliseet are important, both in Christian contexts, and for wakes and "noon-day singing." A *Micmac Hymnal* with accompanying cassette was published in 1985 by the Micmac Association for Cultural Studies. As in other areas, fiddle music is both distinctive and popular in contemporary communities. Probably the best-known Micmac fiddler is Lee Cremo (interviewed in [Cronk] *The Sound of the Drum* 1990).

The Wendat (Huron)

Bruce Trigger's detailed historical research (especially *The Children of Aataentsic: A History of the Huron People to 1660*, 1976), has facilitated access to extensive documentary sources for studying Wendat history, especially the early "historical" period from the alliance with Champlain in 1615 and the establishment of "Huronia" on Georgian Bay to their defeat by the Iroquois by 1650 and their consequent dispersal northeast to the Île d'Orléans (later Lorette), and southwest to the Petun or the Odawa at Michilimackinac. With the Odawa Nation, a century-long alliance was formed and they moved together to Chequamegon (on the south shore of Lake Superior) and back, driven by the Sioux. This southern group are called Wyandot in the literature whereas "Huron" was more long-standing in literature about northern groups. With the establishment of peace between the French and Iroquois Nations in 1701, some moved to the Lake St. Clair area, together with Potawatomi and Odawa people. Allied with Pontiac in 1763, but split in their allegiance during the War of 1812, some (the Sandusky Wyandot) established settlement in the Ohio valley only to be forced to cede lands after the US Removal Act of 1830 which engineered the forced relocation of Indians to lands west of the Mississippi. In 1843 they moved to Kansas and on to Oklahoma where the Delaware and Seneca welcomed them to their lands. The northern communities, on the other hand, were in close contact with the Montagnais and Attikamek. They effected a change in economic activity to place more emphasis on hunting, fishing, and trapping in the late nineteenth century. During the same period, a handicraft industry developed which continues to thrive.

Like the western Abenaki and Algonquin, the proximity of the provincial capital of Quebec has put the Wendat Nation at the crossroads of cultures. The Conseil Attikamek Montagnais together with the Education Committee of that council, which has effectively reshaped curricula in Quebec/Labrador communities, is located at Village Huron. They have also adopted a role as cultural ambassadors to the larger public for many decades. A succession of dance troupes, including Cabir-Coubat (dir. Marguerite Vincent, active in the 1960s), Le Huron (dir. Max Gros-Louis, active in the 1970s) and Sandowka (dir. M. Picard, active in the mid-1980s) have been at the centre of these cross-cultural performances, dancing choreographed pieces such as the Dance of the Eagle Feather or Calumet Dance and a number of social dances which continue to function at community social events, especially the "snake dance," about which the following legend circulates in the Village Huron near Quebec City:

Un énorme serpent hantait la rivière St.-Charles, c'est-à-dire "Cabir-Coubat," qui signifie "rivière aux nombreux détours." Ce serpent était surnommé "Oyalé Owek." Les Hurons entendirent le sifflement du monstre sous les chutes. Il tint les habitants en émoi et fit le désespoir des Jésuites. Les missionnaires décidèrent d'avoir recours à la prière, par contre les vieillards épuisèrent en vain leur sagesse, les guerriers leur bravoure, les sorciers leurs incantations et, selon leur croyance superstitieuse, dansèrent pour chasser le mauvais esprit représentant le même élément. (Vincent 1984: 293)

The Huron musical instruments examined in the course of this project come from only two main sources, Barbeau's collection at Lorette and in Oklahoma ca. 1911 and the present-day collection at the local museums in the Village Huron. The early group includes (a) primarily full cowhorn rattles resembling those of the Wabanaki Confederacy, though sometimes adorned differently; (b) gourd rattles; and (c) a flute with external block.

The later group includes (d) a moose hoof rattle which resembles one other rattle seen in a Wabanaki collection. With the fur and dew claws left on, the vessel of this rattle looks like an animal's head. We were told that the white "collar" and beaded coloured rings indicate clan.

Among the newest instruments created, at least in part, for the transcultural performances of the dance troupes are (e) single- and double-membrane frame drums (stitched with random running stitches, unlike those of their neighbours); (f) globe rattles adorned with colourful fluff feathers; and (g) a clay disc rattle occasionally available for sale as a craft item.

Iroquois Confederacy

The Five Iroquoian Nations who developed one of the most important political structures in North American history had established their Confederacy long before the colonial period (the period of the founding of the Confederacy is still debated and placed variably between 1400 and 1600; see discussion in Tooker SH 15: 420). In the seventeenth century, they engaged in what Trigger describes as "commercially motivated warfare" (SH 15: 345) to secure their territory and control of its resources. In the late sixteenth century they moved up the St. Lawrence toward Tadoussac and by 1603, northeast into Algonquin and Montagnais lands. Between 1615 and 1640, they moved east toward the Mahican; from 1642-45, west to defeat the Huron, Petun, Neutral, and Erie. They began to move south to the Delaware and Susquehanna where they intensified efforts in the 1659-63 period. War with the Susquehanna was concluded in 1676, but the Seneca continued to fight the Illinois in the 1680s, and French attacks on Iroquoian communities continued through the 1690s. A more lasting peace was effected with the French (together with the alliance of northern Algonquian Nations) in 1701. Even Nations defeated by the Iroquois were treated with respect in an alliance which Doxtator (1990) labels a "tributary" alliance. The Delaware are a good case in point; they served in diplomacy efforts in the eighteenth century with the Susquehanna in particular. After the American Revolution, many Delaware came to Six Nations (with the addition of the Tuscarora), and their brothers, the Munsee, were established at Allegany and Walpole Island.

Within that structure, Iroquois territory (in what is now New York State and Ontario) was organized like a conceptual Longhouse with the numerically dominant Seneca Nation as keepers of the western doorway, the Mohawk Nation keepers of the eastern doorway, and the centrally placed Onondaga as firekeepers and keepers of the wampum. The sixth Nation, the Tuscarora, were "adopted" ca. 1720 as "children" of the Oneida and as a "younger brother" in the Confederacy, following the League's efforts in mediating the damaging struggles with settlers in the Carolinas from 1711-13.

The early eighteenth century is usually regarded as a peaceful and prosperous time, but after the Treaty of 1763 in which the English gained control in New England, Confederacy power declined. The Iroquois Nations were persuaded to sell interests in the Ohio Valley (west of the Alleghany Mountains) and, thereby, had less interaction with Delaware, Wyoming, and Shawnee. The period following the American Revolution was worse; forced to sign treaties with the new American government, they lost much of their New York land and were confined to reservations by agreements such as the Treaty of Big Tree, 1797. Some Loyalist Iroquois, together with some Delaware, Nanticoke, Tutelo, Creek, and Cherokee, moved north with Joseph Brant in 1784 to the Grand River or Bay of Quinte areas (Tyendinaga established 1793). Brant subsequently sold part of their land allotment to settlers.

The devastating negotiations with the new American government and social upheavals contributed to a demoralizing atmosphere within the League Nations. In this environment, beginning in 1799, Handsome Lake began having a series of visions which led him to preach a new code of living. After his death in 1815, his grandson continued preaching his "Code," first recorded in 1845 by Ely S. Parker. The Handsome Lake Code became the basis for the Longhouse religion. The Longhouse tradition was firmly established in New York and Six Nations in the nineteenth century but came to the Kahnawake and St. Regis reserves only in the 1920s and 1930s.

Christian missionary attempts were received variously among the Iroquois Nations. A Moravian mission was established for a short while from 1750-55 among the Cayuga and Onondaga. Presbyterianism (brought by Samuel Kirkland in 1767) and later Anglicanism or Methodism flourished at Oneida where the Handsome Lake movement had less impact.

For the Iroquois, as for other Nations, the nineteenth century involved reaction to and struggle over government policies of assimilation, and in the US, forced relocation to lands west of the Mississippi. The manipulation of land deals was often clouded, not merely by the overt government agenda of "removal," but by other corrupt processes. In 1838, for example, Iroquois lands were sold to New York State by Iroquois who profited handsomely but who were not representative of their government. Widespread recognition that this deal was invalid led to a revised treaty in 1842 in which Allegany and Cattaraugus were restored. The compromise sale of Tonawanda resulted in a temporary separation of people there until the land was bought back in 1857.

The Seneca reservation was established in Kansas in 1838 and subsequently in northeastern Oklahoma. In the course of these struggles, some Oneidas moved to land purchased from the Menominee in Wisconsin in 1823 while others went to the area near London, Ontario, around 1840. Not all people living with the six Nations opposed a shift to European-style farming and education. Ojibwe Peter Jones on the Mississauga Reserve near New Credit promoted agriculture and schools among his own people to whom he served as a Christian missionary.

The twentieth century has seen some reinstatement of lands after the US Indian Reorganization Act of 1935. On the other hand, projects such as the Kinzua dam, which flooded a large portion of the Allegany Reservation and necessitated the move of the Coldspring Longhouse to Steamburg, were major setbacks.

At present, Iroquoian communities maintain a rich ceremonial and social musical life, centred around the Longhouse. Haudenosaunee culture is an ongoing way of life, based in part on the *Gaiwi:yo:h*, or "Good Message" of Seneca prophet Handsome Lake, and on the Great Law of the Iroquoian Confederacy. In these communities, singing is an integral part of celebration and healing; it is one way of relating to and communicating with the world around.

There are three basic types of traditional Longhouse songs: social dance songs, or *yoedza'ge-ka:'* ("the earth kind"); ceremonial songs, thanking the Creator and other forces for their continued help; and songs for curing societies. Ceremonial songs such as the Great Feather Dance, and songs for curing societies such as the Wooden Face Societies, have been extensively discussed in the ethnographic literature, but Iroquoian people have concerns about non-Native interest in these repertoires which, in their own communities, are restricted to safeguard the ceremonial and curing songs from misuse and exploitation.

In many communities, people get together for social events, some of them following Longhouse ceremonies. Like all Longhouse events, socials begin with the recitation of the " Thanksgiving Address" by a designated speaker acknowledging all the environmental and spiritual forces "from the earth to beyond the sky" which help humanity survive. The first two-dance set is the Standing Quiver, a type of "unaccompanied Stomp Dance, in which the lead singer and other dancers alternate short phrases in a call-response style as they move around the Longhouse. This is followed by the Moccasin dance. After that, song sets may be chosen from among the more than thirty different types of social dances, each with characteristic melodies, rhythmic patterns, and dance steps. Many of the social dances are accompanied by a small water drum, played by the lead singer, and cowhorn rattle.

One social dance, the *eskanyeh*, or "ladies shuffle dance" (sung by men or women but only danced by women), although one of the oldest repertoires, is the preferred genre for newly created songs. Twice a year, singing societies from different communities get together for a "sing," a type of intercommunity social at which each group performs one set of *eskanyeh* (seven songs twice through). *Eskanyeh* songs may borrow or adapt music from other songs, and their texts, consisting of vocables and/or short phrases in Seneca or occasionally in English, are often humorous. Singing societies are primarily charitable organizations, raising money or otherwise helping as needed.

A wide variety of traditional musical instruments continues to be used in Iroquoian communities. A small water drum and one or many (truncated) cowhorn rattles serve as the usual accompaniment for social dancing and at "sings." Turtle rattles are used ceremonially for the Great Feather Dance of mid-winter and in medicine society doings. Hickory and elm bark rattles as well as tincan rattles are also used by medicine societies. Box turtle rattles are associated with the women's *towisa* society. Two unusual hemispheric Mohawk drums collected in Kahnawake in the 1930s and currently in the McCord Museum are not recognized in Iroquoian communities in the 1990s.

The Innu: Naskapi, Montagnais, and Attikamek

Unlike the Huron, for whom a detailed historical and ethnohistorical record has been reconstructed, the Innu of Labrador and Quebec have been represented with the conventional dichotomy between history and ethnography operative. The difference between the historical record presented for this group (in relation to that of, for example, the Iroquois) in a reference source such as the Smithsonian *Handbook of North American Indians* is striking evidence of this split. Recent studies (of the seventeenth century by Leacock and Goodman 1976, or the eighteenth and nineteenth by Morantz 1977 and 1983) have redressed the problems of an historical picture by focusing on the impact of and response to institutions such as the Christian church or fur trade.

Although urged by the French to fight the Iroquois/English alliance, the Montagnais resisted warfare except where their land was directly threatened. Capable of navigating the rugged interior of northern Quebec and Labrador, a single group could travel a vast area; in the sixteenth and seventeenth centuries, trade along the St. Lawrence was part of the annual cycle, and the missions at

Tadoussac and Sillery became focal points. For the Montagnais, Leacock (1980) has demonstrated that part of the Jesuit agenda for colonization played upon this cycle of extended travel; women and children were encouraged to stay close to the mission and, hence, were separated from families and areas where traditional culture operated most strongly. Trading posts were first established in Ungava Bay (Fort Chimo, 1830) and among the Cree, along the east Main (Great Whale River) in the early nineteenth century.

On the west Main, on the other hand, a trading sloop had wintered at Fort Albany since 1698 and Hudson Bay Company posts were established from the company's founding in 1670 (Rupert House 1668, Moose Factory 1671). In the late seventeenth century, these Cree-centred posts received visitors from other nations, especially the Ojibwe who travelled north to trade. To compete with the Northwest Company, the HBC extended its operation after 1720, establishing posts on the north shore of Lake Superior. Following the merger of the NWC with the HBC in 1821, smaller posts were disbanded and settlement consolidated around larger ones. Indian trappers had less power since they could dictate little to the trader monopoly after this. Although a Jesuit mission existed at Fort Albany for a few years from 1686-93, missionary efforts only became intensive in this late nineteenth-century period. Both Anglican/Church of England (York Factory, 1823, or Fort George, 1852) and Oblates (Moose Factory since 1847 with circuits to outlying communities) were active.

The Attikamek of the St. Maurice River in Quebec had also been active in the seventeenth-century fur trade, especially at Tadoussac and Sillery. Raided by the Iroquois in 1651-52 and dispersed after a smallpox epidemic in 1669-70, they were in a weak position. Some records suggest that, in the 1690s, a group whom the French called Têtes de Boule moved to the area from Lake Superior or Hudson Bay. By the late eighteenth century, communities were consolidating around trading posts, especially Weymontachingue, established in 1774 by the Northwest Company. Missionaries arrived in 1837. Commercial logging began in 1851 and remains an economic mainstay, but only a few Attikamek were hired until the period of WWII. Attikamek hunting patterns were seriously disturbed by the construction in 1910 of the La Tuque-Abitibi rail line, which cut their territory in half, and by the flooding of their villages and lands by the La Loutre Dam, constructed 1914-17. Summer schools operated in the 1920s, but reserves were not established until the 1940s. The Nation revived the Attikamek name in 1972, and three years later a political alliance with the Montagnais resulted in the creation of the Conseil Attikamek Montagnais (CAM).

In Labrador, the very isolation of the Innu area has made it the selected location for NATO low-flying aircraft testing, an activity which disturbs wildlife patterns and terrifies humans. A major protest opposed this development throughout the late 1980s and into the 1990s.

For the Naskapi and Montagnais (as well as for the Cree) of northern Quebec, much traditional cultural knowledge relating to music as well as to other domains is associated with the hunt (especially the caribou hunt) and with life in the forest, a domain which is distinguished from life in the village setting (see Tanner 1979). Contemporary cultural renewal projects such as the Montagnais *Nutshimiu Atusseun* ("Work in the Country") recognize the cultural importance of the forest by taking young people for a period of several months into this setting in order to teach them traditional knowledge and life skills.

The most valued song repertoire related to hunting, however, are *nikamuna* (singular, *nikamun*, also spelled *nikamowin, nagamon, nakamun*) which are accompanied with the snare-strung frame drum called the *teueikan. Nikumana* are received in dreams in which they may be associated with a particular animal or object relating to the hunt (e.g., a canoe, snowshoes), or with a person of special importance to the singer. The performance of songs from this repertoire could serve to help a hunter locate game or it could be a celebration of success in the hunt.

The double-rimmed frame drum called the *teueikan* is regarded as an important symbol of Montagnais identity. Drum-makers can distinguish between drums made in different communities, on the other hand, by looking at the lacing style (some regions drill holes in the rims while others wind the rawhide around the outer rims) and membrane configuration (Betsiamites sometimes uses a double layer of rawhide for the membrane; Innu from Davis Inlet or St. Augustine make single-membrane drums). All varieties of this instrument, however, have an E/W snare crossing the diameter on the top of the membrane and a N/S snare on the bottom of the membrane. Drums are rarely highly decorated, but red outer rims and various configurations of red dots are commonplace. Snares have quill, bone, or carved wooden rattlers, the latter more recent. The

drum is hand-held by a loop at the top or suspended from a ridge pole or angled stick, if out-of-doors. Using a wooden stick, the hunter/drummer (head always clad in a scarf or hat), first beats a fast "tremolo" beat to start the snares buzzing (the snares are often called "spirit voices") while he sings a song received in a dream. The fast beat gives way to an iambic pattern to which those present dance, symbolically said by some to be recreating the tracks of animals.

By the 1970s and 1980s, *nikumana* were used in social contexts (e.g., dances at weddings, or public receptions and festivals). Together with contemporary repertoires, *nikamuna* may also be heard on Native radio stations such as those operated by SOCAM—the Societé de Communication Attikamek-Montagnaise). In general, songs have two short phrases (often within a narrow pitch range) which are repeated several times.

While no longer extant in most areas, some people share their memories of the shaking tent, a divination ritual in which an individual communicated with spirits who entered a specially constructed tent, causing it to shake without human intervention. Songs were used in this context (see, e.g., Preston 1976). Healing ceremonies involved specific types of rattles as in the Anishnabe area. An unusual Naskapi rattle constructed from two caribou shoulder blades is found in two museum collections. Museum documentation for one of these (see HEY 23/6638) associates this rattle type with the sweat lodge.

Other traditional Naskapi/Montagnais rattles which are widely distributed are membrane-covered disc rattles, frequently described in museum documentation as babies' rattles, or smaller substitutes for the *teueikan*. As in Anishnabe areas, some disc rattles are handleless; we were told that these were played by spirits in the contexts of ceremonies. Disc rattle membranes are often painted with a central circle (red or blue, usually), and/or a red perimeter ring. Bits of red and blue and/or green cloth or yarn are sometimes caught in the stitching around the perimeter. Museum collections also contain tin-can rattles from the Montagnais areas closest to the Cree and Attikamek.

Whistles are made in the bush in the springtime and birch-bark moose calls in the late fall or early winter. Two varieties of buzzers (one type a bull-roarer) are found in the ethnographic collections described here. Bull-roarers are said to make the wind rise so that the snow would become hard, facilitating travel in the springtime.

There are several song repertoires which are not regarded as *nikumana*. Women compose lullabies (called *bebe kataushu* or *bebe ataushu* in northern Quebec and Labrador) which feature a refrain using vocables such as "bai, bai." Short songs may also be performed in the context of myth narration; most sub-Arctic Algonquian Nations make a careful distinction between the classic myths (*atnuhan*) and other stories relating to contemporary or recent experiences (*tipatshimun*).

Interaction between Native and European musics in this area has a long history. Fiddle music and Christian hymns, for example, have been actively adapted to create distinctive styles, and newly created pieces have been composed within the Native communities since the late sixteenth and early seventeenth centuries; hence, these repertoires are regarded as "traditional" music in many communities. Among the earliest Christian converts, many Naskapi and Montagnais men and women have large repertoires of hymns and cantiques in their own languages. These constitute one sort of "prayer" for people who are devout in their Roman Catholic beliefs. A major annual celebration is the Feast of St. Anne in late July when thousands of Native people travel to sacred places (such as the shrine of St. Anne de Beaupré, Quebec) to worship together using their own language and hymns.

Fiddle music has been particularly popular in Algonquin and Attikamek communities. In addition, a contemporary song movement began, among the Montagnais, with singer/guitarist Philippe McKenzie in the 1970s. Composing mostly in a style called "folk Innu," dozens of groups have emerged since that time, the most commercially successful, as of 1990, being Kashtin (Florent Vollent and Claude McKenzie) whose albums have had major mainstream success. Since 1985, a major annual festival, Innu Nikamu ("the Indian sings") has showcased both contemporary and traditional musics at Maliotenam, near Sept-Îles, Quebec.

Like the Montagnais, the Attikamek have a double-rimmed *teueikan* and disc rattle, the latter often identifiably Attikamek in that the membranes are separated so that the stitching looks like the V-lacing on the drum. Small can rattles and one can-shaped bark rattle have been collected from this area. One type of buzzer is represented in the collections described here.

The Attikamek are skilled workers in birch bark, a material used, among other things, for root-sewn moose calls. Styles of decoration have changed during the twentieth century. Bitten designs were sometimes made by skilled artisans.

In the 1960s, layered patterns were collected but more realistic flowers, birds, and fish were the norm during the 1970s when the demand for sale items intensified.

The Anishnabek: Cree, Ojibwe, Algonquin, Odawa, and Nipissing

Immediately to the west of the Montagnais-Attikamek area are the Algonquin and Nipissing who, in the seventeenth century, played a critical role as mediators between French and English from their central location at Trois-Rivières. For the Northern Alliance they obtained European trade goods throughout the seventeenth century. They negotiated an early peace with the Mohawk in 1634 and were instrumental in several other treaty attempts around mid-century. Following the Iroquois success against the Huron in 1649, they dispersed to Lac St. Jean and Sillery. Around this time the Nipissing, friends of the Huron, had been attacked in the march on Huronia, and they fled west to Lake Nipigon, from where they traded with the Cree as far north as James Bay. In the early eighteenth century, a mission established at the Lake of Two Mountains served Algonquian, Iroquois, and Nipissing; the Abenaki moved into the St. Lawrence area with the permission of the Algonquin around this time. By the mid-nineteenth century, reserves were established on the Gatineau and Ottawa Rivers. The Nipissing joined the Maniwaki Algonquin. The "period" ended when, in 1877, the church at Lake of Two Mountains burned.

Playing a dominant role in both political and cultural developments was the largest Algonquian Nation, the Ojibwe. The Nation is described in different publications with different terminology and in different (outsider-imposed) categories which perhaps cloud the image of the enormous strength and richness of the Ojibwe cultural tradition. The southwestern branches of the Nation came to be known as Chippewa in the United States. The Smithsonian Institution's *Handbook of North American Indians*, for example, discusses the northern and southern branches in different volumes (6 and 15). As in the case of the Cree, an eastern/western split also occurs in ethnographic writing about the Ojibwe, the former grouped with Eastern Woodlands and the latter with the Plains areas.

Together with the Odawa and Potawatomi they formed the Three Fires Confederacy in the nineteenth century, and the liaison continues to function in Ontario and Quebec in the 1990s. In general, these nations supported the northern alliance with the French in the seventeenth and eighteenth centuries although support was shifted to the British in the American Revolution. Some find in the historical record (see H. Hickerson 1962, 1963) evidence that the westward migration of the Ojibwe began in the post-contact period and started around the south shore of Lake Superior. The oral history of Anishnabe migration, however, implies that the Ojibwe began their journey on the eastern seaboard. Some sources (Hickerson 1962) also suggest that the Manitoba Saulteaux may be more closely related to the Southwestern Ojibwe.

As a result of the fur trade, northern Ojibwe shifted from hunting to trapping in the late seventeenth and eighteenth centuries. Northern groups had considerable interaction with the Cree in the period from 1670 to ca. 1740 since they travelled north to the Hudson Bay posts to trade. After about 1740, posts were established on the north shore of Lake Superior and the northern path was less used. As with the Cree, the period after 1821 saw a disempowering of Indian hunters as the depletion of certain animal stocks and the monopoly of traders took effect. In Canada, a series of treaties, such as Treaty No. 3 (1873), defined reserve land and government obligations in a paternalistic fashion. In southern Ontario, Ojibwe groups were resident along the north shores of Lake Erie and Ontario, east to the Bay of Quinte as early as the 1690s and at Detroit and the straits between Lakes Huron and Superior in the early eighteenth century (together with the Odawa and Potawatomi). With Pontiac, they tried to oust the British from Detroit in 1763, and subsequent treaties forced land cessions to the British.

The eighteenth century saw a move of some southern groups to the Michigan and southern Ontario areas. Wild-rice harvesting became an economic staple for these groups. In the early nineteenth century, a southwestern branch fought the Fox and subsequently the Dakota for control of Minnesota lands. In their drive against the Dakota, some settled as far west as the Turtle Mountains, North Dakota. Mid-nineteenth-century treaties with the Canadian and US governments saw the severe diminishing of their land base as with other Nations and the establishment of reservations in Wisconsin and Minnesota. In the late nineteenth century, the land base and the strength of the band was further eroded by the US Allotment Act of 1887 by which reservation land could be sold to individuals. It is in this context that the Drum Dance was brought to Wisconsin Ojibwe from the Plains.

In the twentieth century, the technology of resource development has been an important issue

for virtually all Aboriginal groups, but especially for both the Innu and Anishnabe, whose northern lands are so resource rich. The environmental and cultural implications of dams on northern rivers in order to produce hydro-electric power was hotly contested around the James Bay I agreement in the mid-1970s and continues to be a major issue with an ongoing environmental assessment of James Bay in the 1990s.

In the 1980s, the Anishnabek assumed an important role in the revival of Algonquian spiritual traditions. Knowledge of teachings relating to such instruments as the big drum is shared by elders at events such as Elders Conferences, ceremonies and gatherings. A basic vision for the Anishnabek is related in their migration legend, a story which recounts the seven "fires," or stopping places, of the people in their journey from the east coast toward the west on the North American continent. The "fires" constitute both a historical record and a set of "teachings." Traditional Anishnabek see themselves as the generation of the Seventh Fire, and accept a role in bringing back many of their traditions.

The migration legend also recounts the giving of the Midewiwin to the Anishnabe people at the time of the fourth fire. Among the Ojibwe of northwestern Ontario, the Midewiwin is a fundamental religious institution. Ceremonies are held in an elongated lodge which is a metaphor for the cosmos and the pathway of life. The great myth of Nanabush tells of the Midewiwin origin and teaches the ritual process for the various degrees of initiation ceremonies. The sounds of the Midewiwin are distinctive: water drums, gourd rattles, and metal (preferably copper) or bark rattles accompany various types of ceremonial songs. We were told that the flute was brought into the Midewewin lodge by the women. Two drum types are central to Midewiwin lodge ceremonies. Currently the most widely used is the "little boy," a drum which is paradoxically virtually absent from museum collections. It is smaller than the "grandfather" and the membrane is held down with seven stones tied within the arches formed by the lacing points in the hide. The stones are said to signify strength, weight, and confirmation as well as the seven fires or teachings and the seven prophecies of the Anishnabe people. This drum is the "helper" of the grandfather drum and was given to reach all the people. When used, the rope which holds the seven stones can be tied in a variety of manners (forty-nine different patterns can be produced as appropriate for the ceremony or the part of the ceremony). The patterns are formed on the bottom of the drum and held in place with the drummer's foot.

More widely found in historical collections, however, is the grandfather, a water drum made from a taller, hollowed log. The grandfather drum, like many musical instruments, is regarded as a gift from the Creator (see, for example, James Redsky's description in *Great Leader of the Ojibway: Mis-quona-quab*, [1972], or commentaries in chapter 2). The symbolism of the loon who flew down to beat the drum is evident in the abstract bird-shaped drumsticks which were described as older than other types such as those made from two crossed wooden pieces. In the 1990s, membership in the Midewiwin is active and growing.

Music plays an important part in other healing activity, in sweat lodges or other ceremonies. Disc rattles (skin-covered discs with circular wooden "frames" which extend to form a handle) function as medicine rattles; the type of skin and rattlers relate to the function of the rattle. Fish-skin rattles or those made from the stomach lining of a bird are valued for their healing power. Small-frame drum/rattles, described in the documentation of some museums as *wabeno* drums, were also medicine tools. Certain groups had specific types of medicine rattles, often reflecting the birds, animals, or other natural materials of the area in which they lived.

Ojibwe elders identify several types of horizontal drums: at the 1986 Elders and Traditional Peoples' Conference at Trent University, Eddie Benton-Benai spoke of the "peace drum," the pow-wow drum, the hand drum, which he also called the dream drum, and medicine drums. The latter are usually suspended from four posts in the four directions. The curved posts have ceremonial significance.

The peace or ceremonial drum is the same as that called the dance drum in much of the literature. It was given to the Anishnabe people with spiritual teachings which are embodied in its structure and use—its orientation in relation to the four directions, bipartite membrane surface (often painted red and blue with a black line running across the diameter from east to west), cross lacing, careful dressing, and tobacco offerings. The drum constitutes an important way of life for many young Anishnabe men. Ceremonial drums frequently have their own repertoire of songs which must be performed before any other music at public events. Drumsticks are usually straight with a padded distal end. Some museum artifacts had a middle fur-wrapped section. The dance drum is imitated in the powwow

drum which may be a commercial bass drum, significantly turned in a horizontal direction.

The hand drum called the dream drum originated in the warrior societies according to Anishnabe elders. Artwork on the rawhide membrane represents the vision/dream of the carrier. It can be used for healing, or for sustaining a fast. Young Anishnabe men who follow traditional teachings continue to undertake fasts during which they are often the recipients of songs given to them by spirits, sometimes in the context of dreams. The images painted on drums, or the specific construction of a musical instrument may be related to the directives received in a dream. Drums documented in archival collections as dream drums sometimes refer to instruments received in this intensive individual context and sometimes to large horizontal drums which were used by Dreamers Societies.

Anishnabe flutes are usually described in association with courting. Song stanzas were alternated with flute renditions of the same tune (see Vennum 1989: 13). A revival of interest in flute-making and playing occurred in the 1980s.

It is not always possible to identify the type or function of a musical instrument from its physical form. The way in which it was created or acquired may be significant. Furthermore, while many instrument types appear similar for different Anishnabe Nations, each also has distinctive sound producers or distinctive designs. Cree frame drums, for example, more frequently use the colours blue and yellow, as well as a parallel snare configuration across the E/W membrane diameter. Generalizations must be qualified, however, since many different drum types are used by members of the same Nation. Our documentation records four different types of Cree frame drums, for example. A single Cree drum among those documented had a double rim on both sides of a frame, like the Montagnais double-membrane *teueikan* described above. This particular drum (see Colour Plate 12) is a spectacular instrument, painted dark green, very large, with quill snares and a variety of cloths, ties, and offerings. Other frame drums were equally large but had a single rim, top and bottom. A third type resembles the Ojibwe, double-membrane, frame drum (or drum/rattle) in which membranes are stitched around the frame perimeter to completely cover the wood. As in the case of the similar Ojibwe drum, this type was regarded as "powerful," especially when the image of birds—sometimes facing one another in a mirror effect—was painted on the membrane. Finally, a fourth structural type consists of a single membrane, overcast to the bottom of the frame and laced on the underside with thongs which are joined in the middle to form a hand-hold. This type resembles Plains Cree drums and may, in some instances, be wrongly attributed to Eastern Woodlands groups by museums.

Cree drumsticks, like those of other Nations, are also diverse. The aforementioned green drum has a stick made of wood and root material, the latter curved into a circle at the distal end, and covered with cloth. Several elders pointed out the similarity of this drumstick and a lacrosse racquet. The drumstick is sometimes even equipped with a net. A specially shaped, carved wooden stick was identified as a "sacred" type by a Cree elder. Its unusual shape resembles the supports of the large peace drum. Other carved shapes, one almost symmetrical with slight flares at both proximal and distal ends, were also documented.

Two Algonquin drum types were documented in museum collections. A snare-strung frame drum like that of the Attikamek and Montagnais appears rarely in the collections described here where it is said to be associated with shamanism. The Algonquin also use a drum which is structured like the traditional double-rim *teueikan* of the Montagnais but shaped taller, like a Euro-American military snare drum. Stars and crescent moons were often painted on the frame of this tall drum, although other styles of both realistic and abstract designs were sometimes adopted. Photographs from the 1940s and 1950s show this drum played in processionals together with fiddles, the latter an instrument which remains extremely popular in some communities. The tall drum is described as the dance drum in some museum documentation.

Other musical traditions specific to individual Nations continue to exist. For example, the Algonquin of northern Ontario use a large moose-hoof rattle (the *shinaueshikan*) which is unknown in other areas. In the early twentieth century, other instrument types are described in the ethnographic literature for this Nation: Johnson (MS, Heye Archives V-L) describes a drum "made of a hollow cedar log with a skin head fastened to hoops on both ends. The heads were tightened by lashings pulling on the loops." He also noted a rattle "made by stringing bear's teeth and mud-turtle's claws alternately on a small stick" (ibid.). Algonquin moose calls were often decorated with alternate layers of positive and negative design reflecting an image of several layers of the universe.

Among those documented in our project, Cree disc rattles are the most varied with regard to membrane type. Of special note are the fish-skin covered rattles which are associated with healing ceremonies. Translucent membranes, identified in one case as the ejected stomach lining of a bird, as well as bird skin and caribou are used on other rattles. Each is a specific type with specific uses and powers. Most Cree disc rattles have straight handles, unlike ones made further east. Further west, the handles are made longer and are often sheathed in one or more materials (leather, tape, etc.). Some disc rattles have a blue pattern of concentric (or just centric) circles similar to the red Montagnais ones.

Two Cree instruments which we heard about but did not see are the *nukuman* (a large bone buzzer which is looped around a tree and played with both hands), and a fiddle made by stringing sinew across the arc of a caribou shoulder blade. A sinew-strung bow was used to play this. The repertoire described by elder James Carpenter for this instrument was varied and included ceremonial songs. On the other hand, European fiddles are widely used in Cree communities to accompany dance.

Whistles and bull-roarers are also represented in the collections which we documented.

Contemporary Intertribal Celebrations

Contemporary powwows, generally traced to the war dance and grass dance complexes of the Plains, are open-air events which occur in many Anishnabe as well as Iroquoian communities generally on summer weekends. The "drums" (a term referring to the ensembles as well as the instruments) reside under a central arbour at the heart of the dance space. Their sound is frequently described as the "heartbeat" of the Nations. Many drummers explain that the military bass drum was taken from European culture and "turned," thereby usurping European strength and changing the power of the drum in the direction of Aboriginal culture. The powwow drum itself never rests directly on the earth, but is usually placed on a special blanket.

Traditionally the powwow drum is played only by men, although women have been drumming in recent years. While men drum and sing at the drum, women encircle the men and join in the singing part way through each strophe; they sing an octave higher and sometimes finish the verse on their own as the men drop out to retake the high notes of the next strophe. Thus women are said to hold the circle together and to finish what the men start in each strophe. Although the tradition of specific Nations or communities varies, each day of a powwow usually begins with an invocation and a "grand entry" of all participants. Both specific dances and "inter-tribals," in which all participants dance together, follow. Honour songs may pay tribute to individuals, groups, or other living entities (e.g., the earth). At competitive powwows, dancers register in categories defined by costume, musical repertoire, and dance steps (e.g., " Traditional," Fancy," "Grass," and "Jingle-dress"). The "grass dance" and "jingle-dress" categories arose in the 1980s, based on an older tradition in the case of the former or inspired by a relatively recent vision in the case of the latter. The intense, often pulsated singing style and descending step-like musical contour is derived from Plains tradition. Specific dance types are distinguished by the tempi and rhythmic patterns of the songs, the latter often relating to the dance motion. Drummers, drum keepers, and singers speak eloquently about the great respect paid to this drum and offer some of its teachings. For many individuals, however, the spiritual dimensions are not their focus; for them, powwows are pleasurable occasions on which to renew acquaintances and affirm Indian identity.

Notes

1   See, for example, Ruth Whitehead's *The Old Man Told Us: Excerpts from Micmac History 1500-1950* (1991).
2   An indication of the complexity of this issue alone is suggested by the "Synonymy" sections in region-specific volumes of the Smithsonian Institution's *Handbook of North American Indians*, Washington, 1978-.
3   John Grant's *Moon of Wintertime: Missionaries and the Indians of Canada in Encounter since 1534* (1984) is one noteworthy example.
4   Phrase used on the cover of Miller's *Skyscrapers Hide the Heavens: A History of Indian-White Relations in Canada* (1989).
5   The re-visioning of Native history relates, in the opinion of some scholars (see, e.g., Edward Bruner,

"Ethnography as Narrative," in Turner and Bruner, *The Anthropology of Experience* [1986]) to a fundamental change in paradigm in which the "Golden Age," which was seen as a period in the past, is now seen as a period in the future. In spite of this, the phrase "Golden Age" has appeared frequently in the newer histories to indicate a period (often relatively early in the colonial period) when the integrity of Aboriginal governments was not yet eroded. Schmalz (1991; also see his recent *Ojibwa of Southern Ontario* [1990]), for example, writes of the early eighteenth century as the "golden age" of the Southern Ontario Ojibwe when they were masters of the Great Lakes. Trigger cites Bailey's *The Conflict of European and Algonkian Cultures 1504-1700* (1937) as a turning point in the historical study of native peoples. Trigger's own history (*Natives and Newcomers* 1985) of Indian-European relations in the seventeenth century is subtitled *Canada's "Heroic Age" Reconsidered.*
6   Unpublished historical writing by Deborah Doxtator, especially her "One Heart, One Mind, One Body: The Meaning of Alliance in Iroquoia 1700-1760" (MS 1990) was especially helpful in our study. So too were local histories such as Pierre Gill's *Les Premiers Habitants du Saguenay-Lac St. Jean* (1987) or Marguerite Vincent Tehariolina's history of her Nation *La Nationne Huronne. Son histoire, sa culture, son esprit* (1984).
7   See some discussion of this in Chapter Four. The literature on Native representation is now enormous. In the Canadian context significant studies include, in addition to Doxtator's *Fluffs and Feathers*, referenced in that earlier discussion, her thesis "Iroquoian Museums and the Idea of the Indian: Aspects of the Political Role of Museums" (M.A. thesis, Museum Studies Programme, University of Toronto, 1983). The imaging of Native culture in literature and film has been extensively studied in recent decades. Two early Canadian landmarks in this regard are Leslie Monkman's *A Native Heritage: Images of the Indian in Native Canadian Literature* (1981) and Carol Carpenter's *Many Voices* (1979).
8   See chapters by Bock and Reynolds in the Smithsonian *Handbook of North American Indians*, Vol. 15: *The Northeast* (1978).

Bibliography

Abler, Thomas S. 1987. Dendrogram and Celestial Tree: Numerical Taxonomy and Variants of the Iroquoian Creation Myth. *Canadian Journal of Native Studies* 7/2:195-222.

Ahenakew, Freda. 1987. *Cree Language Structures: A Cree Approach*. Winnipeg: Pemmican Publications.

Ames, Michael, *et al.* 1988. Proposed Museum Policies for Ethnological Collections and the Peoples They Represent. *Muse* 6/3:47-57.

An Antane Kapesh/Anne André. 1976. *Eukuan Nin Matshimanitu Innu-Iskueu /Je Suis une Maudite Sauvagesse*. Ottawa: Lemeac.

André, Mathieu. 1984. *Moi Mestanapeu*. Sept-Îles: Edition Innu.

Appadurai, Arjun. 1988. Introduction: Place and Voice in Anthropological Theory. *Cultural Anthropology* 3/1:16-20.

Arima, Eugene Y., and Magnus Einarsson. 1976. Whence and When the Eskimo Fiddle? *Folk* 18:23-40.

Assiniwi, Bernard. 1972. *À l'Indienne*. Ottawa: Lemeac.

Aubin, George F. 1975. *A Proto-Algonquian Dictionary*. Mercury Series. Canadian Ethnology Service Paper 29. Ottawa: National Museums of Canada.

Austin, Alberta, Ron LaFrance, *et al.* 1987. *Seneca Language Topic Reference Guide*. Gowanda, NY: Title VII Education Bilingual Program.

Babcock, Barbara. 1987. Taking Liberties, Writing from the Margins, and Doing It with a Difference. *Journal of American Folklore* 100:390-411.

Bailey, A.G. [1937] 1969. *The Conflict of European and Algonkian Cultures 1504-1700: A Study in Canadian Civilization*. Toronto: University of Toronto Press.

Baraga, R.R. [1878-80] 1973. *A Dictionary of the Otchipwe Language*. Minneapolis: Ross and Haines.

Barsh, Russel Lawrence. 1987. Are Anthropologists Hazardous to Indians' Health? *The Journal of Ethnic Studies* 15/4:1-38.

Basile, Marie, and Gerard McNulty. 1971. *Atanukana*. Quebec: Centre d'études nordiques, Université Laval.

Bateson, Gregory. [1968] 1972. Redundancy and Coding. In *Animal Communication: Techniques of Study and Results of Research*, ed. Thomas A. Sebeok. Reprinted in *Steps to an Ecology of Mind*, pp. 411-25.

____. 1972. *Steps to an Ecology of Mind*. New York: Ballantine.

____, and Mary Catherine Bateson. 1987. *Angels Fear: Towards an Epistemology of the Sacred*. New York: Macmillan.

Battiste, Marie. 1987. Mi'kmaq Linguistic Integrity: A Case Study of Mi'kmawey School. In *Indian Education in Canada*. Vol. 2, *The Challenge*, ed. J. Barman *et al.*, pp. 107-25. Vancouver: University of British Columbia Press.

____. 1986. Micmac Literacy and Cognitive Assimilation. In *Indian Education in Canada*. Vol. 1: *The Legacy*, ed. J. Barman *et al.*, pp. 23-44. Vancouver: University of British Columbia Press.

Bauman, R., and J. Sherzer. 1974. *Explorations in the Ethnography of Speaking*. London: Cambridge University Press.

Bauman, Richard. 1986. *Story, Performance, and Event*. Cambridge: Cambridge University Press.

Beck, Peggy V., and A.L. Walters. 1977. *The Sacred: Ways of Knowledge, Sources of Life*. Tsaile, AZ: Navajo Community College.

Becker, Judith. 1988. Earth, Fire, Sakti and the Javanese Gamelan. *Ethnomusicology* 32/3:385-91.

Benedict, Michael Les. 1986. Historians and the Continuing Controversy Over Fair Use of Unpublished Manuscript Materials. *American Historical Review* 91/4:859-81.

Benton-Benai, Eddie. 1987 (November-December). The Seventh Fire: Native Cultural Renaissance. *Boozhoo*, 7-11.

Berger, Peter L., and Thomas Luckmann. 1966. *The Social Construction of Reality*. Garden City, NY: Doubleday.

Berkhofer, Robert F., Jr. 1979. *The White Man's Indian*. New York: Vintage Books.

Black, Mary B. 1977. Ojibwe Taxonomy and Percept Ambiguity. *Ethos* 5/1:90-118.

____. 1977. Ojibwa Power Belief System. In Raymond D. Fogelson and R.N. Adams, *The Anthropology of Power: Ethnographic Studies from Asia, Oceania, and the New World*, 141-51. New York: Academic Press.

Blessing, Fred K. 1969. Medicine Bags and Bundles of Midewiwin. *The Minnesota Archaeologist*, 30/4:79-121.

____. 1977. *The Ojibway Indians Observed*. St. Paul: Minnesota Archeological Society.

Blum, Stephen, Philip Bohlman, and Daniel Neuman, eds. 1990. *Ethnomusicology and Modern Music History*. Urbana: University of Illinois Press.

Bonvillain, Nancy, ed. 1980. Studies in Iroquoian Culture. *Occasional Publications in Northeastern Anthropology* 6:59-70.

Bourdieu, Pierre. 1991. *Language and Symbolic Power*. Edited and introduced by John B. Thompson. Translated by Gino Raymond and Matthew

Adamson. Cambridge, MA: Harvard University Press.

____. 1977. *Outline of a Theory of Practice*. Trans. R. Nice. Cambridge: Cambridge University Press.

Brant, Beth. 1984. *A Gathering of Spirit*. Toronto: The Women's Press.

Brightman, Robert A. 1989. *Acaoohkiwina and Acimowina: Traditional Narratives of the Rock Cree Indians*. Mercury Series, Paper 113. Ottawa: Canadian Museum of Civilization.

Brincard, Marie-Thérèse, ed. 1989. *Sounding Forms: African Musical Instruments*. New York: The American Federation of Arts.

Brown, Donald Nelson. 1967. The Distribution of Sound Instruments in the Prehistoric Southwestern United States. *Ethnomusicology* 11/1:71-90.

____. 1971. Ethnomusicology and the Prehistoric Southwest. *Ethnomusicology* 15/3:363-78.

Brown, Jennifer S.H., and R. Brightman, eds. 1988. *The Orders of the Dreamed: George Nelson on Cree and Northern Ojibwe Religion and Myth, 1823*. Winnipeg: University of Manitoba Press.

Bruner, Edward. 1988. *Text, Play and Story: The Construction and Reconstruction of Self and Society*. Prospect Heights, IL: Waveland Press.

____. 1986. Ethnography as Narrative. In *The Anthropology of Experience*, ed. Edward Bruner and Victor Turner, pp. 139-58. Urbana and Chicago: University of Illinois Press.

Bruyas, Rev. James. [1862] 1970. *Radical Words of the Mohawk Language: With Their Derivatives*. New York: AMS Press.

Burlin, Natalie Curtis. [1907] 1968. *The Indians Book*. New York: Dover.

Burnham, Dorothy K. 1992. *To Please the Caribou: Painted Caribou-Skin Coats Worn by the Naskapi, Montagnais, and Cree Hunters of the Quebec-Labrador Peninsula*. Toronto: Royal Ontario Museum.

Butler, Judith P. 1990. *Gender Trouble: Feminism and the Subversion of Identity*. New York: Routledge.

Capps, Walter Holden, and Åke Hultkrantz. 1976. *Seeing with a Native Eye*. New York: Harper & Row.

Cardinal, Douglas. 1977. *Of the Spirit: Writings by Douglas Cardinal*, ed. George Melnyk. Edmonton: NeWest Press.

Carpenter, Carole. 1979. *Many Voices: A Study of Folklore Activities in Canada and Their Role in Canadian Culture*. Ottawa: National Museums of Canada.

Cavanagh, Beverley. *See also* Diamond Cavanagh, Beverley.

Cavanagh, Beverley. 1985-86. Les myths et la musique naskapis. *Recherches amérindiennes au québec* 15/4:5-18.

____. 1987. The Performance of Hymns in Eastern Woodland Indian Communities. In *Sing Out the Glad News: Hymn Tunes in Canada*, ed. John Beckwith, pp. 45-56. CanMus Documents, 1. Toronto: Institute for Canadian Music.

____. 1987. Problems in Investigating the History of an Oral Tradition: Reconciling Different Types of Data about Inuit Drum Dance Traditions. *Annuario musical* (Barcelona) 42:29-51.

____. 1988. The Transmission of Algonkian Indian Hymns: Between Orality and Literacy. In *Musical Canada: Words and Music Honouring Helmut Kallmann*, ed. Beckwith, J. and F. Hall, pp. 3-28. Toronto: University of Toronto Press.

Chafe, Wallace L. 1963. *Handbook of the Seneca Language*. Bulletin 388. Albany: New York State Museum.

____. 1983. *Onödowa'ga:' Gawë:no' Oiwa'shö'öh: Words of the Seneca Language*. Salamanca, NY: Seneca Bilingual Education Program.

____. 1967. *Seneca Morphology and Dictionary*. Washington: Smithsonian.

____. 1961. *Seneca Thanksgiving Rituals*. Bulletin 183. Washington: Bureau of American Ethnology.

Clark, Jeremiah S., ed. 1902. *Rand's Micmac Dictionary*. Charlottetown: Patriot Publishing.

Clarke, Sandra. 1982. *North-West River (Sheshatshit) Montagnais: A Grammatical Sketch*. Canadian Ethnology Service Paper No. 80. Ottawa: National Museums of Canada.

Clifford, James. 1988. *The Predicament of Culture: Twentieth-Century Ethnography, Literature, and Art*. Cambridge, MA: Harvard University Press.

____, and George E. Marcus, eds. 1986. *Writing Culture: The Poetics and Politics of Ethnography*. Berkeley: University of California Press.

Coe, Ralph T. 1976. *Sacred Circles: Two Thousand Years of North American Indian Art*. London: Arts Council of Great Britain.

Conklin, Harold C., and W.C. Sturtevant. 1953. Seneca Indian Singing Tools at Coldspring Longhouse. *Proceedings of the American Philosophical Society* 97:262-90.

Corbière, Melvina. *Nishinabenda pu-ne/Let's Talk Ojibwe*. N.p.: Ojibwe Cultural Foundation, n.d.

Cove, John. 1987. *Shattered Images: Dialogues and Meditations on Tsimshian Narratives*. Ottawa: Carleton University Press.

Cringan, Alexander T. 1903. Iroquois Folk Songs. *Annual Archeological Report*. Toronto: Ontario Provincial Museum.

____. 1900. Pagan Dance Songs of the Iroquois. *Annual Archeological Report*. Toronto: Ontario Provincial Museum.

[Cronk, M. Sam, comp.]. 1990. *The Sound of the Drum*. Brantford: Woodland Cultural Centre.

Cronk, M. Sam. 1988. Writing While They're Singing: A Conversation about Longhouse Social Dance Songs. *New York Folklore* 14/3-4:49-60.

DeBlois, Don A., and Alphonse Metallic. 1983. *Micmac Lexicon*. Ottawa: National Museums of Canada.

Densmore, Frances. [1910-13] 1972. *Chippewa Music*. Introduction by Thomas Vennum. New York: Da Capo Press.

DeVale, Sue Carole, ed.. 1990. *Issues in Organology: Selected Reports in Ethnomusicology*. Vol. 8. Los Angeles: University of California.

____. 1990. Musical Instruments and Ritual: A Systematic Approach. *Journal of the American Musical Instrument Society* 16:126-60.

Diamond. *See also* Diamond Cavanagh *and* Cavanagh.

Diamond, Jody. 1990. There Is No They There. *MusicWorks* 47:12-23.

Diamond Cavanagh, Beverley. 1989. Music and Gender in the Sub-Arctic Algonkian Area. In *Women in North American Indian Music: Six Essays*, ed. R. Keeling. SEM Special Series No. 6. Bloomington, IN: Society for Ethnomusicology.

____. 1992. Christian Hymns in Eastern Woodlands Communities: Performance Contexts. In *Musical Repercussions of 1492: Explorations, Encounters, and Identities*, ed. Carol E. Robertson, pp. 381-94. Washington: Smithsonian Institution.

____, Sam Cronk, and Franziska von Rosen. 1988. Vivre ses traditions. In *Recherches amérindiennes au Québec* 18/4:5-21.

Dickason, Olive P. 1992. *Canada's First Nations: A History of Founding Peoples from Earliest Times*. Toronto: McClelland & Stewart.

Dixon, Susan R., ed. 1990. *Unbroken Circles: Traditional Arts of Contemporary Woodland Peoples. Northeast Indian Quarterly* (special issue) 7/4.

Dournon, Geneviève. 1992. Organology. In *Ethnomusicology: An Introduction*, ed. Helen Myers. New York: Norton.

Doxtator, Deborah. 1988. *Fluffs and Feathers*. Brantford, ON: Woodland Cultural Centre.

____. 1983. Iroquoian Museums and the Idea of the Indian: Aspects of the Political Role of Museums. Master's thesis, Museum Studies Programme, University of Toronto.

____. 1990. One Heart, One Mind, One Body: The Meaning of Alliance in Iroquoia 1700-1760. Manuscript.

Druck, Mary A. 1980. The Concept of Personhood in Seventeenth and Eighteenth Century Iroquois Ethnopersonality. In *Studies on Iroquoian Culture*, ed. Nancy Bonvillain. *Occasional Publications in Northeastern Anthropology* 6:59-70.

Duffek, Karen, and Tom Hill, eds. 1989. *Beyond History*. Vancouver: Vancouver Art Gallery.

Etienne, Mona, and Eleanor Leacock, eds. 1980. *Women and Colonization: Anthropological Perspectives*. New York: Praeger.

Fabre, Père Bonaventure. [1695] 1970. *Racines Montagnais*. Transcribed by Gerard McNulty and Associates, Travaux. Divers, PQ: Centre d'études Nordiques de l'université Laval.

Feld, Steven. 1982. *Sound and Sentiment: Birds, Weeping, Poetics, and Song in Kaluli Expression*. Philadelphia: University of Pennsylvania Press.

Fenton, W.J. 1985. On Traditional Literatures: This Island, the World on a Turtle's Back. In *Critical Essays in Native American Literature*, ed. A. Wiget, pp. 133-53. Boston: G.K. Hall.

Foster, Michael. 1974. *From the Earth to Beyond the Sky: An Ethnographic Approach to Four Longhouse Iroquois Speech Events*. Ottawa: National Museums of Canada.

____, Jack Campisi, and Marianne Mithun. 1984. *Extending the Rafters: Interdisciplinary Approaches to Iroquoian Studies*. Albany: State University of New York.

Foucault, Michel. 1972. *The Order of Things*. New York: Vintage.

____. 1984. *The Foucault Reader*, ed. Paul Rabinow. New York: Pantheon.

Francis, Daniel. 1992. *The Imaginary Indian: The Image of the Indian in Canadian Culture*. Vancouver: Arsenal Pulp Press.

Freeman, John F. 1966; 1982 (Supplement). *A Guide to Manuscripts Relating to the American Indian in the Library of the American Philosophical Society*. Philadelphia: American Philosophical Society.

Frisbie, Charlotte. 1987. *Navajo Medicine Bundles or Jish: Acquisition, Transmission, and Disposition in the Past and Present*. Albuquerque: University of New Mexico Press.

____. 1980. Vocables in Navajo Ceremonial Music. *Ethnomusicology* 24/3:347-92.

Fuks, Victor. 1990. Waiapi Musical Instruments: Classification, Symbols and Meanings. In Sue Carole DeVale, *Issues in Organology: Selected Reports in Ethnomusicology*, Vol. 8, pp. 143-74. Los Angeles: University of California.

Gessain, R., and P.-E Victor. 1973. Le tambour chez les Ammassalimiut. *Objets et mondes* 13/3:129-60.

Geyshick, Ron. 1989. *Tebwewin (Truth): Stories by an Ojibway Healer*. Compiled by Judith Doyle. Toronto: Summerhill.

Gill, Pierre. 1987. *Les Premiers Habitants du Saguenay-Lac St. Jean*. [Pointe-Bleue]: Mishinikan.

Gill, Sam. 1987. *Native American Religious Action: A Performance Approach to Religion*, ed. Frederick Denny. Columbia: University of South Carolina Press.

Goffmann, Erving. 1959. *The Presentation of Self in Everyday Life*. New York: Doubleday (Anchor Books).

Grant, John Webster. 1984. *Moon of Wintertime: Missionaries and the Indians of Canada in Encounter since 1534*. Toronto: University of Toronto Press.

Green, Rayna. 1988. Poor Lo and Dusky Ramona: Scenes from an Album of Indian America. In *Folk Roots, New Roots: Folklore in American Life*, ed. Jane S. Becker and Barbara Franco, pp. 77-102. Lexington, MA: Museum of Our National Heritage.

____. 1984. *That's What She Said: Contemporary Poetry and Fiction by Native American Women*. Bloomington: Indiana University Press.

Gregoire, Michel. 1989. *La Langage de la chasse*. Translation and Commentary by Richard Dominique. Sillery: Les Presses de l'Université de Québec.

Grenier, Line, and Jocelyne Guilbault. 1990. Authority Revisited: The "Other" in Anthropology and Popular Music Studies. *Ethnomusicology* 34/3:381-97.

Griffiths, Linda. 1989. *The Book of Jessica*. Toronto: Coach House Press.

Grossberg, Lawrence, Cary Nelson and Paula Treichler, eds. 1992. *Cultural Studies*. New York: Routledge.

Guilbault, Jocelyne. 1987. The La Rose and La Marguerite Organizations in St. Lucia: Oral and Literate Strategies in Performance. *Yearbook for Traditional Music* 19:97-116.

Gunn Allen, Paula. 1986. *The Sacred Hoop: Recovering the Feminine in American Indian Traditions*. Boston: Beacon Press.

Haefer, J. Richard. 1981. Musical Thought in Papago Culture. Ph.D. thesis, University of Illinois at Urbana-Champaign.

____. 1976. North American Indian Musical Instruments: Some Organological Distribution Problems. *Journal of the American Musical Instrument Society* 14:56-85.

Halliday, M.A.K., and R. Hassan. 1989. *Language, Context, and Text: Aspects of Language in a Social-Semiotic Perspective*. Oxford: Oxford University Press.

Hallowell, A. Irving. 1955. *Culture and Experience*. Philadelphia: University of Pennsylvania Press.

____. 1960. Ojibwa Ontology, Behavior, and World View. In *Culture and History: Essays in Honour of Paul Radin*, ed. Stanley Diamond. New York: Columbia University Press.

Hamell, George R. 1992. The Iroquois and the World's Rim: Speculations on Colour, Culture and Contact. *American Indian Quarterly* 16/4:451-70.

Hamm, Charles. 1983. *Music of the New World*. New York: Norton.

Handler, Richard. 1983. On Dialogue and Destructive Analysis: Problems in Narrating Nationalism and Ethnicity. *Journal of Anthropological Research* 41/2: 171-81.

____. 1986. Authenticity. *Anthropology Today* 2/1:2.

____. 1991. Who Owns the Past? History, Cultural Property, and the Logic of Possessive Individualism. In *The Politics of Culture*, ed. Brett Williams. Washington and London: Smithsonian Institution.

Harrington, Mark E. 1921. *Religion and Ceremonies of the Lenape*. New York: Museum of the American Indian, Heye Foundation.

Harrison, Julia D. (Response B. Trigger). 1988. "The Spirit Sings" and the Future of Anthropology. *Anthropology Today* 4/6:6-10.

Harrison, Regina. 1989. *Signs, Songs, and Memory in the Andes: Translating Quechua Language and Culture*. Austin: University of Texas Press.

Hassan, Scheherezade Qassim. 1980. *Les Instruments de Musique en Iraq et Leur Role dans la Société Traditionnelle*. Cahier de l'Homme, Nouvelle Série XXI. Paris: Mouton Editeur.

Hauser, Michael. 1978. Inuit Songs from Southwest Baffin Island in Cross-cultural Context. *Études/Inuit/Studies* 2/1:55-83; 2/2:71-105.

Helm, June, ed. 1981. *Subarctic: Handbook of North American Indians*. Vol. 6 (Series editor, William Sturtevant). Washington: Smithsonian Institution. Abbreviated *SH 6*.

Henry, Reginald, and Marianne Mithun. 1982. *Watewayéstanih: A Cayuga Teaching Grammar*. Brantford, ON: Woodland Indian Cultural Educational Centre.

Heth, Charlotte. 1980. Stylistic Similarities in Cherokee and Iroquois Music. *Journal of Cherokee Studies* 4:128-62.

____, ed. 1992. *Native American Dance: Ceremonies and Social Traditions*. Washington: National Museum of the American Indian, Smithsonian Institution with Starwood Publishing, Inc.

____, ed. 1991. *Sharing a Heritage: American Indian Arts*. 2d ed. Los Angeles: University of California Press.

Hewitt, J.N.B. 1899-1900; 1925-26. *Iroquoian Cosmology*. Annual Reports of the Bureau of American Ethnology 21:127-339; 43:449-819.

Hickerson, Harold. 1970. *The Chippewa and Their Neighbours: A Study in Ethnohistory*. New York: Holt, Rinehart and Winston.

____. 1962. The Southwestern Chippewa: An Ethnohistorical Study. *Memoirs of the American Anthropological Association* 92.

____. 1963. The Sociohistorical Significance of Two Chippewa Ceremonials. *American Anthropologist* 68/1:1-26.

Hill, Jonathan. 1979. Kamayura Flute Music. *Ethnomusicology* 23/3:417-32.

Hoffman, Bernard G. 1955. The Historical Ethnography of the Micmac of the 16th and 17th Centuries. Ph.D. thesis (Anthropology), University of California.

Hoffman, Walter James. 1891. *The Midewiwin or "Grand Medicine Society" of the Ojibwa*. 7th Report. Washington: Bureau of American Ethnology.

Hofmann, Charles. 1972. *Musical Instruments of the Indians of the Americas*. Drawings by Edward G. Cornwell, Jr. Rochester: Rochester Museum and Science Centre.

Hofstadter, Douglas. 1985. *Metamagical Themas: Questing for the Essence of Mind and Pattern*. New York: Basic.

hooks, bell. 1990. *Yearning: Race, Gender, and Cultural Politics*. Toronto: Between the Lines.

Horse Capture, George. 1991. Survival of Culture. *Museum News* 70/1:49-51.

Howley, James P. [1915] 1975. *The Beothuks or Red Indians*. Toronto: Coles.

Hoxie, Frederick E. 1988. *Indians in American History*. Arlington Heights, IL: Harlan Davidson.

Hymes, Dell. 1973. *Breakthrough into Performance*. Urbino: Università di Urbino.

____. 1981. *In Vain I Tried to Tell You: Essays in Native American Ethnopoetics*. Philadelphia: University of Pennsylvania Press.

Isaacs, Hope L. 1977. "Orenda" and the Concept of Power among the Tonawanda Seneca. In *The Anthropology of Power*, ed. R.D. Fogelson and R. Adams, pp. 167-84. New York: Academic Press.

Izikowitz, Karl Gustav. [1935] 1970. *Musical and Other Sound Instruments of the South American Indians*. 2d ed. Goteborg: Elanders Boktryckeri Aktieb.

Jakobson, Roman. 1962. *Selected Writings*. 4 vols. The Hague: Mouton.

Jauvin, Jerge. 1993. *Aitnanu: The Lives of Hélène and William Mathieu Mark*, ed. Daniel Clement. Ottawa: Canadian Museum of Civilization.

Johnson, Frederick. 1928. The Algonquin at Golden Lake, Ontario. In Heye Foundation Series: *Indian Notes*, 5/2:173-78. New York: Museum of the American Indian, Heye Foundation.

____. 1929. Notes on the Ojibwa and Potawatomi of the Parry Island Reservation, Ontario. In Heye Foundation Series: *Indian Notes* 6/3:193-216. New York: Museum of the American Indian, Heye Foundation.

____. 1930. An Algonquin Band at Lac Barrière, Province of Ontario. In Heye Foundation Series: *Indian Notes* 7/1:27-39. New York: Museum of the American Indian, Heye Foundation.

____. 1943. Notes on Micmac Shamanism. *Primitive Man* 16:53-80.

Jones, Rev. Peter (Kaykewaquonaby). [1861] 1970. *History of the Ojebway Indians; with Especial Reference to Their Conversion to Christianity*. Freeport, NY: Books for Libraries Press.

Kallmann, Helmut, *et al.*, eds. 1992. *Encyclopedia of Music in Canada*. 2d ed. Toronto: University of Toronto Press.

Kartomi, Margaret. 1991. *On Concepts and Classifications of Musical Instruments*. Chicago: University of Chicago Press.

Keeling, Richard, ed. 1989. *Women in North American Indian Music: Six Essays*. SEM Special Series, 6. Bloomington: Society for Ethnomusicology.

King, J.C.H. 1982. *Thunderbird and Lightning: Indian Life in Northeastern North America 1600-1900*. London: British Museum Publications.

King, Thomas, ed. 1990. *All My Relations: An Anthology of Contemporary Canadian Native Fiction*. Toronto: McClelland and Stewart.

Kirk, Sylvie van. [1980 or 1981]. *"Many Tender Ties": Women in Fur-Trading Society in Western Canada, 1670-1870*. Winnipeg, MB: Watson and Dwyer.

Kohl, Johann G. [1860] 1956. *Kitchi-gami: Wanderings Round Lake Superior*. Minneapolis: Ross & Haines.

Kondo, Dorinne. 1990. *Crafting Selves: Power, Gender, and Discourses of Identity in a Japanese Workplace*. Chicago: University of Chicago Press.

Kress, Gunther R., and Robert Hodge. 1979. *Language as Ideology*. London: Routledge and Kegan Paul.

Kuanutin Nutshimiu-Atusseun. 1988. Sept-Îles: Epishiminishkueu.

Kuper, Adam. 1988. *The Invention of Primitive Society: Transformations of an Illusion*. London: Routledge.

Kurath, Gertrude P. 1968. *Dance and Song Rituals of Six Nations Reserve, Ontario*. Ottawa: National Museums of Canada.

____. 1964. *Iroquois Music and Dance: Ceremonial Arts of Two Seneca Longhouses*. Bulletin 187. Washington: Bureau of American Ethnology.

____. 1951. Local Diversity in Iroquois Music and Dance. In *Symposium on Local Diversity in Iroquois Culture*, ed. William N. Fenton. Bulletin 149. Washington: Bureau of American Ethnology.

Lavie, Smadar, *et al.*, eds. 1993. *Creativity/Anthropology*. Ithaca: Cornell University Press.

Le Clercq, Chrétien. [1610] 1910. *New Relation of Gaspesia with the Customs and Religion of the Gaspesian Indians*. Trans. and ed. by W.F. Ganong. Toronto: Champlain Society.

Leacock, Eleanor B., and Jacqueline Goodman. 1976. Montagnais Marriage and the Jesuits in the Seventeenth Century: Incidents from the Relations of Paul LeJeune. *Western Canadian Journal of Anthropology* 6/3:77-91.

____, and Richard Lee, eds. 1982. *Politics and History in Band Societies*. Cambridge: Cambridge University Press.

Leavitt, Robert. 1985. Confronting Language Ambivalence and Language Death: The Roles of the University in Native Communities. *Canadian Journal of Native Studies* 5/2:262-67.

____. 1989. *Maritime Native Studies*. Fredericton: Micmac-Maliseet Institute, University of New Brunswick.

Lee, Benjamin, ed. 1982. *Psychosocial Theories of the Self*. New York: Plenum Press.

Lee, Dorothy Sara. 1979. *Native North American Music and Oral Data: Catalogue of Sound Recordings, 1893-1976*. Foreword by Willard Rhodes. Bloomington: Indiana University Press.

Leppert, Richard, and Susan McClary, eds. 1987. *Music and Society: The Politics of Composition, Performance and Reception*. Cambridge: Cambridge University Press.

Lescarbot, Marc. [1618] 1907-14. *The History of New France*. Trans. W.L. Grant. 3 vols. Toronto: Champlain Society.

Levine, Victoria Lindsay. 1990. Arzelie Langtry and a Lost Pan-tribal Tradition. In *Ethnomusicology and Modern Music History*, ed. Stephen Blum, Philip Bohlman, and Daniel Neuman. Urbana: University of Illinois Press.

Lichtenwanger, William. 1974. *A Survey of Musical Instrument Collections in the United States and Canada*. Chapel Hill, NC: N.p.

Linnekin, Jocelyn. 1991. Cultural Invention and the Dilemma of Authenticity. *American Anthropology* 93:446-49.

Lippard, Lucy R. 1990. *Mixed Blessings: New Art in a Multicultural America*. New York: Pantheon.

____. 1992. *Partial Recall with Essays on Photographs of Native North Americans*. New York: New Press.

Lutz, Hartmut. 1991. *Contemporary Challenges: Conversations with Canadian Native Authors*. Saskatoon: Fifth House Publishers.

Lutz, Maija. 1982. *Musical Traditions of the Labrador Coast Inuit*. Ottawa: National Museums of Canada.

Lyford, Carrie A. 1983. *Iroquois Crafts*. Stevens Point, WI: R.C. Schneider.

____. 1982. *Ojibwa Crafts*. Stevens Point, WI: R.C. Schneider.

Mailhot, José, and Kateri Lescop. 1977. *Lexique Montagnais-Français du dialecte de Schefferville, Sept-Îles et Maliotenam*, Dossier 29. Québec: Ministère des Affaires culturelles.

Mallery, Garrick. [1988-89] 1972. *Picture-Writing of the American Indians*. 2 vols. New York: Dover.

Maracle, David. 1985. *Iontewennaweienhastáhkwa': Mohawk Language Dictionary*. London: University of Western Ontario, Native Language Centre.

Marcus, George E., and Michael M.J. Fischer. 1986. *Anthropology as Cultural Critique: An Experimental Moment in the Human Sciences*. Chicago: University of Chicago Press.

Mason, Bernard S. [1938] 1972. *Drums, Tomtoms and Rattles: Primitive Percussion Instruments for Modern Use*. Drawings by Frederic H. Kock. New York: Dover.

Mathews, Zena Pearlstone, and Aldona Jonaitis, eds. 1982. *Native North American Art History: Selected Readings*. Palo Alto, CA: Peek Publications.

Mavor, James W., Jr., and Byron E. Dix. 1989. *Manitou: The Sacred Landscape of New England's Native Civilization*. Rochester, VT: Inner Traditions International.

McAllester, David. 1956. An Apache Fiddler. *Ethnomusicology Newsletter* 8:1-5.

McCaffrey, M.T., B. Jameson, C. Chapdelaine, R. Holmes Whitehead, L. Muller-Wille, and T. Qumaq. 1992. *Wrapped in the Colours of the Earth: Cultural Heritage of the First Nations*. Montreal: McCord Museum.

McClary, Susan. 1991. *Feminine Endings: Music, Gender, and Sexuality*. Minnesota: University of Minnesota Press.

McElwain, Thomas. 1987. Seneca Iroquois Concepts of Time. *Canadian Journal of Native Studies* 7/2:267-77

McGee, Timothy. *Music in Canada*. Toronto: University of Toronto Press, 1985.

McKenzie, Marguerite. N.d. The Language of the Montagnais and Naskapi in Labrador. Manuscript.

McMaster, Gerald, and Lee-Ann Martin, eds. 1992. *Indigena: Contemporary Native Perspectives*. Hull: Canadian Museum of Civilization.

McNulty, Gerard E., and Marie-Jeanne Basile. 1981. *Lexique Montagnais-Français du parler de Mingan*. Québec: Université Laval.

Mechling, William H. 1958-59. The Malecite Indians, with Notes on the Micmacs, 1916. *Anthropologica* 7:1-160; 8:161-274 (this includes his 1911 work).

Medicine, Beatrice. 1987. My Elders Tell Me. In *Indian Education in Canada: The Challenge*, ed. Jean Barman, *et al.* Vancouver: University of British Columbia Press.

Merriam, Alan P. 1967. *Ethnomusicology of the Flathead Indians*. New York: Wenner-Gren Foundation.

____. 1951. Flathead Indian Instruments and Their Music. *Musical Quarterly* 37:368-75.

Micmac Association for Cultural Studies. 1985. *Micmac Hymnal*. Sydney: Micmac Association for Cultural Studies.

Miller, J.R. 1989. *Skyscrapers Hide the Heavens: A History of Indian-White Relations in Canada*. Toronto: University of Toronto Press.

Mitchell, Frank. 1978. *Navaho Blessingway Singer: The Autobiography of Frank Mitchell*, ed. Charlotte J. Frisbie and David P. McAllester. Tucson: University of Arizona Press.

Mokakit Indian Education Research Association. 1988. *Selected Papers from the 1986 Conference*. Vancouver: Mokakit Indian Education Research Association.

Monkman, Leslie. 1981. *A Native Heritage: Images of the Indian in Native Canadian Literature*. Toronto: University of Toronto Press.

Morantz, Toby. 1977. James Bay Trading Captains of the 18th Century: New Perspectives on Algonquian Social Organization. In *Actes du huitième congrès des algonquinistes*, ed. W. Cowan, pp. 77-89. Ottawa: Carleton University.

____. 1983. *An Ethnohistoric Study of Eastern James Bay Cree Social Organization, 1700-1850*. Ottawa: National Museums of Canada.

Morgan, Lewis Henry. [1851] 1962 (Reprint). *League of the Iroquois*. Secaucus, NJ: Citadel Press.

Morrison, Kenneth M. 1984. *The Embattled Northeast: The Elusive Ideal of Alliance in Abenaki-Euroamerican Relations*. Berkeley: University of California Press.

____. 1986. Montagnais Missionization in Early New France: The Syncretic Imperative. *American Indian Culture and Research Journal* 10/3:1-23.

Murray, David. 1991. *Forked Tongues: Speech, Writing and Representation in North American Indian Texts*. Bloomington: Indiana University Press.

Nettl, Bruno. 1989. *Blackfoot Musical Thought: Comparative Perspectives*. Kent, OH: Kent State University Press.

____. 1954. *North American Indian Musical Styles*. Philadelphia: American Folklore Society.

____. 1969. Musical Areas Reconsidered: A Critique of North American Indian Research. In *Essays in Musicology in Honor of Dragan Plamenac*, ed. G. Reese and R.J. Snow. Pittsburgh: University of Pittsburgh Press.

Obomsawin, Alanis. 1977. Sounds and Voices from Our People. In *Stones, Bones and Skin: Ritual and Shamanic Art*, pp. 49-57. Toronto: The Society for Art Publications.

Ögwehöwe:ka:—Native Languages for Communication. 1987. New York State Syllabus. Albany: University of New York, State Education Department.

Ong, Walter. 1982. *Orality and Literacy*. London: Methuen.

Ortiz, Alfonso. 1977. Some Concerns Central to the Writing of "Indian" History. *Indian Historian* 10/1:17-22.

Pacifique. 1939. *Leçons grammaticales théoriques et pratiques de la langue micmaque*. Sainte-Anne de Restigouche: Bureau du messenger micmac.

Paper, Jordan. 1988. *Offering Smoke: The Sacred Pipe and Native American Religion*. Moscow, ID: University of Idaho Press.

____. N.d. Through the Earth Darkly: The Female Spirit in Native American Religions. Manuscript.

Parker, Arthur. 1908. *Myths and Legends of the New York State Iroquois*. Bulletin 125. Albany: New York State Museum.

Parsons, Elsie C. 1925. Micmac Folklore. *Journal of American Folk-Lore* 38:55-133.

Parthun, Paul. 1978. Conceptualization of Traditional Music among the Ojibwe of Manitoba and

Minnesota. *Anthropological Journal of Canada* 16/3:27-32.

Penney, David W. 1991. Floral Decoration and Culture Change: An Historical Interpretation of Motivation. *American Indian Culture and Research Journal* 15/1:53-77.

____, ed. 1989. *Great Lakes Indian Art*. Detroit: Wayne State University Press and the Detroit Institute of Arts.

Perreault, Jeanne, and Sylvia Vance, eds. 1990. *Writing the Circle: Native Women of Western Canada*. Edmonton: NeWest.

Phillips, Ruth B. 1987. Like a Star I Shine: Northern Woodlands Artistic Traditions. In *The Spirit Sings: Artistic Traditions of Canada's First Peoples*. Toronto: McClelland & Stewart.

Picken, Lawrence E.R. 1975. *Folk Musical Instruments in Turkey*. London: Oxford University Press.

Piggott, G.L. 1983. *Ojibwe Lexicon*. Ottawa: National Museums of Canada.

Posluns, Michael. 1990. Original Institutions and Crisis Management: The First Nations before and after Meech Lake. Public lecture presented at York University.

Powers, William K. 1987. *Beyond the Vision: Essays on American Indian Culture*. Norman: University of Oklahoma Press.

____. 1987. Cosmology and the Reinvention of Culture: The Lakota Case. *Canadian Journal of Native Studies* 7/2:165-80.

____. 1980. Oglala Song Terminology. *Selected Reports in Ethnomusicology* 3/2:23-41.

Poynton, Cate. 1989. *Language and Gender: Making the Difference*. Oxford: Oxford University Press.

Preston, Richard. 1976. *Cree Narrative: Expressing the Personal Meaning of Events*. National Museum of Man Mercury Series No. 30. Ottawa: National Museums of Canada.

____. 1985-86. Transformations musicales et culturelles chez les Cris de l'Est. *Recherches amérindiennes au Québec* 15/4:19-28.

Prince, J. Dyneley. 1897. The Passamaquoddy Wampum Records. *Proceedings of the American Philosophical Society* 36:479-95.

____. 1901. Notes on Passamaquoddy Literature. *Annals of the New York Academy of Sciences* 13/4:381-86.

Radin, Paul. 1928. Ethnological Notes on the Ojibwa of Southeastern Ontario. *American Anthropologist* 30/4:659-68.

Rand, Silas T. 1888. *Dictionary of the Language of the Micmac Indians Who Reside in Nova Scotia, New Brunswick, Prince Edward Island, Cape Breton, and Newfoundland*. Halifax: Nova Scotia Printing.

____. 1894. *Legends of the Micmacs*. New York and London: Longmans, Green.

Randel, Don, ed. 1986. *The New Harvard Dictionary of Music*. Cambridge, MA: Harvard University Press.

Redsky, James. [1972]. *Great Leader of the Ojibway: Mis-quona-quab*. Edited by James R. Stevens. Toronto: McClelland and Stewart.

Rhodes, Willard. [1952] 1967. Acculturation in North American Indian music. In *International Congress of Americanists, Proceedings of the 19th Congress*, ed. Sol Tax. New York: Cooper Square Publications.

Richardson, Boyce. 1989. *Drum Beat: Anger and Renewal in Indian Country*. Toronto: Summerhill Press for the Assembly of First Nations.

Richter, D.K., and J.H. Merrell, eds. 1987. *Beyond the Covenant Chain: The Iroquois and Their Neighbours in Indian North America, 1600-1800*. Syracuse: Syracuse University Press.

Ridington, Robin. 1993. A Sacred Object as Text. *American Indian Quarterly* 17/1:83-99.

____. 1988. *Trail to Heaven: Knowledge and Narrative in a Northern Community*. Vancouver: Douglas & McIntyre.

____. 1990. *Little Bit Know Something: Stories in a Language of Anthropology*. Vancouver: Douglas & McIntyre.

Rita Joe. 1978. *Poems of Rita Joe*. Halifax: Abenaki Press.

River Desert Education Authority. [1987]. *Algonquin Lexicon*. Prepared by Ernest McGregor. Maniwaki: River Desert Education Authority.

Robertson, Marion. 1973. *Rock Drawings of the Micmac Indians*. Halifax: The Nova Scotia Museum.

Rose, Richard. 1987. The Morgan Collection at the Rochester Museum and Science Center. *American Indian Art Magazine* 12:32-37.

Ross, Rupert. 1992. *Dancing with a Ghost: Exploring Indian Reality*. Markham: Reed Books Canada.

Rouget, Gilbert. 1985. *Music and Trance*. Chicago: University of Chicago Press.

Sachs, Curt, and Erich M. von Hornbostel. 1961. Classification of Musical Instruments. Trans. Anthony Baines and Klaus P. Wachsmann. *The Galpin Society Journal* 14:3-29.

Said, Edward W. 1982. Opponents, Audiences, Constituencies, and Community. In *The Politics of Interpretation*, ed. W.J.J. Mitchell, pp. 7-32. Chicago: University of Chicago Press.

____. 1978. *Orientalism*. New York: Pantheon.

____. 1991. *Musical Elaborations*. New York: Columbia University Press.

Savard, Remi. 1979. *Contes indiens de la Basse Côte-Nord du Saint-Laurent*. Ottawa: Musées nationaux du Canada.

Schmalz, Peter S. 1991. *The Ojibwa of Southern Ontario*. Toronto: University of Toronto Press.

Scollon, Ron, and S.B.K. Scollon. 1981. *Narrative, Literacy, and Face in Interethnic Communication*. Norwood, NJ: Ablex.

Seeger, Anthony. 1986. The Role of Sound Archives in Ethnomusicology Today. *Ethnomusicology* 30/2: 261-76.

____. 1987. *Why Suya Sing*. Cambridge: Cambridge University Press.

Shea, John Gilmary. 1861. Micmac or Recollect Hieroglyphics. *The Historical Magazine* 5/10:289-92.

Shelemay, Kay Kaufman, 1980. "Historical Ethnomusicology": Reconstructing Falasha Liturgical History. *Ethnomusicology* 24/2:233-58.

Sherzer, Joel. 1987. *Native American Discourse: Poetics and Rhetoric*. Cambridge: Cambridge University Press.

Shimony, Annemarie A. 1961. *Conservatism Among the Iroquois at the Six Nations Reserve*. Yale University Publications in Anthropology No. 65. New Haven: Yale University Press.

Short, T.L., and J. Deely. 1986. *Frontiers in Semiotics*. Bloomington: Indiana University Press.

Simeon, Thomas. 1979. *Nikanshets Utettsewunwow. 1. Pusslagan* (Le travail de mes grands-parents. 1. Le casseau d'ecorce). Hull: N.p.

Skinner, Alanson. 1915. Associations and Ceremonies of the Menominee Indians. *Anthropological Papers of the American Museum of Natural History* 13/2:167-215.

____. 1921. *Material Culture of the Menominee*. Indian Notes and Monographs. New York: Museum of the American Indian, Heye Foundation.

____. 1911. Notes on the Eastern Cree and Northern Saulteaux. *Anthropological Papers of the American Museum of Natural History* 9/1:1-179.

____. 1923-25. Observations on the Ethnology of the Sauk Indians. *Bulletin of the Public Museum of the City of Milwaukee*, 5/1-3.

Solie, Ruth, ed. 1993. *Musicology and Difference*. Berkeley: University of California Press.

Solomon, Art. 1990. *Songs for the People: Teachings on the Natural Way*. Toronto: NC Press.

Speck, Frank. 1982. The Double-curve Motif in North-eastern Algonkian Art. In *Native North American Art History*, ed. Z.P. Mathews and A. Jonaitis, pp. 383-428. Palo Alto, CA: Peek Publications.

____. 1935. *Naskapi Savage Hunters of the Labrador Peninsula*. Norman: University of Oklahoma Press.

____. 1985. *A Northern Algonkian Source Book*. Edited with an Introduction by E.S. Rogers. New York: Garland.

____. [1940] 1970. *Penobscot Man: The Life History of a Forest Tribe in Maine*. Philadelphia: University of Pennsylvania Press; New York: Octagon Books.

____. 1919. Penobscot Shamanism. *American Anthropological Association, Memoirs* 6:237-88.

____. 1927. Symbolism in Penobscot Art. In *Anthropological Papers of the American Museum of Natural History*. Vol. 29, Part 2. New York.

Bibliography

Spindler, George, and Louise Spindler. 1971. *Dreamers with Power: The Menominee*. Prospect Heights, IL: Waveland Press.

Spitall, William Guy. 1961. A Brief Note on Iroquois Musical Instruments. *American Indian Tradition* 7/4:137.

Spivak, Gayatri Chakravorty. 1988. *In Other Worlds: Essays in Cultural Politics*. New York: Routledge.

____. 1990. *The Post-Colonial Critic: Interviews, Strategies, Dialogues*. New York and London: Routledge.

Subotnik, Rose R. 1991. *Developing Variations*. Minneapolis: University of Minnesota Press.

Sullivan, Lawrence E. 1988. *Icanchu's Drum: An Orientation to Meaning in South American Religions*. New York: Macmillan.

Tanner, Adrian. 1979. *Bringing Home Animals: Religious Ideology and Mode of Production of the Mistassini Cree Hunters*. Social and Economic Studies No. 23, Institute of Social and Economic Research. St. John's: Memorial University of Newfoundland.

Taylor, Garth. 1980. *Canoe Construction in a Cree Culture Tradition*. Ottawa: National Museums of Canada.

Tedlock, Barbara. 1992. *The Beautiful and the Dangerous: Encounters with the Zuni Indians*. New York: Viking.

____. 1984. The Beautiful and the Dangerous: Zuni Ritual and Cosmology as an Aesthetic System. *Conjunctions* 6:246-65.

____, ed. 1987. *Dreaming: Anthropological and Psychological Interpretations*. Cambridge: Cambridge University Press.

____, and D. Tedlock. 1985. Text and Textile: Language and Technology in the Arts of the Quiche Maya. *Journal of Anthropological Research* 41/2:121-46.

Tedlock, Dennis. 1982. *The Spoken Word and the Work of Interpretation*. Philadelphia: University of Pennsylvania Press.

Thomas, Jake. N.d. *The Great Law of Peace*. N.p.: Iroquoian Institute.

Tehanetorens. N.d. *Wampum Belts*. Onchiota: Six Nations Indian Museum.

Thwaites, Reuben G., ed. [1896-1901] 1959. *The Jesuit Relations and Allied Documents: Travel and Explorations of the Jesuit Missionaries in New France, 1610-1791*. 73 vols. New York: Pageant. Abbreviated *JR*.

Todd, Loretta. 1992. *See* McMaster and Martin, eds., 1992.

Toelken, Barre. 1976. Seeing with a Native Eye: How Many Sheep Will It Hold? In *Seeing with a Native Eye*, ed. Walter Holden Capps and Åke Hultkrantz, pp. 9-24. New York: Harper & Row.

____, and Tacheeni Scott. 1981. Poetic Retranslation and the "Pretty Languages" of Yellowman. *Traditional Literatures of the American Indian: Texts and Interpretations*, ed. Karl Kroeber. Lincoln: University of Nebraska Press.

Tooker, Elizabeth. 1987. The Speck Iroquois Collection in the University Museum. *Expedition* 29:49-53.

Trigger, Bruce. 1976. *The Children of Aataentsic: A History of the Huron People to 1660*. Montreal: McGill-Queen's University Press.

____. 1985. *Natives and Newcomers: Canada's "Heroic Age" Reconsidered*. Kingston and Montreal: McGill-Queen's University Press.

____. 1986. The Historians' Indian: Native Americans in Canadian Historical Writing from Charlevoix to the Present. *Canadian Historical Review* 67/3:315-42.

____, ed. 1978. *The Northeast: Handbook of North American Indians*. Vol. 15 (Series editor: William Sturtevant.) Washington: Smithsonian Institution. Abbreviated *SH 15*.

Tuck, James. 1976. *Ancient People of Port au Choix: The Excavation of an Archaic Indian Cemetery in Newfoundland*. St. John's: Institute of Social and Economic Research, Memorial University of Newfoundland.

Turnbull, Colin. 1990. Liminality: A Synthesis of Subjective and Objective Experience. In *By Means of Performance: Intercultural Studies of Theatre and Ritual*, ed. Richard Schechner and Willa Appel. Cambridge: Cambridge University Press.

Turner, Lucien M. 1888. The Single-headed Drum of the Naskopie (Nagnagnot) Indians, Ungava District, Hudson Bay Territory. *Proceedings of the United States National Museum* 11:434-44.

____. [1894] 1979. *Indians and Eskimos in the Quebec-Labrador Peninsula: Ethnology of the Ungava District, Hudson Bay Territory*. Quebec: Comeditex.

Vachon, Daniel. 1987. Language and Generation. Manuscript.

Vachon, Daniel / Tamien Pashau. 1985. *Umue Tipatshimun Innut Ute Uashat / L'Histoire Montagnaise de Sept-Îles*. Sept-Îles: Editions Innu.

Vander, Judith. 1988. *Songprints: The Musical Experience of Five Shoshone Women*. Urbana and Chicago: University of Illinois Press.

Vastokas, Joan M., *et al.* 1990. *Perspectives of Canadian Landscape: Native Traditions*. Toronto: Robarts Centre for Canadian Studies, York University.

____, and R. Vastokas. 1973. *Sacred Art of the Algonkians*. N.p.: Mansard Press.

Vennum, Thomas. 1982. *The Ojibwe Dance Drum: Its History and Construction*. Washington: Library of Congress.

____. 1989. *Ojibway Music from Minnesota: A Century of Song for Voice and Drum*. St. Paul: Minnesota Historical Society Press.

Vincent Tehariolina, Marguerite. 1984. *La Nation Huronne: son histoire, sa culture, son esprit*. Québec: Éditions du Pelican.

Vizenor, Gerald. 1984. *The People Named Chippewa.* Minneapolis: University of Minnesota Press.

Voegelin, Erminie W. 1943. Shawnee Musical Instruments. *American Anthropologist* n.s. 44:463-75.

Wachsmann, Klaus. 1984. Classification. In *The New Grove Dictionary of Musical Instruments*, ed. Stanley Sadie, vol. 1, pp. 407-14. London: Macmillan.

Wallis, Wilson D., and Ruth S. Wallis. 1955. *The Micmac Indians of Eastern Canada.* Minneapolis: University of Minnesota Press.

____. 1957. *The Malecite Indians of New Brunswick.* Bulletin 148. Ottawa: National Museums of Canada.

Watson, Graham. 1987. Make Me Reflexive—But Not Yet: Strategies for Managing Essential Reflexivity in Ethnographic Discourse. *Journal of Anthropological Research* 43/1:29-41.

Webster, Gloria Cranmer. 1988. The "R" Word. *Muse* 6/3:43-44.

Whidden, Lynn. 1983. The Evolution of a Powwow Drum. *Troubadour* 6/3:7-9.

____. 1985-86. Les hymnes, une anomalie parmi les chants traditionnels des Cris du Nord. *Recherches amérindiennes au Québec* 15/4:29-36.

Whitehead, Ruth Holmes. 1982. *Micmac Quillwork.* Halifax: The Nova Scotia Museum.

____. 1987. I Have Lived Here Since the World Began: Atlantic Coast Artistic Traditions. In *The Spirit Sings: Artistic Traditions of Canada's First Peoples*, pp. 17-50. Toronto: McClelland and Stewart.

____. 1991. *The Old Man Told Us: Excerpts from Micmac History, 1500-1950.* Halifax: Nimbus.

____. 1988. *Stories from the Six Worlds: Micmac Legends.* Halifax: Nimbus.

Widdess, Richard. 1992. Historical Ethnomusicology. In *Ethnomusicology: An Introduction*, ed. Helen Myers, pp. 219-37. New York: Norton.

Williams, Alice. 1989. The Spirit of My Quilts. *Canadian Women's Studies* 10/2-3:49-54.

Witherspoon, Gary. 1977. *Language and Art in the Navajo Universe.* Ann Arbor: University of Michigan Press.

Witmer, Robert. 1990. Stability in Blackfoot Songs, 1909-1968. In *Ethnomusicology and Modern Music History*, ed. Stephen Blum, Philip Bohlman, and Daniel Neuman. Urbana: University of Illinois Press.

Worth, Sol, and John Adair. [1972] 1975. *Through Navajo Eyes.* Bloomington: Indiana University Press.

Wright, Ronald. 1992. *Stolen Continents: The "New World" through Indian Eyes.* Toronto: Penguin.

Young, David E. 1985. The Need for a Cognitive Approach to the Study of Material Culture. *Culture* 5/2:53-67.

Young, M. Jane. 1985. Images of Power and the Power of Images: The Significance of Rock Art for Contemporary Zunis. *Journal of American Folklore* 98:3-48.

Zemp, Hugo. 1978. `Aré `aré Classification of Musical Types and Instruments. *Ethnomusicology* 22/1:37-67.

____. 1979. Aspects of `Aré `aré Musical Theory. *Ethnomusicology* 23/1:5-48.

____. 1971. *Musique Dan.* Paris: Mouton.

Index

Index

WE AS A PEOPLE WERE ENTRUSTED WITH ENSUR-
ING THAT THAT SOUND WOULD GO ON FOREV-
ER AND THAT IT WOULD BE AT THE CENTRE OF
OUR PEOPLE. AND THOUGH WE WERE TOLD THAT WE
MAY SUFFER AS A PEOPLE MORE THAN EVEN THE OTHER
NATIONS ON THIS ISLAND, THAT ONE DAY WE WOULD
HAVE TO TAKE OUR RIGHTFUL PLACE BECAUSE WE
WERE ENTRUSTED WITH THAT SOUND, THAT ORIGINAL
SOUND, AND BECAUSE WE WERE ENTRUSTED WITH
THOSE TEACHINGS THAT OTHERS ONE DAY WOULD BE
SEARCHING FOR.

(Jim Dumont, Birch Island, August 3, 1986)